D1716503

Psychoeducational Assessment and Intervention for Ethnic Minority Children

APPLYING PSYCHOLOGY
IN THE SCHOOLS
BOOK SERIES

Psychoeducational Assessment and Intervention for Ethnic Minority Children

EVIDENCE-BASED APPROACHES

Edited by

SCOTT L. GRAVES, Jr., and JAMILIA J. BLAKE

American Psychological Association • Washington, DC

Published by
American Psychological Association
750 First Street, NE
Washington, DC 20002
www.apa.org

To order
APA Order Department
P.O. Box 92984
Washington, DC 20090-2984
Tel: (800) 374-2721; Direct: (202) 336-5510
Fax: (202) 336-5502; TDD/TTY: (202) 336-6123
Online: www.apa.org/pubs/books
E-mail: order@apa.org

In the U.K., Europe, Africa, and the Middle East, copies may be ordered from
American Psychological Association
3 Henrietta Street
Covent Garden, London
WC2E 8LU England

Typeset in Goudy by Circle Graphics, Inc., Columbia, MD

Printer: Sheridan Books, Inc., Ann Arbor, MI
Cover Designer: Mercury Publishing Services, Inc., Rockville, MD

The opinions and statements published are the responsibility of the authors, and such opinions and statements do not necessarily represent the policies of the American Psychological Association.

Library of Congress Cataloging-in-Publication Data

Names: Graves, Scott L., editor. | Blake, Jamilia J., editor.
Title: Psychoeducational assessment and intervention for ethnic minority
   children : evidence-based approaches / [edited by] Scott L. Graves, Jr.,
   and Jamilia J. Blake.
Description: Washington, DC : American Psychological Association, [2016] |
   Series: School psychology | Includes bibliographical references and index.
Identifiers: LCCN 2015030762 | ISBN 9781433821745 | ISBN 1433821745
Subjects: LCSH: Children of minorities—Education—United States. | Children
   of minorities—Psychological testing—United States.
Classification: LCC LC3731 .P89 2016 | DDC 371.829/0973—dc23 LC record available at
http://lccn.loc.gov/2015030762

British Library Cataloguing-in-Publication Data
A CIP record is available from the British Library.

Printed in the United States of America
First Edition

http://dx.doi.org/10.1037/14855-000

CONTENTS

CONTRIBUTORS

Candice Aston, MSEd, Duquesne University, Pittsburgh, PA
Jamilia J. Blake, PhD, Texas A&M University, College Station
Matthew K. Burns, PhD, University of Missouri, Columbia
Sara M. Castro-Olivo, PhD, Texas A&M International University, Laredo
Kristine Cramer, MA, University of California, Riverside
Laura B. Frame, MA, Texas A&M University, College Station
Nicole M. Garcia, MA, University of California, Riverside
Scott L. Graves, Jr., PhD, Duquesne University, Pittsburgh, PA
Stephanie Hargrove, BS, George Mason University, Fairfax, VA
Lori Helman, PhD, University of Minnesota, Minneapolis
Alyce M. Hopple, MEd, Indiana State University, Terre Haute
Laurice M. Joseph, PhD, Ohio State University, Columbus
Ahoo Karimian, MA, Pepperdine University, Los Angeles, CA
Alicia D. Knight, PhD, Cypress Independent School District, Houston, TX
Allison McCobin, MS, Duquesne University, Pittsburgh, PA
Jennifer McComas, PhD, University of Minnesota, Minneapolis
Kara E. McGoey, PhD, Duquesne University, Pittsburgh, PA
Leah M. Nellis, PhD, Indiana State University, Terre Haute
Markeda Newell, PhD, Loyola University Chicago, Chicago, IL

Kayla Nichols, MSEd, Duquesne University, Pittsburgh, PA

Sherrie L. Proctor, PhD, Queens College, City University
of New York, Queens

Sandra M. Pulles, MA, University of Minnesota, Minneapolis

Cyrell C. B. Roberson, BS, University of California, Berkeley

David Shriberg, PhD, Loyola University Chicago, Chicago, IL

Chamane Simpson, PhD, The Graduate Center, City University
of New York, Manhattan

Leann V. Smith, MA, University of Texas at Austin

Alexander J. Steiner, MA, Alliant International University, Los Angeles, CA

April D. Thames, PhD, University of California Los Angeles Semel Institute
for Neuroscience and Human Behavior

Tiffany G. Townsend, PhD, Georgetown University School of Medicine,
Washington, DC

Lindsey G. Venesky, PhD, Duquesne University, Pittsburgh, PA

Rebecca R. Winters, MEd, Texas A&M University, College Station

Frank C. Worrell, PhD, University of California, Berkeley

SERIES FOREWORD

Outside of their homes, children spend more time in schools than in any other setting. From tragedies such as Sandy Hook and Columbine to more hopeful developments such as the movement toward improved mental health and academic achievement, there is an ongoing need for high-quality writing that speaks to ways in which children, families, and communities associated with schools worldwide can be supported through the application of sound psychological research, theory, and practice.

For the past several years, the American Psychological Association (APA) Books program and Division 16 (School Psychology) have partnered to produce the Applying Psychology in the Schools book series. The mission of this series is to increase the visibility of the science, practice, and policy for children and adolescents in schools and communities. The result has been a strong collection of scholarly work that appeals not only to psychologists but also to individuals from all fields who have reason to seek and use what psychology has to offer in schools.

This volume continues the strong tradition of the series. In particular, this volume provides an extremely thorough overview of ways in which evidence-based approaches can be used to inform assessment of and intervention with ethnic minority children. As such, this volume is an invaluable resource for practitioners, researchers, and graduate students alike from all applied psychology and education disciplines.

Since its initiation, many individuals have made significant contributions to this book series. I thank previous series editors Sandra L. Christensen, Catherine Christo, Jan Hughes, R. Steve McCallum, David McIntosh, LeAdelle Phelps, Linda Reddy, Susan Sheridan, and Christopher H. Skinner for their wonderful service. I also thank Linda Malnasi McCarter and Beth Hatch of APA Books for their editorial work and support, as well as all of the people at APA Books who have worked behind the scenes to bring this book to fruition. Finally, I thank Drs. Graves and Blake for identifying the need for this book, recruiting such a talented group of chapter authors, and doing such a superb editing job.

The leadership of Division 16 welcomes your comments about this volume as well as your ideas for other topics that you would like to see explored in this series. To share your thoughts, please visit the Division 16 website at http://www.apadivisions.org/division-16/.

David Shriberg, PhD
Series Editor

Psychoeducational Assessment and Intervention for Ethnic Minority Children

INTRODUCTION

SCOTT L. GRAVES, JR., AND JAMILIA J. BLAKE

> You don't make progress by standing on the sidelines, whimpering and
> complaining. You make progress by implementing ideas.
> —Shirley Chisholm, *Unbossed and Unbought*

The landscape of the U.S. student population is changing. By 2024, ethnic and racial "minority" students will constitute the numerical majority of students in U.S. public schools (Kena et al., 2015). Although scholars have long projected this shift in racial and ethnic diversity of the school-age youth population, few training programs and resources focus on evidence-based strategies for delivering mental health services to ethnically diverse students. Thus, the purpose of this volume is to provide a comprehensive resource for the psychoeducational assessment of and interventions for ethnic minority children.

This volume is based on two important premises. First, empirical research is necessary to inform psychological practice with ethnic minority children. This idea is supported by the *Guidelines on Multicultural Education, Training, Research, Practice, and Organizational Change for Psychologists* (American

http://dx.doi.org/10.1037/14855-001
Psychoeducational Assessment and Intervention for Ethnic Minority Children: Evidence-Based Approaches,
S. L. Graves, Jr., and J. J. Blake (Editors)

Psychological Association [APA], 2003) and the *Guidelines for Research in Ethnic Minority Communities* (Council of National Psychology Associations for the Advancement of Ethnic Minority Interests, 2000). But although each of these sets of guidelines provides general principles, more specific information is needed to apply the principles to actual practice. This text addresses this need by explaining how the history of assessment and intervention informs current practices with ethnic minority students and then by applying the guidelines in a way that addresses these historical influences.

The second premise is that ethnic minority students are not homogeneous, and this reality requires cultural and context-specific research and interventions. All individuals exist within a context of historical, economic, and political circumstances, and psychologists are frequently called on to understand how these environmental systems influence individuals' behavior (APA, 2003). Our intent in this book is not to provide a definitive approach or solutions to all issues related to ethnic minority children, but rather to provide a practical starting point for stakeholders to consider when conducting research, conducting clinical assessments, and developing interventions. Directions for future research are highlighted in each chapter.

The scope of the volume is broad. Contributors cover fundamentals such as the history of assessment related to ethnic minorities, including how the revision of the standards for educational assessment affects ethnic minority students; cultural considerations in assessment practices for ethnic minority students (e.g., neuropsychological, early childhood, social–emotional assessment); and evidence-based intervention strategies to improve the performance of these students.

This book strives to integrate the current theory, research, and practice of assessment and intervention for ethnic minority students into one comprehensive resource. Although other texts cover assessment and intervention, they do not focus specifically on empirically proven intervention strategies for ethnic minority populations. This volume focuses on strategies that have proven to be effective with ethnic minority populations and programs that school-focused researchers and practitioners can implement. It guides readers through the process of assessing and intervening with ethnic minority populations.

This volume consists of three parts. Part I (Chapters 1–3) describes the historical context of U.S. schooling for ethnic minority children. Chapters in this section provide a foundation from which to understand the need for improved assessment and intervention practices for minority students, including a historical overview, theoretical frameworks, and national standards for educational and psychological testing as it relates to ethnic minority children. In Chapter 1, Graves and Aston provide a comprehensive overview of the history of assessment with ethnic minority populations. Given the controversial nature of intellectual assessment with diverse populations, it is important to have a reference point to frame subsequent chapters. In Chapter 2, Blake, Smith, and Knight focus on theoretical frameworks to explain achievement outcomes in ethnic minority children. Given longstanding academic achievement gaps, it is imperative that the theoretical frameworks and ideologies that guide educational policy are relevant for diverse populations. In Chapter 3, Worrell and Roberson examine the recently updated *Standards for Educational and Psychological Testing* (American Educational Research Association, American Psychological Association, & National Council on Measurement in Education, 2014) that provide a framework for evaluating tests and testing practices in the fields of psychology, education, and psychometrics. The authors provide an overview of previous versions of the *Standards* and discuss how the content affects diverse populations.

Part II (Chapters 4–8) provides a theoretical foundation for understanding assessment practices in relation to ethnic minority youth; it also provides discusses applications for assessing this population. In particular, chapters in this section document culturally appropriate assessment practices in the areas of intelligence, academic achievement, social–emotional assessment, early childhood, and neuropsychology. In Chapter 4, Graves and Nichols provide a historical overview and the current state of intellectual assessment of ethnic minority children in the United States. Because of the ongoing debate regarding bias in norm-referenced assessment instruments and ethnic minority children, researchers and practitioners must understand these issues. In Chapter 5, Nellis and Hopple focus on the assessment of academic skills and achievement within the context of special education evaluation and identification. With schools being tasked with assessing students' academic performance, it is important to understand what is measured, how it is measured, and how the information is used. In Chapter 6, Blake, Winters, and Frame provide essential information that professionals should understand when assessing students of ethnically diverse backgrounds for social–emotional and behavioral concerns. These authors discuss assessment criteria in light of criteria established by the Individuals with Disabilities Education Improvement Act of 2004 and the *Diagnostic and Statistical Manual of Mental Disorders*. In Chapter 7, McGoey, McCobin, and Venesky review the recommended assessment practices in early childhood and provide specific recommendations for working with diverse families. In Chapter 8, Thames, Karimian, and Steiner highlight essential findings from the disciplines of cultural neuroscience and cultural neuropsychology that have informed and influenced current clinical practice. These considerations include economic disadvantage, educational quality, the use of ethnic and racial corrected norms, the use of interpreters, culturally familiar test content, bilingualism, stereotype threat, and test-taking anxiety.

Finally, Part III (Chapters 9–14) documents the current state of intervention practices for ethnic minority youth. The section aims to provide a theoretical foundation for understanding intervention practices in relation to ethnic minority youth, as well as practical applications for intervening with this population. This section describes interventions for reading, social–emotional development, and other subjects. It also presents general guidance for improving educational and mental health service delivery for ethnic minority populations. In Chapter 9, Burns, Pulles, Helman, and McComas demonstrate how screening data from the curriculum-based measurement of oral reading fluency with first-grade students could be used to evaluate student response to the core curriculum and to identify the need for Tier 1 interventions. In Chapter 10, Castro-Olivo, Cramer, and Garcia describe a research agenda for culturally validated interventions that best serve the social–emotional and academic needs of diverse children. In Chapter 11, Newell reviews the evidence on consultation with racial minority students and discusses methods and approaches for conducting high-quality consultation research with racial minority students. In Chapter 12, Townsend and Hargrove explore health vulnerabilities faced by African American girls. In addition, they offer a conceptual model that considers contextual factors, which researchers may find helpful in guiding intervention development. In Chapter 13, Joseph discusses the advantages and usefulness of single-subject research designs with culturally and linguistically diverse populations. In Chapter 14, Proctor and Simpson discuss how multicultural training within psychology graduate programs can improve service delivery to ethnically and racially diverse prekindergarten to 12th-grade students. These authors also make recommendations for multicultural practices that can be initiated to prepare psychologists to work with ethnically and racially diverse school-age students.

REFERENCES

American Educational Research Association, American Psychological Association, & National Council on Measurement in Education. (2014). *Standards for educational and psychological testing*. Washington, DC: Author.

American Psychological Association. (2003). Guidelines on multicultural education, training, research, practice, and organizational change for psychologists. *American Psychologist, 58*, 377–402.

Chisholm, S. (1970). *Unbossed and unbought*. New York, NY: Houghton Mifflin.

Council of National Psychology Associations for the Advancement of Ethnic Minority Interests. (2000). *Guidelines for research in ethnic minority communities*. Washington, DC: American Psychological Association.

Kena, G., Musu-Gillette, L., Robinson, J., Wang, X., Rathbun, A., Zhang, J., . . . Dunlop Velez, E. (2015). *The condition of education 2015* (NCES 2015-144). Washington, DC: U.S. Department of Education, National Center for Education Statistics.

I

HISTORICAL CONTEXT AND CURRENT ISSUES RELATED TO THE ASSESSMENT OF ETHNIC MINORITY CHILDREN

1

HISTORY OF PSYCHOLOGICAL ASSESSMENT AND INTERVENTION WITH MINORITY POPULATIONS

SCOTT L. GRAVES, JR., AND CANDICE ASTON

The assessment and intervention practices for ethnic minorities are long debated topics and are pertinent to current psychological practices. To understand the controversy behind the psychological assessment of ethnic minority populations, it is important to consider the history of assessment in the United States. The purpose of this chapter is to provide this history.

EARLY HISTORY OF PSYCHOLOGICAL ASSESSMENT

Psychological testing originated more than 100 years ago in laboratory studies that focused on sensory discrimination, motor skills, and reaction time (McReynolds, 1987). The term *mental test* was coined in the 1890s by

http://dx.doi.org/10.1037/14855-002
Psychoeducational Assessment and Intervention for Ethnic Minority Children: Evidence-Based Approaches,
S. L. Graves, Jr., and J. J. Blake (Editors)

James McKeen Cattell and was used to describe a set of tests, which included measures of sensation, reaction time, human memory span, and rate of movement (Gregory, 2004). However, it was Alfred Binet's and Victor Henri's later explanation and classification of mental processes that served as the framework for advancing psychological measurement. In fact, Alfred Binet is noted as a founding father of the psychometric movement. Because of his success, Binet was asked by the French government in 1904 to help decide which students would likely experience difficulty in schools due to the implementation of a new law requiring all French children to attend school. Binet collaborated with Theodore Simon, a medical doctor, to develop a series of questions that focused on cognitive processes not taught in school, such as attention, memory, and problem-solving skills. The Binet-Simon scale developed from this process became the basis for intelligence tests that are still used today.

Binet, despite his psychometric contribution to intelligence, did not believe his psychometric instrument could assess a single, permanent, and inborn level of intelligence (Kamin, 1995). However, this is often overlooked, as evidenced by the later use of his test to identify intellectual differences between racial groups in the United States. As recognition for the Binet-Simon scale grew in the United States, Stanford psychologist Lewis Terman adapted the test and standardized it on American participants, publishing it in 1916 as the Stanford–Binet Intelligence Scale. This scale quickly became the standard intelligence test administered in the United States. The Stanford–Binet used a single number, known as the intelligence quotient (or IQ), to represent an individual's score on the test. Dividing the test taker's mental age by his or her chronological age and then multiplying this number by 100 generated this score.

The Stanford–Binet has remained a popular assessment tool through the years. In 1937, the test was revised to extend the age downward to 2 and upward to 22. To date, a major criticism of the Stanford–Binet is its deliberate exclusion of Mexican American, African American, and other children of color from the original standardization sample (Valencia & Suzuki, 2000). Despite being revised in 1937 (Terman & Merrill, 1937) and in 1960 (Terman & Merrill, 1973), there continued to be only White children included in the standardization sample. This resulted in 6 decades during which children of color were routinely administered a test for which they were not represented in the normative group. It was not until the 1972 Stanford–Binet revision that minority children were added to the standardization sample (Terman & Merrill, 1973). The exclusion of minority children in the Stanford–Binet standardization sample is one example of the inequitable assessment practices that existed during that time.

EMERGENCE OF INTELLIGENCE TESTING
DURING WORLD WAR I

World War I created several opportunities for the advancement of the field of psychology. The testing program that was used by the U.S. Army during World War I is credited with the spread of intelligence testing; it also helped substantiate psychology as both a science and profession in America from 1914 to 1918 (Boake, 2002).

While the United States prepared for World War I, army officials sought out psychologists to develop a method to screen army recruits for duty. Robert Yerkes, president of the American Psychological Association (APA) during the time, developed two tests known as the Army Alpha and Beta tests (Yerkes, 1921). The Alpha test was based on the work of Otis (1918) and consisted of eight verbally loaded tests for average and high-functioning recruits. The Beta test was nonverbal in nature and administered to illiterate individuals or recruits whose first language was not English (Guthrie, 2004). The test consisted of several visual perceptual and motor tasks and was administered through demonstration or gestures. By the end of the war, 1.75 million men had been administered either the Alpha or Beta test in an effort to help the army determine which men were well suited for specific positions and management roles in the military (McGuire, 1994). However, this screening process was not for ethnic minorities. Regardless of how African American men performed on the Army test, they were predominately used for hard manual labor and often as experimental subjects for research (Guthrie, 2004).

The army test received criticism because of inconsistencies in its administration and issues of validity, specifically for people of color. One alarming finding from the army tests was that the average mental age of recruits was 13, with a 12 being the cutoff for feeblemindedness; this suggests that it was not a valid assessment of intellectual functioning (Guthrie, 2004). In spite of these criticisms, at the end of World War I these intelligence tests were being used in a variety of situations outside the military with individuals of all ages, racial and ethnic backgrounds, and nationalities. For example, IQ tests were utilized at Ellis Island to screen new immigrants for mental defects as they entered the United States (Boake, 2002). This resulted in the use of inappropriate tests to make far-reaching and inaccurate generalizations about entire populations and led some test experts to urge Congress to enact immigration restrictions (Kamin, 1995). This case is just one instance of the multitude of hardships caused by the inappropriate administration of mental tests. More egregious uses of intelligence tests to substantiate prejudices toward ethnic minorities were developed after the war by utilizing data collected from the army tests.

For example, a study conducted at Colgate University focused on differences in test scores based on skin color. The results from this study were published in the journal *School and Society* and purported that lighter skinned individuals performed better on intelligence measures than darker skinned individuals (Guthrie, 2004). Findings from the Colgate study and others like it furthered the belief of racial inferiority and led to the ban of interracial marriage, reduced funds for Black schools, and increased support for legal segregation. Scholars such as W. E. B. Du Bois and Horace Mann Bond, who publicly criticized the use of intelligence testing, wholly refuted these claims. Horace Mann Bond investigated the scores obtained on the army tests by race and found that Blacks from northern states such as Illinois, New York, Ohio, and Pennsylvania scored higher than Whites from the southern states of Mississippi, Kentucky, Arkansas, and Georgia (Urban, 1989). His findings were used to refute claims of genetic explanations for racial differences and dispelled the notion of racial inferiority. Albert Beckham, who extensively researched intelligence testing and is noted as one of the first Black school psychologists, attempted to refute the numerous claims of inherent inferiority of African Americans (Graves, 2009). Because of the dearth of research refuting Black inferiority hypotheses, most Black social scientists had no choice but to focus their research on intelligence testing. Unfortunately, Beckham's work, like that of many Black social scientists at the time, was discounted because of the dearth of research challenging the scientific merit of scientific inferiority claims. The discounting of ethnic minority psychologists' opinions would change after the civil rights era.

LARRY P. v. RILES

During the post-civil rights era, Black psychologists had opposing views regarding psychological testing. In response to decades of research illustrating racial and ethnic differences in IQ, Black psychologists worked in conjunction with social agencies such as the National Association for the Advancement of Colored People to prohibit intelligence testing of African American children. One of the best-known cases in the social sciences regarding this topic is *Larry P. v. Riles* (1979). In their presentation to the court, the plaintiffs argued that the Wechsler Intelligence Scale for Children, the revised Wechsler Intelligence Scale for Children, and the Stanford–Binet IQ tests were biased and inappropriate for testing minority children. The court ruled that the use of intelligence testing with African Americans for the purpose of placing them in special education was illegal in California. The attorney for Larry P. argued that the disproportionate number of African Americans represented in the educable mentally retarded (EMR) classes, with IQ test scores being the primary factor for placement, violated the equal protection clause of the Fourteenth Amendment (Hilliard, 1983). The judge, Robert Peckham, ruled that standardized intelligence tests are racially and culturally biased, have a discriminatory impact on Black children, and have not been validated to make permanent placement decisions regarding education. As a result, if an African American child's performance was suspected to fall in the EMR range, an alternative form of placement testing, other than IQ tests, had to be administered. In addition to this ruling, one of the most compelling arguments against using intelligence testing with African American children came from the Association of Black Psychologists (Williams, 2008). The official position statement of the association called for a moratorium on the use of all psychological and educational tests with African American children (Holliday, 2009).

In 1986, the court revised the Larry P. court order to extend the intelligence testing ban to all African American children. The California Department of Education and the public interest lawyers who represented Larry P. obtained an order from Judge Peckham to ban the use of standardized intelligence tests for African American children for assignment to special education programs (Guthrie, 2004). However, African American children could still take intelligence tests to be considered for the state-supported gifted and talented education program. To this day, schools in California are still not allowed to use intelligence tests with African American children for special education placement decisions. Despite the outcome of the Larry P. case, many states in the United States continue to rely primarily on intelligence testing for special education placement decisions of minority children.

PARENTS IN ACTION ON SPECIAL EDUCATION v. HANNON

While the news of the Larry P. case was circulating in California, a similar case came to trial in Illinois. *Parents in Action on Special Education v. Hannon* (1980) was a class action lawsuit filed on behalf of two African American children who had been placed in special classes for the educable mentally handicapped on the basis of IQ test scores. Parents argued that the use of IQ tests for African American children violates the equal protection clause of the Constitution and many federal statutes (Hilliard, 1983). However, unlike the ruling in the Larry P. case, Judge Grady reached the opposite decision, ruling that IQ tests were not biased in regard to African

American children. As a result of issues regarding assessments and culturally fair practices, several ethnic psychological associations emerged.

ASSOCIATION OF BLACK PSYCHOLOGISTS

Ethnic minority psychologists have historically faced many challenges when attempting to enter the field of psychology. Few Blacks, Latinos, Asians, or American Indians were admitted to doctoral study in psychology from the field's early stages, and fewer received doctorates (Guthrie, 2004). However, in 1968 a small number of Black psychologists from around the country formed the Association of Black Psychologists (ABPsi) at the annual convention of the APA (Pickren & Rutherford, 2010). This organization was formed to actively address the serious problems facing Black psychologists and the larger Black community. Guided by the principle of self-determination, these psychologists began building an institution through which they could address the long-neglected needs of Black professionals (Williams, 2008).

ABPsi has since become a successful organization that has made many contributions to the advancement of psychological practices, especially practices for African Americans. To advance public policy and disseminate research regarding African Americans, ABPsi established an extensive publication program that includes the quarterly *Journal of Black Psychology* and the monthly newsletter *Psych Discourse* (Holliday, 2009). These publications helped advance the research base of studies regarding African Americans, which ultimately led to the development of other ethnic-based journals such as the *Journal of Latina/o Psychology*, *Asian American Journal of Psychology*, and *Journal of Indigenous Research*. ABPSi has played an integral role in the formation of later minority-led psychological organizations with similar aims.

NATIONAL LATINA/O PSYCHOLOGICAL ASSOCIATION

The National Latina/o Psychological Association was formed to help improve psychological practices in the Latino community. Educational psychologist Edward Casavantes devoted much of his work toward Latino educational and civil rights (Padilla & Olmedo, 2009) In 1969, Casavantes founded the Association of Psychologists Por La Raza, which held their first meeting at the APA convention in 1970 (Padilla & Olmedo, 2009). The organization was later renamed the National Latina/o Psychological Association, but the mission did not change. The mission of the National Latina/o Psychological

Association is to advance the psychological education and training, scientific practice, and organizational change to enhance the overall well-being of Hispanic and Latina/o populations.

SOCIETY OF INDIAN PSYCHOLOGISTS

Unlike those of other ethnic groups, the history of American Indian and Alaska Native psychology is limited (Trimble & Clearing-Sky, 2009). Carolyn Attneave devoted much of her work to developing culturally based activities for American Indian and Alaskan Native populations. The Society of Indian Psychologists was founded in the 1970s from the Network of Indian Psychologists (Trimble & Clearing-Sky, 2009). One of the primary aims of the society is to provide an organization for Native American indigenous people to advance the research and knowledge on Native people and address issues affecting Native mental health (Trimble & Clearing-Sky, 2009). An overarching goal of this organization is to connect Native psychologists and support their mission of addressing issues regarding Native mental health.

ASIAN AMERICAN PSYCHOLOGICAL ASSOCIATION

Similarly, the Asian American Psychological Association (AAPA) emerged in the early 1970s when two brothers from the San Francisco area, Derald and Stanley Sue, organized a series of meetings on mental health issues in the Asian community. The meetings led to the official founding of the organization in 1972 by Dr. Stanley Sue, the first president of AAPA. One of the organization's main objectives is to investigate the unique mental health needs of Asian Americans (Leong & Okazaki, 2009) and provide a network to support current Asian psychologists. From its inception, the association has worked to advocate for and address the concerns of Asian Americans. In 1980, the AAPA successfully urged the U.S. Bureau of the Census to include Asian American subgroups in its census data (Leong & Okazaki, 2009). This association has also been successful at advancing the multicultural psychology movement and has led the APA to establish a board of minority affairs (Leong & Okazaki, 2009).

Collectively, these professional organizations have helped to ensure culturally fair assessment practices and have increased the research base on minority mental health. These minority-focused organizations continue to work on removing the barriers faced by minority psychologists and to ultimately make the field of psychology more inclusive.

HISTORICAL ISSUES IN INTERVENTION RESEARCH
WITH MINORITY POPULATIONS

As with the history of intellectual assessment, intervention research and mental health service delivery with ethnic minorities populations have faced many criticisms (see Chapters 10 and 14, this volume). Because of the rising numbers of ethnic minorities in the United States, the mental health field as a whole has begun to advocate for more culturally competent research practices. These concerns were prompted by the limited number of ethnic minority participants in research studies and the heavily documented mental health disparities among ethnic and racial groups (Schulman et al., 1999). Because of the lack of participation of minorities in research studies, it is difficult to confirm whether evidence-based interventions would have an equally effective outcome.

As indicated by Evans (2010), it is imperative to find out what works for whom and under what conditions. Nation et al. (2003) determined that intervention program relevance is a direct function of the degree to which a community's norms, cultural beliefs, and practices have been integrated into program content, delivery, and evaluation. For instance, treatment disparities may be reduced if interventions are perceived to be more relevant and applicable from the perspective of ethnically diverse families (Serpell, Clauss-Ehlers, & Lindsey, 2007).

Evidence-based practice in psychology is the integration of the best available research with clinical expertise in the context of client characteristics, culture, and preferences (APA Presidential Task Force on Evidence-Based Practice, 2006). As previously mentioned, one of the essential requirements for interventions to be evidence-based is that they are evaluated on the populations for which they will be used (APA Task Force on Evidence-Based Practice for Children and Adolescents, 2008). Although the evidence-based practice movement is gaining momentum, several questions frame current debates about the role of student characteristics in this movement. Among these questions, arguably none is more important than intervention effectiveness across diverse populations.

Although it would be ideal for psychologists and educators to have a research base that documents participant intervention characteristics, research summaries have indicated that diverse participants in intervention research have not been studied extensively. For example, in the highly cited National Research Council's synthesis of minority students in gifted and special education, Donovan and Cross (2002) found that understanding the effects of race and ethnicity on educational outcomes was difficult because many research studies did not specify the racial composition of their samples or were limited by insufficient sample sizes to disaggregate outcomes. In addition, according to the United States Surgeon General (U.S. Department of Health and Human Services, 1999), specific treatments exist for most mental disorders; however, diverse individuals are largely absent from the efficacy studies that make up this evidence base. The Surgeon General's report titled *Mental Health: Culture, Race and Ethnicity* (U.S. Department of Health and Human Services, 2001) found that of the 9,266 participants involved in the efficacy studies forming the major treatment guidelines for bipolar disorder, schizophrenia, depression, and attention-deficit/hyperactivity disorder, only 561 Black, 99 Latino, 11 Asian Americans and Pacific Islanders, and 0 American Indians and Alaskan Natives were included. Consequently, few of these studies had the statistical power necessary to examine treatment efficacy by ethnicity.

In addition, content analysis of psychological journals has also found limited inclusion of diverse children (Graham, 1992; Lindo, 2006). Research that examined clinical trials funded by the National Institute of Mental Health published between 1995 and 2004 reported no significant progress in the reporting of participants' ethnicity or racial background during the previous decade across leading journals in the field (Mak, Law, Alvidrez, & Pérez-Stable, 2007). In an analysis of school psychology journals, Grunewald et al. (2014) found that only 15% of articles have diversity as a focus. Results from a longitudinal content analysis of early childhood behavior literature (published between 1984 and 2003) by Conroy, Dunlap, Clark, and Alter (2005) found that participants' race and ethnicity were reported in only 7% of the studies. In addition, participants' socioeconomic status was reported in only 7% of the studies.

Given that significant information is missing from the psychological intervention literature (i.e., socioeconomic status, geographic location, and participants' race), practitioners and teachers must ask themselves whether these treatments generalize to the populations they work with. The intervention efficacy literature provides some insight into this area, although it is not specific to the field of school psychology. In a meta-analysis of 76 studies that evaluated culturally adapted interventions, there was a moderately strong effect for this type of intervention modification (Griner & Smith, 2006). Specifically, interventions that targeted a specific cultural group were 4 times more efficacious than interventions developed broadly for a group of individuals. Because an adapted versus standard intervention research base is not yet available, practitioners must use caution when using interventions on populations for which they were not intended (Ingraham & Oka, 2006). School-based professionals must realize that a client's individual characteristics may affect intervention efficacy and that they may have to modify their interventions accordingly. Unfortunately, this type of consistent trial and error modification takes time, which is one of the most significant barriers to the implementation of evidence-based practices in schools (Forman, Olin,

Hoagwood, Crowe, & Saka, 2009). When researchers design and implement interventions, they should adhere more to the recommendations, such as the ones made by the Task Force on Evidence-Based Interventions. By using these resources, researchers can ensure they are not excluding information that is necessary for successful intervention implementation.

The history of assessment and intervention with ethnic minority populations has been a heavily deliberated topic. Despite all the controversy surrounding intellectual assessment, few would argue for a complete abandonment of intellectual testing. Thus, intelligence testing is likely to be present for many years to come and will retain an integral role in the practice of psychology (see Chapter 4, this volume). Therefore, it is important that research on intellectual assessment continues to evolve and become more diverse with respect to ethnic minority populations. In addition, intervention research should document outcomes by ethnic background. The expansion of a research agenda that aims to address the need to adapt intervention programming for ethnic minority populations is vital (see Chapter 10, this volume). In sum, continued efforts are needed to ensure that both assessments and intervention assessments are held to a high standard in regard to cultural competence.

REFERENCES

American Psychological Association Task Force on Evidence-Based Practice for Children and Adolescents. (2008). *Disseminating evidence-based practice for children and adolescents: A systems approach to enhancing care*. Washington, DC: American Psychological Association.

APA Presidential Task Force on Evidence-Based Practice. (2006). Evidence-based practice in psychology. *American Psychologist, 61,* 271–285. http://dx.doi.org/10.1037/0003-066X.61.4.271

Boake, C. (2002). From the Binet–Simon to the Wechsler–Bellevue: Tracing the history of intelligence testing. *Journal of Clinical and Experimental Neuropsychology, 24,* 383–405. http://dx.doi.org/10.1076/jcen.24.3.383.981

Conroy, M. A., Dunlap, G., Clark, S., & Alter, P. J. (2005). A descriptive analysis of positive behavioral intervention with young children with challenging behaviors. *Topics in Early Childhood Special Education, 25,* 157–166. http://dx.doi.org/10.1177/02711214050250030301

Donovan, S., & Cross, C. (2002). *Minority students in special and gifted education*. Washington, DC: National Academy Press.

Evans, S. (2010). School mental health: Moving forward and facing our challenges. *School Mental Health, 2,* 1–2. http://dx.doi.org/10.1007/s12310-010-9031-8

Forman, S., Olin, S., Hoagwood, K., Crowe, M., & Saka, N. (2009). Evidence-based interventions in schools: Developers views of implementation barriers and facilitators. *School Mental Health, 1*, 26–36. http://dx.doi.org/10.1007/s12310-008-9002-5

Graham, S. (1992). "Most of the subjects were White and middle class": Trends in published research on African Americans in selected APA journals, 1970–1989. *American Psychologist, 47*, 629–639. http://dx.doi.org/10.1037/0003-066X.47.5.629

Graves, S. L. (2009). Albert Sidney Beckham: The first African American school psychologist. *School Psychology International, 30*, 5–23. http://dx.doi.org/10.1177/0143034308101847

Gregory, R. J. (2004). *Psychological testing: History, principles, and applications.* Boston, MA: Allyn & Bacon.

Griner, D., & Smith, T. B. (2006). Culturally adapted mental health intervention: A meta-analytic review. *Psychotherapy: Theory, Research, Practice, Training, 43*, 531–548. http://dx.doi.org/10.1037/0033-3204.43.4.531

Grunewald, S., Shriberg, D., Wheeler, A. S., Miranda, A. H., O'Bryon, E. C., & Rogers, M. R. (2014). Examining diversity research literature in school psychology from 2004 to 2010. *Psychology in the Schools, 51*, 421–433. http://dx.doi.org/10.1002/pits.21764

Guthrie, R. V. (2004). *Even the rat was white: A historical view of psychology* (2nd ed.). Boston, MA: Pearson Education.

Hilliard, A. G. (1983). IQ and the courts: *Larry P. vs. Wilson Riles* and *PASE vs. Hannon. Journal of Black Psychology, 10*, 1–18.

Holliday, B. G. (2009). The history and visions of African American psychology: Multiple pathways to place, space, and authority. *Cultural Diversity and Ethnic Minority Psychology, 15*, 317–337. http://dx.doi.org/10.1037/a0016971

Ingraham, C., & Oka, E. (2006). Multicultural issues in evidence-based interventions. *Journal of Applied School Psychology, 22*, 127–149. http://dx.doi.org/10.1300/J370v22n02_07

Kamin, L. J. (1995). The pioneers of IQ testing. In R. Jacoby & N. Glauberman (Eds.), *The bell curve debate: History, documents, opinions* (pp. 81–105). New York, NY: Times Books.

Larry P. v. Riles, 793 F. Supp. 926 (N.D. Cal. 1979).

Leong, F. T., & Okazaki, S. (2009). History of Asian American psychology. *Cultural Diversity and Ethnic Minority Psychology, 15*, 352–362. http://dx.doi.org/10.1037/a0016443

Lindo, E. (2006). The African American presence in reading intervention experiments. *Remedial and Special Education, 27*, 148–153. http://dx.doi.org/10.1177/07419325060270030301

Mak, W. W., Law, R. W., Alvidrez, J., & Pérez-Stable, E. J. (2007). Gender and ethnic diversity in NIMH-funded clinical trials: Review of a decade of published research. *Administration and Policy in Mental Health and Mental Health Services Research, 34*, 497–503. http://dx.doi.org/10.1007/s10488-007-0133-z

McGuire, F. (1994). Army alpha and beta tests of intelligence. In R. J. Sternberg (Ed.), *Encyclopedia of human intelligence* (pp. 125–129). New York, NY: Macmillan.

McReynolds, P. (1987). Lightner Witmer: Little-known founder of clinical psychology. *American Psychologist, 42,* 849–858. http://dx.doi.org/10.1037/0003-066X.42.9.849

Nation, M., Crusto, C., Wandersman, A., Kumpfer, K. L., Seybolt, D., Morrissey-Kane, E., & Davino, K. (2003). What works in prevention: Principles of effective prevention programs. *American Psychologist, 58,* 449–456. http://dx.doi.org/10.1037/0003-066X.58.6-7.449

Otis, A. S. (1918). An absolute point scale for the group measurements of intelligence. Part I. *Journal of Educational Psychology, 9,* 239–261. http://dx.doi.org/10.1037/h0072885

Padilla, A. M., & Olmedo, E. (2009). Synopsis of key persons, events, and associations in the history of Latino psychology. *Cultural Diversity and Ethnic Minority Psychology, 15,* 363–373. http://dx.doi.org/10.1037/a0017557

Parents in Action on Special Education v. Hannon, 506 F. Supp. 831 (N.D. Ill. 1980).

Pickren, W. E., & Rutherford, A. (2010). *A history of modern psychology in context.* Hoboken, NJ: Wiley.

Schulman, K. A., Berlin, J. A., Harless, W., Kerner, J. F., Sistrunk, S., Gersh, B. J., . . . Escarce, J. J. (1999, February 25). The effect of race and sex on physicians' recommendations for cardiac catheterization. *The New England Journal of Medicine, 340,* 618–626. http://dx.doi.org/10.1056/NEJM199902253400806

Serpell, Z. N., Clauss-Ehlers, C. S., & Lindsey, M. A. (2007). Schools' provision of information regarding mental health and associated services to culturally diverse families. In S. W. Evans, M. Weist, & Z. Serpell (Eds.), *Advances in school-based mental health* (Vol. 2, pp. 18-1–18-17). Kingston, NJ: Civic Research Institute.

Terman, L. M., & Merrill, M. A. (1937). *Measuring intelligence: A guide to the administration of the new revised Stanford–Binet tests of intelligence.* Boston, MA: Houghton Mifflin.

Terman, L. M., & Merrill, M. A. (1973). *Stanford–Binet Intelligence Scale: Manual for the third revision, Form L–M.* Boston, MA: Houghton Mifflin.

Trimble, J. E., & Clearing-Sky, M. (2009). An historical profile of American Indians and Alaska Natives in psychology. *Cultural Diversity and Ethnic Minority Psychology, 15,* 338–351. http://dx.doi.org/10.1037/a0015112

Urban, W. J. (1989). The black scholar and intelligence testing: The case of Horace Mann Bond. *Journal of the History of the Behavioral Sciences, 25,* 323–334. http://dx.doi.org/10.1002/1520-6696(198910)25:4<323::AID-JHBS2300250403>3.0.CO;2-J

U.S. Department of Health and Human Services. (1999). *Mental health: A report of the surgeon general.* Rockville, MD: U.S. Department of Health and Human Services.

U.S. Department of Health and Human Services. (2001). *Mental health: Culture, race, and ethnicity. A supplement to Mental health: A report of the surgeon general.* Rockville, MD: U.S. Department of Health and Human Services.

Valencia, R. R., & Suzuki, L. A. (2000). *Intelligence testing and minority students: Foundations, performance factors, and assessment issues* (Vol. 3). Thousand Oaks, CA: Sage.

Williams, R. L. (2008). A 40-year history of the Association of Black Psychologists (ABPsi). *Journal of Black Psychology, 34,* 249–260. http://dx.doi.org/10.1177/0095798408321332

Yerkes, R. M. (Ed.) (1921). Psychological examining in the United States Army. *Memoirs of the National Academy of Sciences, 15,* 1–890.

2

THEORETICAL FRAMEWORKS OF ETHNIC MINORITY YOUTH ACHIEVEMENT

JAMILIA J. BLAKE, LEANN V. SMITH, AND ALICIA D. KNIGHT

The racial–ethnic achievement gap is a pressing societal issue that plagues the American educational system. In the United States, American Indian students earn the lowest reading and math scores and represent the largest percentage of high school dropouts of all youth, followed by Black and Latino students (Faircloth & Tippeconnic, 2010; National Center for Education Statistics [NCES], 2013; Rampey, Lutkus, Weiner, & Rahman, 2006). Unfortunately, the limited research on American Indian student achievement leaves this population virtually absent from the achievement gap discourse pushing the academic underperformance of Black and Latino students to the forefront of research, practice, and policy devoted to eradicating racial and ethnic educational disparities. In light of the dearth of theoretical and empirical research on the educational experiences of American Indian youth, this chapter focuses on theoretical models to explain achievement outcomes in Black and Latino youth.

http://dx.doi.org/10.1037/14855-003
Psychoeducational Assessment and Intervention for Ethnic Minority Children: Evidence-Based Approaches,
S. L. Graves, Jr., and J. J. Blake (Editors)

In 2013, 17% of Black and 22% of Latino eighth-grade students read at or above the proficient level (NCES, 2013). This translates into approximately 73% to 78% of Black and Latino eighth-grade students failing to read at grade level. Equally alarming is the high school dropout rates for these populations. According to the NCES 2013 report, Black and Latino students' high school dropout rates exceeded the overall dropout rate for the adolescent population in 2012 by 1% for Black youth and almost 6% for Latino youth (NCES, 2013).

Similar trends have also been found in the racial and ethnic distributions of school discipline sanctions. There appears to be a pushing out, if you will, of economically disadvantaged students and students of Black and Latino ancestry from schools by way of exclusionary discipline practices (Blake, Butler, Lewis, & Darensbourg, 2011; Losen & Martinez, 2013). The 2014 report by the U.S. Department of Education Office of Civil Rights revealed that rates of suspension for Black youth were double that of their overall enrollment in U.S. public schools in the 2011–2012 academic year. Although Latino youths' suspension rates were not greater than their enrollment in public schools in 2011–2012, their suspension rates were 13% higher than that of White students (U.S. Department of Education, 2014). Due to the likelihood that students subject to frequent exclusionary discipline will have early and continued contact with the criminal justice system, the prospect of high school completion for these students is low (Appleseed, 2007; Kim, Losen, & Hewitt, 2010; Marchbanks et al., 2014), suggesting that the disparate impact of exclusionary discipline provides another mechanism to further widen the racial and ethnic achievement gap (Gregory, Skiba, & Noguera, 2010).

The societal benefits of ensuring the educational attainment of all students makes the racial and ethnic achievement gap not only a national educational issue but also a public health concern. Research suggests that higher educational attainment is associated with increased earning potential, lower lifetime unemployment rates (Ryan & Siebens, 2012), and decreased involvement in criminal offending during adulthood (Ford & Schroeder, 2010). The current trend in Black and Latino students' achievement and school noncompletion suggests that if racial and ethnic disparities in education persist, Black and Latino youth will face an opportunity gap that will not only limit their individual ability to compete in society to attain gainful employment but will also have profound implications for the nation's economy. Thus, the task for educators, policymakers, and achievement scholars is not whether they should intervene but how best to forge collective efforts to eliminate educational disparities for all youth. Before addressing inequitable educational practices, however, we must first evaluate the predominant theoretical frameworks and ideologies that guide the current conceptualization of racial and ethnic disparities in education. The consideration of new theoretical frameworks is critical for identifying more effective remedies to narrow the achievement gap.

BEYOND DEFICIT-BASED FRAMEWORKS: THE INTERSECTION OF CULTURE AND CONTEXT

The traditional framework for understanding racial and ethnic disparities in achievement is through racial and ethnic group comparisons. This approach has resulted in White youths' achievement and learning-related behaviors serving as the standard by which all racially and ethnically diverse youth are evaluated. The advantage of a comparative framework is that it elucidates racial and ethnic differences in achievement and highlights which racial and ethnic groups are underachieving relative to same-aged peers. However, the disadvantage of this approach is that it assumes a monolithic view of racial and ethnic groups and is deficit oriented (Hilliard, 2003). Failing to recognize the within-group cultural variation in racial and ethnic populations (e.g., variations in socioeconomic status among racial and ethnic groups, regional differences among racial and ethnic groups situated in various parts of the country) limits the identification of individual and systemic processes that cause discrepancies in achievement in some subpopulations of racial and ethnic groups but not in others (e.g., African Americans vs. Caribbean American youth, Colombian vs. Mexican American youth). Furthermore, a monolithic perspective of racial and ethnic groups allows educational scholars and practitioners to focus solely on students' racial and ethnic status as the cause of the achievement gap, as opposed to considering how members from racial and ethnic minority groups' historical experiences with structural racism and individual discrimination in the United States have shaped and influenced their risk of underachievement. The view that racial–ethnic educational disparities are solely attributed to race and ethnicity also results in the tendency for scholars and psychologists to falsely ascribe racial and ethnic achievement discrepancies to genetic, heritable traits (Skiba, 2012).

A call has been issued for the adoption of culturally grounded strengths-based theories to understand racial and ethnic disparities in student achievement that focus on within group cultural heterogeneity and assets that promote academic success (Boykin & Allen, 2000; Okeke-Adeyanju et al., 2014). Culturally grounded competency frameworks provide the most culturally sensitive and ethically appropriate way to understand student achievement and to deliver psychological and educational services to ethnically diverse youth. These models are favored over deficit-based theories, which attribute the source for racial and ethnic minority students' underachievement to cultural disadvantage because they alter the long-standing portrayal of Black and Latino youth as being born into conditions of unavoidable risks without any supports or means to overcome these risks. To date, there are at least three culturally driven competency models that attempt to explain ethnically diverse students' achievement by addressing the intersecting nature of culture and context in shaping youths' achievement: the phenomenological variant of ecological systems theory, the talent development model of schooling, and the stereotype threat framework.

PHENOMENOLOGICAL VARIANT OF ECOLOGICAL SYSTEMS THEORY

The phenomenological variant of ecological systems theory (PVEST) is a framework that is heavily rooted in developmental and ecological theory and can be used to examine the strengths and resiliency of ethnic minority youth. PVEST operates under the premise that risks and protective factors are present in various contexts and may differ depending on one's stage of development; for example, a support that is in place during early childhood may not have the same relevance during adolescent maturation. In addition, a child's or adolescent's perception of these experiences, whether they be normative or atypical, will shape how they prepare or orient themselves to future experiences. To understand this process, the PVEST framework focuses on discovering the supports and strengths present in the face of developmental (e.g., puberty) and/or contextual challenges (e.g., unexpected life events) that facilitate successfully overcoming adversity for all children. Approaching challenges in this way reveals intrapersonal resilience and identifies potential supports for future challenges. This is in contrast to traditional theoretical approaches to understanding ethnic minority youths' development, which labels individual risks without identifying the individual strengths that help youth navigate these obstacles.

Media and empirical portrayals of ethnic minority youth emphasize that youth face discrimination; poverty; limited access to social, psychological, and educational resources; and other risks. However, strengths and opportunities for success are rarely presented; thus, people of color are viewed as only having exorbitant levels of risks and hardships (Pope, 2013). PVEST moves away from focusing solely on deficits and challenges to considering how these risks may be lessened with resilience. Adopting this approach encourages psychologists to consider how youth who are perceived to be most at risk of social and economic adversity can achieve success when faced with these challenges.

Success in overcoming challenges is indicative of having protective factors, such as supports or strengths, readily available. PVEST explores these protective factors by examining coping processes, life outcomes, and current stressors to examine future variables of strength and support for the individual. Cultural strengths such as spirituality, interdependence, and the adherence to cultural traditions are considered common protective factors that aid some ethnic minority youth in overcoming life challenges (Jagers, Smith, Mock, & Dill, 1997; Russell, Chu, Crockett, & Lee, 2010; Sinha & Rosenberg, 2013). Socializing youth racially and ethnically, teaching racial pride to navigate experiences of discrimination for Black youth, and ensuring cultural traditions, values, and norms are retained in Latino youth are examples of cultural strengths that have garnered the most empirical support in reducing adverse experience for ethnically diverse youth (Boykin & Toms, 1985; Pessar, 1995). Racial and ethnic socialization has been found to moderate the effect of exposure to violence on engaging in violent behaviors in Black males (DeGruy, Kjellstrand, Briggs, & Brennan, 2012); to increase overall adaptive functioning in underresourced Black youth (Elmore & Gaylord-Harden, 2013); and to explain lower levels of depression in Black, Latino, and Asian youth (Liu & Lau, 2013). In addition to their benefits to youths' overall functioning, racial and ethnic socialization practices predict early childhood achievement values (Suizzo, Pahlke, Yarnell, Chen, & Romero, 2014) and later achievement outcomes during the adolescence of ethnically diverse youth (Strambler, Linke, & Ward, 2013).

McGee and Pearman (2014) used the PVEST model to explain the risks encountered and success attained as high-achieving African American males progressed from kindergarten to eighth grade. Through the PVEST model, they classified protective and risk factors as either internal or external to create a table of assets, resources, challenges, and distress encountered by youth. For example, intrinsic motivation for learning math (an internal protective factor) and strong family socialization (an external protective factor) were labeled as an asset and a resource, respectively; fatigue over being subjected to racial stereotypes (an internal risk) and being a victim of childhood trauma (an external risk) were categorized as a distressful challenges. From this detailed collection of assets and resources, McGee and Pearman offered recommendations on ways to increase Black male achievement in fields related to science, technology, engineering, and math (STEM). Their findings suggest that encouraging Black father figures to participate in school activities, developing culturally relevant math-related curricula, and creating summer or after-school programs for high-achieving students may be practices that can enhance Black student achievement. Although research specifically using PVEST is still developing, elements of PVEST in the form of incorporating cultural assets and strengths of adolescents to better understand their development is observed in positive youth development (PYD) research.

PVEST and PYD both reframe youth developmental risks as challenges that can be overcome using interpersonal characteristics and coping strategies the youths bring with them to social and educational contexts. Both frame-works also have inspired empirical questions and interventions that empha-size adolescents' assets and strengths. Cultural adaptation and ethnic identity are two cultural variables that are often included in the promotion of healthy development and achievement in Latin American youth (N. A. Gonzales, Fabrett, & Knight, 2009; Quintana & Scull, 2009). *Cultural adaptation* refers to the way in which an individual navigates the values, beliefs, and behaviors of two different cultures. Three components of cultural adaptation are *acculturation* (adaptation to the host culture), *enculturation* (adaptation in favor of one's heritage culture), and *biculturalism* (an integration of both cultures). *Ethnic identity*, a similar yet different construct, refers to the degree to which a person defines him- or herself as a member of his or her ethnic group and the level of attachment he or she feels toward that group. Acevedo-Polakovich et al. (2014) used an asset-orientation model to study whether the relation between ethnic identity and youths' social–developmental assets (e.g., leader-ship, social responsibility, academic engagement) differed for Latino youths on the basis of their level of cultural adaptation. They found that Latino youths who were bicultural reported lower levels of leadership and respon-sibility; a positive relationship between ethnic identity and leadership was strongest for acculturated youth. Acevedo-Polakovich et al.'s findings sug-gest that developing an identity as a Latino is related to better outcomes for youths who have adapted their values, beliefs, and traditions to American culture. This finding shifts practitioners and scholars from promoting ethnic identity as vital for healthy development of all Latino youth and highlights that a more complex relationship may exist.

Focusing on the assets and strengths that ethnic minority youth bring to a learning environment may lead to a better conceptualization of what clients are experiencing, which in turn allows interventions to be better tailored to their needs. PVEST and PYD are both frameworks for unveiling the strengths that ethnic minority youths possess both internally and through their access to external supports. The talent development model of schooling capitalizes on the cultural strengths identified through PVEST and PYD frameworks by extending them to their application to the school setting to facilitate better educational outcomes among ethnically diverse youth.

TALENT DEVELOPMENT MODEL OF SCHOOLING

The recognition that the integration of cultural elements in the school could help ethnic minority students learn served as the launching pad for Boykin's (2000) talent development model for schooling (TDM). Like PVEST, TDM assumes that all youths possess certain strengths that may be advantageous for their social and academic development and that both context and culture are essential in shaping ethnic minority youths' academic success. Unique to TDM is the emphasis placed on the integration of student strengths with their academic potential and the infusion of culture in the instructional and cocurricular values of educational systems. TDM asserts that all children can learn and will do so when the environment sets high expectations for students to meet rigorous academic standards. TDM emphasizes changing the instructional environment to better fit the needs and talents of students. The framework focuses on building children's personal assets and viewing these assets as a form of social capital valuable to the educational system. Among ethnic minority youth, these assets can be homemaking, caretaking responsibilities, and other skills developed through cultural traditions (e.g., bilingualism). For example, there is some research that has suggested that caretaking responsibilities may foster greater self-confidence, empathy, and leadership (Burton, 2007). If ethnic minority youths' assets are viewed as forms of social capital, these qualities will be viewed as adaptive and may be useful in the classroom (Boykin, 2000; Richardson & van Brakle, 2013). TDM shifts traditional pedagogy that labels students on the basis of their abilities to a model that changes the school structure and academic supports to help and value all students with differing learning styles. By altering the culture and values of the educational system instead of attempting to change the learner, TDM situates the problem outside the child and prevents educators from blaming students for their academic difficulties.

TDM focuses on six themes that should be integrated into the education of ethnically diverse youth. First, there should be a focus on assets and strengths. This theme is consistent with moving away from the deficit-based models for understanding youth achievement and closely aligns with PVEST and PYD theoretical orientations. An example of how a school can build on the assets of ethnic minority youth is the inclusion of bilingual education for students from Spanish-speaking households. Ramirez, Perez, Valdez, and Hall (2009) analyzed the long-term effects of a bilingual program implemented in an elementary school for kindergarten to third grade limited-English-proficient Mexican American students. The program incorporated English and Spanish education, as well as the development of bicultural identities. Thirty years after its completion, the researchers investigated whether the program had a significant impact on school dropout, standardized test scores, and ethnic identity. Findings suggested that, compared with the control group, program participants had lower dropout rates, scored higher on measures of both Mexican and American identities, and did not differ significantly on standardized test scores. This finding illustrates how capitalizing on the assets of ethnically diverse students (e.g., bilingual language instruction for Spanish-speaking Latino youth) may improve school retention. Research on the strengths and assets of Black youths also shows evidence for them being incorporated in educational settings.

The second theme of TDM underscores the importance of providing social and academic support (e.g., offering mentoring to incoming freshman students) across key developmental transitions, such as the transitions from elementary to middle school and middle school to high school, to facilitate students' optimal adjustment and growth. The third theme is to replace instructional practices that reinforce passive rote learning with instructional strategies that encourage constructivist and activist learning. *Constructivism* posits that learners actively extract meaning from information presented to them. To this end, problem-solving and critical analyses are hallmarks of constructivist learning styles. *Activists* learn by doing and enjoy being actively engaged during instruction. Brainstorming, group discussions, puzzles, and role-playing are ways to include activist practices in instruction. These approaches differ from common "drill and kill" methods of instruction that emphasize rote memorization and regurgitation.

Preparation for the 21st century through developing communication and higher level numeracy skills is the fourth theme of TDM. An illustration of this theme can be found in an information technology (IT) and STEM after-school program implemented by Duran, Hoft, Lawson, Medjahed, and Orady (2014) for students who were female, who were from underrepresented ethnic minority groups, or who had special needs. The 2-year program implemented in four urban high schools sought to supplement the students' basic learning by giving them mentors and workshops and facilitating their completion of an IT/STEM inquiry-based final project that was presented to key STEM businesses and scholars in a science-fair format. The results showed that students gained significant skills in common technology usage (e.g., typing, web searching), but more important, gained programming skills (e.g., robotics programming). The program also had a positive impact on the career aspirations of the students, in that 55% exited the program with increased or sustained interest in IT/STEM careers. Duran et al.'s study provided preliminary evidence that advanced technology and information systems skills can be developed in urban areas with ethnically diverse students.

The fifth theme of TDM is that the school should operate as a community. Schools that have a shared goal and communicate that all students are valued and belong in the classroom not only enhance the educational outcomes of its students (Lee & Smith, 1996) but also build the morale of the staff (Boyer, 1995). This collective approach to education makes students feel empowered to learn while simultaneously encouraging teachers and staff to feel vital to the child's learning. One example of a community building strategy for schools involves how teachers interact and provide feedback to students. Strambler and Weinstein (2010) found that the interactions between teachers and students had important implications for students' attitudes toward learning. In their study of Black and Latino elementary students, they found that these students on average showed high levels of academic valuing. However, this changed when teacher feedback was considered. For Black and Latino students, higher perceived negative teacher feedback predicted more devaluing of academics, and greater perceived teacher care predicted less devaluing. This study demonstrated how impactful teachers' perceived attitudes toward students and feedback delivery style were on ethnic minority youths' perception of education. It also lent some support to the importance of TDM's community building theme for enhancing academic success of ethnically diverse youth.

The final theme of TDM is that meaningful and connected learning occurs when it is relevant to the child's life and future job security. Showing students why what they are learning is important and how it relates to their larger goals may foster positive attitudes toward achievement that in turn lead to better academic outcomes (Darensbourg & Blake, 2014; Mickelson, 1990; Strambler & Weinstein, 2010; Wang & Eccles, 2013). Mickelson (1990) found that although all high school students possessed abstract achievement values, marked by a general valuing of school, for Black students, concrete achievement values related to the utility of education were more predictive of their achievement outcomes than abstract values. Thus, learning is more meaningful for Black students when the task is connected to relevant aspects of their lives and communities.

TDM asserts that when all six of these themes are addressed, elements of students' culture are integrated within instruction and valued by the educational systems, and school–community partnerships are central to educational institutions, positive student outcomes will be achieved by all students. Although empirical evidence for incorporating all six TDM themes is developing, conventional wisdom suggests that if evidence exists for each theme independently, integrating all themes should lead to greater levels of academic success for ethnically diverse youth.

STEREOTYPE THREAT THEORY

Stereotype threat is a phenomenon that has received substantial attention in the achievement gap literature. Stereotype threat is essential to understanding the academic achievement of ethnic minority youth, in that it has been found to affect students' in-class task performance, overall standardized test performance, and performance on intelligence tests (Nussbaum & Steele, 2007; Steele, 1997; Steele & Aronson, 1995). The stereotype threat theory is similar to TDM and PVEST in its attention to culture and context and recognition that the cultural experiences of ethnic minority youth play a significant and unique role in ethnically diverse students' psychosocial and educational outcomes. However, unlike the other models, stereotype threat places more emphasis on ethnic minority experiences of discrimination and exposure to stereotypes, making it more applicable to ethnically diverse adolescents who have the cognitive ability to recognize stereotypes than the other models that are more heavily rooted in developmental and pedagogical theory.

Stereotype threat is characterized by an individual's decreased task performance in the presence of stimuli that increase the individual's awareness of stereotypes about their group's underperformance in the assessed task domain (Steele & Aronson, 1995). Steele (1997) asserted that when a racial or ethnic minority member's race is salient and they encounter or are reminded of the negative stereotypes that exist in a particular domain for their racial or ethnic group, internalized anxiety is activated and task performance is undermined. This process results in a continuous cycle of anxiety activation and task underperformance that can eventually lead the individual to no longer desire to participate in that domain out of fear that they will confirm the stereotypes that exist for their group or that compromise their performance in the domain when the stereotype for their racial or ethnic group is activated.

Strong, converging evidence supports stereotype threat and has shown it to be true for more than just ethnically diverse populations. Research has shown that women in male-dominated fields (e.g., STEM; S. J. Spencer, Steele, & Quinn, 1999), White males in sports when presented with negative messages of White athleticism (Stone, 2002), White males when compared with Asian males in math tests (Aronson et al., 1999), and people with low socioeconomic status (B. Spencer & Castano, 2007) all experience stereotype threat and underperform on a given task when exposed to stereotypes related to their race/ethnicity or gender. In their meta-analysis on stereotype threat in Black and Latino populations, Nadler and Clark (2011) found that both Latino and Black students experience stereotype threat and that their experiences do not differ significantly. However, it is important to note that stereotype threat does not appear to affect all ethnic minority students, even those from the same ethnic group, in similar ways. The differential effect of stereotype threat for individuals of the same ethnic group underscores the importance of considering the heterogeneity within ethnic groups when evaluating the impact of stereotypes and discrimination on youth.

Operating from a stereotype threat framework requires an understanding of the larger context in which these stereotypes and messages of inadequacy are being delivered and perpetuated. It also requires an understanding of individuals and how they see themselves; thus, it requires the use of variables that speak to the importance of group membership (e.g., ethnic identity) rather than merely group membership status (e.g., being a member of a racial or ethnic group). This means that stereotype threat is most likely to be activated when youth have the cognitive sophistication to develop an ethnic identity (Quintana et al., 2006). For stereotype threat to occur, a number of elements must be considered: (a) the affiliation or value of the task domain, (b) the salience of the individual's ethnicity, and (c) the knowledge of stereotypes related to their ethnic group. The individual must identify with and value the task domain (e.g., a math major completing a math exam; Steele, 1997). People who identify with the domain have the ability and interest in succeeding but still experience stereotype threat when presented with negative information about the intellectual ability of their social group (Brown & Pinel, 2003). Findings also revealed that people who have greater ethnic identity are more likely to underperform when their status in that group is highlighted and associated with negative stereotypes (Davis, Aronson, & Salinas, 2006; P. M. Gonzales, Blanton, & Williams, 2002). A person whose racial or ethnic group membership is highly salient to their identity is more affected by the negative messages they hear about their group and experience more pressure to try and avoid confirming those negative stereotypes. Last, *ethnic stigma consciousness*, an overall awareness of the stigmas that plague a member's racial or ethnic group (e.g., Blacks' stigma of being anti-intellectual), also interferes with optimal task performance (Brown & Pinel, 2003; Schmader, Johns, & Forbes, 2008). Understanding the elements that make a person more vulnerable for stereotype threat, racial or ethnic identity, ethnic stigma consciousness, and academic identity can aid psychologists in identifying and assisting students who may be experiencing stereotype threat effects.

There is a wealth of research on ways the negative impact of stereotype threat can be circumvented; however, much of this work has been conducted with college-age students. There is some intervention research with school-age populations showing that teaching students to reattribute intellectual ability and performance on standardized achievement tests to malleable external rather than internal characteristics and writing interventions that focus on self-affirmations can buffer the effect of stereotype threat on achievement outcomes (Good, Aronson, & Inzlicht, 2003; Sherman et al., 2013). Hanselman, Bruch, Gamoran, and Borman (2014) implemented a self-affirmation intervention in 11 different middle schools of varying levels of ethnic diversity. Schools were classified as being high-potential-threat and low-potential-threat schools on the basis of the level of ethnic diversity of the school and its corresponding academic standards. High-potential-threat schools were operationalized as less ethnically diverse and as having higher achievement standards than low-potential-threat schools, which were defined as evidencing greater ethnic diversity among students and heterogeneity in student achievement and socioeconomic status. Students were also grouped on the basis of their susceptibility to stereotype threat effects. Black and Latino students were grouped together as being most susceptible to stereotype threat, and White and Asian students were labeled as least susceptible. The intervention was designed to counteract ethnic and/or gender identity threat of students by having them write short, self-affirming essays as part of their language arts class activities three to four times during the school year. Students were randomly assigned to either write an essay about their most important values from a list of options or to write about their least important value from the same list and why this may be important to someone else. Findings revealed that self-affirmations reduced by 12.5% the racial–ethnic achievement gap in overall grade point average of Black and Latino youth who were in high-threat schools compared with nonsusceptible youth. This provides preliminary evidence that the deleterious effect of stereotype threat on performance can be reduced.

Although stereotype threat does not fully explain the achievement gap, its contribution to understanding ethnic minority learners, primarily those situated in more racialized and stereotype-rich environments, is important. Stereotype threat situates the learner in the school context, but also suggests that larger social contexts (i.e., society) shape the experiences of ethnic minority youth and that experiences of discrimination and stereotyping may have powerful implications for ethnically diverse students' achievement.

CONCLUSION

The underachievement of Black and Latino students is a national issue that warrants strategic efforts to alter these students' negative educational trajectory. Historically, racial and ethnic disparities have been framed from a deficit-oriented perspective in which adaptive characteristics of ethnically diverse youth (e.g., resilience) that prove beneficial in educational settings have been overlooked. The theoretical frameworks presented in this chapter— phenomenological variant of ecological systems theory, talent development model of schooling, and stereotype threat theory—are culturally grounded, strength-based theories that highlight how examining the intersecting role of context and culture from an asset building framework can positively influence ethnically diverse youths' social and educational outcomes. It is important that these frameworks replace traditional models for understanding ethnic minority youths' achievement, given that they emphasize the promotion of assets and resiliency in ethnically diverse youth, which have the power to influence these youths' academic success. It is important to note that although these models might also generalize to socially marginalized youth from other racial and ethnic backgrounds (e.g., Southeast Asians, Native Americans), supporting evidence is minimal, if not altogether absent. Because the empirical research evaluating the application of these models to other diverse populations is limited, caution is encouraged in the extension of these models to other populations without additional empirical support.

REFERENCES

Acevedo-Polakovich, I. D., Cousineau, J. R., Quirk, K. M., Gerhart, J. I., Bell, K. M., & Adomako, M. S. (2014). Toward an asset orientation in the study of U.S. Latina/o youth: Biculturalism, ethnic identity, and positive youth development. *The Counseling Psychologist, 42,* 201–229. http://dx.doi.org/10.1177/0011000013477904

Appleseed, T. (2007). Texas' school-to-prison pipeline: Dropout to incarceration. *The impact of school discipline and zero tolerance.* Austin, TX: Author.

Aronson, J., Lustina, M. J., Good, C., Keough, K., Steele, C. M., & Brown, J. (1999). When White men can't do math: Necessary and sufficient factors in stereotype threat. *Journal of Experimental Social Psychology, 35,* 29–46. http://dx.doi.org/10.1006/jesp.1998.1371

Blake, J. J., Butler, B. A., Lewis, C. L., & Darensbourg, A. (2011). Unmasking the inequitable discipline experiences of urban Black girls: Implications for urban stakeholders. *The Urban Review, 43,* 90–106. http://dx.doi.org/10.1007/s11256-009-0148-8

Boyer, E. (1995). *The basic school: A community for learning.* New York, NY: Carnegie.

Boykin, A. W. (2000). The talent development model of schooling: Placing students at promise for academic success. *Journal of Education for Students Placed at Risk, 5,* 3–25. http://dx.doi.org/10.1080/10824669.2000.9671377

Boykin, A. W., & Allen, B. A. (2000). Beyond deficit and difference: Psychological integrity in developmental research. In C. C. Yeakey (Ed.), *Edmond W. Gordon: Producing knowledge, pursuing understanding* (pp. 15–34). Stamford, CT: JAI Press. http://dx.doi.org/10.1016/S1479-358X(00)80007-8

Boykin, A. W., & Toms, F. D. (1985). Black child socialization: A conceptual framework. In H. P. McAdoo & J. L. McAdoo (Eds.), *Black children: Social, educational, and parental environments* (pp. 33–52). Newbury Park, CA: Sage.

Brown, R. P., & Pinel, E. C. (2003). Stigma on my mind: Individual differences in the experience of stereotype threat. *Journal of Experimental Social Psychology, 39,* 626–633. http://dx.doi.org/10.1016/S0022-1031(03)00039-8

Burton, L. (2007). Childhood adultification in economically disadvantaged families: A conceptual model. *Family Relations, 56,* 329–345. http://dx.doi.org/10.1111/j.1741-3729.2007.00463.x

Darensbourg, A. M., & Blake, J. J. (2014). Examining the academic achievement of Black adolescents: Importance of peer and parental influences. *Journal of Black Psychology, 40,* 191–212. http://dx.doi.org/10.1177/0095798413481384

Davis, C., Aronson, J., & Salinas, M. (2006). Shades of threat: Racial identity as a moderator of stereotype threat. *Journal of Black Psychology, 32,* 399–417. http://dx.doi.org/10.1177/0095798406292464

DeGruy, J., Kjellstrand, J. M., Briggs, H. E., & Brennan, E. M. (2012). Racial respect and racial socialization as protective factors for African American male youth. *Journal of Black Psychology, 38,* 395–420. http://dx.doi.org/10.1177/0095798411429744

Duran, M., Hoft, M., Lawson, D. B., Medjahed, B., & Orady, E. A. (2014). Urban high school students' IT/STEM learning: Findings from a collaborative inquiry- and design-based afterschool program. *Journal of Science Education and Technology, 23,* 116–137. http://dx.doi.org/10.1007/s10956-013-9457-5

Elmore, C. A., & Gaylord-Harden, N. K. (2013). The influence of supportive parenting and racial socialization messages on African American youth behavioral outcomes. *Journal of Child and Family Studies, 22,* 63–75. http://dx.doi.org/10.1007/s10826-012-9653-6

Faircloth, S. C., & Tippeconnic, J. W. (2010). *The dropout/graduation crisis among American Indian and Alaska Native students: Failure to respond places the future of Native peoples at risk.* Los Angeles, CA: The Civil Rights Project/Proyecto Derechos Civiles at UCLA.

Ford, J. A., & Schroeder, R. D. (2010). Higher education and criminal offending over the life course. *Sociological Spectrum, 31,* 32–58. http://dx.doi.org/10.1080/02732173.2011.525695

Gonzales, N. A., Fabrett, F. C., & Knight, G. P. (2009). Acculturation, enculturation, and the psychological adaptation of Latino youth. In F. A. Villarruel et al. (Eds.), *Handbook of U.S. Latino psychology: Developmental and community-based perspectives* (pp. 115–134). Thousand Oaks, CA: Sage.

Gonzales, P. M., Blanton, H., & Williams, K. J. (2002). The effects of stereotype threat and double-minority status on the test performance of Latino women. *Personality and Social Psychology Bulletin, 28,* 659–670. http://dx.doi.org/10.1177/0146167202288010

Good, C., Aronson, J., & Inzlicht, M. (2003). Improving adolescents' standardized test performance: An intervention to reduce the effects of stereotype threat. *Journal of Applied Developmental Psychology, 24,* 645–662. http://dx.doi.org/10.1016/j.appdev.2003.09.002

Gregory, A., Skiba, R. J., & Noguera, P. A. (2010). The achievement gap and the discipline gap two sides of the same coin? *Educational Researcher, 39,* 59–68. http://dx.doi.org/10.3102/0013189X09357621

Hanselman, P., Bruch, S. K., Gamoran, A., & Borman, G. D. (2014). Threat in context: School moderation of the impact of social identity threat on racial/ethnic achievement gaps. *Sociology of Education, 87,* 106–124. http://dx.doi.org/10.1177/0038040714525970

Hilliard, A. G., III. (2003). No mystery: Closing the achievement gap between Africans and excellence. In T. Perry, C. Steele, & A. G. Hilliard III, (Eds.), *Young, gifted, and Black* (pp. 131–165). Boston, MA: Beacon Press.

Jagers, R. J., Smith, P., Mock, L. O., & Dill, E. (1997). An Afrocultural social ethos: Component orientations and some social implications. *Journal of Black Psychology, 23*, 328–343. http://dx.doi.org/10.1177/00957984970234002

Kim, C. Y., Losen, D. J., & Hewitt, D. T. (2010). *The school-to-prison pipeline: Structuring legal reform.* New York, NY: New York University Press.

Lee, V., & Smith, J. (1996). Collective responsibility for learning and its effects on gains in achievement for early secondary school students. *American Journal of Education, 104*, 103–147. http://dx.doi.org/10.1086/444122

Liu, L. L., & Lau, A. S. (2013). Teaching about race/ethnicity and racism matters: An examination of how perceived ethnic racial socialization processes are associated with depression symptoms. *Cultural Diversity and Ethnic Minority Psychology, 19*, 383–394. http://dx.doi.org/10.1037/a0033447

Losen, D. J., & Martinez, T. (2013). *Out of school and off track: The overuse of suspensions in American middle and high schools* (pp. 1–105). Los Angeles, CA: The Civil Rights Project at UCLA.

Marchbanks, M. P., Blake, J. J., Booth, E. A., Carmichael, D., Seibert, A., & Fabelo, T. (2014). The economic effects of exclusionary discipline on grade retention and high school dropout. In D. Losen (Ed.), *Closing the school discipline gap: Research to practice* (pp. 59–74). New York, NY: Teachers' Press.

McGee, E. O., & Pearman, F. A. (2014). Risk and protective factors in mathematically talented Black male students: Snapshots from kindergarten through eighth grade. *Urban Education, 49*, 363–393. http://dx.doi.org/10.1177/00420859 14525791

Mickelson, R. A. (1990). The attitude–achievement paradox among Black adolescents. *Sociology of Education, 63*, 44–61. http://dx.doi.org/10.2307/2112896

Nadler, J. T., & Clark, M. H. (2011). Stereotype threat: A meta-analysis comparing African Americans to Hispanic Americans. *Journal of Applied Social Psychology, 41*, 872–890. http://dx.doi.org/10.1111/j.1559-1816.2011.00739.x

National Center for Education Statistics. (2013). *The nation's report card: A first look: 2013 mathematics and reading* (NCES 2014-451). Washington, DC: Institute of Education Sciences, U.S. Department of Education.

Nussbaum, A. D., & Steele, C. M. (2007). Situational disengagement and persistence in the face of adversity. *Journal of Experimental Social Psychology, 43*, 127–134. http://dx.doi.org/10.1016/j.jesp.2005.12.007

Okeke-Adeyanju, N., Taylor, L. C., Craig, A. B., Smith, R. E., Thomas, A., Boyle, A. E., & DeRosier, M. E. (2014). Celebrating the strengths of Black youth: Increasing self-esteem and implications for prevention. *The Journal of Primary Prevention, 35*, 357–369. http://dx.doi.org/10.1007/s10935-014-0356-1

Pessar, P. (1995). *A VISA for a dream: Dominicans in the United States.* New York, NY: Allyn & Bacon.

Pope, R. J. (2013). Reflections of a Black male counseling psychology doctoral student: Lessons learned from APA Division 45 Commentary and the role of social justice for counseling psychologists. *Journal for Social Action in Counseling and Psychology, 5*, 103–115.

Quintana, S. M., Aboud, F. E., Chao, R. K., Contreras-Grau, J., Cross, W. E., Hudley, C., . . . Vietze, D. L. (2006). Race, ethnicity, and culture in child development: Contemporary research and future directions. *Child Development, 77*, 1129–1141. http://dx.doi.org/10.1111/j.1467-8624.2006.00951.x

Quintana, S. M., & Scull, N. C. (2009). Latino ethnic identity. In F. A. Villarruel, G. Carlo, J. M. Grau, M. Azmitia, N. J. Cabrera, & T. J. Chahin (Eds.), *Handbook of U.S. Latino psychology: Developmental and community-based perspectives* (pp. 81–98). Thousand Oaks, CA: Sage.

Ramirez, M., Perez, M., Valdez, G., & Hall, B. (2009). Assessing the long-term effects of an experimental bilingual-multicultural programme: Implications for dropout prevention, multicultural development and immigration policy. *International Journal of Bilingual Education and Bilingualism, 12*, 47–59. http://dx.doi.org/10.1080/13670050802149523

Rampey, B. D., Lutkus, A. D., Weiner, A. W., & Rahman, T. (2006). *National Indian Education Study, Part I: The performance of American Indian and Alaska Native fourth- and eighth-grade students on NAEP 2005 reading and mathematics assessments* (NCES 2006-463). Washington, DC: U.S. Department of Education, Institute of Educational Sciences, National Center for Education Statistics.

Richardson, J. B., & van Brakle, M. (2013). The everyday struggle: Social capital, youth violence, and parenting strategies for urban, low-income black male youth. *Race and Social Problems, 5*, 262–280. http://dx.doi.org/10.1007/s12552-013-9103-0

Russell, S. T., Chu, J. Y., Crockett, L. J., & Lee, S. (2010). Interdependent independence: The meanings of autonomy among Chinese American and Filipino American adolescents. In S. T. Russell, L. J. Crockett, & R. K. Chao (Eds.), *Asian American parenting and parent–adolescent relationships* (pp. 101–116). New York, NY: Springer Science. http://dx.doi.org/10.1007/978-1-4419-5728-3_6

Ryan, C. L., & Siebens, J. (2012). *Educational attainment in the United States: 2009 population characteristics*. Washington, DC: U.S. Census Bureau, U.S. Department of Commerce, Economics and Statistics Administration. Retrieved from http://www.census.gov/prod/2012pubs/p20-566.pdf

Schmader, T., Johns, M., & Forbes, C. (2008). An integrated process model of stereotype threat effects on performance. *Psychological Review, 115*, 336–356. http://dx.doi.org/10.1037/0033-295X.115.2.336

Sherman, D. K., Hartson, K. A., Binning, K. R., Purdie-Vaughns, V., Garcia, J., Taborsky-Barba, S., . . . Cohen, G. L. (2013). Deflecting the trajectory and changing the narrative: How self-affirmation affects academic performance and motivation under identity threat. *Journal of Personality and Social Psychology, 104*, 591–618. http://dx.doi.org/10.1037/a0031495

Sinha, J. W., & Rosenberg, L. B. (2013). A critical review of trauma interventions and religion among youth exposed to community violence. *Journal of Social Service Research, 39*, 436–454. http://dx.doi.org/10.1080/01488376.2012.730907

Skiba, R. (2012). As nature has formed them: The history and current status of racial difference research. *Teachers College Record, 114,* 1–49.

Spencer, B., & Castano, E. (2007). Social class is dead. Long live social class! Stereotype threat among low socioeconomic status individuals. *Social Justice Research, 20,* 418–432. http://dx.doi.org/10.1007/s11211-007-0047-7

Spencer, S. J., Steele, C. M., & Quinn, D. M. (1999). Stereotype threat and women's math performance. *Journal of Experimental Social Psychology, 35,* 4–28. http://dx.doi.org/10.1006/jesp.1998.1373

Steele, C. M. (1997). A threat in the air: How stereotypes shape intellectual identity and performance. *American Psychologist, 52,* 613–629. http://dx.doi.org/10.1037/0003-066X.52.6.613

Steele, C. M., & Aronson, J. (1995). Stereotype threat and the intellectual test performance of African Americans. *Journal of Personality and Social Psychology, 69,* 797–811. http://dx.doi.org/10.1037/0022-3514.69.5.797

Stone, J. (2002). Battling doubt by avoiding practice: The effects of stereotype threat on self-handicapping in white athletes. *Personality and Social Psychology Bulletin, 28,* 1667–1678. http://dx.doi.org/10.1177/014616702237648

Strambler, M. J., Linke, L. H., & Ward, N. L. (2013). Academic identification as a mediator of the relationship between parental socialization and academic achievement. *Contemporary Educational Psychology, 38,* 99–106. http://dx.doi.org/10.1016/j.cedpsych.2012.11.001

Strambler, M. J., & Weinstein, R. S. (2010). Psychological disengagement in elementary school among ethnic minority students. *Journal of Applied Developmental Psychology, 31,* 155–165. http://dx.doi.org/10.1016/j.appdev.2009.11.006

Suizzo, M. A., Pahlke, E., Yarnell, L., Chen, K. Y., & Romero, S. (2014). Home-based parental involvement in young children's learning across U.S. ethnic groups: Cultural models of academic socialization. *Journal of Family Issues, 35,* 254–287. http://dx.doi.org/10.1177/0192513X12465730

U.S. Department of Education. (2014). *Civil rights data collection: Data snapshot: School discipline* (Issue Brief No. 1). Washington, DC: U.S. Department of Education, Office for Civil Rights.

Wang, M. T., & Eccles, J. S. (2013). School context, achievement motivation, and academic engagement: A longitudinal study of school engagement using a multidimensional perspective. *Learning and Instruction, 28,* 12–23. http://dx.doi.org/10.1016/j.learninstruc.2013.04.002

3

2014 *STANDARDS FOR EDUCATIONAL AND PSYCHOLOGICAL TESTING*: IMPLICATIONS FOR ETHNIC MINORITY YOUTH

FRANK C. WORRELL AND CYRELL C. B. ROBERSON

In the current educational arena, testing looms large for teachers (Baker et al., 2010; Worrell et al., 2014) as well as students (Barton, 1999; Weingarten, 2011), and the stakes on many of these tests are tremendously high because they are used in determining educational and career trajectories. At the same time, much of the nation is engaged in an educational endeavor called the Common Core State Standards Initiative (2014). Adopted by 43 states and the District of Columbia for English and language arts (42 for mathematics), the Common Core is the closest that the United States has come to national standards for kindergarten through 12th-grade education, and if implemented with fidelity, it is expected to increase the rigor of education that American students receive. There are also hopes in some policy circles (e.g., Powers, 2014) that the Common Core will reduce the longstanding and seemingly intractable achievement gaps (American Psychological Association [APA] Presidential Task Force on Education Disparities, 2012; Aud, Fox, &

http://dx.doi.org/10.1037/14855-004
Psychoeducational Assessment and Intervention for Ethnic Minority Children: Evidence-Based Approaches,
S. L. Graves, Jr., and J. J. Blake (Editors)

KewalRamani, 2010) and excellence gaps (Plucker, Burroughs, & Song, 2010; Plucker, Hardesty, & Burroughs, 2013; Warne, 2014) among U.S. racial and ethnic groups.

It is in this context that we take a look at the *Standards for Educational and Psychological Testing* (referred to as the *Standards* henceforth; American Educational Research Association [AERA], APA, & National Council on Measurement in Education [NCME], 2014) that were recently released, as well as the six previous editions. "The purpose of the *Standards* is to provide criteria for the development and evaluation of tests and testing practices and to provide guidelines for assessing the validity of interpretations of test scores for the intended test uses" (AERA, APA, & NCME, 2014, p. 1).

The issue of the appropriate use of test scores provides a raison d'etre for this chapter because there are individuals who believe that commonly used tests of cognitive and academic functioning should not be used with ethnic minority youth. From the point of view of these critics, test scores are biased and do not result in valid interpretations for ethnic minority youth (e.g., Ford & Helms, 2012). Our goal in this chapter is to provide an overview of the history of the *Standards* from the initial versions published in the 1950s to the 2014 edition, with specific emphasis on the applicability to ethnic minority populations. In addition to briefly summarizing the content of these documents, we also discuss whether and how they address the issues of bias and fairness in testing. However, before beginning our overview of the editions of the *Standards*, we provide a brief discussion of the criticisms of tests that have made the *Standards* particularly salient for individuals involved in testing ethnic minority youth.

CRITICISMS ABOUT TEST SCORES IN MINORITY POPULATIONS

The use of standardized tests of cognitive abilities assessing g, also referred to as intelligence or IQ, with certain groups has generated considerable controversy for several decades. In 1996, Neisser et al. summarized the extant literature on intelligence, concluding that "intelligence test scores predict individual differences in school achievement moderately well, correlating about .50 with grade point average and .55 with the number of years of education that individuals complete," but pointing out that "population levels of school achievement are not determined solely or even primarily by intelligence or any other individual-difference variable" (p. 96). In a more recent review of the literature on intelligence, Nisbett et al. (2012, p. 131) came to similar conclusions, some of which had been reported considerably earlier (see Jenkins, 1939).

Because scores on tests are frequently used in determining eligibility for special education classification or for assigning students to programs for the gifted and talented (GATE), groups with lower mean scores on these measures, such as African Americans, are overrepresented in special education (McCray, Webb-Johnson, & Neal, 2003) and underrepresented in GATE programs (Erwin & Worrell, 2012; Ford, 1998), and several researchers have interpreted the differences in means among racial and ethnic groups as evidence of bias in these test scores (Ford, 1998, 2008). Neisser et al. (1996, p. 93) addressed this issue specifically, distinguishing between *outcome bias* and *predictive bias*. Although lower mean scores resulting in negative outcomes are indicative of outcome bias, intelligence tests predict school performance similarly for all groups, including African Americans, indicating that when used "as predictors of future performance, the tests do not seem to be biased against African Americans" (Neisser et al., p. 93). In other words, intelligence test scores are not contaminated with predictive bias.

VERSIONS OF THE STANDARDS

We now turn our attention to the *Standards* themselves. There are six previous versions of the *Standards*: 1954, 1955, 1966, 1974, 1985, and 1999. Although the goals of the earlier editions were generally the same, the most recent versions have been much more explicit in dealing with bias and fairness, issues relevant to testing ethnic minority students.

The 1954 and 1955 Recommendations

The first edition of what is now called the *Standards* was entitled *Technical Recommendations for Psychological Tests and Diagnostics* (APA, AERA, & National Council on Measurements Used in Education [NCMUE], 1954) and was the result of the first joint effort of the sponsoring organizations to help test users select and interpret tests and to assist test producers in communicating the information needed by test users in selection and interpretation. Prior to the 1954 publication, test producers used their own judgment in deciding which standards should apply to the tests they developed, resulting in a lack of coherence and inconsistent information being provided on published tests. Thus, the goals of the 1954 *Standards* were to develop universal, professional standards for reporting information about tests used in psychological testing and to increase transparency in the testing industry for all stakeholders, including test producers, tests users (institutions and employers), and test takers.

"The essential principle . . . is that a test manual should carry information sufficient to enable any qualified user to make sound judgments regarding the usefulness and interpretation of the test" (APA, AERA, & NCMUE, 1954, p. 2). Although the opening sentence of the 1954 document referenced both educational and psychological tests, as noted in the title, it was specific to psychological and diagnostic testing, and a companion volume—*Technical Recommendation for Achievement Tests* (AERA & NCMUE, 1955)—was published a year later by two of the three organizations with education as their specific charge—that is, AERA and NCMUE. The 1954 and 1955 documents had a similar organizational structure, consisting of an introduction discussing development and scope of the recommendations and six sections with recommendations or standards: (a) Dissemination of Information, (b) Interpretation, (c) Validity, (d) Reliability, (e) Administration and Scoring, and (f) Scales and Norms. Much of the text in the 1954 and 1955 editions is the same, with differences generally made to invoke psychological versus educational tests. The sections containing the recommendations each began with a relatively short introduction, except in the case of "Validity," which had a longer discussion introducing four types of validity: content, predictive, concurrent, and construct. Each of the six sections with standards was also subdivided by topic, with an overarching standard (e.g., A1, B4) followed by several standards explicating the overarching standard (e.g., A1.1, B4.4).

General principles established in these first manuals that also apply to the most recent edition include (a) excluding tests used primarily for research purposes from the viewpoint of the *Standards*, (b) recognizing that test development requires a reasonable balance among costs, time, and the final product, (c) refusing to give specific numerical guidance on the size of validity or reliability coefficients, (d) indicating that test users should have appropriate qualifications to be using and interpreting tests, and (e) acknowledging the need for periodic revision of the *Standards* related to changes in tests and to advances in knowledge and psychometric theory.

Finally, both the 1954 and 1955 editions included three levels of standards: "ESSENTIAL standards indicate what information will be genuinely needed for most tests in their usual applications," "VERY DESIRABLE is used to draw attention to types of information which contribute greatly to the user's understanding of the test," and "DESIRABLE includes information which would be helpful, but less so than the ESSENTIAL and VERY DESIRABLE information" (APA, AERA, & NCMUE, 1954, pp. 5–6). The authors recognized that some information, although *very desirable*, may not be available for inclusion in a manual at the time a test is released (e.g., long-term validity coefficients). The *Standards* specifically stated that the purpose was not to stifle growth or innovation but to help test producers develop assessments that were appropriate, valid, and suitable for a wide a variety of purposes while working to make tests are as useful as possible for test users.

The 1954 and 1955 *Technical Recommendations* did not address testing ethnic minority students as a specific topic. However, they did reflect issues that would eventually be raised by individuals concerned with using tests with ethnic minority populations. These issues came up in several sections. For example, the "Interpretation" sections began with an acknowledgement that test users are "responsible for making inferences as to the meaning and *legitimate* [emphasis added] uses of scores" (AERA & NCMUE, 1955, p. 13). This section in the 1955 edition also contained *essential* standards related to drawing attention to frequent misinterpretations of scores (B1.3) and differentiating interpretations appropriate for groups versus individuals (B5.2) and a *very desirable* recommendation about considering appropriate background factors (B6). The equivalent essential standards in the 1954 edition were B1.23 and B5.2, respectively. There were also essential standards in several other sections, including "Validity," "Reliability," and "Scales and Norms," which addressed the issues of making inferences across groups. These standards included C2.1, C13, C113.1, C13.3, C13.6, D3, D3.2, D3.4, F7.1, F7.11, F7.31, and F7.6. Standard F4 in 1954 (F5 in 1955) also stated that in some circumstances, local norms may be more useful than published norms, a point that several researchers writing on identifying ethnic minority students for placement in gifted and talented programs have made in the recent past (cf. Lohman, 2005; Worrell & Erwin, 2011).

The 1966 Edition

In 1966, a revised edition of the *Technical Recommendations* was published. This 40-page edition, the *Standards for Educational and Psychological Tests and Manuals* (APA, AERA, & NCME, 1966), included standards for both educational and psychological tests. The joint committee decided that "in view of the similarity in the nature of many (but not all) problems in both educational and psychological measurement . . . it was advantageous to issue one set of standards" (APA, AERA, & NCME, 1966, p. 1). In keeping with all subsequent revisions, the joint committee used the extant literature and sought broad input from interested stakeholders in testing and measurement to inform the revision. The format and structure of the 1966 *Standards* were similar to that of the two previous editions and consisted of the same sections. As in previous editions, issues related to testing ethnic minorities were alluded to in discussions of appropriate reference groups or bias in sampling, but the term *ethnic minority* was not specifically mentioned nor were any specific ethnic minority groups.

The 1974 Edition

The 1974 edition, entitled the *Standards for Educational and Psychological Tests*, retained some elements of the 1966 edition, including all of the sections in the previous edition, as well as the distinction among *essential*, *very desirable*, and *desirable* standards. However, it also represented a substantial revision of the *Standards*, both in terms of structure and with regard to acknowledging that the document had to address concerns regarding selecting individuals for employment or admitting students to educational institutions and had to speak specifically to issues such as "discrimination again members of groups such as minorities or women" (APA, AERA, & NCME, 1974, p. 1).

With regard to structure, there were several changes in the 1974 edition. First, this edition contained 10 chapters with standards divided into three sections (see Table 3.1), in contrast to the six chapters in the three previous editions. This was the first edition in which standards for validity and reliability were grouped together, making up the second section. This edition also separated standards for use from the standards for the tests themselves, with two of the additional chapters resulting from this distinction. Chapter C, for example, focused on what a test producer must put in a manual with regard to administration and scoring, in contrast with Chapter I, which focused on how a test user administered and scored the test. Similarly, Chapter B focused on the information that test producers had to include in tests and test manuals to aid interpretation, whereas Chapter J focused on how the user should interpret scores. The other two new foci, which had chapters in their own right, were also related to test users—that is, qualifications and concerns of test users (Chapter G) and choosing or developing tests (Chapter H).

The other major change in the 1974 edition was the specific attention to ethnic minorities, which manifested in several ways. First, the word *ethnic* was included in lists of groups to pay attention to (e.g., Standard D2.2, an

TABLE 3.1
Major Sections in the 1974 *Standards*

Title	No. of standards
Introduction	
Standards for Tests, Manuals, and Reports	
A. Dissemination of Information	16
B. Aids to Interpretation	21
C. Directions for Administration and Scoring	14
D. Norms and Scales	28
Standards for Reports of Research on Reliability and Validity	
E. Validity	82
F. Reliability and Measurement Error	26
Standards for the Use of Tests	
G. Qualifications and Concerns of Users	9
H. Choice or Development of Test or Method	9
I. Administration and Scoring	16
J. Interpretation of Scores	24
Total	245

essential standard). Ethnicity was also specifically referenced in Standard E6.1, another essential standard, and in the comments to D2.2, E6.1 and three other essential standards (e.g., D2, H2.1, J5). The term *minority group* is also used. Second, this edition introduced the concept of fairness in testing and tied that concept to bias. In the introduction, the 1974 *Standards* noted that test performance can be influenced by cultural background and that "unfairness can be built into a test" (APA, AERA, & NCME, 1974, p. 2); test users were explicitly cautioned about their role in contributing to fair assessment. However, the 1974 *Standards* also pointed out that test abuse and inappropriate use of test scores do not provide a compelling reason for banning the use of tests for at least two reasons. First, to the extent that decisions will continue to be made without test scores, the decisions will be less well informed than decisions made involving the appropriate use of test scores. Second, because many tests are used for finding potential talent, restricting test use can reduce the probability of finding outstanding talent in the very groups that are underrepresented.

Finally, in 1974, the *Standards* introduced two important principles with regard to bias and validity across groups that are still not well understood today. With regard to bias, the 1974 *Standards* noted that "a simple difference in group means does *not* by itself identify an unfair test, although it should stimulate research to explore the question of fairness" (APA, AERA, & NCME, 1974, p. 43). Rather, bias is related to differential validity and can be examined using a variety of methods. With regard to validity, the *Standards* indicated that "no test is valid for all purposes or in all situations or for all groups of individuals" (p. 31). Thus, "it is incorrect to use the unqualified phrase 'the validity of the test'" (p. 31).

It is perhaps not surprising that the 1974 edition of the *Standards* was the first to address issues of bias directly. The previous 2 decades had witnessed the growth of the civil rights and Black Power movements (Altman, 1997; Smith, 2003) and the violent backlash against African Americans, reflected in the assassinations of Malcolm X in 1965 and Martin Luther King, Jr. in 1968. The Civil Rights Act banning housing discrimination and the election of the first African American woman to Congress also took place in that period, and Cross's (1971) original nigrescence theory—one of the seminal cultural identity theories—was published in 1971 (see Worrell, 2012). Thus, the joint committee that prepared the 1974 *Standards* would have been extremely remiss if they had not dealt with the issue of testing ethnic minority populations.

The 1985 Edition

The 1985 edition of the *Standards* maintained the organizational structure of grouping chapters into sections (see Table 3.2) and consisted of 16 chapters—six

TABLE 3.2

Major Sections in the 1985 *Standards*

Title	No. of standards
Introduction	
Part I: Technical Standards for Test Construction and Evaluation	
1. Validity	25
2. Reliability and Errors of Measurement	12
3. Test Development and Revision	25
4. Scaling, Norming, Score Comparability, and Equating	9
5. Test Publication: Technical Manuals and User's Guides	11
Part II: Professional Standards for Test Use	
6. General Principles of Test Use	13
7. Clinical Testing	6
8. Educational Testing and Psychological Testing in Schools	12
9. Test Use in Counseling	9
10. Employment Testing	9
11. Professional and Occupational Licensure and Certification	5
12. Program Evaluation	8
Part III: Standards for Particular Applications	
13. Testing Linguistic Minorities	7
14. Testing People Who Have Handicapping Conditions	8
Part IV: Standards for Administrative Procedures	
15. Test Administration, Scoring, and Reporting	11
16. Protecting the Rights of Test Takers	10
Glossary	
Bibliography	
Total	180

more than the previous edition—grouped into four sections related to technical standards, test use, particular applications, and administrative procedures. The 1985 edition changed the terms used to indicate the levels of standards—that is, *essential, highly desirable,* and *desirable*—to *primary, secondary,* and *conditional* standards. Primary standards were ones that all tests needed to meet (in essence, they were essential); secondary standards were desirable, but usually "beyond reasonable expectation in many situations" (AERA, APA, & NCME, 1985, p. 3); and conditional standards were ones that varied according to the testing application. Thus, conditional standards could be primary in some applications but secondary in others.

Perhaps in keeping with the importance of validity and reliability, these chapters were placed at the beginning of the section on technical standards immediately after the introduction and have been in the same place up to the current edition. In addition, the 1985 *Standards* made it clear that the categories of validity—that is, content, predictive, and so on—are not different types of validity, but different types of validity evidence that are useful in supporting the inferences being made on the basis of test scores.

Chapters on test development and revision, score comparability, scaling and norming, and manuals and user guides were also included in this first section. Part II in 1985 included seven chapters with standards for test use, including the first set of standards targeted at testing in different types of contexts, including clinical, counseling, educational, employment, and licensure and certification, as well as standards for program evaluation. Part IV included a chapter on administration, scoring, and reporting and one on protecting the rights of test takers.

Part III included standards that were specific to testing in special populations, including linguistic minorities (Chapter 13, seven standards) and individuals with disabilities (Chapter 14, eight standards). As the first standard in Chapter 13 indicated, for individuals who are not native speakers of English or who speak certain dialects of English, "testing should be designed to minimize threats to test reliability and validity that may arise from language differences" (AERA, APA, & NCME, 1985, p. 74). Other standards in this chapter focused on the importance of (a) evidence in support of reliability, validity, and comparability of scores for translated tests, (b) information on appropriate test use and interpretation in linguistically diverse samples, and (c) language proficiency levels in employment workforce testing not exceeding the level required for the actual job, among others. The standards in Chapter 14 raised addressed issues related to psychometric evidence of modified tests and use of appropriate norming samples and qualified test administrators. With regard to ethnic minorities, the 1985 edition contained many of the changes introduced in 1974 (e.g., including ethnic groups as an important demographic variable, suggesting local norms when necessary) and also reiterated the discussion of differential prediction with regard to making claims about bias in test scores.

The 1999 Edition

The evolution of the *Standards* continued with the 1999 edition (AERA, APA, & NCME). This edition contained 15 chapters in three sections (see Table 3.3). There were a number of substantive changes from the 1985 edition that were aptly summarized by Camara and Lane (2006). First, this edition did not label standards as primary versus secondary or conditional, or as essential versus desirable. All standards were expected to apply to tests in the appropriate contexts. Second, there was a concerted attempt to clarify that the use of *testing* in the title was not intended to restrict the *Standards*; indeed, the standards were intended to apply to the range of tests, assessment, and classification systems that are used in formal decision making across a broad set of situations, from the individual psychologist's office to credentialing and licensure and testing in schools and the workplace. Third, the chapters on

TABLE 3.3
Major Sections in the 1999 *Standards*

Title	No. of standards
Introduction	
Part I: Test Evaluation, Construction, and Documentation	
1. Validity	24
2. Reliability and Errors of Measurement	20
3. Test Development and Revision	27
4. Scales, Norms, and Score Comparability	21
5. Test Administration, Scoring, Reporting, and Interpretation	16
6. Supporting Documentation for Tests	15
Part II: Fairness in Testing	
7. Fairness in Testing and Test Use	12
8. The Rights and Responsibilities of Test Takers	13
9. Testing Individuals of Diverse Linguistic Backgrounds	11
10. Testing Individuals with Disabilities	12
Part III: Testing Applications	
11. The Responsibilities of Test Users	24
12. Psychological Testing and Assessment	20
13. Educational Testing and Assessment	19
14. Testing in Employment and Credentialing	17
15. Testing in Program Evaluation and Public Policy	13
Glossary	
Total	264

clinical testing and test use in counseling were combined into a single chapter on psychological testing, as were the chapters on employment testing and licensure and certification. Camara and Lane pointed out that 91% of the standards had comments in 1999, compared with 50% in 1985.

Of particular relevance in this chapter was the addition of an entire chapter on fairness in testing, which was the first chapter in a section on fairness; additional chapters in the "Fairness" section focused on the rights and responsibilities of test users and on testing individuals from diverse linguistic backgrounds and individuals with disabilities. The new chapter on fairness included discussions of fairness and validity issues for subgroups such as construct-irrelevant variance, appropriateness of testing accommodations, and the effects of assessment and accountability programs for subgroups (Camara & Lane, 2006). Fairness in testing is a controversial topic. Critics often question whether testing will ever be fair for every test taker. As noted in the 1999 edition, although there is a broad consensus that tests should be free from bias and all test takers should always be treated fairly during testing, no evaluative device is ever perfectly fair. However, when tests are properly designed and used, they advance society's goals of increasing equal opportunities. The inclusion of tests in admissions processes was one step in removing barriers to educational opportunities for underrepresented individuals. In addition, testing settings are interpersonal environments. Thus, fair interactions between test administrators and test takers are just as important as developing technically fair tests.

Several different views of fairness were covered in the 1999 *Standards*: fairness as lack of bias, fairness as equitable treatment in the testing process, fairness as equality in outcomes of testing, and fairness as opportunity to learn. The first two definitions of fairness are related to eliminating all biases when developing tests and treating all test takers fairly. The third characterization of fairness in testing communicates the principle that individuals with the same ability should perform similarly on achievement tests despite group membership (e.g., race, gender, class). The last view is related to the idea that every test taker should have the same opportunity to learn the material covered on any given achievement test.

The chapter also discussed two types of test biases: content-related sources of test bias and response-related sources of test bias. The first type of test bias is due to inappropriate selection of content on a test. Content is inappropriate if members of different groups interpret the content differently or if the language used is offensive or emotionally charged for a particular group of test takers. Response-related test bias occurs when one group consistently responds to an item incorrectly because of cultural factors, linguistic factors, or a lack of motor skills. Last, before listing the standards for fairness in testing, the chapter included information on fairness in selection and prediction. Bias can also be found in the relationship between test and criterion scores when used for selection and prediction. Generally, if the relationship between test and criterion scores is different for different groups, selection decision rules should also differ for each group in question. The many types of test biases support the principle that tests should be one part of a holistic process when selecting individuals for educational and employment opportunities.

The 2014 *Standards*

The 2014 *Standards* has 13 chapters and three sections (see Table 3.4). There were several changes in the 2014 *Standards*, which are summarized on page 4 of the document; however, we only address the issue of fairness in this chapter. In response to the call for public comments related to the revision of the 1999 *Standards*, there were requests to expand the section on fairness and include chapters on additional groups (e.g., older individuals, racial and ethnic minorities). The joint committee that prepared the 2014 *Standards* chose a different approach. Rather than approaching the concept of fairness

TABLE 3.4
Major Sections in the 2014 *Standards*

Title	No. of standards
Introduction	
Part I: Foundations	
1. Validity	26
2. Reliability/Precision and Errors of Measurement	21
3. Fairness in Testing	20
Part II: Operations	
4. Test Design and Development	26
5. Scores, Scales, Norms, Score Linking, and Cut Scores	24
6. Test Administration, Scoring, Reporting, and Interpretation	17
7. Supporting Documentation for Tests	15
8. The Rights and Responsibilities of Test Takers	13
9. The Rights and Responsibilities of Test Users	24
Part III: Testing Applications	
10. Psychological Testing and Assessment	18
11. Workplace Testing and Credentialing	16
12. Educational Testing and Assessment	19
13. Uses of Tests for Program Evaluation, Policy Studies, and Accountability	9
Glossary	
Total	248

from the perspective of several different groups, they focused on fairness as an overarching principle in testing akin to validity and reliability:

> Fairness is a fundamental validity issue and requires attention throughout all stages of test development and use. . . . In the current version [2014] of the *Standards*, these issues are presented in a single chapter to emphasize that fairness to all individuals in the intended population of test takers is an overriding, foundational concern. (AERA, APA, & NCME, 2014, p. 49)

In other words, all test takers across all demographic subgroups are entitled to tests and a testing process that is fair.

In keeping with this interpretation of fairness, the 2014 *Standards* defined *fairness* as "responsiveness to individual characteristics and testing contexts so that test scores yield valid interpretations for intended uses" (AERA, APA, & NCME, 2014, p. 50). In other words, test scores should reflect the construct they are intended to measure and be as free as possible from construct-irrelevant variance. In this regard, the 2014 *Standards* include discussions of four general views of fairness. The first involves being fairly treated during the testing process so that one's scores are not affected by how one is treated but actually reflect what one is being tested on. Standardization helps in this process, although for some groups a change from the standardized procedures may be necessary to increase score comparability. The second view of fairness is related to lack of measurement bias. Test scores should have the same meaning for all test takers, irrespective of background and demographic characteristics. Investigating differential item functioning, differential test functioning, and predictive bias are some of the ways in which we test developers and researchers can examine this concern.

The third view of fairness is related to access to the construct as it is being measured. In other words, demographic factors such as gender, age, race, ethnicity, disability status, or first language, as well as combinations of any of these characteristics, should not confer an advantage or result in a disadvantage to any individual in a testing situation. The validity of test score interpretations for their intended uses represents the fourth general view of fairness. For example, performance on a test administered in English may result in erroneous interpretations of the test taker's competence if the test taker is an English language learner. The 2014 *Standards* also provide an overview of four potential threats to fairness interpretations of test scores. One of these is opportunity to learn, which was hinted at in 1985, but explicitly highlighted in 1999. Another threat is test content, which should be appropriate so it does not favor any specific group or result in different levels of engagement, motivation, or distress across subgroups. A third threat is test response, in terms of ability to respond on the basis of test response formats, the ways in which tests are scored, and the types of responses elicited; none of these should disadvantage specific subgroups.

The fourth threat is test context. As in 1999, the *Standards* acknowledge that in some situations, the interaction between the person administering the test and the test taker can increase construct-irrelevant variance in the test scores. Moreover, there is also a recognition that test users should be cognizant of the growing body of literature on fairness issues that may result in new insights between editions of the *Standards:*

> As research on contextual factors (e.g., stereotype threat [Steele, 1997]) is ongoing, test developers and test users should pay attention to the emerging empirical literature on these topics so that they can use this information if and when the preponderance of evidence dictates that it is appropriate to do so. (AERA, APA, & NCME, 2014, p. 55)

This acknowledgement places the onus on individuals who develop tests and on those who interpret test scores to consider not only the *Standards* as written but also the new evidence that will inform subsequent versions of the *Standards*. Finally, in addition to the stand-alone chapter on fairness, the 2014 *Standards* indicate that one additional change in this edition was the inclusion of fairness concerns across all the chapters.

CONCLUSION

In assessing how the *Standards* have handled issues relevant to ethnic minority youth over the years, we conclude this chapter with a question: Looking across the seven issues of the *Standards*, do we see an increased recognition of and concern about issues relevant to these groups? There are some who will answer this question in the negative. They will point out that the 1985 and 1999 editions had a section devoted to fairness issues and that the 2014 edition has only one chapter, and they will point to the fact that there is still no chapter devoted specifically to ethnic minority issues.

However, we disagree with that interpretation. It is possible to argue that the *Standards* have always been concerned with issues of bias and fairness, and there is evidence of this in the first edition in 1954, as we have pointed out. However, although these issues were recognized, ethnic groups were not explicitly mentioned in 1954, 1955, and 1966. In 1974, ethnic groups were introduced as one of the specific subgroups to pay attention to, as was the concept of fairness in testing. This attention was heightened with the introduction of the special applications section in 1985 (Section 3), which included a chapter devoted to linguistic minorities. This section was relabeled "Fairness," was expanded to four chapters, and became the second section in the 1999 edition. In 2014, the fairness section was eliminated, but the fairness chapter was moved into Section I "to emphasize accessibility and fairness as fundamental issues in testing" (AERA, APA, & NCME, 2014, p. 4), and fairness issues were also included across the volume. Thus, the big two in testing—validity and reliability—have been expanded into the big three: validity, reliability, and fairness. From our perspective, this expansion is a positive development that will result in greater attention to concerns regarding testing ethnic minority youth.

REFERENCES

Altman, S. (1997). *The encyclopedia of African American heritage*. New York, NY: Facts on File.

American Educational Research Association, American Psychological Association, & National Council on Measurement in Education. (1985). *Standards for educational and psychological testing*. Washington, DC: American Psychological Association.

American Educational Research Association, American Psychological Association, & National Council on Measurement in Education. (1999). *Standards for educational and psychological testing*. Washington, DC: American Educational Research Association.

American Educational Research Association, American Psychological Association, & National Council on Measurement in Education. (2014). *Standards for educational and psychological testing.* Washington, DC: American Educational Research Association.

American Educational Research Association & National Council on Measurements Used in Education. (1955). *Technical recommendations for achievement tests.* Washington, DC: National Education Association.

American Psychological Association, American Educational Research Association, & National Council on Measurements Used in Education. (1954). *Technical recommendations for psychological tests and diagnostic techniques.* Washington, DC: American Psychological Association.

American Psychological Association, American Educational Research Association, & National Council on Measurement in Education. (1966). *Standards for educational and psychological tests and manuals.* Washington, DC: American Psychological Association.

American Psychological Association, American Educational Research Association, & National Council on Measurement in Education. (1974). *Standards for educational and psychological tests.* Washington, DC: American Psychological Association.

American Psychological Association Presidential Task Force on Education Disparities. (2012). *Ethnic and racial disparities in education: Psychology's contributions to understanding and reducing disparities.* Retrieved from http://www.apa.org/ed/resources/racial-disparities.aspx

Aud, S., Fox, M., & KewalRamani, A. (2010). *Status and trends in the education of racial and ethnic groups* (NCES 2010-015). Washington, DC: U.S. Government Printing Office.

Baker, E. L., Barton, P. E., Darling-Hammond, L., Haertel, E., Ladd, H. F., & Linn, R. L., . . . Shepard, L. A. (2010). *Problems with the use of student test scores to evaluate teachers.* Retrieved from http://www.epi.org/page/-/pdf/bp278.pdf

Barton, P. E. (1999). *Too much testing of the wrong kind; too little of the right kind in K–12 education.* Retrieved from http://www.ets.org/Media/Research/pdf/PICTOOMUCH.pdf

Camara, W. J., & Lane, S. (2006). A historical perspective and current views on the standards for educational and psychological testing. *Educational Measurement: Issues and Practice, 25*(3), 35–41. http://dx.doi.org/10.1111/j.1745-3992.2006.00066.x

Common Core State Standards Initiative. (2014). *Preparing America's students for success.* Retrieved from http://www.corestandards.org/

Cross, W. E., Jr. (1971). The Negro-to-Black conversion experience. *Black World, 20*(9), 13–27.

Erwin, J. O., & Worrell, F. C. (2012). Assessment practices and the underrepresentation of minority students in gifted and talented education. *Journal of Psychoeducational Assessment, 30,* 74–87. http://dx.doi.org/10.1177/0734282911428197

Ford, D. Y. (1998). The underrepresentation of minority students in gifted education: Problems and promises in recruitment and retention. *The Journal of Special Education, 32*, 4–14. http://dx.doi.org/10.1177/002246699803200102

Ford, D. Y. (2008). Intelligence testing and cultural diversity: The need for alternative instruments, policies, and procedures. In J. L. VanTassel-Baska (Ed.), *Alternative assessments with gifted and talented students* (pp. 107–128). Waco, TX: Prufrock Press.

Ford, D. Y., & Helms, J. E. (2012). Overview and introduction: Testing and assessing African Americans: "Unbiased" tests are still unfair. *Journal of Negro Education, 81*, 186–189.

Jenkins, M. D. (1939). The mental ability of the American Negro. *Journal of Negro Education, 8*, 511–520. http://dx.doi.org/10.2307/2292647

Lohman, D. F. (2005). An aptitude perspective on talent: Implications for identification of academically gifted minority students. *Journal for the Education of the Gifted, 28*, 333–360.

McCray, A. D., Webb-Johnson, G., & Neal, L. I. (2003). The disproportionality of African Americans in special education: An enduring threat to equality and opportunity. In C. C. Yeakey & R. D. Henderson (Eds.), *Surmounting the odds: Education, opportunity, and society in the new millennium* (pp. 455–485). Greenwich, CT: Information Age.

Neisser, U., Boodoo, G., Bouchard, T. J., Jr., Boykin, A. W., Brody, N., Ceci, S. J., . . . Urbina, S. (1996). Intelligence: Knowns and unknowns. *American Psychologist, 51*, 77–101. http://dx.doi.org/10.1037/0003-066X.51.2.77

Nisbett, R. E., Aronson, J., Blair, C., Dickens, W., Flynn, J., Halpern, D. F., & Turkheimer, E. (2012). Intelligence: New findings and theoretical developments. *American Psychologist, 67*, 130–159. http://dx.doi.org/10.1037/a0026699

Plucker, J. A., Burroughs, N., & Song, R. (2010). *Mind the (other) gap!* Bloomington: Center for Evaluation and Education Policy, Indiana University.

Plucker, J. A., Hardesty, J., & Burroughs, N. (2013). *Talent on the sidelines: Excellence gaps and America's persistent talent underclass*. Storrs: Center for Education Policy Analysis, Neag School of Education, University of Connecticut.

Powers, K. (2014, March). *Closing the academic achievement gap with Common Core*. Retrieved from http://www.aeaonline.org/blogs/closing-academic-achievement-gap-common-core

Smith, R. C. (2003). *Encyclopedia of African-American politics*. New York, NY: Facts in File.

Steele, C. M. (1997). A threat in the air: How stereotypes shape intellectual identity and performance. *American Psychologist, 52*, 613–629. http://dx.doi.org/10.1037/0003-066X.52.6.613

Warne, R. T. (2014). Using above-level testing to track growth in academic achievement in gifted students. *Gifted Child Quarterly, 58*, 3–23. http://dx.doi.org/10.1177/0016986213513793

Weingarten, R. (2011, August 14). Are we testing too much? *The Huffington Post.* Retrieved from http://www.huffingtonpost.com/randi-weingarten/are-we-testing-too-much_b_876107.html

Worrell, F. C. (2012). Forty years of Cross' nigrescence theory: From stages to profiles, from African Americans to all Americans. In J. M. Sullivan & A. M. Esmail (Eds.), *African American identity: Racial and cultural dimensions of the Black experience* (pp. 3–28). Lanham, MD: Lexington Books.

Worrell, F. C., Brabeck, M. M., Dwyer, C. A., Geisinger, K. F., Marx, R. W., Noell, G. H., & Pianta, R. C. (2014). *Assessing and evaluating teacher education programs.* Washington, DC: American Psychological Association.

Worrell, F. C., & Erwin, J. O. (2011). Best practices in identifying students for gifted and talented education (GATE) programs. *Journal of Applied School Psychology, 27,* 319–340. http://dx.doi.org/10.1080/15377903.2011.615817

II

ASSESSMENT OF ETHNIC MINORITY STUDENTS

4

INTELLECTUAL ASSESSMENT OF ETHNIC MINORITY CHILDREN

SCOTT L. GRAVES, JR., AND KAYLA NICHOLS

The intellectual assessment of ethnic minority populations is a contentious topic in the field of psychology. The controversy stems primarily from the use of standardized measures of intelligence to diagnose learning and intellectual disabilities. This is coupled with the overrepresentation of certain minority groups in special education for intellectual disabilities. Although multiple criteria exist (e.g., Individuals With Disabilities Education Improvement Act, *Diagnostic and Statistical Manual of Mental Disorders, International Classification of Diseases*), each includes the consideration of an individual's overall cognitive processing abilities, which are typically measured with norm-referenced intelligence tests (i.e., Kaufman Assessment Battery for Children, Wechsler Intelligence Scale for Children, Woodcock–Johnson Tests of Cognitive Abilities). There has been an ongoing debate as to whether these measures are biased in regard to ethnic minority populations and whether their use is the primary reason that there is an overrepresentation of specific groups (i.e., Latinos and African

http://dx.doi.org/10.1037/14855-005
Psychoeducational Assessment and Intervention for Ethnic Minority Children: Evidence-Based Approaches,
S. L. Graves, Jr., and J. J. Blake (Editors)

Americans) in special education (Helms, 2006; Jensen, 1980). To address these controversies, this chapter provides a historical overview of intellectual assessment, discussion of the presence of bias in assessment instruments, and the current state and future directions for the intellectual assessment of ethnic minority populations in the United States.

HISTORICAL CONTEXT OF INTELLECTUAL ASSESSMENT

There is a substantial history on the intellectual assessment of ethnic minority populations dating back to the early 1900s (see Guthrie, 1998; Thomas, 1984; Valencia & Suzuki, 2001, for comprehensive reviews). Mass testing in earnest was institutionalized during World War I, as the Army Alpha and Beta tests were administered to over 1,700,000 enlisted men and officers (Wasserman, 2012). This testing period led to the development of individualized standardized measures of intelligence such as the Wechsler Intelligence Scale for Children (WISC). Following this development, major criticisms and accusations of the inherent bias in intelligence tests for ethnic minority populations surfaced.

ARE INTELLECTUAL ASSESSMENT INSTRUMENTS BIASED FOR ETHNIC POPULATIONS?

In the most recent version of the *Standards for Educational and Psychological Testing* (American Educational Research Association, American Psychological Association, & National Council on Measurement in Education, 2014) the concept of bias is addressed as a fairness doctrine. For instance, Standards for Fairness, Standard 3.0, states:

> All steps in the testing process, including test design, validation, development, administration, and scoring procedures, should be designed in such a manner as to minimize construct-irrelevant variance and to promote valid score interpretations for the intended uses for all examinees in the intended population.

These guidelines give a clear indication that bias and fairness should be taken into account for developing instruments to be used in ethnic minority populations (see Chapter 3, this volume).

Thus, bias occurs when the test constructs or factors result in a systematically different meaning across examinee subgroups. Although score differences between racial groups were thought to be indicative of test score bias, this is not always the case. Statistical procedures such as item response theory, confirmatory factor analysis, and multigroup structural equation modeling have improved psychologists' ability to detect bias in assessments. Establishing measurement invariance is an essential step in determining the validity of any assessment instrument. If constructs are not measured similarly across groups, comparisons of scores between ethnic groups should not be made (see Reynolds & Lowe, 2009, for a review of assessment bias).

Current research has indicated that several of the most commonly used instruments for intellectual assessment have undergone the aforementioned statistical procedures. For instance, Edwards and Oakland (2006) examined the factorial invariance of the Woodcock–Johnson III Tests of Cognitive Abilities (WJ III COG). The results of that study indicated that although the mean scores differed between African American and Caucasian students, the factor scores were not statistically different between groups. Similarly Dale, Finch, Mcintosh, Rothlisberg, and Finch (2014) investigated the utility of the Stanford–Binet (5th ed.) on diverse populations, using African American and Caucasian preschoolers matched on age, gender, and parent education level. Results indicated that African American and Caucasian preschool children did not vary in the level or the pattern of their performance. These findings were replicated on a separate matched sample of African American and Caucasian preschoolers. In addition, results of the study indicated that African American and Caucasian preschool children did not differ statistically on overall cognitive ability as measured by Full Scale IQ. This type of analysis was also done on the Kaufman Assessment Battery for Children (2nd ed.; KABC–II) with a referred sample of African American and Caucasian preschoolers. A profile analysis by Dale, McIntosh, Rothlisberg, Ward, and Bradley (2011) documented the similar performances of African American and Caucasian children on Cattell-Horn-Carroll broad abilities of the KABC–II. In particular, children had similar patterns of highs and lows and performed at the same level with no significant difference between the two groups in their overall mean IQ. Relatedly, Nakano and Watkins (2013) tested the structural validity of the WISC–IV with a sample of 176 Native American children referred for evaluation. Confirmatory factor analysis replicated the normative first-order factor structure and a higher order general ability factor for the WISC–IV with this sample. In sum, the current research on psychometric statistical bias has demonstrated that current assessment instruments such as the KABC–II and WJ III COG do not demonstrate notable statistical bias for ethnic minority populations. That is, current IQ tests measure the same constructs in ethnic minority populations as they do in majority populations (Neisser et al., 1996).

Although commonly used intellectual assessment measures do not exhibit predictive bias in ethnic minority populations, ethnically diverse youth do generally score lower in comparison with majority-race students on selected measures of cognitive ability. The cause of this phenomenon has been the most contentious topic in the field of psychology for the last half century (Helms, 2006; Rushton & Jensen, 2005; Suzuki & Aronson, 2005).

ETHNIC MINORITY PERFORMANCE ON MEASURES OF COGNITIVE ABILITY

Previous research has demonstrated that there is an intellectual test score gap, with African Americans and Latinos scoring approximately one standard deviation below Caucasians, and Asians scoring .5 standard deviations above Caucasians (Rushton & Jensen, 2005). These differences in intellectual performance purportedly exist in international samples as well (Lynn, 2006). Furthermore, the IQ difference between Black and White Americans stands at 1.1 standard deviations and is as large today as it was nearly 100 years ago, according to data from military and convenience samples (Rushton & Jensen, 2005). However, using nationally representative standardization samples of frequently used standardized intelligence measures, Dickens and Flynn (2006) found that African Americans gained 4 to 7 IQ points on non-Hispanic Whites between 1972 and 2002.

Similarly, when attempting to replicate international findings of intellectual performance of Black populations in Africa, Wicherts, Dolan, and van der Maas (2010) could not duplicate Lynn's (2006) results. Specifically, these authors argued that Lynn's review of the literature was unsystematic and too nonspecific to allow replication by independent raters because of the inconsistent use of rules to determine the representativeness and, hence, selection of samples (Wicherts, Dolan, Carlson, & van der Mass, 2010). According to Wicherts, Dolan, Carlson, and Van der Mass (2010), Lynn's assessment of study sample representativeness was not associated with any objective sampling characteristics, but rather with the average IQ in the sample. This suggests that Lynn purposefully excluded samples of Africans with IQ scores above 75 because he deemed these samples to be unrepresentative on the basis of the samples' relatively high IQs. This exclusion was based on previous research by Lynn that purportedly demonstrated that the average IQ test score of Black populations in Africa was 67.

Similarly, Kamin (2006) reviewed the work of past studies that repeatedly indicated that the mean IQ for Black populations in Africa is about 70, which is 15 points lower than that of African Americans and of South Africans (Lynn & Vanhanen, 2002; Rushton & Jensen, 2005). Kamin's results demonstrated another issue in the selective use of convenience samples. Some of the issues noted in his review included the inappropriate conversion of matrices scores into IQ scores, the inclusion of children who had never attended school, the inclusion of children with infections (i.e., malaria), and the translation of IQ tests into languages without any renorming of the measure according to culture. These issues clearly call into question test validity and the subsequent results, given that they did not administer any particular test and simply provided a selective and restrictive review of the literature.

According to the standardization samples of currently used intelligence tests, the current IQ gap between African Americans and Whites ranges from 7.9 to 11.5 points, which is less than the assumed 15-point gap documented in convenience samples. Edwards (2006) indicated that this information should be made readily available by publishers in test manuals, which is generally not the case. The lack of information on the obtained scores in standardization samples of ethnic minorities is even more far reaching for non-African American or White groups. Given that the majority of the intellectual comparison research has been focused on Black–White differences, the intelligence scores of Latino, Native American, and Asian American groups is rarely provided by test publishers (see the KABC–II manual for an exception). For an examination of the current percentage of ethnic minority children represented in commonly used cognitive assessment battery norms, see Chapter 8, this volume.

Taken as a whole, this literature questions the immutability of the ethnic minority–White IQ gap. As such, a renewed focus on understanding the actual performance of ethnic minority populations is warranted, given the advances made in test development and statistical sampling procedures. In addition, given the inability to replicate previous findings that documented the extreme differences in IQ in Black populations in Africa, a reexamination of these issues is warranted. These ubiquitous assessment issues are further complicated by the fact that even when well-normed standardized measures are used, they do not document the performance of populations in a similar fashion.

ARE ALL INTELLECTUAL ASSESSMENTS THE SAME?

Crystallized intelligence is largely influenced by one's cultural background and exposure to vocabulary and general information (i.e., *g* loadings). It has been documented that the higher the *g* loadings of an assessment, the greater predictive validity of that assessment. For example, on the popular WISC, the best measures of *g* are the subtests measuring vocabulary, information, similarities, and arithmetic (Weiss, Keith, Zhu, & Chen, 2013). Historically, this finding has been used to support the theory that ethnic group differences in intelligence are genetic in origin because differences in *g* loadings correlated at a .60 level with ethnic group differences in intelligence (Jensen, 1998). Emerging research, however, is contributing new information in the area.

Analyzing the results of 23 independent and representative samples of twin studies ($N = 7,852$), Kan, Wicherts, Dolan, and van der Maas (2013) investigated how heritability coefficients vary across specific cognitive abilities. Importantly, they assessed the cultural influence of various cognitive abilities by taking the average percentage of test items that were adjusted when the test was adapted for use in 13 different countries. Their major finding in samples of both adults and children was that measures with the greatest cultural load tended to demonstrate the greatest heritability coefficients compared with culture-reduced subtests (e.g., the more the test was associated with IQ). Specifically, this means that the higher the g loadings, the more culturally based the assessment task is. Given that verbal ability and general information knowledge are largely dependent on the quality of a child's educational and home environment (i.e., parental education level, attendance to preschool and quality of preschool attended, print exposure by way of number of books in a home), these abilities are primarily environmental in nature (Lareau, 2011). However, these findings are counter to other explanations for the ethnic minority intellectual performance gap and should be explored further. This documented cultural specificity in general intelligence only has implications when accurately measuring crystalized intelligence, given that IQ test batteries may not also measure the same constructs.

Although it is hypothesized that all well-normed standardized measures of IQ measure the same underlying general factor of intelligence (i.e., g), research has demonstrated that not all standardized intellectual assessment measures produce the same outcomes. Decisions by practicing psychologists regarding specific test administration are influenced by the IQs yielded by the batteries they administer. Considering that the most commonly used intelligence tests have been used interchangeably, the exchangeability of assessment test battery scores would seem to pose no problems. However, this has not been the case for commonly administered assessments in school settings. In Floyd, Clark, and Shadish's (2008) examination of the exchangeability of IQ scores between test batteries, they found that one in four individuals taking an intelligence test battery will receive an IQ more than 10 points higher or lower when taking another battery. Similarly, Silverman et al. (2010) compared 74 adults identified as intellectually disabled, using the Stanford–Binet and WAIS to address concerns of validity of intelligence score inferences across different assessments. Results showed that IQ scores obtained from the WAIS Full Scale IQ were higher than that of the Stanford–Binet Composite IQ, with a mean difference of 16.7 points. The implications of such differences are profound in that they can significantly affect initial diagnostic decisions and the reidentification of individuals diagnosed with learning and intellectual disabilities. Given that the assessment of intellectual abilities using standardized measures of intelligence has been associated with the aforementioned problems and additional issues, such as the overrepresentation of minority students in special education, researchers have long sought different and more equitable means of assessment.

FORMAL DIAGNOSIS OF LEARNING DISABILITIES

As mentioned previously, there are several methods and criteria used to test for learning disabilities, depending on the setting. The most common settings necessitating the assessment of learning disabilities are clinical settings and schools. The assessment process for each of these settings is discussed in this section.

Formal Diagnosis in Clinical Settings

In clinical settings, the *International Classification of Diseases* (10th rev.; *ICD–10*; World Health Organization [WHO], 2012) and the *Diagnostic and Statistical Manual of Mental Disorders* (5th ed.; *DSM–5*; American Psychiatric Association, 2013) are the two guidelines by which professionals make their diagnosis. The *ICD* codes diseases, abnormal findings, complaints, social circumstances, and external causes of injury or diseases, as classified by WHO. This international coding system allows various nations to record prevalence and mortality data for health conditions in a similar manner. The *ICD* coding system has been adopted by the United States and is used by the U.S. Centers for Medicare and Medicaid Services and the Centers for Disease Control and Prevention's National Center for Health Statistics. According to *ICD–10*, specific learning disabilities fall under the classification of "Specific developmental disorders of scholastic skills," specifically defined as follows:

> Disorders in which the normal patterns of skill acquisition are disturbed from the early stages of development. This is not simply a consequence of a lack of opportunity to learn, it is not solely a result of mental retardation, and it is not due to any form of acquired brain trauma or disease. (WHO, 2012, "Specific developmental disorders of scholastic skills," para. 1)

ICD–10 also allows for the following specifiers: F81.0 Specific reading disorder, F81.1 Specific spelling disorder, F81.2 Specific disorder of arithmetical skills, F81.3 Mixed disorder of scholastic skills, F81.8 Other developmental disorders of scholastic skills, and F81.9 Developmental disorder of scholastic skills, unspecified.

DSM–5 also provides a common language and standard criteria for the classification of mental disorders. At the time of *DSM–5*'s release, the official coding system used by the United States was *ICD–9* (WHO, 1979). However, for continuity, *DSM–5* included codes for both *ICD–9* and *ICD–10*. In the fourth edition of the *DSM* (*DSM–IV*; American Psychiatric Association, 1994), the diagnostic category of Learning Disorders was placed under the section titled "Usually First Diagnosed in Infancy, Childhood, or Adolescence." *DSM–5* placed the renamed diagnostic category of Specific Learning Disorder under the section titled "Neurodevelopmental Disorders." *DSM–IV* had placed Learning Disability into one of three categories: Specific Reading Disorder, Specific Math Disorder, and Disorders of Written Expression. Given the fact that substantial overlap occurs between the three categories, *DSM–5* revised the diagnosis into a single category, Specific Learning Disorder (American Psychiatric Association, 2013). This adjustment now allows mental health professionals to specify the area of the disorder and document its severity (e.g., mild, moderate, or severe). In the evaluation of an individual for a learning disability diagnosis according to *ICD–10* and *DSM–5*, there is an examination and synthesis of information pertaining to development, medical history, family circumstances, and educational reports, in addition to the administration of standardized psychoeducational assessment tools.

Formal Diagnosis in Schools

In addition to a *DSM* diagnosis, school-based criteria for learning disability classification exist as well. There are two primary models proposed for the identification of individuals with learning disorders: (a) aptitude–achievement discrepancy and (b) response to intervention. Each of these modalities is described in detail here.

Aptitude–Achievement Discrepancy

The most common approach to determining an aptitude–achievement discrepancy is by identifying an inconsistency between the results of a standardized measure of intelligence (i.e., IQ test) and a test of achievement. This is generally accomplished by examining the discrepancy between a composite measure of IQ and academic achievement as measured by a standardized battery such as the Woodcock–Johnson Tests of Achievement or the Wechsler Individual Achievement Test. The discrepancy approach is based on two features: intellectual ability and academic achievement. To determine the existence of a "severe discrepancy," both the educational and clinical communities generally require the administration of standardized ability (IQ) tests and academic achievement tests, followed by a comparison of the standard scores of the tests. If this comparison shows that the student's achievement is well below his or her ability in at least one area (e.g., reading, mathematics), the student may be diagnosed with a learning disorder (Dombrowski, Kamphaus, & Reynolds, 2004).

Unfortunately, the discrepancy model represents an assessment modality that has not demonstrated adequate validity and reliability in regard to classifying students (Glass, Ryan, Charter, & Bartels, 2009; Watkins, 2003). Frequently referred to as the "wait-to-fail model," the ability–achievement discrepancy paradigm makes it difficult to identify children in early elementary school because students typically do not demonstrate a discrepancy in their intellectual functioning and academic achievement prior to third grade (Haager, 2007; White, Polly, & Audette, 2012). In addition, research has demonstrated that the discrepancy model does not provide assistance to children who are struggling academically but who do not manifest a discrepancy between ability and achievement. The typical intellectual profile of these children includes scores that are in the low average (e.g., 75–85) on intelligence and academic test batteries. Although these children may need learning supports, they do not qualify on the basis of the discrepancy criteria. The criticism of this methodology, along with the overrepresentation of ethnic minority students in special education, has brought about the conceptualization of response to intervention (RTI) methodologies, which are now endorsed by the U.S. Department of Education as viable methods of assessing learning disabilities in school settings (Graves & Mitchell, 2011).

Response to Intervention

Origins of Response to Intervention. Before special education laws were formally established, Lloyd Dunn (1968) expressed concern about the high numbers of African American students in special classes. Special classes were formed during the 1890s to address the needs of students with a range of abilities. An additional function after the *Brown v. Board of Education* (1954) verdict was the use of these special education classes to exclude and segregate African American students from general education (Newell et al., 2010).

The enactment of the Education for All Handicapped Children Act of 1975 (EAHCA) brought the first formalized attempt to improve the accuracy with which children were placed in special education. The EAHCA included provisions for ensuring due process, administering nondiscriminatory assessment, and testing in the child's native language. By 1982, the National Research Council report was published recommending the use of evidence-based interventions before any Black student could be referred for a special education evaluation to prevent and/or reduce the number of Black students referred for special education (Heller, Holtzman, & Messick, 1982). This recommendation marked a shift from focusing on special education to a focus on general education. That is, educators must ensure that ethnic minority students are receiving adequate instruction and supports in general education before being referred for a special education evaluation.

In 1990, the EAHCA was reauthorized and renamed the Individuals With Disabilities Education Act (IDEA). However, it was not until the reauthorization of IDEA in 1997 that specific changes were made to the legislation that addressed the number of African American students in special education. Specifically, states were required to collect special education data disaggregated by race and ethnicity. By collecting these data, states could determine whether significant disproportionality was occurring in placement, settings, and/or discipline. If significant disproportionality was found, states were allowed to use up to 15% of their federal education funds for early intervention services. However, *significant disproportionality* was not defined. Moreover, once states identified significant disproportionality there was no guidance on the strategies that should be used to address the problem. Although these provisions have been helpful in collecting data and, to some extent, identifying disproportionality, African Americans have continued to be overrepresented in the learning disabilities category (Losen & Orfield, 2002).

In the reauthorization of IDEA, the Individuals With Disabilities Education Improvement Act of 2004 (IDEIA), the use of an RTI model was added, in part, to address disproportionate representation. As documented by Fuchs, Fuchs, and Speece (2002), RTI has the potential to reduce the number of African American children misidentified and placed in special education, which was consistent with the focus on general education suggested by the National Research Council in 1982 (Heller et al., 1982) and 2002 (Donovan & Cross, 2002).

With the passage of the current version of IDEIA, states now have the option of discontinuing the use of the intelligence–achievement test discrepancy model that has served as the dominant special education assessment framework. Instead, states are allowed to use an RTI assessment model (IDEIA, 2004, Section 614(b)6). This procedural change has resulted in many states examining their standards for learning disabilities assessment and making changes to their eligibility criteria. Currently, 14 states have forbidden the use of intelligence testing in the identification of a learning disability, with several others allowing for the use of a hybrid model of intelligence test use or RTI (Harr-Robins, Shambaugh, & Parrish, 2009; Sawyer, Holland, & Detgen, 2008). Although these changes may be a step in the right direction, there are many unknowns regarding the appropriateness of an RTI assessment framework.

Issues With Response to Intervention. Although there are numerous conceptualizations of RTI, its premise is based on an adequate or inadequate change in a student's academic performance in relation to implementing empirically based interventions (Gresham, 2002; Proctor, Graves, & Esch, 2012). Touted benefits of shifting to an intervention-based assessment model include the early identification of academic difficulties, the framing of student issues from a risk rather than deficit model, and the reduction of identification biases in the special education process (Newell & Kratochwill, 2006). Although the call for discontinuing the use of intelligence tests with African American students may be coming to fruition, there are also significant issues with the RTI alternative. Advocates of the intervention-based assessment approach to identifying children with learning disabilities have suggested it will likely be fairer than IQ-discrepancy models to students from diverse backgrounds because it involves less reliance on standardized testing (Newell & Kratochwill, 2006). Although this may be the case, supposedly empirically based interventions rarely include African American children in their samples. In particular, there is a significant gap in the treatment and intervention research regarding the development and adaptation of treatments with ethnically diverse populations (Bernal & Scharrón-del-Río, 2001; Council of National Psychological Associations for the Advancement of Ethnic Minority Interests, 2003; Miranda, Nakamura, & Bernal, 2003).

There is also little evidence that RTI methods improve disproportionality or special education rates. In a comprehensive review of studies that focused on special education referral and placement rates and RTI, the National Center for Learning Disabilities/RTI Action Network found that overall referral and placement rates stayed fairly constant, with few studies showing decreases (Hughes & Dexter, 2008). Although emerging data indicate that RTI may not lead to increased special education placements, it is hard to make firm conclusions, given that many studies did not clearly describe (a) how they identified children who did not respond to interventions, (b) the need for more information on the procedures used to identify children for placement, and (c) the lack of African Americans in the samples (with the exception of Marston, Muyskens, Lau, & Canter, 2003). Consequently, these authors recommended that more longitudinal research is needed to answer the question regarding the impact of RTI on special education placement rates.

CONCLUSION

More research has to be done to document the effect of the ever-changing methodology of learning disabilities identification and its impact on ethnic minority students (Proctor et al., 2012). As documented by the changing criteria of *DSM–5* and IDEIA, significant research has to be conducted to determine how these new classification criteria affect the assessment of ethnic minority children. In addition, ethnic minority students who are diagnosed with learning disabilities have limited preparation for college and are at increased risk of incarceration (Blanchett, 2010). Furthermore, students diagnosed with learning and intellectual disabilities compared with students without disabilities have much greater difficulty finding employment after high school and have fewer postsecondary education opportunities (Kortering, Braziel, & McClannon, 2010; Newman et al., 2009). As a result of these dismal outcomes, understanding appropriate methods used to diagnose ethnic minority students with learning disabilities is essential.

REFERENCES

American Educational Research Association, American Psychological Association, & National Council on Measurement in Education. (2014). *Standards for educational and psychological testing.* Washington, DC: American Educational Research Association.

American Psychiatric Association. (1994). *Diagnostic and statistical manual of mental disorders* (4th ed.). Washington, DC: Author.

American Psychiatric Association. (2013). *Diagnostic and statistical manual of mental disorders* (5th ed.). Arlington, VA: Author.

Bernal, G., & Scharrón-del-Río, M. R. (2001). Are empirically supported treatments valid for ethnic minorities? Toward an alternative approach for treatment research. *Cultural Diversity and Ethnic Minority Psychology, 7,* 328–342. http://dx.doi.org/10.1037/1099-9809.7.4.328

Blanchett, W. J. (2010). Telling it like it is: The role of race, class, & culture in the perpetuation of learning disability as a privileged category for the White middle class. *Disability Studies Quarterly, 30*(2). Retrieved from http://dsq-sds.org/article/view/1233/1280

Brown v. Board of Educ., 347 U.S. 483 (1954).

Council of National Psychological Associations for the Advancement of Ethnic Minority Interests. (2003). *Psychological treatments of ethnic minority populations.* Washington, DC: Association of Black Psychologists.

Dale, B. A., Finch, M. H., Mcintosh, D. E., Rothlisberg, B. A., & Finch, W. H. (2014). Utility of the Stanford–Binet Intelligence Scales with ethnically diverse preschoolers. *Psychology in the Schools, 51,* 581–590. http://dx.doi.org/10.1002/pits.21766

Dale, B. A., McIntosh, D. E., Rothlisberg, B. A., Ward, K. E., & Bradley, M. H. (2011). Profile analysis of the Kaufman assessment battery for children, with African American and Caucasian preschool children. *Psychology in the Schools, 48,* 476–487. http://dx.doi.org/10.1002/pits.20571

Dickens, W. T., & Flynn, J. R. (2006). Black Americans reduce the racial IQ gap: Evidence from standardization samples. *Psychological Science, 17,* 913–920. http://dx.doi.org/10.1111/j.1467-9280.2006.01802.x

Dombrowski, S. C., Kamphaus, R. W., & Reynolds, C. R. (2004). After the demise of the discrepancy: Proposed learning disabilities diagnostic criteria. *Professional*

Psychology: Research and Practice, 35, 364–372. http://dx.doi.org/10.1037/0735-7028.35.4.364

Donovan, M. S., & Cross, C. T. (2002). *Minority students in special and gifted education*. Washington, DC: National Academy Press.

Dunn, L. M. (1968). Special education for the mildly retarded—Is much of it justifiable? *Exceptional Children, 35*, 5–22.

Education for All Handicapped Children Act of 1975, Pub. L. No. 94-142, 89 Stat. 773 (1975).

Edwards, O. W. (2006). Special education disproportionality and the influence of intelligence test selection. *Journal of Intellectual and Developmental Disability, 31*, 246–248. http://dx.doi.org/10.1080/13668250600999178

Edwards, O. W., & Oakland, T. D. (2006). Factorial invariance of Woodcock–Johnson III scores for African Americans and Caucasian Americans. *Journal of Psychoeducational Assessment, 24*, 358–366. http://dx.doi.org/10.1177/0734282906289595

Floyd, R. G., Clark, M. H., & Shadish, W. R. (2008). The exchangeability of IQs: Implications for professional psychology. *Professional Psychology: Research and Practice, 39*, 414–423. http://dx.doi.org/10.1037/0735-7028.39.4.414

Fuchs, L. S., Fuchs, D., & Speece, D. L. (2002). Treatment validity as a unifying construct for identifying learning disabilities. *Learning Disability Quarterly, 25*, 33–45. http://dx.doi.org/10.2307/1511189

Glass, L. A., Ryan, J. J., Charter, R. A., & Bartels, J. M. (2009). Discrepancy score reliabilities in the WISC–IV standardization sample. *Journal of Psychoeducational Assessment, 27*, 138–144. http://dx.doi.org/10.1177/0734282908325158

Graves, S., & Mitchell, A. (2011). Is the moratorium over? African American psychology professionals' views on intelligence testing in response to changes to federal policy. *Journal of Black Psychology, 37*, 407–425. http://dx.doi.org/10.1177/0095798410394177

Gresham, F. M. (2002). Responsiveness to intervention: An alternative approach to the identification of learning disabilities. In R. Bradley, L. Donaldson, & D. Hallahan (Eds.), *Identification of learning disabilities* (pp. 467–519). Mahwah, NJ: Erlbaum.

Guthrie, R. (1998). *Even the rat was white: A historical view of psychology* (2nd ed.). Needham Heights, MA: Allyn & Bacon.

Haager, D. (2007). Promises and cautions regarding using response to intervention with English language learners. *Learning Disability Quarterly, 30*, 213–218. http://dx.doi.org/10.2307/30035565

Harr-Robins, J. J., Shambaugh, L. S., & Parrish, T. (2009). *The status of state-level response to intervention policies and procedures in the west region states and five other states* (Issues & Answers Report REL 2009-No. 077). Washington, DC: U.S. Department of Education, Institute of Education Sciences, National Center for Education Evaluation and Regional Assistance, Regional Educational Laboratory West.

Heller, K. A., Holtzman, W. H., & Messick, S. (Eds.). (1982). *Placing children in special education: A strategy for equity*. Washington, DC: National Academy.

Helms, J. E. (2006). Fairness is not validity or cultural bias in racial-group assessment: A quantitative perspective. *American Psychologist, 61,* 845–859. http://dx.doi.org/10.1037/0003-066X.61.8.845

Hughes, C., & Dexter, D. D. (2008). *Field studies of RTI programs, revised*. Retrieved from http://www.rtinetwork.org/learn/research/field-studies-rti-programs

Individuals With Disabilities Education Act, 20 U.S.C. §§ 1400–1487 (1997, 2004).

Jensen, A. R. (1980). *Bias in mental testing*. New York, NY: Free Press.

Jensen, A. R. (1998). *The g factor: The science of mental ability*. Westport, CT: Praeger.

Kamin, L. J. (2006). African IQ and mental retardation. *South African Journal of Psychology, 36,* 1–9. http://dx.doi.org/10.1177/008124630603600101

Kan, K. J., Wicherts, J. M., Dolan, C. V., & van der Maas, H. L. J. (2013). On the nature and nurture of intelligence and specific cognitive abilities: The more heritable, the more culture dependent. *Psychological Science, 24,* 2420–2428. http://dx.doi.org/10.1177/0956797613493292

Kortering, L. J., Braziel, P. M., & McClannon, L. J. (2010). Career ambitions: A comparison of youth with and without SLD. *Remedial and Special Education, 31,* 230–240. http://dx.doi.org/10.1177/0741932508324404

Lareau, A. (2011). *Unequal childhoods: Race, class, and family life* (2nd ed.). Oakland: University of California Press.

Losen, D. J., & Orfield, G. (2002). *Racial inequity in special education*. Cambridge, MA: Harvard Education Press.

Lynn, R. (2006). *Race differences in intelligence: An evolutionary analysis*. Whitefish, MT: Washington Summit.

Lynn, R., & Vanhanen, T. (2002). *IQ and the wealth of nations*. Westport, CT: Praeger.

Marston, D., Muyskens, P., Lau, M., & Canter, A. (2003). Problem-solving model for decision-making with high-incidence disabilities: The Minneapolis experience. *Learning Disabilities Research & Practice, 18,* 187–200. http://dx.doi.org/10.1111/1540-5826.00074

Miranda, J., Nakamura, R., & Bernal, G. (2003). Including ethnic minorities in mental health intervention research: A practical approach to a long-standing problem. *Culture, Medicine and Psychiatry, 27,* 467–486. http://dx.doi.org/10.1023/B:MEDI.0000005484.26741.79

Nakano, S., & Watkins, M. W. (2013). Factor structure of the Wechsler Intelligence Scales for Children—Fourth Edition among referred Native American students. *Psychology in the Schools, 50,* 957–968. http://dx.doi.org/10.1002/pits.21724

Neisser, U., Boodoo, G., Bouchard, T. J., Jr., Boykin, A. W., Brody, N., Ceci, S. J., . . . Urbina, S. (1996). Intelligence: Knowns and unknowns. *American Psychologist, 51,* 77–101. http://dx.doi.org/10.1037/0003-066X.51.2.77

Newell, M., & Kratochwill, T. (2006). The integration of response to intervention and critical race theory-disability studies: A robust approach to reducing racial discrimination in evaluation decisions. In S. Jimerson, M. Burns, & A. VanDerHeyden (Eds.), *Handbook of response to intervention: The science and practice of assessment and intervention* (pp. 65–79). New York, NY: Springer.

Newell, M. L., Nastasi, B. K., Hatzichristou, C., Jones, J. M., Schanding, G. T., Jr., & Yetter, G. (2010). Evidence on multicultural training in school psychology: Recommendations for future directions. *School Psychology Quarterly, 25,* 249–278. http://dx.doi.org/10.1037/a0021542

Newman, L., Wagner, M., Cameto, R., Knokey, A.-M., Buckley, J. A., & Malouf, D. (2009). *Post-high school outcomes of youth with disabilities up to 4 years after high school.* Retrieved from http://ies.ed.gov/ncser/pdf/20093017.pdf

Proctor, S. L., Graves, S., & Esch, R. (2012). Assessing African American students for specific learning disabilities: The promises and perils of response to intervention. *Journal of Negro Education, 81,* 268–282.

Reynolds, C., & Lowe, P. (2009). The problem of bias in psychological assessment. In T. B. Gutkin & C. R. Reynolds (Eds.), *The handbook of school psychology* (4th ed., pp. 332–374). New York, NY: Wiley.

Rushton, J. P., & Jensen, A. R. (2005). Thirty years of research on race differences in cognitive ability. *Psychology, Public Policy, and Law, 11,* 235–294. http://dx.doi.org/10.1037/1076-8971.11.2.235

Sawyer, R., Holland, D., & Detgen, A. (2008). *State policies and procedures and selected local implementation practices in response to intervention in the six Southeast Region states* (Issues & Answers Report, REL 2008; No. 063). Retrieved from http://ies.ed.gov/ncee/edlabs/regions/southeast/pdf/REL_2008063_sum.pdf

Silverman, W., Miezejeski, C., Ryan, R., Zigman, W., Krinsky-McHale, S., & Urv, T. (2010). Stanford–Binet and WAIS IQ differences and their implications for adults with intellectual disability (aka mental retardation). *Intelligence, 38,* 242–248. http://dx.doi.org/10.1016/j.intell.2009.12.005

Suzuki, L., & Aronson, J. (2005). The cultural malleability of intelligence and its impact on the racial/ethnic hierarchy. *Psychology, Public Policy, and Law, 11,* 320–327. http://dx.doi.org/10.1037/1076-8971.11.2.320

Thomas, W. (1984). Black intellectuals, intelligence testing in the 1930s and the sociology of knowledge. *Teachers College Record, 85,* 477–501.

Valencia, R., & Suzuki, L. (2001). *Intelligence testing and minority students: Foundations performance factors and assessment issues.* Thousand Oaks, CA: Sage.

Wasserman, J. D. (2012). A history of intelligence assessment: The unfinished tapestry. In D. P. Flanagan & P. L. Harrison (Eds.), *Contemporary intellectual assessment: Theories, tests, and issues* (3rd ed., pp. 3–55). New York, NY: Guilford Press.

Watkins, M. W. (2003). IQ subtest analysis: Clinical acumen or clinical illusion? *The Scientific Review of Mental Health Practice, 2,* 118–141.

Weiss, L. G., Keith, T. Z., Zhu, J., & Chen, H. (2013). WISC–IV and clinical validation of the four-and five-factor interpretive approaches. *Journal of Psychoeducational Assessment, 31,* 114–131. http://dx.doi.org/10.1177/0734282913478032

White, R. B., Polly, D., & Audette, R. H. (2012). A case analysis of an elementary school's implementation of response to intervention. *Journal of Research in Childhood Education, 26*, 73–90. http://dx.doi.org/10.1080/02568543.2011.632067

Wicherts, J. M., Dolan, C. V., Carlson, J. S., & van der Maas, H. L. J. (2010). Another failure to replicate Lynn's estimate of the average IQ of sub-Saharan Africans. *Learning and Individual Differences, 20*, 155–157. http://dx.doi.org/10.1016/j.lindif.2010.03.010

Wicherts, J. M., Dolan, C. V., & van der Maas, H. L. J. (2010). A systematic literature review of the average IQ of sub-Saharan Africans. *Intelligence, 38*, 1–20. http://dx.doi.org/10.1016/j.intell.2009.05.002

World Health Organization. (1979). *International classification of diseases* (9th rev.). Geneva, Switzerland: Author.

World Health Organization. (2012). *International classification of diseases* (ICD). Retrieved from http://www.who.int/classifications/icd/en

5

ACADEMIC ASSESSMENT OF DIVERSE STUDENTS

LEAH M. NELLIS AND ALYCE M. HOPPLE

In schools today, educators are frequently assessing students' academic performance and growth for a variety of reasons, including planning and evaluating the effectiveness of instruction, determining placement in special programs and services, and fulfilling accountability requirements. Each of these assessment purposes raises unique questions and concerns about what is measured, how it is measured, and how the information is used. These concerns are heightened for students who are linguistically and/or culturally diverse (e.g., Abedi, 2004; Abedi & Gándara, 2006) and contribute to the substantial differences in educational opportunities and academic achievement that continue to exist between English learners (EL) and non-ELs and students of historically underserved racial and ethnic groups (Hemphill & Vanneman, 2011; National Center for Education Statistics, 2014; National Education Association [NEA], 2007; Sullivan, 2010). The nature of school-based assessment practices and decisions has also been identified as a significant factor

http://dx.doi.org/10.1037/14855-006
Psychoeducational Assessment and Intervention for Ethnic Minority Children: Evidence-Based Approaches,
S. L. Graves, Jr., and J. J. Blake (Editors)

in the overrepresentation of certain racial and ethnic groups in special education and their underrepresentation in high ability and gifted programs (Donovan & Cross, 2002; NEA, 2007; Sullivan, 2011).

Although only one piece of the assessment puzzle, educational evaluations conducted during the special education identification process should include a careful review and consideration of information gathered prior to the referral for evaluation. In addition, such evaluations pose an opportunity for school teams to intentionally collect additional assessment data that reflect the specific needs, background, and experiences of the individual student. This is important for all students but critically so for culturally and linguistically diverse students because of the existing disproportionality in special education and high ability programming. Although much has been written about best practices and recommendations for assessing diverse students, we see two limitations—first, the primary focus has been on the assessment of cognitive abilities, and second, considerations relevant to students who are diverse due to cultural, ethnic, and experiential differences but are not ELs are not differentiated from those for students who are linguistically diverse. Thus, this chapter focuses on the assessment of academic skills and achievement within the context of special education evaluation and identification by highlighting challenges, potential strategies, and considerations that apply to both ELs and students who are culturally diverse due to nonlinguistic factors.

CONCEPTUALIZING DIVERSITY

As noted by Sullivan (2012a), the dimensions of school diversity are numerous, including race, ethnicity, language, gender, disability, religion, class, and sexual orientation, and have collectively resulted in schools experiencing significant and growing levels of student diversity. Various terms such as *limited English proficient* (LEP), *English language learner* or *English learner*, *language minority*, and *culturally and linguistically diverse* (CLD) are used to refer to a heterogeneous group of diverse students. Having multiple definitions and terms has led to confusion and differences of opinion regarding grouping criteria (Frisby, 2009; Rhodes, Ochoa, & Ortiz, 2005). For example, although CLD references cultural diversity, much of the existing research and literature on this topic is relevant to those who are both linguistically and culturally diverse as opposed to those who are only culturally diverse.

For the purposes of this chapter, we focus on students who are diverse because of race, ethnicity, and/or language. We use the term *emerging bilingual* (EB; Klingner & Eppolito, 2014) to refer to students who are in the process of learning and becoming proficient in English. This term is intended to be more positive and strength-based than descriptors such as LEP and to differentiate

EB students from those who are native English speakers; it is in no way meant to diminish the cultural differences that exist among students who are learning English as a second language. Indeed, such students are an increasingly heterogeneous group with varying backgrounds and experiences related to factors such as culture and acculturation, immigration, and socioeconomic status (Sullivan, 2012b). EB students include those who are both foreign and U.S. born; those who have learned two languages either at the same time or who began learning English after first learning another language; and those who have varying skills in the areas of reading, writing, listening, and speaking (O'Bryon, 2014).

Similarly, we use *culturally diverse* (CD) to refer to students who are native English speakers but who are members of racial and ethnic subgroups that are the focus of special education disproportionality. Nationally, African American students are the group most often overrepresented, Latino students are overrepresented in some states in the categories of learning disability and speech and language impairment, and American Indian and Alaskan Native groups are overrepresented in learning disability numbers (Waitoller, Artiles, & Cheney, 2010). The distinction between EB and CD groups is made to assist practitioners who are working primarily with one of the groups and to facilitate a deepening awareness that schools without linguistically diverse students or English language learners still have diversity issues that should and must be addressed.

ASSESSMENT CHALLENGES AND CONCERNS

Several concerns and challenges associated with assessing linguistically and/or CD learners have been identified. In this section, we review those that are most relevant to academic assessment. However, it is important to acknowledge the relative lack of research in this area. Noltemeyer, Proctor, and Dempsey (2013) summarized the findings of four key studies investigating the diversity-related content in school psychology journals and noted the continued need for such research, especially with a focus on race and ethnicity and multiracial students. Brown, Shriberg, and Wang (2007) reviewed publications in five school psychology journals from the years 2000 to 2003 and found that 20.4% ($n = 21$) were focused on diversity-related assessment practices, including cognitive, academic, mental health, behavior, and curriculum-based methods. It is unknown how many focused on academic assessment practices specifically or provided explicit recommendations for practice.

Validity and Norm-Referenced Measures

The most fundamental concern focuses on the validity of the assessment measures being used and the subsequent decisions and actions made by schools and educators (Braden, 1999). *Validity* is the degree to which the interpretations and actions based on assessment data and information are appropriate and adequate for a given student (Messick, 1991). Validity requires assessment instruments and methods to actually measure the constructs, skills, and attributes they claim to measure and for which they are being utilized. For EB students, this is a critical challenge because other factors such as language proficiency and cultural knowledge are often also measured, to some degree, by most assessment measures (Pitoniak et al., 2009). Rhodes et al. (2005) identified the influence of differences in culture and cultural knowledge as being "one of the most influential factors operating within the context of any evaluation" (p. 136). Variables such as language acquisition and proficiency, acculturation, and prior educational and environmental experiences introduce what has been termed *construct-irrelevant variance* and may limit the degree to which assessment results reflect what a student can and cannot do in the academic area being assessed.

Individually administered, standardized, norm-referenced tests are commonly used to assess academic achievement as part of special education identification. One basic concern about the use of such measures is that the standardization samples often do not represent the diversity and characteristics of the students being assessed (Rhodes et al., 2005). When a student's language or cultural background is considerably different from that of the standardization group, test results should not be considered valid (Sattler, 2008). S. O. Ortiz and Ochoa (2005) emphasized that "stratification in the norm sample on the basis of race is not equivalent to stratification on the basis of culture" (p. 158). They further noted that there were no tests available with norm samples that have controlled for differences in cultural knowledge or acculturation. Similar concerns exist about the representativeness of norm samples for EB students. Norm samples that include, for example, monolingual Spanish speakers do not represent the linguistically diverse students in the United States who are experiencing bilingualism as immigrants or second- or third-generation ELs (Pollard-Durodola, Cardenas-Hagan, & Tong, 2014).

Several studies explored the performance of ELs on achievement tests and indicated that a major factor in the performance discrepancy between EL and non-EL students is the linguistic complexity of the assessment instrument and the fact that students may not understand the directions for the task or the questions being asked of them because of vocabulary and syntax (Abedi, 2004; Abedi & Gándara, 2006; Abedi, Hofstetter, & Lord, 2004; Chu & Floress, 2011; Geva, Yaghoub-Zadeh, & Schuster, 2000). Abedi (2004) postulated that the confounding of language and academic content knowledge is so substantial that it undermines validity and utility of academic achievement testing for ELs as well as other groups, including CD students.

The Culture–Language Interpretive Matrix (C–LIM; Flanagan, Ortiz, & Alfonso, 2013) was developed to help practitioners determine the degree to which a student's performance on cognitive assessments was influenced by cultural and/or linguistic variables. The C–LIM does not include subtests from academic assessments although most would be considered high in terms of cultural loading and linguistic demand (Flanagan, Ortiz, & Alfonso, 2013). Thus, performance on academic assessments reflects a student's level of acquired knowledge that is heavily based on language development and is difficult to separate from formal instruction and schooling. S. Ortiz (personal communication, August 25, 2015) recommended that academic assessment data be prioritized as an indicator of educational need and a baseline measure of performance levels. Doing so will increase the likelihood that instruction will be delivered at an appropriate level for the student and optimize the opportunity for progress and learning.

Language of Assessment

Determining which language(s) to use when assessing EB students is a complex dilemma and one for which there is limited consensus and little clear guidance (S. O. Ortiz, 2014). This issue also introduces challenges associated with using interpreters, test modifications, and having qualified and bilingual staff to conduct evaluations. Further, much of the literature on this issue has focused on assessment in general or cognitive assessment but not academic assessment. Section 300.304(c)(1) of the Individuals With Disabilities Education Act of 2004 (IDEA) states that assessments administered as part of the evaluation process

> (i) Are selected and administered so as not to be discriminatory on a racial or cultural basis;
> (ii) Are provided and administered in the child's native language or other mode of communication and in the form most likely to yield accurate information on what the child knows and can do academically, developmentally, and functionally, unless it is clearly not feasible to so provide or administer;
> (iii) Are used for the purposes for which the assessments or measures are valid and reliable.

However, scholars such as Rivera, Moughamian, Lesaux, and Francis (2008) have emphasized that native language assessment for children who have not or no longer receive native language instruction or support must be interpreted cautiously and should not be used for accountability or evaluative purposes. Pitoniak et al. (2009) noted that using modifications such as translations for only some EB students raises questions about equity if translations are not available for all native languages spoken by students in a school district or state. Flanagan et al. (2013) summarized the benefits and limitations of four basic approaches for addressing concerns about fairness and validity in the assessment of diverse students. One approach involves making modifications or adaptations to a test instrument or materials in an effort to decrease the potential impact of a given student characteristic. Examples include deleting items, removing or modifying time limits, explaining instructions and test items, or using a translator or interpreter. A second approach involves using assessments that require limited or no verbal communication between the examiner and student. Such assessments use gestures, pantomime, and pictures and are often referred to as nonverbal in nature. Native language testing, the third approach, refers to conducting the assessment using instruments designed for individuals who speak the student's non-English language. The fourth approach involves using English-based assessment instruments in a way that takes into consideration the influences of culture and linguistic background on test performance. Although each approach is intended to reduce the potential adverse impact of culture or linguistic background, Flanagan et al. concluded that testing in English and interpreting results in light of the influence of culture and linguistic background provides the most practical and defensible approach. Despite the lack of empirical evidence and practice guidelines on this issue, scholars are in agreement that assessment approach and measures must be chosen, used, and interpreted in a manner that aligns with a given student's native language experience, proficiency levels in native and English language, and instructional experiences in both languages (S. O. Ortiz, 2014).

School Procedures and Practices

As noted earlier, the evaluation process and assessment elements depend greatly on the professional judgment of the professionals involved. School-based practitioners seek to conduct special education evaluations that are consistent with federal and state requirements and with professional practice standards. Flanagan et al. (2013) noted that the "manner and degree to which factors such as limited English proficiency and differences in opportunity to learn cultural knowledge influence [performance on assessments] has been largely overlooked in the current empirical literature and vague in practice guidelines" (p. 295). Thus, practitioners have few examples of specific suggestions for making the types of decisions that are relevant to the assessment of EB and CD students. This has a significant impact on the practices that are subsequently used at a school building and district level, which has the potential to affect identification patterns and disproportionate representation.

Scholars have studied the practices of school staff and teams that are relevant to special education referral and identification. Klingner and Harry (2006) reported that school teams gave only cursory attention to prereferral strategies, and most EL students were moved to special education testing without full consideration of the role of linguistic background and language proficiencies. They further noted that although school staff varied in terms of knowledge about language acquisition issues, many lacked critical information, which led to substantial variation in the quality of meetings and the decisions reached. A more recent study by A. A. Ortiz et al. (2011) found similar results through archival file review for 44 ELs identified with reading-related learning disabilities. They found "serious shortcomings in the district's implementation of special education referral, assessment, eligibility determinations, and placement procedures" (p. 322). Shortcomings included no teacher concerns or specific areas of concern noted on referral paperwork; a lack of interventions, especially those targeting English-language development skills prior to special education referral; a lack of assessment in both of the student's languages; and eligibility decisions based predominately on cognitive and academic achievement. File reviews conducted by an expert clinical panel indicated that only 23% ($n = 10$) of the files contained evidence that the student met special education eligibility criteria.

Figueroa and Newsome (2006) reviewed 19 school-based psycho-educational reports completed for ELs and identified competency issues among school professionals, as well as concerning practices. Specifically, they reported that educational evaluations rarely assessed or considered factors known to be confounding effects of bilingualism. One such example is the association between second-language acquisition and lower fluency in oral expression, listening comprehension, and reading. In fact, many characteristics that are typical of children learning a second language were often cited as the evidence for the disability, and there was difficulty distinguishing between low-language proficiency and learning disabilities (Liu, Ortiz, Wilkinson, Robertson, & Kushner, 2008). Figueroa and Newsome (2006) further noted that psychoeducational reports did not address the reason for referral; the student's language acquisition history and status; or the appropriateness of instruction, intervention, or test results. Flanagan et al. (2013) also reported a tendency for school practitioners to provide a general "interpret with caution" statement regarding test results of ELs in reports but then provide an otherwise traditional interpretation of the results.

Empirical evidence has certainly indicated limitations in the evaluation process for EB students. Less research has been conducted related to school practices for students who are CD, but similar concerns likely apply because of the increased ambiguity about how to address cultural influences on learning and assessment.

Training and Professional Competency

The assessment, teaming, and special education identification practices observed in schools reflect the training and preparation of educators and specialized staff, such as school psychologists. Numerous scholars have addressed the lack of explicit training in areas relevant to CLD students in preparation programs for general educators (Durgunoğlu & Hughes, 2010; Sleeter, 2001; Sullivan & Thorius, 2010), special educators (Darling-Hammond, 2010), and school psychologists (Lopez & Bursztyn, 2013; Newell et al., 2010). Studies have also indicated that a lack of training for bilingual education teachers may affect the inappropriate identification of reading-related learning disabilities among ELs (Liu et al., 2008; Wilkinson, Ortiz, Robertson, & Kushner, 2006). Seidl and Pugach (2009) noted the importance of preparing both general and special educators and other school staff to work collaboratively to assure the effectiveness of general education and the appropriateness of assessment and special education processes for students, regardless of cultural and linguistic backgrounds.

STRATEGIES FOR IMPROVING ASSESSMENT AND SPECIAL EDUCATION EVALUATION PRACTICES

Practices such as response to intervention (RTI) have the potential to improve the instruction and intervention services for diverse students and would address some of the concerns noted regarding prereferral processes (García & Ortiz, 2008; Linán-Thompson & Ortiz, 2009). Readers are referred to Chapter 9 (this volume) for more information about RTI. Considerations applicable to the special education evaluation and identification process are discussed next.

Use of Ecological Approach and Multiple Assessment Methods

According to the National Dissemination Center for Children with Disabilities (2007), the purposes of evaluation under IDEA 2004 include (a) to determine whether the student is a "child with a disability" as defined in IDEA 2004, (b) to gather information that will help determine the student's educational needs, and (c) to guide decision making about educational programming for the student. Each of these purposes is important and may call for different assessment approaches and measures. The focus on identifying the presence of a disability is often paramount and is especially challenging for students who are culturally and/or linguistically diverse.

Although determining the presence of a disability is necessary for eligibility determination, it is not sufficient, because the team also must document the student's need for specialized instruction and services. Assessments that analyze the student's specific academic skills are necessary to both document need and inform decisions about instruction and services (Yell, Busch, & Rogers, 2008). When such information is collected as part of the educational evaluation, it can be used to write the present levels of academic achievement and functional performance statement and measurable annual goals in a student's individualized education program (IEP), if found eligible. Yell et al. (2008) noted that an educational evaluation that incorporates methods such as criterion-referenced tests and curriculum-based assessment (CBA) will be especially helpful in identifying student need and guiding programming decisions. Further, using CBA may prevent a teacher from having to collect additional information to write the IEP and begin specialized instruction. Rhodes (2005) noted that norm-referenced measures of achievement and CBAs should be viewed as complementary assessment methods because each has its own limitations and contribution to the assessment process.

Therefore, the use of multiple and alternative assessment approaches and measures is commonly recommended (S. O. Ortiz, 2014; Rivera et al., 2008; Sullivan, 2012b). Culturally responsive (CR) assessment practices are those that consider a student's cultural and linguistic background and prior experience when selecting and interpreting assessment instruments so that the characteristics and needs of the student can be matched to the assessment practice and instrument (Rhodes et al., 2005; Sullivan, 2012a). Using an ecological framework to conduct special education evaluations is recommended as a more equitable process for identifying students with disabilities (Klingner & Eppolito, 2014), and it provides a structure for the use of CR assessment practices. Such an approach examines the influence of contextual variables (e.g., languages spoken in the home, length of time in the United States, family socioeconomic status, family support structure) and the effectiveness of instruction and intervention and considers learner characteristics such as school history, preschool experiences, first- and second-language acquisition and proficiency, and health. An ecological approach incorporates the use of multiple assessment methods, including interviews, observations, record review, and assessment through methods such as CBA (Hosp & Ardoin, 2008; Klingner & Eppolito, 2014; S. O. Ortiz, 2014).

The concept of *opportunity to learn* is integral in an ecological approach and addresses the question of whether the student has received high-quality instruction using an interactive and meaningful curriculum designed to develop both content knowledge and language skills (Klingner & Eppolito, 2014). This question can be addressed through the use of assessment methods such as curriculum-based measurement (CBM; Deno, 1985) and CBA for instructional design (CBA-ID; Burns & Parker, 2014) used during an intervention period and/or during the special education evaluation process. CBA-ID measures a student's specific academic skills, identifies an instructional level and acquisition rate and can be beneficial in the design of individualized interventions (Shapiro, 2011). However, CBM is a set of standardized, timed assessment procedures designed to measure academic progress (Deno, 1985). Two of the most familiar CBMs are AIMSweb (Shinn & Shinn, 2003) and dynamic indicators of basic early literacy skills (DIBELS; Good & Kaminski, 2002), or IDEL (D. L. Baker & Good, 2006), the Spanish version of DIBELS.

The use of CBM has been recommended for use with EB students by many researchers, especially for the purpose of measuring growth in academic skills (S. K. Baker, Plasencia-Peinado, & Lezcano-Lytle, 1998; Linán-Thompson, Vaughn, Hickman-Davis & Kouzekanani, 2003; Sandberg & Reschly, 2011; Schon, Shaftel, & Markham, 2008) when performance is compared with that of *true peers*, students of similar linguistic and cultural background and status (Sullivan, 2012b). Literature reviews of CBM research have indicated moderate to strong reliability and criterion-related validity coefficients for the curriculum-based measurement of oral reading fluency (CBM-R) for EL students (Wayman, Wallace, Wiley, Tichá, & Espin, 2007) and mixed results regarding rates of progress of ELs compared with non-ELs (Sandberg & Reschly, 2011).

Although there appears to be adequate evidence for the use of CBM for progress monitoring and RTI, there is less evidence regarding its utility for higher stake decisions, such as special education identification. A study conducted by Klein and Jimerson (2005) indicated that ethnicity and home language together influenced the predictive validity of oral reading tasks, a common CBM measure. The performance on high-stakes assessments of Hispanic students whose home language was Spanish was overpredicted and that of English-speaking Caucasian students was underpredicted. Quirk and Beem (2012) also reported that oral reading fluency measures overestimated the reading comprehension skills for a substantial number of EL students, resulting in potential misidentification of reading problems for more than 55% of students in Grades 2, 3, and 5 in their sample. Despite this lack of empirical evidence, the majority (51%) of school psychologists in a study conducted by McCloskey and Athanasiou (2000) reported using CBM as one assessment method when determining special education eligibility for EL students.

The use of CBM with students from diverse racial and ethnic backgrounds has been the focus of limited research, and existing findings have varied. Kranzler, Miller, and Jordan (1999) reported that the meaning of oral reading fluency scores differed across race and ethnicity at particular grade levels in their sample. Performance on CBM measures overestimated the reading comprehension skills of African American students in Grades 4 and 5 and underestimated that of Caucasian students. However, Hintze, Callahan, Matthews, Williams, and Tobin (2002) examined the differential predictive bias of oral reading fluency and reported that ethnicity was not a significant predictor of reading comprehension once socioeconomic status, age, and oral reading fluency skill were controlled. CBM scores predicted similar reading comprehension performance for Caucasian and African American students. Hintze et al. concluded that CBM-R is appropriate for use as a screening, referral, and progress measure for racially and ethnically diverse students.

Despite their limitations, norm-referenced measures of academic achievement will continue to be used as part of special education evaluations. Practitioners should take care to select measures and interpret results in light of the student's background and experiences. In addition, practitioners may find it helpful to conduct error analysis and quantify the impact of confounding variables by calculating the number and percentage of missed items that appear to be related to linguistic and/or cultural influences. Task features that have been shown to differentially impact performance include

- the complexity of the directions for the task or the questions asked of the student due to vocabulary; sentence length; use of prepositional phrases, comparative structures, and discourse; subordinate, conditional, and relative clauses; passive voice; and negation (Abedi, 2004);
- the use of idioms, figurative language, and words with multiple meanings (Klingner & Eppolito, 2014);
- timed or speed-based tasks (Figueroa & Newsome, 2006);
- the inclusion of phonemes that are not present in the student's native language on phonological awareness activities (August & Shanahan, 2006);
- response formats that require extensive writing or oral communication, as opposed to those that allow diagrams or charts; and
- the use of context for fictional questions (e.g., math reasoning) that is unfamiliar to the student (Pitoniak et al., 2009).

Improving the Quality and Consistency of School Practices

Multidisciplinary teams have been known to make special education eligibility decisions on the basis of students' perceived need for services rather than on data-based evidence. Such practices create inconsistency and potentially result in overidentification and misclassification (Mellard, Deshler, & Barth, 2004). When definitions about what constitutes disability and eligibility criteria are lacking or vague, school practitioners base decisions on professional judgment rather than data and evidence (Kavale & Forness, 2000). Lichtenstein (2008) warned against the use of a great deal of professional judgment because it raises concerns not only about consistency but also about accuracy and objectivity in the decision-making process. District-wide policies and procedures can reduce inconsistency and misclassification by creating a structure for decision making that reduces errors in practices (Lichtenstein, 2008; Page, 2002).

The importance of clarity regarding disability identification and special education eligibility is heightened in the context of serving linguistically and culturally diverse students because of the complexity of the relationship between language acquisition, proficiency, and academic performance and the documented lack of training and expertise among educators and school staff regarding this population of students. Thus, the development of local guidance and procedures has the potential to significantly improve practices at a school building and district level. Nellis (2013) addressed the importance of local guidance and identified benefits such as increased specificity regarding the type of assessment data that will be collected and how results will be interpreted for CLD students. Such guidance fills a void that has been noted in the literature and it facilitates a shared understanding among staff—school psychologists, speech-language therapists, teachers, and administrators—and families regarding how language acquisition, cultural differences, and educational opportunities will be considered when making decisions about the presence of a disability for diverse students. Guidance and explicit eligibility considerations also have the potential to foster deeper analysis of student strengths and needs, which could, in turn, lead to better developed instructional programs and services. Improved system-wide practices also have the potential to result in more appropriate special education identification decisions and thus would lessen the presence of disproportionality.

Another element of improved school practices that is especially relevant when working with diverse students is increased teaming and family involvement. Salend and Salinas (2003) noted the importance of including educators trained in assessing EB students as part of the multidisciplinary teams that make decisions about ELs. This may include staff such as English-as-a-second-language (ESL) teachers, bilingual educators, and interpreters. A. A. Ortiz et al. (2011) recommended the involvement of ESL staff because they reportedly "play a critical role in preventing student failure and in supporting struggling learners in their classrooms" (p. 325). In addition, ESL staff can contribute to the team process by providing quality assessment data that offers information related to the student's language acquisition process, language proficiency, and English literacy skills. Sullivan (2012a) also emphasized the need to involve family members as meaningful contributors to intervention teams, problem-solving teams, or special education evaluation teams. Family involvement helps the school staff develop a better understanding of the child, his or her development and background, and how culture and/or language may or may not contribute to learning progress and performance.

CONCLUSION

The assessment of EB and CD students, especially the assessment of academic skills and levels of performance, is a complicated task that affects important decisions and outcomes at student, school, and district levels. Although the topic of assessment of diverse students is often discussed and debated, the existing empirical evidence is relatively limited and the practice recommendations are general and vague. However, school practices can be improved at the local level and, as a result, students will receive more appropriate instruction and learning opportunities and fewer inappropriate special education referrals and determinations will be made. Improving school-wide practices can be a daunting task, but each school professional can contribute through engagement in continued professional learning, collaboration with a colleague, use of a different assessment method, or listening to a student's family talk about prior experiences and concerns. Although each is a small act in itself, collectively they can have a substantial impact when carried out by multiple educators and specialists, on an ongoing basis, for all students.

REFERENCES

Abedi, J. (2004). The No Child Left Behind Act and English language learners: Assessment and accountability issues. *Educational Researcher, 33*, 4–14. http://dx.doi.org/10.3102/0013189X033001004

Abedi, J., & Gándara, P. (2006). Performance of English language learners as a subgroup in large-scale assessment: Interaction of research and policy. *Educational Measurement: Issues and Practice, 25*(4), 36–46. http://dx.doi.org/10.1111/j.1745-3992.2006.00077.x

Abedi, J., Hofstetter, C., & Lord, C. (2004). Assessment accommodations for English-language learners: Implications for policy-based empirical research. *Review of Educational Research, 74*, 1–28. http://dx.doi.org/10.3102/00346543074001001

August, D., & Shanahan, T. (Eds.). (2006). *Developing literacy in second-language learners: A report of the National Literacy Panel on language-minority children and youth.* Mahwah, NJ: Erlbaum.

Baker, D. L., & Good, R. H. (2006). Fluency in oral story. In R. H. Good, D. L. Baker, N. Knutson, & J. M. Watson (Eds.), *Dynamic indicators of reading success* (7th ed., pp. 40–44). Eugene, OR: Dynamic Measurement Group.

Baker, S. K., Plasencia-Peinado, J., & Lezcano-Lytle, V. (1998). The use of curriculum based measurement with language-minority students. In M. R. Shinn (Ed.), *Advanced applications of curriculum-based measurement* (pp. 175–213). New York, NY: Guilford Press.

Braden, J. P. (1999). Straight talk about assessment and diversity: What do we know? *School Psychology Quarterly, 14*, 343–355. http://dx.doi.org/10.1037/h0089013

Brown, S. L., Shriberg, D., & Wang, A. (2007). Diversity research literature on the rise? A review of school psychology journals from 2000 to 2003. *Psychology in the Schools, 44*, 639–650. http://dx.doi.org/10.1002/pits.20253

Burns, M. K., & Parker, D. C. (2014). *Curriculum-based assessment for instructional design: Using data to individualize instruction.* New York, NY: Guilford Press.

Chu, S., & Floress, S. (2011). Assessment of English language learners with learning disabilities. *The Clearing House: A Journal of Educational Strategies, Issues and Ideas, 84*, 244–248.

Darling-Hammond, L. (2010). Teacher education and the American future. *Journal of Teacher Education, 61*, 35–47. http://dx.doi.org/10.1177/0022487109348024

Deno, S. L. (1985). Curriculum-based measurement: The emerging alternative. *Exceptional Children, 52*, 219–232.

Donovan, M. S., & Cross, C. T. (Eds.). (2002). *Minority students in special and gifted education.* Washington, DC: National Academies Press.

Durgunoğlu, A. Y., & Hughes, T. (2010). How prepared are teachers to teach English language learners? *International Journal of Teaching and Learning in Higher Education, 22*, 32–41.

Figueroa, R. A., & Newsome, P. (2006). The diagnosis of LD in English learners: Is it nondiscriminatory? *Journal of Learning Disabilities, 39*, 206–214. http://dx.doi.org/10.1177/00222194060390030201

Flanagan, D. P., Ortiz, S. O., & Alfonso, V. C. (2013). *Essentials of cross-battery assessment* (3rd ed.). Hoboken, NJ: Wiley.

Frisby, C. (2009). Cultural competence in school psychology: Established or elusive construct? In T. B. Gutkin & C. R. Reynolds (Eds.), *The handbook of school psychology* (pp. 855–887). Hoboken, NJ: Wiley.

García, S. B., & Ortiz, A. A. (2008). A framework of culturally and linguistically responsive design of response to intervention models. *Multiple Voices for Ethnically Diverse Exceptional Learners, 11*(1), 24–41.

Geva, E., Yaghoub-Zadeh, Z., & Schuster, B. (2000). Understanding individual differences in word recognition skills of ESL children. *Annals of Dyslexia, 50*, 121–154. http://dx.doi.org/10.1007/s11881-000-0020-8

Good, R. H., & Kaminski, R. A. (Eds.). (2002). *Dynamic indicators of basic early literacy skills* (6th ed.). Eugene, OR: Institute for the Development of Educational Achievement.

Hemphill, F. C., & Vanneman, A. (2011, June). *Achievement gaps: How Hispanic and White students in public schools perform in mathematics and reading on the national assessment of educational progress*. Retrieved from http://nces.ed.gov/nationsreportcard/pdf/studies/2011459.pdf

Hintze, J. M., Callahan, J. E., Matthews, W. J., Williams, S. A., & Tobin, K. G. (2002). Oral reading fluency and prediction of reading comprehension in African American and Caucasian elementary school children. *School Psychology Review, 31*, 540–553.

Hosp, J. L., & Ardoin, S. P. (2008). Assessment for instructional planning. *Assessment for Effective Intervention, 33*, 69–77. http://dx.doi.org/10.1177/1534508407311428

Individuals With Disabilities Education Act of 2004, 20 U.S.C. § 1400 (2004).

Kavale, K. A., & Forness, S. R. (2000). What definitions of learning disability say and don't say: A critical analysis. *Journal of Learning Disabilities, 33*, 239–256. http://dx.doi.org/10.1177/002221940003300303

Klein, J. R., & Jimerson, S. R. (2005). Examining ethnic, gender, language, and socioeconomic bias in oral reading fluency scores among Caucasian and Hispanic students. *School Psychology Quarterly, 20*, 23–50. http://dx.doi.org/10.1521/scpq.20.1.23.64196

Klingner, J., & Eppolito, A. M. (2014). *English language learners: Differentiating between language acquisition and learning disabilities*. Arlington, VA: Council for Exceptional Children.

Klingner, J. K., & Harry, B. (2006). The special education referral and decision-making process for English language learners: Child study team meetings and placement conferences. *Teachers College Record, 108*, 2247–2281. http://dx.doi.org/10.1111/j.1467-9620.2006.00781.x

Kranzler, J. H., Miller, M. D., & Jordan, L. (1999). An examination of racial/ethnic and gender bias on curriculum-based measurement of reading. *School Psychology Quarterly, 14*, 327–342. http://dx.doi.org/10.1037/h0089012

Lichtenstein, R. (2008). Best practices in identification of learning disabilities. In A. Thomas & J. Grimes (Eds.), *Best practices in school psychology V* (Vol. 2, pp. 295–318). Bethesda, MD: National Association of School Psychologists.

Linán-Thompson, S., & Ortiz, A. A. (2009). Response to intervention and English-language learners: Instructional and assessment considerations. *Seminars in Speech and Language, 30*, 105–120. http://dx.doi.org/10.1055/s-0029-1215718

Linán-Thompson, S., Vaughn, S., Hickman-Davis, P., & Kouzekanani, K. (2003). Effectiveness of supplemental reading instruction for second-grade English language learners with reading difficulties. *The Elementary School Journal, 103*, 221–238. http://dx.doi.org/10.1086/499724

Liu, Y., Ortiz, A. A., Wilkinson, C., Robertson, P., & Kushner, M. (2008). From early childhood special education to special education resource rooms: Identification, assessment, and eligibility determinations for English language learners with reading-related learning disability. *Assessment for Effective Intervention, 33*, 177–187. http://dx.doi.org/10.1177/1534508407313247

Lopez, E. C., & Bursztyn, A. M. (2013). Future challenges and opportunities: Toward culturally responsive training in school psychology. *Psychology in the Schools, 50*, 212–228. http://dx.doi.org/10.1002/pits.21674

McCloskey, D., & Athanasiou, M. S. (2000). Assessment and intervention practices with second language learners among school psychologists. *Psychology in the Schools, 37*, 209–225. http://dx.doi.org/10.1002/(SICI)1520-6807(200005)37:3<209::AID-PITS2>3.0.CO;2-#

Mellard, D. F., Deshler, D. D., & Barth, A. (2004). LD identification: It's not simply a matter of building a better mousetrap. *Learning Disability Quarterly, 27*, 229–242. http://dx.doi.org/10.2307/1593675

Messick, S. (1991). Validity of test interpretation and use. In M. C. Alkin (Ed.), *Encyclopedia of educational research* (6th ed., pp. 1487–1495). New York, NY: Macmillan.

National Center for Education Statistics. (2014). *National assessment of educational progress (NAEP), various years, 1990–2013 mathematics and reading assessments.* Retrieved from http://nationsreportcard.gov/

National Dissemination Center for Children with Disabilities. (2007). *Individuals with Disabilities Education Act, Module 9: Introduction to evaluation under IDEA.* Retrieved from http://www.parentcenterhub.org/repository/partb-module9/

National Education Association (NEA). (2007). *Truth in labeling: Disproportionality in special education.* Washington, DC: Author.

Nellis, L. M. (2013). *Consistency in evaluation and eligibility decisions: Importance at the local level.* Unpublished manuscript.

Newell, M. L., Nastasi, B. K., Hatzichristou, C., Jones, J. M., Schanding, G. T., & Yetter, G. (2010). Evidence on multicultural training in school psychology: Recommendations for future directions. *School Psychology Quarterly, 25*, 249–278. http://dx.doi.org/10.1037/a0021542

Noltemeyer, A. L., Proctor, S. L., & Dempsey, A. (2013). Race and ethnicity in school psychology publications: A content analysis and comparison to publications in related disciplines. *Contemporary School Psychology, 17*, 129–142.

O'Bryon, E. C. (2014). Challenges and complexities in the assessment of the bilingual student. In A. B. Clinton (Ed.), *Assessing bilingual children in context: An integrated approach* (pp. 7–24). Washington, DC: American Psychological Association. http://dx.doi.org/10.1037/14320-002

Ortiz, A. A., Robertson, P. M., Wilkinson, C. U., Liu, U. J., McGhee, B. D., & Kushner, M. I. (2011). The role of bilingual education teachers in preventing inappropriate referrals of ELLs to special education: Implications for response to intervention. *Bilingual Research Journal, 34*, 316–333. http://dx.doi.org/10.1080/15235882.2011.628608

Ortiz, S. O. (2014). Best practices in nondiscriminatory assessment. In P. L. Harrison & A. Thomas (Eds.), *Best practices in school psychology: Foundations* (pp. 61–74). Bethesda, MD: National Association of School Psychologists.

Ortiz, S. O., & Ochoa, S. H. (2005). Conceptual measurement and methodological issues in cognitive assessment of culturally and linguistically diverse individuals. In R. L. Rhodes, S. H. Ochoa, & S. O. Ortiz (Eds.), *Assessing culturally and linguistically diverse students: A practical guide* (pp. 153–167). New York, NY: Guilford Press.

Page, S. (2002). *Establishing a system of policies and procedures.* Westerville, OH: Process Improvement.

Pitoniak, M. J., Young, J. W., Martiniello, M., King, T. C., Buteux, A., & Ginsburgh, M. (2009). *Guidelines for the assessment of English-language learners.* Princeton, NJ: Educational Testing Service.

Pollard-Durodola, S. D., Cardenas-Hagan, E., & Tong, F. (2014). Implications of bilingualism for reading assessment. In A. B. Clinton (Ed.), *Assessing bilingual children in context: An integrated approach* (pp. 241–264). Washington, DC: American Psychological Association. http://dx.doi.org/10.1037/14320-011

Quirk, M., & Beem, S. (2012). Examining the relations between reading fluency and reading comprehension for English language learners. *Psychology in the Schools, 49,* 539–553. http://dx.doi.org/10.1002/pits.21616

Rhodes, R. L. (2005). Assessment of academic achievement. In R. L. Rhodes, S. H. Ochoa, & S. O. Ortiz (Eds.), *Assessing culturally and linguistically diverse students: A practical guide* (pp. 202–214). New York, NY: Guilford Press.

Rhodes, R. L., Ochoa, S. H., & Ortiz, S. O. (Eds.). (2005). *Assessing culturally and linguistically diverse students: A practical guide.* New York, NY: Guilford Press.

Rivera, M. O., Moughamian, A. C., Lesaux, N. K., & Francis, D. J. (2008). *Language and reading interventions for English language learners and English language learners with disabilities.* Portsmouth, NH: RMC Research Corporation, Center on Instruction.

Salend, S. J., & Salinas, A. (2003). Language differences or language difficulties: The work of the multidisciplinary team. *Teaching Exceptional Children, 35*(4), 36–43.

Sandberg, K. L., & Reschly, A. L. (2011). English learners: Challenges in assessment and the promise of curriculum-based measurement. *Remedial and Special Education, 32,* 144–154. http://dx.doi.org/10.1177/0741932510361260

Sattler, J. M. (2008). *Assessment of children: Cognitive applications* (5th ed.). San Diego, CA: Jerome M. Sattler.

Schon, J., Shaftel, J., & Markham, P. (2008). Contemporary issues in the assessment of culturally and linguistically diverse students. *Journal of Applied School Psychology, 24,* 163–189. http://dx.doi.org/10.1080/15377900802089395

Seidl, B., & Pugach, M. C. (2009). Support and teaching in the vulnerable moments: Preparing special educators for diversity. *Multiple Voices for Ethnically Diverse Exceptional Learners, 11,* 57–75.

Shapiro, E. S. (2011). *Academic skills problems: Direct assessment and intervention* (4th ed.). New York, NY: Guilford Press.

Shinn, M. M., & Shinn, M. R. (2003). *Administration and scoring of early literacy measures for use with AIMSweb.* Eden Prairie, MN: Edformation.

Sleeter, C. E. (2001). Preparing teachers for culturally diverse schools: Research and the overwhelming presence of whiteness. *Journal of Teacher Education, 52,* 94–106. http://dx.doi.org/10.1177/0022487101052002002

Sullivan, A. (2010). Preventing disproportionality: A framework for culturally responsive assessment. *NASP Communique, 39*(3), 1 & 24.

Sullivan, A. (2011). Disproportionality in special education identification and placement of English language learners. *Exceptional Children, 77,* 317–334. http://dx.doi.org/10.1177/001440291107700304

Sullivan, A. (2012a). Culturally responsive practice. In A. L. Noltemeyer & C. S. McLoughlin (Eds.), *Disproportionality in education and special education: A guide to creating more equitable learning environments* (pp. 181–198). Springfield, IL: Charles C Thomas.

Sullivan, A. (2012b). Patterns and correlates of the disproportionate representation of linguistic minority students in special education. In A. L. Noltemeyer & C. S. McLoughlin (Eds.), *Disproportionality in education and special education: A guide to creating more equitable learning environments* (pp. 181–198). Springfield, IL: Charles C Thomas.

Sullivan, A. L., & Thorius, K. A. (2010). Considering intersections of differences among students identified as disabled and expanding conceptualizations of multicultural education. *Race, Gender, & Class, 17*(1-2), 93–109.

Waitoller, F. R., Artiles, A. J., & Cheney, D. A. (2010). The miner's canary: A review of overrepresentation research and explanations. *The Journal of Special Education, 44,* 29–49. http://dx.doi.org/10.1177/0022466908329226

Wayman, M. M., Wallace, T., Wiley, H. I., Tichá, R., & Espin, C. A. (2007). Literature synthesis on curriculum-based measurement in reading. *The Journal of Special Education, 41,* 85–120. http://dx.doi.org/10.1177/00224669070410020401

Wilkinson, C. Y., Ortiz, A. A., Robertson, P. M., & Kushner, M. I. (2006). English language learners with reading-related LD: Linking data from multiple sources to make eligibility determinations. *Journal of Learning Disabilities, 39,* 129–141. http://dx.doi.org/10.1177/00222194060390020201

Yell, M., Busch, T. W., & Rogers, D. C. (2008). Planning instruction and monitoring student performance. *Beyond Behavior, 17,* 31–38.

6

SOCIAL–EMOTIONAL AND BEHAVIORAL ASSESSMENT

JAMILIA J. BLAKE, REBECCA R. WINTERS, AND LAURA B. FRAME

Racially and ethnically diverse youth who experience mental health challenges, particularly low-income Latino, Black, and American Indian children, may be at risk of not receiving needed psychological support because of financial and social barriers to mental health care access (Blake, Nero, & Rodriguez, 2011; Kataoka, Zhang, & Wells, 2002; Novins & Bess, 2011). Considering the significant amount of time that children spend at school, schools represent an ideal setting to provide mental health services to youth who lack resources for continuous psychological treatment. When considering how to best support the mental health needs of youth from ethnically diverse backgrounds, scholars and psychologists must consider the intertwining and confounding effects of a variety of factors, including individual and community poverty, exposure to violence and trauma, and systems of oppression that may be inherent in social constructs of race and gender (Collins, 2000). Failure to examine such key aspects of youths' experience can lead to potential errors in the

http://dx.doi.org/10.1037/14855-007
Psychoeducational Assessment and Intervention for Ethnic Minority Children: Evidence-Based Approaches,
S. L. Graves, Jr., and J. J. Blake (Editors)

assessment process and attenuate the effects of any supports or treatment provided. Therefore, from the beginning of the assessment process, it is critical to evaluate the strengths and difficulties of ethnically diverse youth from an intersectionality framework by considering the degree to which influential factors combine to affect the manifestation of social, emotional, or behavioral symptoms.

The overarching purpose of this chapter is to provide essential information that psychologists must know when assessing students of ethnically diverse backgrounds for social–emotional and behavioral concerns. In this chapter, we discuss how cultural manifestations of symptoms may influence assessment practices for ethnically diverse students using the criteria specified in the Emotional Disturbance (ED) category of the Individuals With Disabilities Educational Improvement Act of 2004 (IDEIA; 34 CFR Section 300.8 (c)(4)(i)) that most closely align with the *Diagnostic and Statistical Manual of Mental Disorders* (5th ed.; *DSM–5*; American Psychiatric Association, 2013) symptoms for childhood disorders. We also outline recommendations for best practices for the social–emotional assessment process with ethnically diverse students.

IDEIA EMOTIONAL DISTURBANCE

Efforts to provide assessment and intervention for youth with social, emotional, or behavioral difficulties in schools are currently guided by a framework specified within IDEIA. Under this federal law, students with social, emotional, or behavioral symptoms of a certain severity may be qualified to receive special education or related services in school, as outlined in an Individualized Education Plan. Although they may meet criteria under any category that best fits their individual needs, students with serious emotional and behavioral difficulties that are not rooted in another disorder (e.g., autism, an intellectual disability) are most often considered for the ED category.

When determining whether a student should be identified as a child or adolescent with an ED, psychologists must consider whether the child is

> exhibiting one or more of the following characteristics over a long period of time and to a marked degree that adversely affects a child's educational performance: a) an inability to learn that cannot be explained by intellectual, sensory, or health factors; b) an inability to build or maintain satisfactory interpersonal relationships with peers and teachers; c) inappropriate types of behavior or feelings under normal circumstances; d) a general pervasive mood of unhappiness or depression; e) a tendency to develop physical symptoms or fears associated with personal or school problems. (IDEIA 34 CFR Section 300.8 (c)(4)(ii))

IDEIA further dictates that students who have been diagnosed with schizophrenia may qualify for services as ED (34 CFR Section 300.8 (c)(4)(ii)).

Several factors inherent in the federal definition of ED render its use challenging, particularly when evaluating the psychological well-being of ethnic minority students. Controversy has surfaced about how to interpret the individual criteria, because evaluating the emotional and behavioral manifestations of youth can be a fairly subjective process. Students' ability to build and maintain relationships, their demonstration of physical symptoms or fears, and more could be determined and interpreted in various ways according to cultural norms surrounding behavior and affective expression. Further, the exclusionary criteria attached to this category make the assessment process particularly complex and subjective.

The IDEIA criteria specify that children who are considered to be "socially maladjusted" may not qualify for services. The original intent of this clause, from a legal perspective, was (a) to ensure that students were not affixed with an ED label because of the manifestation of typical adolescent behavior and (b) to avoid providing services to students who would be more appropriately placed within the criminal justice system (Smith, Katsiyannis, Losinski, & Ryan, 2015). Whereas significant attention has been devoted to addressing the problems with the ED social maladjustment exclusionary clause, less emphasis has been placed on how students' cultural backgrounds may influence the manifestation of emotional and behavioral symptoms and prevent them from receiving the mental health and educational supports they require.

Racial and Ethnic Distributions for Emotional Disturbance

The disproportionate representation of ethnic minority students in the ED category has been discussed extensively (Coutinho, Oswald, Best, & Forness, 2002; McKenna, 2013; Wiley, Brigham, Kauffman, & Bogan, 2013). Current statistics based on 2012 data from the Office of Special Education and the 2012 U.S. Census reveal that Black students are twice as likely to be identified with ED as White students (odds ratio [OR] = 2; U.S. Bureau of the Census, 2013; U.S. Department of Education, Office of Special Education Programs, 2012). In contrast, Latino (OR = .78) and Asian (OR = .2) students were less likely to be identified with ED than their White peers. Over- or underrepresentation in the ED category may be due to any number of factors, depending on the racial or ethnic group and the unique cultural environment of each student and the school they attend. Factors such as student demographics, instructional practices, the perception of ethnically diverse students held by school staff (due to racial bias), the definition of ED used to determine eligibility, and students' socioeconomic status (SES) have been regarded as influential in determining representation (McKenna, 2013).

Whereas some scholars have suggested that the disproportionate representation of ethnically diverse youth in the ED category is attributable to race or ethnicity, others have argued that this ED disproportionality is primarily due to SES. Mixed findings have resulted from studies attempting to elucidate the relationship between student SES and race or ethnicity and over- and underrepresentation in special education. For example, in examining potential risk factors for ED placement, it is widely acknowledged that Latino youth, who are underrepresented in the ED category, are typically overrepresented among those living in poverty (Wiley et al., 2013). Although not a direct test of the role of racial or ethnic bias in ED placement decisions, these findings do suggest that SES alone may not fully explain racial or ethnic over- and underrepresentation in the ED category.

Need for Culturally Sensitive Assessment Practices

In summary, the need to examine factors related to diversity and racial and ethnic bias within the assessment process continues to grow as concerns regarding disproportionate representation surface throughout the United States. This need is particularly important in light of the lack of cultural sensitivity and room for interpretation inherent in the ED criteria, which may result in the over- or underrepresentation of students from racially and ethnically diverse backgrounds with mental health concerns. Given that the conceptualization of ED depends on the cultural lens from which symptoms are perceived, it is important to consider that behavioral expectations are not uniform across cultures. What is labeled as deviant behavior by school personnel may not be regarded as such in outside settings among other cultural groups, and some students may lack the social prowess to meet the demands of each setting. Thus, practitioners must consider the way that cultural variables intertwine to affect internalizing and externalizing behaviors to truly understand the nature of students' experience and determine their mental health needs.

CULTURAL MANIFESTATIONS OF EMOTIONAL DISTURBANCE SYMPTOMATOLOGY

When evaluating students of diverse cultural backgrounds for qualification under the category of ED, it is imperative to first understand how youth across cultures may exhibit social–emotional and behavioral symptoms. Although it is difficult to disentangle the effects of variables such as gender and SES from the effects of race and ethnicity, some studies have found trends in psychological symptoms among ethnically diverse populations. Students of Black, Latino, and Indigenous American origin tend to report the highest level of unmet mental health needs (Campbell & Evans-Campbell, 2011; Ringel & Sturm, 2001); this may be related to similarities in environmental variables, such as low SES, that are linked to psychological difficulties (Brown & Grumet, 2009).

Although similar psychological ailments may be found among youth of various ethnic groups, they are often expressed in distinct ways (Zayas & Gulbas, 2012). These manifestations, termed *idioms of distress*, indicate psychological conflict and suffering in a manner that is culturally meaningful to the individual, according to his or her experiences and socialization (Nichter, 2010). Thus, similar psychosocial stressors across home and school settings may result in different social, emotional, and physical responses across cultures that communicate the need for psychological support. Child mental health professionals who work with students of diverse backgrounds must be aware of cross-cultural similarities and differences in emotional and behavioral expression to ensure accurate assessment and identification for special education services. This section reviews cross-cultural findings in relation to symptoms of depression, anxiety, and schizophrenia that are associated with the IDEIA criteria for ED. Because of the limited research on Native American youths' display of internalizing and psychotic symptoms, this section focuses on the psychological functioning of Black, Latino, and Asian youth.

Depression

Depressive symptoms are expressly specified within the IDEIA criteria as being indicative of an ED. Research in recent years has emphasized that symptom development and presentation of depression are likely to differ across ethnic groups (Austin & Chorpita, 2004).

Black Youth

In examining depression among Black youth, some studies have found higher prevalence rates in comparison with Caucasian youth (e.g., Allen-Meares, Colarossi, Oyserman, & DeRoos, 2003; Franko et al., 2005; Kistner, David, & White, 2003), whereas others have found lower rates (Angold et al., 2002; Doerfler, Felner, Rowlison, Raley, & Evans, 1988). Inconsistencies in reported prevalence rates may be due to methodological differences between studies, particularly in population characteristics and measurement tools. Several consistencies have been found, however, in relation to the risk factors and variables that may affect the development of depression in Black youth. According to the 2000 U.S. Census, 31% of Black youth live in poverty, a rate that is 2.5 times greater than that of their Caucasian counterparts (Grant et al., 2004). Myriad investigations have linked poverty and economic disadvantage to depression, resulting from high stress, lack of resources and opportunity, increased risk of victimization, compromised parenting skills, and lack of social support from family or community (Fitzpatrick, 1993; Gaylord-Harden, Elmore, Campbell, & Wethington, 2011). Regardless of SES, perceived racism and discrimination are associated with low self-concept and depression across studies, because Black youth face oppression in various forms (Hammack, 2003; Nyborg & Curry, 2003).

With regard to the measurement of depression, the tendency of Blacks to endorse fewer symptoms in many studies has led researchers to question the application of current DSM–5 criteria to this population (Ofonedu, Percy, Harris-Britt, & Belcher, 2013). Studies such as that of Iwata, Turner, and Lloyd (2002) have found that Black participants are less likely to report feelings of sadness than Caucasian participants, and they may be prone to report anger as a way to mask such feelings (Davis & Stevenson, 2006). This finding is attributed to cultural stigma in the Black community, in which sadness is perceived as a sign of weakness or vulnerability. Thus, although Black youth may experience classic internalizing feelings of hopelessness, isolation, and withdrawal similar to peers in other ethnic groups, they often present with symptoms such as irritability, anger, blaming, and other externalizing behaviors as a protective mechanism (Baker, 2001; Ofonedu et al., 2013). Given the common association of these behaviors with conduct disorders and the overdiagnosis of conduct problems in Black youth, they might not be easily recognized as culturally specific coping strategies for depression (Davis & Stevenson, 2006). Therefore, practitioners must be prepared to inquire about both internalizing and externalizing behaviors when investigating depression among Black youth, because externalizing symptoms may be indicative of disorders that are typically conceptualized with internalizing symptoms.

Latino Youth

In general, studies have found that Latino youth, particularly adolescent girls, exhibit symptoms of depression and suicidality at a higher rate than White or Black peers (Polo & López, 2009; Zayas & Gulbas, 2012). Although cultural nuances in the nature of depressive symptoms have not yet been emphasized in studies of Latino youth, many have examined cultural differences in the development of symptoms and treatment-seeking behaviors. Overall, the finding that Latino youth exhibit a higher level of depression has been linked to a number of risk factors that they often experience, including exposure to influences such as poverty, violence, familial stress, immigration, and discrimination. The association between these variables and internalizing symptoms, particularly depression, has been established by a growing literature base (Tarshis, Jutte, & Huffman, 2006). Although some researchers have found that acculturative stress and English language proficiency related to immigration lead to negative outcomes such as depression (Polo & López,

2009), others have revealed a higher level of symptomology for Latinos who have resided in the United States for longer periods. Dawson and Williams (2008) found that although language status was not associated with internalizing symptoms among young Latino children, being born in the United States was a significant factor. Others have likewise found that, consistent with the "immigrant paradox," Latino youth born in the United States report more negative mental health outcomes than those born elsewhere (Ortega, Rosenheck, Alegría, & Desai, 2000), suggesting that they may experience marginalization among peers of other cultures as well as within their own group. Therefore, Latino youth may be at risk of experiencing depression regardless of their degree of acculturation.

One model that has been used to explain differences in the manifestation of internalizing symptoms among Latino youth is the problem suppression–facilitation model (Weisz, 1989), which suggests that cultural beliefs, values, and parenting practices influence the development of psychological difficulties. According to this model, internalizing symptoms may result from expectations of obedience, respect, and self-regulation, in association with the cultural value of *familism*, because they promote the needs of family or community over those of the individual. Whereas support for this model among Latino youth has been inconsistent, perhaps due to within-group differences, it is important to recognize the role of cultural socialization practices when evaluating symptoms in this population (Polo & López, 2009).

Research related to suicidality in Latino youth may be particularly illuminating when examining cultural manifestations of internalizing symptoms. In their review on cultural factors related to suicidality, Chu, Goldblum, Floyd, and Bongar (2010) indicated a rate of 14% for Latinas, which is nearly twice as high as that of White (7.7%) and Black peers (9.9%). For Latino youth, culturally specific factors that may predict suicidality include acculturative stress, lower religiosity, substance use, discrimination, low SES, familial stress, and lack of familial support or cohesion. In particular, females may be at a higher risk as a result of conflicting values and gender-specific expectations found across cultures, which they must navigate in daily life.

Asian Youth

Investigations focusing on depression among Asian youth are relatively limited, and existing studies examining various ethnic groups have consistently found lower rates among Asian youth when compared with White peers (Roberts, Roberts, & Chen, 1997). Austin and Chorpita (2004) examined depression among Chinese Americans, Filipinos, Hawaiians, and Japanese Americans relative to a White comparison group but did not find any significant differences across groups. However, an earlier investigation by Kuo (1984) identified significant differences in rates of depression, with Korean Americans having the highest rates, followed by Filipino Americans, Japanese Americans, and Chinese Americans. In this study, prevalence rates were similar to those of White youth. Some researchers have suggested that low rates of depression among Asian youth may be due to a smaller symptom range, which impedes them from meeting criteria for depression according to diagnostic expectations, even if their level of impairment is similar to that of other youth (Hwang, Myers, Abe-Kim, & Ting, 2008). Further studies are needed in this area to determine the degree to which symptoms are expressed and whether it may be necessary to modify diagnostic criteria for Asian youth.

Research on suicidality trends among Asian youth has revealed some cultural manifestations in how they may develop and exhibit symptoms. As described by Chu and colleagues (2010), interpersonal difficulties, family shame or negative events, discrimination, and low SES may be predictive of suicidal ideation among Asian youth. Mixed results have been found with regard to acculturation level. Cheng et al. (2010) found that familial conflict and community belonging or support may be particularly predictive of suicidality in this population. Furthermore, when symptoms are exhibited, they are often less likely to be expressed in Asian youth because of a desire to avoid shame, and thus may be manifested as somatic symptoms rather than classic expressions of depression. It has been suggested that when evaluating Asian youth for suicidal thoughts, they are more likely to be revealed in an individual interview than in traditional questionnaires (Chu et al., 2010). Given the association between suicidality and depression, practitioners may wish to consider these risk factors and cultural differences when evaluating symptoms among Asian youth.

Anxiety

Although symptoms of anxiety are not delineated as a condition for ED placement, the criteria asserting that students with ED can display a tendency to develop physical symptoms or fears associated with personal or school problems align with anxiety-related symptomatology.

Black Youth

Although the literature on anxiety in Black youth is relatively limited, extant studies of adults and children suggest that it is common among this population (Barbarin & Soler, 1993; Kingery, Ginsburg, & Alfano, 2007). However, studies have found that it may be more frequently manifested through somatic symptoms than classic cognitive or behavioral signs. Given the tendency of Black adults to seek help for psychological difficulties from medical practitioners rather than mental health professionals (Snowden & Pingitore, 2002), this finding is likely related to cultural stigma associated with mental illness. A key investigation by White and Farrell (2006) examined the prevalence of headaches and abdominal pain among a large sample of Black adolescents and found that 40% reported experiencing headaches and 36% experienced abdominal pain. These symptoms alone were linked to increased anxiety over a period of 6 months. Another study by Kingery and colleagues (2007) examined a larger range of somatic symptoms and found that 83% of Black adolescents reported experiencing at least one somatic symptom in the 2 previous weeks. These rates are similar or higher than those found in studies conducted among other ethnic groups (e.g., Garber, Walker, & Zeman, 1991). Somatic symptoms also significantly predicted anxiety levels at both initial evaluation and at 6-month follow-up. The most common symptoms reported included feeling tense (44%), being restless or on edge (27%), feeling sick to the stomach (26%), experiencing chest pains (20%), and having sweaty or cold hands (19%). Therefore, extant evidence suggests that somatic symptoms may be particularly important indicators of anxiety among Black youth, which has implications for the assessment of anxiety-related disorders.

Latino Youth

A number of studies have indicated the prevalence of anxiety among Latino children and adolescents is higher than that of peers in other ethnic groups (McLaughlin, Hilt, & Nolen-Hoeksema, 2007; Pina & Silverman, 2004). Specifically, Latino youth and their parents have reported a higher level of worry, separation anxiety, and harm avoidance (Ginsburg & Silverman, 1996; McLaughlin et al., 2007; Varela et al., 2004). Researchers have suggested that, similar to Black youth, somatization may be a key element of anxiety manifestation among Latinos. Many existing studies have found that Latino adults endorse a higher level of somatic symptoms than do members of other racial or ethnic groups (Canino, Rubio-Stipec, Canino, & Escobar, 1992), and Latino youth also appear to report an increased level of somatization (McLaughlin et al., 2007; Pina & Silverman, 2004). However, others have found fewer somatic symptoms in comparison with symptoms of panic and separation anxiety (Martinez, Polo, & Carter, 2012).

Considering the large within-group differences found among Latino youth, studies have also begun to examine specific variables and patterns associated with internalizing symptoms. Those focusing on immigrant populations have revealed that, in general, this group is at risk of experiencing internalizing symptoms such as social anxiety (Polo & López, 2009). However, fewer symptoms of anxiety have been found among those with longer residency and higher levels of English proficiency (Polo & López, 2009; Potochnick & Perreira, 2010). In addition, the adherence of families to traditional cultural values may be associated with the presence of anxiety. Emphasis on family obligations, close relationships, obedience, and expectations of loyalty, for example, are often an essential part of the socialization process for Latino youth. Some studies have found, however, that children whose values aligned more closely with this socialization orientation, relative to peers of other groups, exhibit higher levels of anxiety symptoms including panic, separation anxiety, and harm avoidance (McLaughlin et al., 2007). Therefore, it is important to consider variables such as length of residency, language status, socialization, and stressful life events, as well as other environmental factors when evaluating anxiety among Latino youth.

Asian Youth

Few studies have examined the prevalence and manifestation of anxiety in Asian youth. In their investigation of various Asian subgroups, Austin and Chorpita (2004) found that Asian youth reported significantly more symptoms of social anxiety, separation anxiety, obsessive–compulsive disorder, and panic disorder than their White counterparts. Specifically, Hawaiian participants reported the highest levels of separation anxiety and Chinese American participants reported more social anxiety than other groups. It has been suggested that the manifestation of social anxiety may be associated with expectations found within Asian families and communities to perform well, in addition to the desire to avoid negative shame-inducing events, such as those related to violating social norms. Similar to findings related to depression in Asian youth, some studies have found that this group is more likely to express symptoms through somatization than by describing feelings that are more commonly associated with anxiety (Hwang et al., 2008).

Schizophrenia

The inclusion of schizophrenia as a criterion for ED placement may be problematic for a number of reasons, particularly in relation to Black youth. First, according to standard diagnostic criteria, age of onset for schizophrenia typically occurs in late adolescence or early adulthood (American Psychiatric Association, 2013). Therefore, prevalence rates of true cases of schizophrenia in school-age children should be limited. Yet, the few studies that have examined schizophrenia in the literature have found that it is most frequently diagnosed among Black participants at a rate that is 2 to 3 times higher than that of other ethnicities (Hwang et al., 2008). Whaley (2001, 2011), suggesting that Black individuals may be misdiagnosed due to culture-specific behaviors that are associated with schizophrenia, mainly paranoia. This assertion is supported by studies that have found clinician biases, in that Black clinicians diagnosing Black patients with schizophrenia were less likely to find symptoms of paranoia than non-Black clinicians (Trierweiler et al., 2006). Whaley (2011) therefore discussed the need for clinicians to differentiate between "functional" or clinical paranoia, which is part of the diagnostic criteria for schizophrenia, and "cultural paranoia," which may be due to a mistrust of clinicians. Clinicians who misinterpret cultural behaviors as psychological symptoms may unknowingly introduce cultural biases into their diagnostic practices. Although recent studies investigating this potential bias have found the promising result that clinicians are able to identify cultural mistrust (Whaley, 2011), this suggests that training in cultural competence related to appropriate identification may also be beneficial for practitioners within the school setting.

BEST PRACTICES IN THE ASSESSMENT OF SOCIAL–EMOTIONAL AND BEHAVIORAL DISORDERS

Efforts to ensure accurate assessment and identification of ethnically diverse students with social–emotional and behavioral concerns must begin as early as the prereferral stage. The decision of whether to refer a student is extremely important, and the costs and benefits of being placed in special education in relation to achievement and educational opportunity have been weighed extensively in the literature (Artiles, Kozleski, Trent, Osher, & Ortiz, 2010; Wiley et al., 2013). This determination may be particularly important for students who are evaluated for placement under the category of ED, given the doubly detrimental effect this label may have for ethnic minority students who are already socially marginalized. For many students, social–emotional or behavioral difficulties may not be sufficiently severe as to warrant special education placement, whereas it may represent an opportunity for others to receive needed supports that will enable them to succeed in school.

The Prereferral Team

The prereferral team has an important role in determining the need for a comprehensive special education evaluation. Therefore, members should be selected carefully according to the needs of each school and its population. When working with ethnically diverse youth, special consideration must be taken to ensure that an individual who is knowledgeable about the student culture and culturally responsive practices participates in the team (Moreno & Gaytán, 2013). A primary responsibility of this individual is to help determine whether a referral is reflective of true social, emotional, or behavioral difficulties or is related to cultural issues in the classroom. He or she may also assist with ensuring that information is sought regarding students' strengths, their overall learning and social environment, and whether the academic curriculum is being taught in such a way that it can provide an equal educational opportunity. Finally, when working with culturally diverse youth, the prereferral team must examine the rate of existing disciplinary referrals for each student and carefully consider whether the root of the difficulties is truly related to behavioral issues or other variables, such as a lack of cultural synchrony between teachers/administrators and students, difficulties with the curriculum, or other aspects of instruction (Graves & Howes, 2011). After these considerations have been addressed, the team may recommend a student for prereferral intervention before further evaluation.

Specific Assessment Methods

Once students have been referred for a comprehensive evaluation with the possibility of ED classification, there are several aspects of assessment that deserve particular attention for youth of diverse cultural backgrounds.

Clinical Interview

The clinical interview is a vital part of the evaluation process, particularly for culturally diverse youth, because it enables collection of data in relation to individual and environmental characteristics. Student, parent, and teacher interviews can elicit unique information that is critical to the assessment; for culturally diverse youth it is recommended that interviews be conducted prior to the formulation of a comprehensive battery, when possible. In determining which individuals have to be interviewed and arranging for interviews, practitioners should consider the cultural background of the family and respect racial and ethnic values that dictate communication between home and school. Practitioners may wish to consider the perception of school and mental health services that a family is likely to have, and they should be aware that students' families might express different views on mental illness that must be respected. School personnel must also strive to be aware of environmental stressors affecting the involvement of families in the assessment process and be understanding when difficulties arise (Moreno & Gaytán, 2013). Finally, the cultural background of the interviewer is also important to consider, particularly when a rift is suspected between the interviewer's perspective and the perspective of the student, teacher, or family.

Specific content to be included in the interview process will differ on an individual basis, but some general areas to address are essential when working with culturally diverse students. Across cultural groups, attention should be paid to the sociocultural factors that may influence student behavior, such as linguistic background, the availability of resources, and interpersonal issues (Kea, Campbell-Whatley, & Bratton, 2003). The manner in which such factors interact with instructional techniques may be of great importance in determining the etiology of current difficulties. For example, culturally diverse students may benefit from the use of instructional practices that acknowledge and incorporate the cultural background of students (see Chapter 2, this volume).

Functional Behavioral Assessments

The use of functional behavioral assessments (FBAs) has gained a high level of attention in recent years, due to their ability to provide key information regarding the etiology of behaviors and make appropriate recommendations. FBAs have not been explored to a great extent with culturally diverse youth yet, but a growing number of studies have suggested that they may be useful at both the prereferral and evaluation stages in helping to reduce disproportionality across ethnic groups in special education. This is largely due to the fact that FBAs can help minimize the degree of subjectivity that is typically inherent in the identification of behaviors during the interview process, while taking into account a variety of environmental variables that can inform culturally responsive interventions (Moreno & Gaytán, 2013). Studies investigating the use of FBAs with Latino youth referred for behavioral difficulties, in particular, have found that academic variables are often intertwined with behavioral variables, and addressing academic needs can lead to a significant reduction in problem behaviors (Preciado, Horner, & Baker, 2009). This finding may be due to the fact that struggling students, especially those who are learning English, may exhibit difficulties with sustaining attention, remaining seated, and adhering to other behavioral expectations. Therefore, the use of FBAs during the prereferral and comprehensive evaluation process may aid practitioners in addressing the cultural context of students and reduce the potential for assessment bias.

Selection of Culturally Fair Assessment Instruments

The most basic psychometric requirements for an effective social, emotional, and behavioral measure is that it assesses the construct(s) that is intended to measure; however, several additional factors must be considered when selecting instruments to assess emotional and behavioral concerns in culturally diverse youth. Hwang and colleagues (2008) called for practitioners to recognize the potential for cultural bias in standardized measures, because some studies have found that the assessment tool used had a greater influence on the number of students identified for special education than students' actual behaviors (McKenna, 2013). Research on the use of behavior rating scales in diverse populations is limited, and some studies have discovered differences across ethnic groups in their results, particularly when examining teacher ratings of hyperactivity and impulsivity (Epstein et al., 2005). These findings call into question the cultural sensitivity of certain rating scales, suggesting that further investigation is needed to ensure that measures exhibit similar properties when used with diverse populations. Dowdy, Kamphaus,

Twyford, and Dever (2014) emphasized the fact that if a measure was initially developed in a population different from the one in which it is to be used, the ability of that measure to generalize to the current population must first be verified. To ensure adequate psychometric characteristics of rating scales, practitioners must carefully review the manual of any assessment tool prior to administering the test and verify its appropriateness for the target population. In addition, items should be examined from the perspective of an individual who is knowledgeable about the cultural group being assessed to be sure items do not use terms or ideas that are unfamiliar to members of the group. Finally, it is recommended that the measures selected be interpreted by practitioners who understand the cultural context of the community and are experienced in working with culturally diverse students.

Administration and Interpretation

Prior to beginning the assessment process, it is critical for the practitioner to communicate with key stakeholders, such as parents or guardians and teachers. If necessary, he or she may wish to seek the assistance of an individual who is familiar with the language or community to ensure accurate communication. When an interpreter is needed to complete the assessment process, practitioners should locate one who has been appropriately trained in interpreting practices as well as the ethical principles of psychological assessment, including confidentiality and management of emotional content. Therefore, the use of children as interpreters or cultural brokers should be avoided, particularly given research findings that their involvement in such activities may place them at risk of elevated psychological symptoms (Dowdy et al., 2014).

When interpreting test results, practitioners must first incorporate multiple sources of information to ensure accuracy in reported symptoms. Although the process of ED assessment is perhaps the most highly subjective of all special education eligibility assessments, by examining consistencies across data sources it is possible to obtain a clearer idea of the student's educational experience. Practitioners should also be knowledgeable about trends in psychological symptom manifestation among the student's cultural group and use this information to determine whether those symptoms exhibited by the student are truly indicative of ED. Finally, information obtained during the assessment process must be interpreted in a way that links student needs to appropriate services. Practitioners can be most proficient in this area when they are familiar with culturally responsive interventions that are established by the research literature. Therefore, increasing knowledge of these practices should be a continuous pursuit in order to provide services with the highest likelihood of helping students reach their potential.

REFERENCES

Allen-Meares, P., Colarossi, L., Oyserman, D., & DeRoos, Y. (2003). Assessing depression in childhood and adolescence: A guide for social work practice. *Child & Adolescent Social Work Journal, 20,* 5–20. http://dx.doi.org/10.1023/A:1021411318609

American Psychiatric Association. (2013). *Diagnostic and statistical manual of mental disorders* (5th ed.). Arlington, VA: Author.

Angold, A., Erkanli, A., Farmer, E. M. Z., Fairbank, J. A., Burns, B. J., Keeler, G., & Costello, E. J. (2002). Psychiatric disorder, impairment, and service use in rural African American and white youth. *Archives of General Psychiatry, 59,* 893–901. http://dx.doi.org/10.1001/archpsyc.59.10.893

Artiles, A. J., Kozleski, E. B., Trent, S. C., Osher, D., & Ortiz, A. (2010). Justifying and explaining disproportionality, 1968–2008: A critique of underlying views of culture. *Exceptional Children, 76,* 279–299. http://dx.doi.org/10.1177/001440291007600303

Austin, A. A., & Chorpita, B. F. (2004). Temperament, anxiety, and depression: Comparisons across five ethnic groups of children. *Journal of Clinical Child and Adolescent Psychology, 33,* 216–226. http://dx.doi.org/10.1207/s15374424jccp3302_2

Baker, F. M. (2001). Diagnosing depression in African Americans. *Community Mental Health Journal, 37,* 31–38. http://dx.doi.org/10.1023/A:1026540321366

Barbarin, O. A., & Soler, R. E. (1993). Behavioral, emotional, and academic adjustment in a national probability sample of African American children: Effect of age, gender, and family structure. *Journal of Black Psychology, 19,* 423–446. http://dx.doi.org/10.1177/00957984930194004

Blake, J. J., Nero, C., & Rodriguez, C. (2011). Mental health delivery in urban schools: It takes a village to empower a child. In L. L. Howell, C. W. Lewis, & N. Carter (Eds.), *Yes, we can! Improving urban schools through innovative educational reform* (pp. 53–76). Charlotte, NC: Information Age.

Brown, M. M., & Grumet, J. G. (2009). School-based suicide prevention with African American youth in an urban setting. *Professional Psychology: Research and Practice, 40,* 111–117. http://dx.doi.org/10.1037/a0012866

Campbell, C. D., & Evans-Campbell, T. (2011). Historical trauma and Native American child development and mental health: An overview. In M. C. Sarche, P. Spicer, P. Farrell, & H. E. Fitzgerald (Eds.), *American Indian and Alaskan children and mental health: Development, context, and prevention* (pp. 2–26). Santa Barbara, CA: Praeger.

Canino, I. A., Rubio-Stipec, M., Canino, G., & Escobar, J. I. (1992). Functional somatic symptoms: A cross-ethnic comparison. *American Journal of Orthopsychiatry, 62,* 605–612. http://dx.doi.org/10.1037/h0079376

Cheng, Y., Newman, I. M., Qu, M., Mbulo, L., Chai, Y., Chen, Y., & Shell, D. F. (2010). Being bullied and psychosocial adjustment among middle school students in China. *The Journal of School Health, 80,* 193–199. http://dx.doi.org/10.1111/j.1746-1561.2009.00486.x

Chu, J. P., Goldblum, P., Floyd, R., & Bongar, B. (2010). The cultural theory and model of suicide. *Applied & Preventive Psychology, 14,* 25–40. http://dx.doi.org/10.1016/j.appsy.2011.11.001

Collins, P. H. (2000). *Black feminist thought: Knowledge, consciousness, and the politics of empowerment* (2nd ed.). New York, NY: Routledge.

Coutinho, M. J., Oswald, D. P., Best, A. M., & Forness, S. R. (2002). Gender and sociodemographic factors and the disproportionate identification of culturally and linguistically diverse students with emotional disturbance. *Behavioral Disorders, 27,* 109–125.

Davis, G. Y., & Stevenson, H. C. (2006). Racial socialization experiences and symptoms of depression among Black youth. *Journal of Child and Family Studies, 15,* 293–317. http://dx.doi.org/10.1007/s10826-006-9039-8

Dawson, B. A., & Williams, S. A. (2008). The impact of language status as an acculturative stressor on internalizing and externalizing behaviors among Latino/a children: A longitudinal analysis from school entry through third grade. *Journal of Youth and Adolescence, 37,* 399–411. http://dx.doi.org/10.1007/s10964-007-9233-z

Doerfler, L. A., Felner, R. D., Rowlison, R. T., Raley, P. A., & Evans, E. (1988). Depression in children and adolescents: A comparative analysis of the utility and construct validity of two assessment measures. *Journal of Consulting and Clinical Psychology, 56,* 769–772. http://dx.doi.org/10.1037/0022-006X.56.5.769

Dowdy, E., Kamphaus, R. W., Twyford, J. M., & Dever, B. D. (2014). Culturally competent behavioral and emotional screening. In M. D. Weist, N. Lever, C. Bradshaw, & J. Owens (Eds.), *Handbook of school mental health: Research, training, practice, and policy* (pp. 311–322). New York, NY: Springer. http://dx.doi.org/10.1007/978-1-4614-7624-5_23

Epstein, J. N., Willoughby, M., Valencia, E. Y., Tonev, S. T., Abikoff, H. B., Arnold, L. E., & Hinshaw, S. P. (2005). The role of children's ethnicity in the relationship between teacher ratings of attention-deficit/hyperactivity disorder and observed classroom behavior. *Journal of Consulting and Clinical Psychology, 73,* 424–434. http://dx.doi.org/10.1037/0022-006X.73.3.424

Fitzpatrick, K. M. (1993). Exposure to violence and presence of depression among low-income, African-American youth. *Journal of Consulting and Clinical Psychology, 61,* 528–531. http://dx.doi.org/10.1037/0022-006X.61.3.528

Franko, D. L., Striegel-Moore, R. H., Bean, J., Barton, B. A., Biro, F., Kraemer, H. C., . . . Daniels, S. R. (2005). Self-reported symptoms of depression in late adolescence to early adulthood: A comparison of African-American and Caucasian females. *Journal of Adolescent Health, 37,* 526–529. http://dx.doi.org/10.1016/j.jadohealth.2004.08.028

Garber, J., Walker, L. S., & Zeman, J. (1991). Somatization symptoms in a community sample of children and adolescents: Further validation of the Children's

Somatization Inventory. *Psychological Assessment: Journal of Consulting and Clinical Psychology, 3*, 588–595. http://dx.doi.org/10.1037/1040-3590.3.4.588

Gaylord-Harden, N. K., Elmore, C. A., Campbell, C. L., & Wethington, A. (2011). An examination of the tripartite model of depressive and anxiety symptoms in African American youth: Stressors and coping strategies as common and specific correlates. *Journal of Clinical Child and Adolescent Psychology, 40*, 360–374. http://dx.doi.org/10.1080/15374416.2011.563467

Ginsburg, G. S., & Silverman, W. K. (1996). Phobia and anxiety disorders in Hispanic and Caucasian youth. *Journal of Anxiety Disorders, 10*, 517–528. http://dx.doi.org/10.1016/S0887-6185(96)00027-8

Grant, B. F., Stinson, F. S., Hasin, D. S., Dawson, D. A., Chou, S. P., & Anderson, K. (2004). Immigration and lifetime prevalence of *DSM–IV* psychiatric disorders among Mexican Americans and non-Hispanic whites in the United States: Results from the National Epidemiologic Survey on Alcohol and Related Conditions. *Archives of General Psychiatry, 61*, 1226–1233. http://dx.doi.org/10.1001/archpsyc.61.12.1226

Graves, S., & Howes, C. (2011). Ethnic differences in social–emotional development in preschool: The impact of teacher child relationships and classroom quality. *School Psychology Quarterly, 26*, 202–214. http://dx.doi.org/10.1037/a0024117

Hammack, P. L. (2003). Toward a unified theory of depression among urban African American youth: Integrating socioecologic, cognitive, family stress, and biopsychosocial perspectives. *Journal of Black Psychology, 29*(2), 187–209. http://dx.doi.org/10.1177/0095798403029002004

Hwang, W.-C., Myers, H. F., Abe-Kim, J., & Ting, J. Y. (2008). A conceptual paradigm for understanding culture's impact on mental health: The cultural influences on mental health (CIMH) model. *Clinical Psychology Review, 28*, 211–227. http://dx.doi.org/10.1016/j.cpr.2007.05.001

Individuals With Disabilities Education Improvement Act, P.L. 108-446, 20 U.S.C. § 1400-87 (2004).

Iwata, N., Turner, R. J., & Lloyd, D. A. (2002). Race/ethnicity and depressive symptoms in community-dwelling young adults. A differential item functioning analysis. *Psychiatry Research, 110*, 281–289. http://dx.doi.org/10.1016/S0165-1781(02)00102-6

Kataoka, S. H., Zhang, L., & Wells, K. B. (2002). Unmet need for mental health care among U.S. children: Variation by ethnicity and insurance status. *The American Journal of Psychiatry, 159*, 1548–1555. http://dx.doi.org/10.1176/appi.ajp.159.9.1548

Kea, C. D., Campbell-Whatley, G. D., & Bratton, K. (2003). Culturally responsive assessment for Black students with learning and behavioral challenges. *Assessment for Effective Intervention, 29*, 27–38. http://dx.doi.org/10.1177/073724770302900104

Kingery, J. N., Ginsburg, G. S., & Alfano, C. A. (2007). Somatic symptoms and anxiety among African American adolescents. *Journal of Black Psychology, 33*, 363–378. http://dx.doi.org/10.1177/0095798407307041

Kistner, J. A., David, C. F., & White, B. A. (2003). Ethnic and sex differences in children's depressive symptoms: Mediating effects of perceived and actual competence. *Journal of Clinical Child and Adolescent Psychology, 32*, 341–350. http://dx.doi.org/10.1207/S15374424JCCP3203_03

Kuo, W. H. (1984). Prevalence of depression among Asian-Americans. *Journal of Nervous and Mental Disease, 172*, 449–457. http://dx.doi.org/10.1097/00005053-198408000-00002

Martinez, W., Polo, A. J., & Carter, J. S. (2012). Family orientation, language, and anxiety among low-income Latino youth. *Journal of Anxiety Disorders, 26*, 517–525. http://dx.doi.org/10.1016/j.janxdis.2012.02.005

McKenna, J. (2013). The disproportionate representation of Blacks in programs for students with emotional and behavioral disorders. *Preventing School Failure, 57*, 206–211. http://dx.doi.org/10.1080/1045988X.2012.687792

McLaughlin, K. A., Hilt, L. M., & Nolen-Hoeksema, S. (2007). Racial/ethnic differences in internalizing and externalizing symptoms in adolescents. *Journal of Abnormal Child Psychology, 35*, 801–816. http://dx.doi.org/10.1007/s10802-007-9128-1

Moreno, G., & Gaytán, F. X. (2013). Reducing subjectivity in special education referrals by educators working with Latino students: Using functional behavioral assessment as a pre-referral practice in student support teams. *Emotional & Behavioural Difficulties, 18*, 88–101. http://dx.doi.org/10.1080/13632752.2012.675132

Nichter, M. (2010). Idioms of distress revisited. *Culture, Medicine and Psychiatry, 34*, 401–416. http://dx.doi.org/10.1007/s11013-010-9179-6

Novins, D. K., & Bess, G. (2011). Systems of mental health care for American Indian and Alaskan Native children and adolescents. In M. C. Sarche, P. Spicer, P. Farrell, & H. E. Fitzgerald (Eds.), *American Indian and Alaskan children and mental health: Development, context, and prevention* (pp. 2–26). Santa Barbara, CA: Praeger.

Nyborg, V. M., & Curry, J. F. (2003). The impact of perceived racism: Psychological symptoms among African American boys. *Journal of Clinical Child and Adolescent Psychology, 32*, 258–266. http://dx.doi.org/10.1207/S15374424JCCP3202_11

Ofonedu, M. E., Percy, W. H., Harris-Britt, A., & Belcher, H. M. E. (2013). Depression in inner-city African American youth: A phenomenological study. *Journal of Child and Family Studies, 22*, 96–106. http://dx.doi.org/10.1007/s10826-012-9583-3

Ortega, A. N., Rosenheck, R., Alegría, M., & Desai, R. A. (2000). Acculturation and the lifetime risk of psychiatric and substance use disorders among Hispanics. *Journal of Nervous and Mental Disease, 188*, 728–735. http://dx.doi.org/10.1097/00005053-200011000-00002

Pina, A. A., & Silverman, W. K. (2004). Clinical phenomenology, somatic symptoms, and distress in Hispanic/Latino and European American youths with anxiety disorders. *Journal of Clinical Child and Adolescent Psychology, 33*, 227–236. http://dx.doi.org/10.1207/s15374424jccp3302_3

Polo, A. J., & López, S. R. (2009). Culture, context, and the internalizing distress of Mexican American youth. *Journal of Clinical Child and Adolescent Psychology, 38*, 273–285. http://dx.doi.org/10.1080/15374410802698370

Potochnick, S. R., & Perreira, K. M. (2010). Depression and anxiety among first-generation immigrant Latino youth: Key correlates and implications for future research. *Journal of Nervous and Mental Disease, 198*, 470–477. http://dx.doi.org/10.1097/NMD.0b013e3181e4ce24

Preciado, J. A., Horner, R. H., & Baker, S. K. (2009). Using a function-based approach to decrease problem behaviors and increase academic engagement for Latino English language learners. *The Journal of Special Education, 42*, 227–240. http://dx.doi.org/10.1177/0022466907313350

Ringel, J. S., & Sturm, R. (2001). National estimates of mental health utilization and expenditures for children in 1998. *The Journal of Behavioral Health Services & Research, 28*, 319–333. http://dx.doi.org/10.1007/BF02287247

Roberts, R. E., Roberts, C. R., & Chen, Y. R. (1997). Ethnocultural differences in prevalence of adolescent depression. *American Journal of Community Psychology, 25*, 95–110. http://dx.doi.org/10.1023/A:1024649925737

Smith, C. R., Katsiyannis, A., Losinski, M., & Ryan, J. B. (2015). Eligibility for students with emotional or behavioral disorders: The social maladjustment dilemma continues. *Journal of Disability Policy Studies, 25*, 252–259. http://dx.doi.org/10.1177/1044207313513641

Snowden, L. R., & Pingitore, D. (2002). Frequency and scope of mental health service delivery to African Americans in primary care. *Mental Health Services Research, 4*, 123–130. http://dx.doi.org/10.1023/A:1019709728333

Tarshis, T. P., Jutte, D. P., & Huffman, L. C. (2006). Provider recognition of psychosocial problems in low-income Latino children. *Journal of Health Care for the Poor and Underserved, 17*, 342–357. http://dx.doi.org/10.1353/hpu.2006.0070

Trierweiler, S. J., Neighbors, H. W., Munday, C., Thompson, E. E., Jackson, J. S., & Binion, V. J. (2006). Differences in patterns of symptom attribution in diagnosing schizophrenia between African American and non-African American clinicians. *American Journal of Orthopsychiatry, 76*, 154–160. http://dx.doi.org/10.1037/0002-9432.76.2.154

U.S. Bureau of the Census. (2013). *State characteristics datasets: Annual state resident population estimates for 6 race groups (5 race alone groups and two or more races) by age, sex, and Hispanic origin: April 1, 2010 to July 1, 2012.* Retrieved from http://www.census.gov/popest/data/state/asrh/2012/SC-EST2012-ALLDATA6.html

U.S. Department of Education, Office of Special Education Programs. (2012). *Children with disabilities receiving special education under Part B of the Individuals With Disabilities Education Act, as amended data.* Retrieved from https://inventory.data.gov/dataset/8715a3e8-bf48-4eef-9deb-fd9bb76a196e/resource/a68a23f3-3981-47db-ac75-98a167b65259

Varela, R. E., Vernberg, E. M., Sanchez-Sosa, J. J., Riveros, A., Mitchell, M., & Mashunkashey, J. (2004). Anxiety reporting and culturally associated interpretation biases and cognitive schemas: A comparison of Mexican, Mexican American, and European American families. *Journal of Clinical Child and Adolescent Psychology, 33*, 237–247. http://dx.doi.org/10.1207/s15374424jccp3302_4

Weisz, J. R. (1989). Culture and the development of child psychopathology: Lessons from Thailand. In D. Cicchetti (Ed.), *Rochester symposium on developmental psychopathology: Vol. 1. The emergence of a discipline* (pp. 89–117). Hillsdale, NJ: Erlbaum.

Whaley, A. L. (2001). Cultural mistrust and the clinical diagnosis of paranoid schizophrenia in Black patients. *Journal of Psychopathology and Behavioral Assessment, 23*, 93–100. http://dx.doi.org/10.1023/A:1010911608102

Whaley, A. L. (2011). Clinicians' competence in assessing cultural mistrust among African American psychiatric patients. *Journal of Black Psychology, 37*, 387–406.

White, K. S., & Farrell, A. D. (2006). Anxiety and psychosocial stress as predictors of headache and abdominal pain in urban early adolescents. *Journal of Pediatric Psychology, 31*, 582–596. http://dx.doi.org/10.1093/jpepsy/jsj050

Wiley, A. L., Brigham, F. J., Kauffman, J. M., & Bogan, J. E. (2013). Disproportionate poverty, conservatism, and the disproportionate identification of minority students with emotional and behavioral disorders. *Education & Treatment of Children, 36*(4), 29–50. http://dx.doi.org/10.1353/etc.2013.0033

Zayas, L. H., & Gulbas, L. E. (2012). Are suicide attempts by young Latinas a cultural idiom of distress? *Transcultural Psychiatry, 49*, 718–734. http://dx.doi.org/10.1177/1363461512463262

7

EARLY CHILDHOOD ASSESSMENT FOR DIVERSE LEARNERS

KARA E. McGOEY, ALLISON McCOBIN, AND LINDSEY G. VENESKY

The essential foundation and building blocks for cognitive, language, social, emotional, adaptive, and motor skills occur within the first years of life. By the age of 5 children reach important developmental milestones in each area. When these milestones are not attained, a child may fall behind his or her peers and begin formal schooling with a deficit (Barnett & Yarosz, 2007). As society emphasizes academic achievement, the ability for every child to enter school ready to learn has become a priority. Preschool children with developmental delays are often not ready to learn in the general education curriculum. Federal legislation such as the Education of the Handicapped Act Amendments of 1986 and subsequent reauthorizations mandated that infants, toddlers, and preschool children be identified for a developmental delay and receive services. The law requires states to find, identify, and serve children with disabilities from birth under the category of a student with a developmental delay. Thus, the ability to identify and assess struggling learners from diverse backgrounds at an early age becomes a priority.

http://dx.doi.org/10.1037/14855-008
Psychoeducational Assessment and Intervention for Ethnic Minority Children: Evidence-Based Approaches,
S. L. Graves, Jr., and J. J. Blake (Editors)

This chapter reviews the recommended assessment practices in early childhood and provides specific recommendations for working with diverse families. First, a general discussion of models of assessment in early childhood is presented. Second, general recommendations for the effective assessment of ethnic minority children are summarized before ending the chapter with a detailed discussion of typical assessment methods in early childhood and appropriate accommodations and modifications for each measure.

ASSESSMENT APPROACHES IN EARLY CHILDHOOD

Assessment in early childhood has a very different focus from assessment of school-age children. Both the National Association of School Psychologists (NASP) and the National Association for the Education of Young Children (NAEYC) have presented detailed position statements outlining recommended approaches and techniques for the assessment of young children. "NASP supports comprehensive and authentic early childhood assessment processes and outcomes that are fair and useful to (a) detect the need for intervention, (b) enhance intervention delivery and individual child response to intervention, and (c) enhance program and system effectiveness" (NASP, 2009, p. 1). The NASP position statement emphasizes that assessment should occur in the child's natural environment and take into account important cultural and familial differences that may affect the assessment process.

NAEYC has conceptualized assessment as an ongoing essential component to every early childhood program and recommends regular assessment of children's strengths, progress, and needs (NAEYC and National Association of Early Childhood Specialists in State Departments of Education [NAECS/SDE], 2003). Assessment methods should be

> developmentally appropriate, culturally and linguistically responsive, tied to children's daily activities, supported by professional development, inclusive of families, and connected to specific, beneficial purposes: (1) making sound decisions about teaching and learning, (2) identifying significant concerns that may require focused intervention for individual children, and (3) helping programs improve their educational and developmental interventions. (NAEYC, NAECS/SDE, 2003, p. 1)

Brassard and Boehm (2007, p. 22) presented six fundamental assumptions that guide preschool assessment and incorporate the beliefs of both NASP and NAEYC.

- Assessment is a dynamic and complex process that addresses various purposes. Moreover, it should be ongoing, reevaluating the changing needs of the child at home and school.

- Children develop embedded in a culture (or cultures) consisting of home, school, and community. They, in turn, change their environment by their presence and their behavior. These sociocultural influences must be accounted for in the assessment process, and assessors must be knowledgeable about local community influences. Family functioning should be a central area of concern.
- Whenever possible, assessment should include observation of the young child in a familiar environment and include meaningful structured and unstructured tasks.
- Assessment and intervention planning centered on instruction and/or behavior change should be considered as reciprocal processes in which assessment guides and evaluates the effectiveness of instruction and intervention strategies.
- Assessment is a collaborative process involving multiple individuals—classroom teachers, caregivers, and early childhood specialists (such as school psychologists, speech therapists, special educators, social workers, occupational and physical therapists, and pediatric physicians and nurses). Family members should be involved as full partners throughout assessment and intervention.
- The focus of assessment can be on consultation with the parent and/or teacher, rather than directly with the child.

As can be seen, consensus exists around the important components of preschool assessment. All agree that assessment in early childhood must have a familial and cultural focus and take these factors into account throughout the assessment process. In fact, Brassard and Boehm (2007) created a model for preschool assessment that incorporates these important tenets. The multifactor eco-cultural model of assessment views assessment "as an ongoing problem-solving task with the goals of understanding the child within his or her daily environments and planning appropriate instruction or other forms of intervention" (p. 24). The model espouses an eco-cultural approach as opposed to an ecological approach to place emphasis on the influence of the young child's cultural, ethnic, and linguistic background and his or her importance in the assessment process. The effect a child's environment has on development is directly assessed and accounted for within this model during every assessment.

In sum, best practices in the assessment of young children consider cultural and familial factors and the environment for every child with the fundamental belief that our testing expectations may not be consistent with the child's past experiences with the world and that these experiences may influence child development and ultimately assessment outcomes.

CONSIDERATIONS WHEN ASSESSING
ETHNICALLY DIVERSE PRESCHOOLERS

Building from the fundamental approach to early childhood assessment, conducting assessment with ethnically diverse children further emphasizes the influence of culture and family on the child's development. Due to the young age of preschoolers, socialization beyond the family and cultural experience may be minimal. As a result, preschoolers from diverse cultures may have little in common with mainstream culture (Santos de Barona & Barona, 2006). Not all children have had early exposure to the same experiences as children in the mainstream culture. Specifically, oral and written linguistic as well as social experiences vary across cultures (e.g., written language and print; familiarity with paper, pencils, and scissors; visits to the library, museums, and schools; Notari-Syverson, Losardo, & Lim, 2003). The variance in experiences then influences a child's ability to understand and perform adequately when assessed using content and materials familiar to the mainstream culture. This leads to an increased risk of school failure for new immigrants, those children from cultures that have oral traditions (e.g., Native Americans and Haitian-Creole), and economically disadvantaged children attending low-quality preschools (Igoa, 1995).

Further, cultures vary in what they consider important for young children to know and develop. Development may vary across cultures according to what is valued as important, which is then fostered in young children, whereas other areas of knowledge and skill may not be addressed (Brassard & Boehm, 2007). For example, the mainstream culture in the United States places an emphasis on individual achievement in specific academic domains, whereas many other cultures (e.g., Latino, Pacific Islander) value the holistic development of the child within the community (Eggers-Pierola, 2002; van Broekhuizen, 2000). Language acquisition can also vary greatly across cultures. Young children acquire their vocabulary from experiencing the world around them; differences in experiences may result in a child from a culturally diverse background being unable to perform at the same level as those children whose experiences are consistent with the mainstream culture from which assessment instruments are derived (Santos de Barona & Barona, 2006). The different experiences inherent across cultures then affect a child's ability to perform on assessment instruments developed with the mainstream culture's frame of reference. Thus, these disparities contribute to the instrument's inability to accurately assess the child's abilities.

Despite the goal of objectivity, assessment practices are closely linked to community values, school practices, and priorities, as well as the attitudes of those administering the instrument (Brassard & Boehm, 2007). The assessment of preschool children is already difficult due to their continually developing verbal ability and lack of behavioral self-regulation that allows them to sit and attend in a testing situation for an extended period of time (McGoey, DuPaul, Haley, & Shelton, 2007; McGoey, Lender, Buono, Blum, Power, & Radcliffe, 2006). In addition, language barriers and differing cultural experiences and expectations for behavior "can generate behaviors that interfere with learning and mimic those generated by disabilities" (Barrera, 1995, p. 54). Therefore, assessment measures may hold limited validity and reliability when assessing young children from a culturally or linguistically diverse background.

When assessing culturally diverse preschoolers, it is important to consider test administration and language (Santos de Barona & Barona, 2006). Both native language and dialect can be relevant to a child's performance. For instance, those children who speak English but who are from other cultures (e.g., Caribbean) use dialects other than standard American English, and there are no assessment tools that use these dialects to make instruments appropriate for those populations (Brassard & Boehm, 2007). These types of linguistic differences affect every aspect of the assessment process and can greatly hinder an instrument's ability to provide an accurate measure of a child's abilities.

In addition to test administration, the interpretation of assessment results can also be influenced by cultural and linguistic diversity. Predictions that can be made from these instruments for children from the mainstream culture may not be applicable to culturally diverse children (Santos de Barona & Barona, 2006). Instruments developed for preschool-age children have lower reliability and validity than others without the added complexity of cultural and linguistic diversity (Santos de Barona & Barona, 2006). These instruments do not take into account cultural influences on content, "contextual influences on the measurement of behavior," or "alternative pathways in development" (Notari-Syverson et al., 2003, p. 40). As a result, the assessment of preschoolers becomes increasingly complex when cultural and linguistic differences are considered. Assessors are encouraged to review the requirements and properties of reliability and validity before administering a test (McGoey, Cowan, Rumrill, & LaVogue, 2010).

Although many assessment instruments may not take into account cultural differences, there are other steps evaluators can take to ensure that the assessment of the child is as accurate as possible. Prior to administering an assessment instrument, an evaluator should consider the influence of the testing environment and may need to adjust the environment so that it is consistent with the child's cultural expectations (e.g., furniture, tools available; Brassard & Boehm, 2007). When assessing young children, context plays a crucial role, which is augmented by the addition of cultural diversity (Notari-Syverson et al., 2003). Because of young children's developing verbal abilities, other information gathered from context can be far more beneficial than any specific response. Further, the evaluator may consider alternative assessment approaches, such as observations of natural activities (Notari-Syverson et al., 2003). As with the case of assessing any preschool-age child, observations of a child from a culturally or linguistically diverse background may provide more accurate information of the child's abilities than assessing the child in a manner that is inconsistent with their current experience.

Overall, the assessment of young children is fraught with difficulty when the child hails from the mainstream culture; this is only made more complex when the child is from an ethnic minority. Assessors must take care to choose appropriate measures and adapt them as necessary. In the remainder of this chapter, we present a sample of screening and assessment measures that are typically used with young children, with discussion of appropriate adaptations embedded in each section.

EARLY CHILDHOOD ASSESSMENT MEASURES

A primary step in the assessment process for young children is the screening of behavior, cognition, social–emotional development, adaptive behavior, and motor abilities. Federal law requires that every state screen young children for developmental delays. Screening can occur with multiple students at a time or on a more individualized level, depending on the need. Screening tools are brief procedures that help evaluate a large number of children to identify students that may be at risk or who are in need of a comprehensive assessment. These tools can take the form of observations, interviews, brief tasks, and/or rating scales. Most scales have both a home and school form that targets specific elements of that setting. Gathering information from multiple settings allows for a comprehensive view of the child and informs the assessor of the child's abilities outside the school setting. There are many different screening tools that can be used to quickly and accurately identify students that may benefit from a more comprehensive evaluation. Some questionnaires and rating scales are multidomain instruments, whereas others simply target one specific domain.

Once young children are identified as exhibiting a developmental delay by reliable and valid screening instruments, a more comprehensive assessment may be warranted. Given the rapid developmental growth during this period, the recommended procedures assess all domains of development, including cognitive, motor, language, adaptive, and social–emotional. Comprehensive assessments may include a measure of intelligence but should always include a full battery to measure all domains. A sample of commonly used comprehensive assessment measures and tests of intelligence are presented next, with particular emphasis on the measures' ability to accurately assess ethnically diverse children.

Observations

Observations are an efficient type of screening method that allows the observer to watch the child's interaction with other family members and peers, as well as evaluate the child's ability level. Unlike rating scales and questionnaires, observations force the observer to objectively identify the child's abilities and behaviors. Observations are often conducted in the child's natural environment, thus meeting the recommended standards for assessing young children.

When screening ethnically diverse young children, observations hold a vital role. Observations can provide information that may not be available during formal assessment due to language and cultural barriers. For example, a young child may not respond to the assessor's command to draw a circle but during observation the child may be seen drawing the sun in a picture. In addition, observations allow the assessor to observe the child in their familial surroundings with attendant cultural norms and expectations. This information can then be used during the interpretation of measures to further explain the child's strengths and weaknesses. After observing a child in the home environment, the assessor may note, for example, that the child is not given the opportunity to independently feed him- or herself because the family relies on older siblings to help the child. Thus, the assessment results should not be interpreted as a child lacking these skills but rather having no opportunity to perform them. Without the important information gathered through observations, a child may be labeled as delayed when in reality she or he has no opportunity or exposure to perform the required mainstream cultural tasks.

Ages and Stages Questionnaire

The Ages and Stages Questionnaire (3rd ed.; ASQ3; Squires & Bricker, 2009) is used to assess developmental delays in children age 4 months to 5½ years. The questionnaire assesses the developmental areas of children's communication, gross motor, fine motor, problem-solving, and personal–social skills. Parental responses to the questionnaire form scores for each of the five domains as well as an ASQ3 total score. In each of the five domains there are six questions regarding the child's mastery of a specific milestone. The statements are answered in a "Yes," "Sometimes," or "Not yet" format. The questionnaire not only identifies areas of concern for a child but also highlights their strengths. There are 19 different age-appropriate forms for parents to complete based on the child's age in months. Each questionnaire contains about 30 items and takes approximately 10 to 15 minutes to complete. At the end of the questionnaire parents are asked whether they have any concerns about their child's development or about the specific skills their child has compared with other children, with a space provided for parents to describe their concern. This feature is important because it allows parents to identify areas that may not have been addressed in the questionnaire. The ASQ3 has a large and diverse national standardization sample of 15,138 children (Squires & Bricker, 2009). The questionnaires are beneficial and efficient in capturing parents' in-depth knowledge of their children.

Hornman, Kerstjens, de Winter, Bos, and Reijneveld (2013) conducted a study to determine the validity and internal consistency of the ASQ3. Their results indicated that the ASQ3 has good internal consistency and construct validity. Results also indicated adequate sensitivity of the questionnaire in identifying children in need of further testing or with developmental delays, with the best sensitivity found using the ASQ3 total score rather than one of the five domains. These results indicate that the ASQ3 is an accurate, valid, and reliable screening tool.

The questionnaire is available in both English and Spanish, allowing Spanish-speaking parents to participate in the screening as well. The reading level of the ASQ3 is reported to be at the fourth- to fifth-grade level, allowing parents with minimal education to complete the form. The ASQ3 may have to be adapted when completed by parents of ethnically diverse children that are not Spanish speaking. Appropriate modifications include reading the items to the parent, asking follow-up questions to ascertain the cultural relevance of items, and observing the child in the home environment to validate items. Tsai, McClelland, Pratt, and Squires (2006) translated the 36-month screener into Chinese, administered it in Taiwan, and found that it accurately captured a child's development in that culture as well. They concluded that the behaviors targeted in the ASQ3 were not dependent on a particular culture and thus could be used throughout multiple cultures. Overall, the ASQ3 allows for flexible parent input on a child's development that may be useful when working with ethnically diverse children.

Battelle Developmental Inventory Screening Test

The Battelle Developmental Inventory Screening Test (BDIST; Newborg, 2005) is an abbreviated version of the Battelle Developmental Inventory–2 (BDI–2; Newborg, 2005). The BDIST is administered to children age 6 months to 8 years. The screening measure was developed by selecting 100 items from the BDI (20 from each domain area) that are the most predictive of performance on the full BDI. The BDIST assesses a child's receptive and expressive language, fine and gross motor skills, personal–social skills, adaptive behavior, and cognitive and academic skills. The screening consists of parent interview, direct assessment, and observation. For each item, a score of two points, one point, or zero points is determined. In addition, for some items, more than one form of measurement can be used to accurately assess the child's abilities in that area. There are basal and ceiling rules for each section, which minimize the number of items the assessor is required to complete. This brief assessment allows for the identification of children at risk or in need of full, comprehensive evaluations (Elbaum, Gattamorta, & Penfield, 2010).

The BDIST was not normed separately from the BDI; rather, the norms and reliability and validity data used for the BDI were also used for the BDIST (Berls & McEwen, 1999). The BDI has strong psychometric properties; the items for the BDIST were selected from items on the BDI, so the psychometric properties established for the BDI were deemed appropriate to use for the BDIST. Elbaum et al. (2010) reviewed the sensitivity and specificity for the BDIST and found high sensitivity, specificity, and classification accuracy. Moreover, examination of the screening tool indicated high item reliability, as well as high domain reliability, which suggests that the items selected from the BDI used in the BDIST are valid and reliable as screening items (Elbaum et al., 2010). Glascoe and Byrne (1993) evaluated 104 children to determine the sensitivity and specificity of the screening tool. Results showed that the BDIST correctly identified 72% of children with disabilities, which indicates adequate sensitivity.

Battelle Developmental Inventory, Second Edition

The Battelle Developmental Inventory, Second Edition (BDI–2; Newborg, 2005), assesses developmental skills of children from birth through 7 years of age. The BDI–2 is individually administered and standardized. The standardization sample includes 2,500 children from birth through 7 years, 11 months, and was matched to percentages of age, sex, geographic region, and socioeconomic levels specified by the 2001 U.S. Census Bureau (Newborg, 2005).

The BDI–2 can be used for a variety of purposes, including the assessment of typically developing children, the assessment and identification of children with a disability or developmental delay, and the planning and implementing of developmental interventions, as well as the evaluations of child-serving programs and services. The administration includes a structured test format that can be completed in 60 to 90 minutes, depending on the age and ability of the child.

The BDI–2 evaluates five developmental domains: adaptive, personal–social, communication, motor, and cognitive. Each domain consists of several subdomains to further highlight specific developmental tasks and skills. Within the Adaptive Domain there are Self-Care and Personal Responsibility subdomains. The Personal–Social Domain includes the Adult Interaction as well as the Self-Concept and Social Role subdomains. The Communication Domain consists of Receptive and Expressive Communication subdomains.

Gross Motor, Fine Motor, and Perceptual Motor combine to form the Motor Domain. Finally, the Cognitive Domain includes Attention and Memory, Reasoning and Academic Skills, and Perception and Concepts subdomains. The five domains are combined to create an overall composite: the BDI–2 Total Score.

Reliability for the BDI–2 was established through internal-consistency, test–retest, and interrater agreement methods. Each method resulted in high reliability for the BDI–2. For instance, internal consistency coefficients for all subdomains ranged from .85 to .95, whereas the domain coefficients ranged from .90 to .96. Test–retest correlations for the subdomains ranged from .77 (Attention and Memory) to .90 (Self-Care), with a median of .80. Domain correlations ranged between .87 and .90. Finally, agreement between scorers ranged from 94% to 99%, indicating a high interrater reliability.

The validity of the BDI–2 has been well established, as indicated by content-related, criterion-related, and construct-related evidence of validity. Content-related evidence was determined through the judgments of researchers and experts in assessment, as well as through empirical item analysis. Criterion-related evidence was established through correlations with a number of other assessments, including the Bayley Scales of Infant Development, Second Edition; Denver Developmental Screening Test–II; and Vineland Social–Emotional Early Childhood Scales. To evaluate the construct-related evidence, age trends were analyzed in addition to the use of intercorrelations and factor analysis among subdomains, domains, and total scores.

The authors of the BDI–2 recognized that administration of this test with English language learners may be difficult, given the reliance on verbal instructions and interview formats. However, the manual does recommend that the examiner make appropriate accommodations as necessary while remembering that the norms are based on the standardized English administration. In addition, the normative information is still valid if the interview items are administered in Spanish, but the items must be presented to the child in English (Newborg, 2005). Williams, Sando, and Soles (2014) conducted a systematic review of the utility of common early childhood cognitive measures for assessment of non–English-speaking children and concluded that the BDI–2 is inadequate for this population. Whenever the BDI–2 is used with ethnically diverse children, the examiner should use observations to validate the standardized assessment results. The allowance of interview and observation to complete the items allows the BDI–2 to be useful with ethnically diverse children.

Brigance Early Childhood Screens III

The Brigance Early Childhood Screens III (Brigance, 2013) are brief assessments used to determine a child's present level of gross-motor skills, fine-motor skills, self-help skills, social–emotional skills, receptive and expressive language, visual and graphomotor skills, articulation and verbal skills, quantitative concepts, personal information, and prereading and reading skills. The Brigance Screens may be useful not only for assessment and identification purposes but also for monitoring progress of skills. There are four different versions of the Brigance Screens: the Infant and Toddler Screen, the Early Preschool Screen, the Preschool Screen, and the Kindergarten and First Grade Screen. Most are administered by the student's teacher or school personnel. The screen requires the child to identify colors, shapes, and objects; draw objects and write; count by rote; identify body parts; follow directions; make visual discriminations; and demonstrate balance and coordination. Item responses from the child receive predetermined point values based on the complexity of the task and the responses by the child. The child's response is scored on a pass–fail rating. The more the child can identify or elaborate on, the more points he or she will receive for that section because each score is multiplied by a specific weight assigned to that section. There are also teacher and parent report forms for the self-help and social–emotional sections of the screens. Responses to the questions on the teacher and parent report forms are reported as "No," "Sometimes," or "Yes." The screening tools are also offered in Spanish, which allows for an accurate measure of abilities for those students with Spanish as a first language (Mantzicopoulos, 1999).

Reliability of the Brigance Early Childhood Screens III was determined by evaluating the test–retest, internal consistency, and interrater reliability. Test–retest reliability was evaluated and scores were considered stable when participants were retested at multiple points in time. Internal consistency was evaluated and determined to be adequate at the item level. Moreover, interrater agreement of observations and ratings of participants was determined to be acceptable. The validity of the Brigance Early Childhood Screens III was established through construct, content, and criterion validity. Content validity was confirmed as adequate through the use of developmental researchers and educators. Construct validity was determined as acceptable for all domains and age levels using differential item analysis. Finally, criterion validity was examined through the comparison of the Brigance Early Childhood Screens III and other tests (Brigance, 2013).

The Brigance Screens III was standardized on a large, nationally representative sample; however, not many accommodations are provided for ethnically diverse families beyond the Spanish translation. In these cases, assessors may have to rely on observations of the child's skills in the classroom or home environment to score the skill, as opposed to asking the child to perform the task. In addition, parents may need assistance in reading the questionnaires and/or understanding the nuances of the questions being asked.

Developmental Profile 3

The Developmental Profile 3 (DP-3; Alpern, 2007) is standardized measure of development for children from birth through 12 years of age, specifically assessing their physical, adaptive, behavior, social–emotional, cognitive, and communication skills. The DP-3 is used to quickly screen children for potential developmental delays. The DP-3 is administered preferably in an interview format, but if this is not possible, it can be administered with the Parent/Caregiver Checklist that the child's primary caregiver completes alone and that is then later scored by the clinician (Alpern, 2007). The screen includes 180 items that each describe a particular skill. However, there are basal and ceiling rules for each developmental domain, so not every item is administered. Responses are based on the parent reports of the child's mastery of the skill and are scored by indicating either yes or no. In addition to scaled scores in each of the five competencies discussed, the child also receives a General Development score. DP-3 responses yield standard scores, percentile ranks, stanines, and age-equivalent scores to aid in interpretation. The DP-3 was normed on 2,216 typically developing children (Alpern, 2007). The distributions of participants' race, ethnicity, geographic location, and socioeconomic status were based on the U.S. population's distribution. The normative sample is considered a valid representation of the population (Alpern, 2007).

The DP-3 places a strong emphasis on the impact of culture on development. One of the purposes of updating the DP-2 was to address cultural changes in society that may have influenced the experience of the child and, therefore, development. The items on the DP-3 attempt to address cultural differences in developmental expectations. The interview format allows parents to elaborate on items and provide a cultural perspective. During development, the standardization sample of the DP-3 included individuals from seven ethnic groups (Asian, Black/African American, Hispanic/Latino, White, Native Hawaiian, Native American, other). Five of the ethnic groups contained a large enough sample to compare the normative data with the full normative data set. Only four of 30 comparisons were clinically significant, thus indicating that the single full normative set is valid for all ethnic groups. Overall, the DP-3 appears to have taken large steps to be culturally sensitive and may be a strong choice for screening ethnically diverse children.

Developmental Assessment of Young Children-2

The Developmental Assessment of Young Children-2 (DAYC-2; Voress & Maddox, 2013) assesses five developmental domains: cognitive, communication, social–emotional, physical, and adaptive. The DAYC-2 is designed for children from birth through 5 years, 11 months. The administration of the DAYC-2 includes a combination of child observation, direct assessment, and parent interview across the five domains. The DAYC-2 was normed on a sample of 1,832 children residing in 20 U.S. states. The percentages of the sample were representative of percentages outlined by the 2010 U.S. Census Bureau (Voress & Maddox, 2013).

Reliability for the DAYC-2 was established using content sampling, test–retest, and interrater reliability methods. The reliability coefficients for the DAYC-2 are high across methods, including a mean of .90 for content sampling, a range of .70 to .91 for test–retest reliability, and .99 for scorer difference reliability. The DAYC-2 has been determined to have content, criterion, and construct validity (Voress & Maddox, 2013).

The DAYC-2 manual presents exact information regarding the inclusion of ethnically and culturally diverse children in the normative sample, allowing the examiner to review this information when working with ethnically diverse children. Because the DAYC-2 allows for observation, interview, and direct assessment, the examiner can make cultural accommodations or rely heavily on observations to score the items.

Differential Ability Scales, Second Edition

The Differential Ability Scales, Second Edition (DAS–II; Elliot, 2007), is an individually administered battery of cognitive subtests for children and adolescents ages 2 years, 6 months, through 17 years, 11 months. The DAS–II includes 20 subtests that are divided into two overlapping batteries, each with its own record form and administration directions. The Early Years battery includes two levels: Lower Level (ages 2 years, 6 months through 3 years, 5 months) and Upper Level (ages 3 years, 6 months, and 6 years, 11 months). The School-Age battery is designed for children ages 7 years through 17 years, 11 months.

The DAS–II subtests include core subtests, which form a composite score of reasoning and conceptual abilities called the General Conceptual Ability, and diagnostic subtests for each battery. Other core composites include Verbal, Nonverbal Reasoning, Spatial, and Special Nonverbal Composites, whereas the diagnostic composites include School Readiness (Early Years battery only), Working Memory, and Processing Speed.

Reliability of the DAS–II was determined by evaluating the internal consistency, test–retest, and interscore agreement. Coefficients across subtests and composites range from .79 to .94 for the Early Years battery and .74 to .96 for the School-Age battery. Test–retest reliability was also found to be adequate, with coefficients ranging across the .70s to the .90s. Further, interscorer agreement was very high, ranging from .98 to .99. The validity of the DAS–II was established by construct and criterion validity. Construct validity was evaluated by using intercorrelations of the subtests and composites, as well as confirmatory factor analysis. The criterion validity was determined by compared the DAS–II with other tests, such as the Wechsler Preschool and Primary Scale of Intelligence; Bayley Scales of Infant and Toddler Development, Third Edition; and Woodcock–Johnson III Tests of Achievement (Elliot, 2007).

During the development of the DAS–II, the authors attempted to reduce bias by establishing an expert review panel to review items, item bias analysis and overrepresentation of African American and Hispanic populations, and an analysis of prediction of achievement for separate subgroups. The analysis showed the DAS–II to be a fair measure of ability for African American and Hispanic children (Marshall, McGoey, & Moschos, 2011). The addition of the DAS–II nonverbal scale allows for flexibility when working with ethnically diverse children or English language learners. In addition, the DAS–II Early Years Spanish Supplement is a Spanish translation of the DAS–II Early Years battery and has been rated as having good utility for administration to Spanish-speaking children (Williams et al., 2014).

Wechsler Preschool and Primary Scale of Intelligence, Fourth Edition

The Wechsler Preschool and Primary Scale of Intelligence, Fourth Edition (WPPSI–IV; Wechsler, 2012), is an individually administered battery of cognitive development for children ages 2 years, 6 months, through 7 years, 7 months. The WPPSI–IV includes 14 subtests that are divided between two separate age bands. The younger age band, which places less of an emphasis on verbal knowledge, includes children ages 2 years, 6 months, through 3 years, 11 months. The older age band includes children ages 4 years, 0 months, through 7 years, 7 months.

The WPPSI–IV subtests include core subtests, which form a Full Scale score comprising the child's crystalized intelligence, conceptual abilities, and reasoning. Additional subtests make up the Primary Index Scale and the Ancillary Index Scale (General Ability Index) scores. Core composites include Verbal Comprehension, Visual Spatial, Working Memory, Fluid Reasoning, and Processing Speed indices, whereas the Ancillary Index Scales include Vocabulary Acquisition, Nonverbal, General Ability, and Cognitive Proficiency composites (Wechsler, 2012).

Reliability of the WPPSI–IV was determined by evaluating the test–retest, internal consistency, and interrater reliability (Syeda & Climie, 2014). Test–retest reliability was determined to be acceptable for both age bands at the subtest level range .75 to .87 and at the composite level range .84 to .89. Coefficients were obtained and found to be adequate at the subtest and composite level, incorporating both age bands, range .75 to ≥ 90. In addition, interrater agreement was exceptional, ranging from .98 to .99. Content validity was determined through comprehensive literature reviews and advisory panel reviews. Criterion validity was examined through comparisons of the WPPSI–IV and other tests, such as the Differential Ability Scale, Second Edition, and Wechsler Intelligence Scale for Children, Fourth Edition (Syeda & Climie, 2014).

The WPPSI–IV manual states that any translation or bilingual administration of the test is a deviation from standardized procedures and is not recommended. The emphasis on verbal directions throughout the test may pose difficulties for ethnically diverse children. In addition, the recommended standard administration procedures may be foreign to some ethnically diverse children not exposed to traditionally schooling. Williams et al. (2014) found the WPPSI–IV to be inadequate for the assessment of non-English speaking children, despite the inclusion of English language learners in the normative sample. Therefore, the WPPSI–IV may not be the first choice test to assess ethnically diverse children and should be interpreted with caution.

CONCLUSION

The field of early childhood education has long held a cultural and familial focus when educating young children, which has extended to assessment practices for young children. However, the published assessment measures available to school psychologists are often limited in their cultural relevance. When working with ethnically diverse children, school psychologists must pay particular attention to the representativeness of the standardization sample, the psychometric properties of a test as they relate to ethnically diverse children, and the ability of a test to allow for accommodations to address cultural and familial differences. Despite progress toward developing screening and assessment instruments that are valid for a more diverse student population, school psychologists and other evaluators maintain the responsibility of using appropriate instruments for the needs of a particular child, including the consideration of any cultural or linguistic differences.

It is recommended that school psychologists take an eco-cultural approach to the assessment of young children and, in particular, of ethnically diverse young children. An eco-cultural model allows an assessment to occur in the child's natural environment and pays particular attention to the child's development within the context of the child's culture and familial expectations. Following this approach, in conjunction with culturally appropriate assessment measures, creates a natural process that is comprehensive and unbiased.

REFERENCES

Alpern, G. D. (2007). *Developmental Profile 3*. Torrance, CA: Western Psychological Services.

Barnett, W. S., & Yarosz, D. J. (2007). Who goes to preschool and why does it matter? *Preschool Policy Matters, 15*. New Brunswick, NJ: NIEER.

Barrera, I. (1995). To refer to not to refer: Untangling the web of diversity "deficit" and disability. *New York State Association for Bilingual Education Journal, 10*, 54–66.

Berls, A. T., & McEwen, I. R. (1999). Battelle Developmental Inventory. *Physical Therapy, 79*, 776–783.

Brassard, M. R., & Boehm, A. E. (2007). *Preschool assessment: Principles and practices*. New York, NY: Guilford Press.

Brigance, A. H. (2013). *Brigance Early Childhood Screens III*. North Billerica, MA: Curriculum Associates.

Education of the Handicapped Act Amendments of 1986. Pub. L. No. 99-457, 20 U.S.C. § 1470 (1986).

Eggers-Pierola, C. (2002). *Connections and commitments: A Latino-based framework for early childhood education*. Newton, MA: Education Development Center. Center for Children and Families.

Elbaum, B., Gattamorta, K. A., & Penfield, R. D. (2010). Evaluation of the Battelle Developmental Inventory, 2nd Edition, Screening Test for use in states' child outcomes measurement systems under the Individuals with Disabilities Education Act. *Journal of Early Intervention, 32*, 255–273. http://dx.doi.org/10.1177/1053815110384723

Elliot, C. D. (2007). *Differential Ability Scales, Second Edition: Introductory and technical handbook*. San Antonio, TX: PsychCorp.

Glascoe, F. P., & Byrne, K. E. (1993). The usefulness of the Battelle Developmental Inventory Screening Test. *Clinical Pediatrics, 32*, 273–280. http://dx.doi.org/10.1177/000992289303200504

Hornman, J., Kerstjens, J. M., de Winter, A. F., Bos, A. F., & Reijneveld, S. A. (2013). Validity and internal consistency of the Ages and Stages Questionnaire 60-month version and the effect of three scoring methods. *Early Human Development, 89*, 1011–1015. http://dx.doi.org/10.1016/j.earlhumdev.2013.08.016

Igoa, C. (1995). *The inner world of the immigrant child*. Mahwah, NJ: Erlbaum.

Mantzicopoulos, P. (1999). Reliability and validity estimates of the Brigance K & 1 screen based on a sample of disadvantaged preschoolers. *Psychology in the Schools, 36*, 11–19. http://dx.doi.org/10.1002/(SICI)1520-6807(199901)36:1<11::AID-PITS2>3.0.CO;2-R

Marshall, S., McGoey, K. E., & Moschos, S. (2011). Test Review: C. D. Elliott Differential Ability Scales-Second Edition. San Antonio, TX: Harcourt Assessment, 2007. *Journal of Psychoeducational Assessment, 29*, 89–93. http://dx.doi.org/10.1177/0734282910368783

McGoey, K. E., Cowan, R. J., Rumrill, P. P., & LaVogue, C. (2010). Understanding the psychometric properties of reliability and validity in assessment. *Work: Journal of Prevention, Assessment & Rehabilitation, 36*, 105–111.

McGoey, K. E., DuPaul, G. J., Haley, E., & Shelton, T. L. (2007). Parent and teacher ratings of attention-deficit/hyperactivity disorder in preschool: The ADHD Rating Scale. *Journal of Psychopathology and Behavioral Assessment, 29*, 269–276.

McGoey, K. E., Lender, W. L., Buono, J., Blum, N. J., Power, T. J., & Radcliffe, J. R. (2006). A model for assessing preschool children with attention and activity regulation problems. *Journal of Infant and Child Psychology, 2*, 117–138.

National Association of Education of Young Children and the National Association of Early Childhood Specialists in State Departments of Education. (2003). *Early childhood curriculum, assessment, and program evaluation: Building an effective, accountable system in programs for children birth through age 8.* Washington, DC: Author.

National Association of School Psychologists. (2009). *Position statement: Early childhood assessment.* Bethesda, MD: Author.

Newborg, J. (2005). *Battelle Developmental Inventory, Second Edition, Examiner's Manual.* Itasca, IL: Riverside.

Notari-Syverson, A., Losardo, A., & Lim, Y. S. (2003). Assessment of young children from culturally diverse backgrounds: A journey in progress. *Assessment for Effective Intervention, 29*, 39–51. http://dx.doi.org/10.1177/073724770302900105

Santos de Barona, M., & Barona, A. (2006). Assessing multicultural preschool children. In B. Bracken & R. Nagle (Eds.), *The psychoeducational assessment of preschool children* (4th ed., pp. 69–92). Mahwah, NJ: Erlbaum.

Squires, J., & Bricker, D. (2009). *Ages and Stages Questionnaire* (3rd ed.). Baltimore, MD: Brooks.

Syeda, M. M., & Climie, E. A. (2014). Review of Wechsler Preschool and Primary Scale of Intelligence–Fourth Edition. *Journal of Psychoeducational Assessment, 32*, 265–272. http://dx.doi.org/10.1177/0734282913508620

Tsai, H. A., McClelland, M. M., Pratt, C., & Squires, J. (2006). Adaptation of the 36-month Ages and Stages Questionnaire in Taiwan: Results from a preliminary study. *Journal of Early Intervention, 28*, 213–225. http://dx.doi.org/10.1177/105381510602800308

van Broekhuizen, D. (2000). *Literacy in indigenous communities.* Honolulu, HI: Pacific Resources for Education and Learning.

Voress, J. K., & Maddox, T. (2013). *Developmental Assessment of Young Children, Second Edition, Examiner's Manual.* Austin, TX: Pro-Ed.

Wechsler, D. (2012). *Wechsler Preschool and Primary Scale of Intelligence–Fourth Edition, Technical and Interpretive Manual.* San Antonio, TX: Psychological Corporation.

Williams, M. E., Sando, L., & Soles, T. (2014). Cognitive tests in early childhood: Psychometric and cultural considerations. *Journal of Psychoeducational Assessment, 32*, 455–476. http://dx.doi.org/10.1177/0734282913517526

8

NEUROPSYCHOLOGICAL ASSESSMENT OF ETHNIC MINORITY CHILDREN

APRIL D. THAMES, AHOO KARIMIAN, AND ALEXANDER J. STEINER

A major imbalance exists between the growing numbers of ethnic/ racial and linguistic minority children in the United States who need neuro-psychological services and the limited number of neuropsychologists trained to handle the cultural complexities characteristic of this subgroup. Further, the neuropsychologist's "tool kit" is often restricted to instruments that have primarily been standardized on White U.S. and Canadian populations, which poses serious threats to reliability and construct validity when attempting to interpret test performance among ethnic and racial minorities. In this chapter, we highlight key findings across studies from the disciplines of cultural neuro-science and cultural neuropsychology that have largely informed and influenced current clinical practice. Rather than focus on particular ethnic and racial subgroups, we outline considerations critical to assessment that disproportionately affect ethnic and racial groups. Such considerations include economic disadvantage, educational quality, use of ethnic and racial corrected

http://dx.doi.org/10.1037/14855-009
Psychoeducational Assessment and Intervention for Ethnic Minority Children: Evidence-Based Approaches,
S. L. Graves, Jr., and J. J. Blake (Editors)

norms, use of interpreters, culturally familiar test content, bilingualism, stereotype threat, and test-taking anxiety. We conclude with recommendations for assessing ethnic and racial minority children and future directions for this line of work.

NEUROPSYCHOLOGICAL ASSESSMENT OF ETHNIC MINORITY CHILDREN

In a neuropsychological evaluation, interpretations are made about relative cognitive strengths and weaknesses as well as possible brain dysfunction by analyzing patterns of performance across various cognitive domains and determining how the individual performs relative to normative standards. Although this may appear relatively straightforward, the assumption that a direct link exists between the brain and behavior has been scrutinized as overly simplistic, particularly as the field continues to evolve. Child neuropsychology and cultural neuropsychology, two overarching topics of this chapter, are subspecialties that have emerged from clinical neuropsychology and that have grown tremendously over the past decade.

NEURODEVELOPMENT

An understanding of the neurodevelopmental process is critical in conducting a child neuropsychological evaluation. Here, we provide a brief review of the neurodevelopmental process; the reader is cautioned that this is not intended to serve as a comprehensive discussion of neurodevelopment (for a more detailed discussion, see Rakic, Bourgeois, Eckenhoff, Zecevic, & Goldman-Rakic, 1986). Broadly, brain development includes several distinct phases that involve neurogenesis, the migration of neurons to their respective location, the differentiation of neurons, and the pruning back of neural connections and cells.

Cell Proliferation and Migration

During the process of normal cell division and proliferation, there is an abundance of axons, synapses, and dendritic spines that develop simultaneously across a number of cortical areas (Rakic et al., 1986). Through the process of cell migration, nerve cell precursors (*neuroblasts*) and glial cell precursors (*glioblasts*) move from their proliferative zones into their permanent locations, also known as *cellular zones*, that further divide and serve their different functions. Although the time to complete cell migration depends on a number of factors, it is estimated that the process is typically complete by 6 to 9 months gestational age; however, glial cells (i.e., cells that aid in a number of protective and supportive functions) may continue to be produced long afterward.

Segregation (Pruning)

Synaptic pruning is a neurological regulatory process in which weak or unwanted neural connections are discarded in lieu of stronger, more efficient neural connections. Improper synaptic pruning has been linked to the development of neuropsychiatric disorders (Paolicelli et al., 2011). Although it was generally believed that pruning ceases in adolescence (Casey, Jones, & Hare, 2008), more recent investigations have suggested that the pruning process continues until the early 20s. In considering this long phase of developmental reorganization of cortical neuronal circuitry, one can appreciate how cortical development can be disrupted by any number of events from the environment (e.g., exposure to drugs, toxins, and poor nutrition).

ENVIRONMENTAL INFLUENCES IN NEURODEVELOPMENT

Many ethnic and racial minority children face the undue burden of dealing with stressors associated with family poverty and limited access to health care and community resources. Consequently, this places them at increased risk of cognitive and emotional delays due to a higher incidence of factors such as low birth weight, poor nutrition, and exposure to prenatal substances and toxins (Evans & English, 2002). For instance, several studies have found that ethnic minority children who live in poverty are at a disproportionately greater risk of exposure to harmful environmental pollutants (Environmental Protection Agency, 2013). In a study that examined the effects of severe malnutrition among Peruvian children, it was found that severe stunting in the second year of life resulted in scores an average of 10 points lower on an IQ battery (i.e., Wechsler Intelligence Scale for Children–Revised) compared with those without severe stunting (Berkman, Lescano, Gilman, Lopez, & Black, 2002). Therefore, gathering information about a child's socioeconomic, health, and nutritional background during a neuropsychological evaluation is absolutely necessary for proper assessment and treatment planning.

Substance abuse, and relatedly, prenatal substance exposure are also highly prevalent in socially disadvantaged and underserved communities (Minnes, Lang, & Singer, 2011). For example, fetal alcohol syndrome (FAS) is a developmental disorder resulting from prenatal exposure to alcohol that manifests in a spectrum of cognitive, behavioral, and physical abnormalities. FAS rates are exceptionally high among low socioeconomic status (SES) African American and Native American populations (Jones, 2011) and therefore should be considered when evaluating children from these communities for neurodevelopmental disorders. Rates of traumatic brain injury are also generally higher among minority youths and adults (Dellinger & Kresnow, 2010). An increasing challenge for child neuropsychologists is how to adequately incorporate these complex factors as well as natural cultural influences in a traditional neuropsychological assessment.

CULTURAL INFLUENCES ON NEURODEVELOPMENT

Research from cultural neuroscience has demonstrated how cultural experience shapes brain development. Perhaps most relevant to this chapter are findings from studies of language and numerical processing. It is imperative for the neuropsychologist to understand how different linguistic skills are represented in the developing brain and how neurological insults (e.g., epileptic lesions) affect the organization of language at different stages of cognitive development.

Studies on developmental speech perception have demonstrated that infants show developmental growth for native language contrasts (Kuhl et al., 2006). Two studies, one conducted using American English /r/ and /l/ sounds among American and Japanese infants at 7 and 11 months (Kuhl et al., 2006) and one conducted using Mandarin Chinese fricative–affricate sounds among American and Taiwanese infants (Tsao, Liu, & Kuhl, 2006), produced an identical pattern of findings. Specifically, at 7 months, infants listening to native-language sounds (American infants listening to English /r/ and /l/ or Chinese infants listening to Chinese sounds) performed identically to infants for whom the contrast was foreign (Japanese infants on /r-l/ and American infants on the Chinese sounds). At 11 months, a change occurred in the ability to discriminate between native and nonnative language. Specifically, infants listening to their native contrast showed a significant increase in performance, whereas infants listening to a foreign-language contrast demonstrated a decrease in performance. These studies provide evidence for a developmental model of language acquisition in which the ability to discriminate between familiar auditory stimuli (e.g., native language) increases with age, whereas the ability to discriminate unfamiliar stimuli decreases.

Although functional neuroimaging has identified universal activity in regions of the left superior posterior temporal gyrus and left inferior frontal gyrus during language processing (Bolger, Perfetti, & Schneider, 2005), other studies have identified cultural differences in language-specific areas.

For instance, the superior temporal gyrus is activated when native English speakers read English words, whereas Chinese characters activate the dorsal extent of the inferior parietal lobe among native Chinese speakers. These variations in brain activation are thought to reflect a basic difference between nonphonetic and phonetic written languages (Tan, Laird, Li, & Fox, 2005). In a study of English and Italian students, it was shown that, in English readers, reading non-words induced greatest activation (relative to a resting state) in the left posterior inferior temporal region and in the inferior frontal gyrus. By contrast, reading non-words generated greatest activation (relative to the resting state) in the left temporoparietal junction in Italian readers (Paulesu et al., 2000), reflecting fundamental differences between the two languages. Moreover, developmental disorders such as dyslexia are associated with dysfunction of the left temporoparietal cortex and the left inferior frontal gyrus in English monolinguals (Shaywitz et al., 1998), whereas in Chinese monolinguals, the association lies in the dysfunction of the left middle frontal gyrus (Siok, Perfetti, Jin, & Tan, 2004). In addition, relative to healthy controls, English dyslexic children exhibited reduced grey matter volume in the left parietal region (Hoeft et al., 2007), whereas Chinese children with reading problems exhibited reduced grey matter volume in the left middle frontal gyrus (Siok, Niu, Jin, Perfetti, & Tan, 2008).

Though specific learning disorders (e.g., dyslexia) occur across cultures, races, and socioeconomic conditions, they may manifest differently as a function of the orthographic and phonological characteristics of the language system (Goswami et al., 2011). For example, native English speakers demonstrate inaccurate reading and are slow to read single words, whereas in other languages that have more direct mapping between sounds and letters (e.g., Spanish, German) and in nonalphabetic languages (e.g., Chinese, Japanese), reading disorders are characterized by slow but accurate reading (Seymour, Aro, & Erskine, 2003). Thus, abnormalities in both functional and anatomical structures of language processing might be language and/or culturally dependent.

The degree of parental involvement has also been demonstrated to influence the rate of vocabulary development. Furthermore, the amount and quality (e.g., longer sentences) of speech that children are exposed to is linked to the rate of vocabulary acquisition (Hoff, 2003; Pan, Rowe, Singer, & Snow, 2005), with similar findings being documented in China (Zhang & Annul, 2008). Other research has demonstrated that vocabulary grows faster in children exposed to a greater quantity of language regardless of socioeconomic status (SES) (Hart & Risley, 1999). Overall, this research has highlighted the importance of evaluating the quantity and quality of parent–child language interactions, which may be independent of, or only partially influenced by, SES.

In addition to studies of language, functional neuroimaging has also provided evidence for cultural differences in numerical processing. Although native English speakers were found to rely on language processes in the left perisylvian cortices for mental calculation, native Chinese speakers engaged the visuo-premotor association network for mental calculation (Tang et al., 2006). A likely explanation for the activation in the visuo-premotor area in Chinese speakers lies in the fact that Chinese characters possess a nonlinear visual complexity, requiring speakers to learn various strokes and space configurations while also memorizing the right location of a subunit (from left to right and top to down) for each character. Furthermore, research has demonstrated that the neural mechanisms that underlie numerical processing differ between Chinese and English speakers (Han & Northoff, 2008).

NEUROPSYCHOLOGICAL ASSESSMENT OF CHILDREN

A number of social and political forces are likely to have contributed to the need for child neuropsychological assessment. First, the passage of the Education for All Handicapped Children Act of 1975 called national attention to the fact that a significant percentage of children experience learning disabilities and other handicaps with a neurodevelopmental etiology (Hynd, Snow, & Becker, 1986). The second force was the number of children surviving neurological trauma as a result of advances in medical care and neuroimaging.

As neurodevelopment was further studied and understood, it became more apparent that the principles that apply to the study of abnormalities of the adult brain do not directly translate to the child brain. Recognizing that child neuropsychological measures could not represent a "mini-version" of adult instruments, child neuropsychologists were under increasing pressure to demonstrate that their assessment tools and methods were valid and reliable when faced with more complex developmental questions and the task of predicting a child's ability to function in a particular context (e.g., school and home settings). Although the child neuropsychologist is ethically obligated to consider the potential impact of the child's culture at each step of the assessment process (American Psychological Association [APA], 2010), there are currently minimal guidelines on how to manage cultural factors in child assessment (Byrd, Arentoft, Scheiner, Westerveld, & Baron, 2008).

Initially, when a child is referred for a neuropsychological evaluation, the purpose is to understand the child's cognitive strengths and weaknesses so that the best educational and/or rehabilitation planning can take place. Laws such as the Individuals With Disabilities Education Act (2004) have changed the face of assessment needs in public schools over the past decade. In short, this law mandates educational services for children who have sustained traumatic brain injuries (TBI). In concordance with this law, public schools are required to provide services that cater to the educational needs of children who have impaired school functioning as a result of TBI. However, the type of information required to guide instructional programming for these children is more complex than that which is provided in the typical school-based evaluation. As such, children with TBI are often referred to neuropsychologists to evaluate their specific strengths and weaknesses and assist in the development of effective educational and treatment plans.

Other examples of common neuropsychological referrals include instances in which a child fails to acquire academic skills as expected and when the presence of medical risk factors (e.g., seizure disorder, TBI) are suspected to affect learning (Yeates, 2000). The results of the assessment may then be used to design individual treatment programs tailored to the child's specific strengths and weaknesses, to evaluate changing treatment needs, and to monitor treatment effectiveness (Root, D'Amato, & Reynolds, 2005).

Educational assessments and neuropsychological assessments both use similar tests that have been deemed to be psychometrically valid in the scientific community; however, the critical difference between the two pertains to the construct being measured, the purpose of their use, and the implications for diagnosis on the basis of the referral questions and assessment findings. In a psychoeducational assessment, the focus is on test scores and how these scores pertain to learning outcomes and behavior. It is relatively common for Individualized Education Plans to be developed or modified on the basis of the results of these types of evaluations. In contrast, a neuropsychological assessment focuses on the pattern of scores across different tests to define a pattern of strengths and weaknesses. For example, a child may have difficulty following a direction because he or she did not pay attention to the direction, did not understand the direction, or did not remember the direction. Hence, the neuropsychologist's primary role is to determine the point(s) at which the child's ability to follow the direction is compromised. As another example, a low score on a test of memory may be indicative of any number of factors (e.g., poor attention, auditory processing problems).

Recommendations that are provided in a child neuropsychological evaluation are critical to how learning accommodations are applied. Examples of treatment recommendations include accommodations such as allowing a child with processing speed difficulties more time to take a test or changing the format of a written to test to an oral test for a child with severe dyslexia and intact auditory processing. Recommendations such as these can significantly affect the course of the child's academic trajectory and allow access to educational resources that might otherwise have been forfeited because of misdiagnosis or inaccurate inferences of intellectual capacity based solely on academic performance.

CULTURAL NEUROPSYCHOLOGY

Many of the cultural considerations in neuropsychological assessment have been gathered from adult populations, but the emergence of the pediatric subspecialty in clinical neuropsychology has brought attention to and raised serious concerns about the practical limitations of the field. As a result of the work that has emerged from cultural neuropsychology, the importance of considering cultural factors in neurocognitive assessments has become increasingly recognized, particularly given that a variety of important legal, medical, and vocational decisions are often influenced by the results of these types of evaluations. Research in the field of cultural neuropsychology has laid the groundwork for better understanding what types of sociocultural issues to consider when conducting neuropsychological assessment with ethnic and racial minorities. Although the literature pertaining specifically to ethnic and racial minority children is sparse, findings from the adult literature (described later) provide a theoretical foundation on which work in pediatrics can be applied.

ETHNICITY-BASED CORRECTIONS IN NEUROPSYCHOLOGICAL ASSESSMENT

A critical component of neuropsychological test interpretation is the existence of valid normative data. Unfortunately, normative scores are limited in that they are only applicable for the group from which the norms were derived (Pedraza & Mungas, 2008). A major concern is the fact that many of the standardized norms for neuropsychological measures available thus far were primarily developed using White U.S. and Canadian populations. If and when ethnic minorities were included in these standardization samples, their performance data were merged with those of the majority group. Many practitioners have since realized that the application of majority group or mixed norms to ethnic subcultures can introduce systematic bias into the examination process. This concern is supported by a number of studies demonstrating ethnic and racial group differences on neuropsychological testing (Heaton, Taylor, & Manly, 2003; Manly, Schupf, Tang, & Stern, 2005). As such, it has been suggested that measures should be flexible to allow for comparison across groups, with careful consideration in the selection of a specific normative dataset so as to yield better sensitivity and specificity and ultimately lead to diagnostic validity (Pedraza & Mungas, 2008).

On the basis of the work on cultural neuropsychology, more informed neuropsychologists are well aware that ethnic and racial minorities are more likely to be misclassified as cognitively impaired when normative testing procedures are used (Heaton et al., 1995; Heaton, Grant & Matthews, 1991). One solution to this problem is demographic corrections, which provide a method of interpreting raw test data that boost specificity for diagnostic purposes (Heaton et al., 1991). In response, the field has made considerable efforts to develop demographically corrected racial norms for several neuropsychological and IQ tests. In 2004, Robert Heaton and Igor Grant produced a revised version of the 1991 Comprehensive Norms for an expanded Halstead-Reitan Battery that provided ethnicity- and race-corrected norms for African Americans and Hispanics.

These demographically corrected norms were designed to equate scores among racial groups to minimize misclassifying individuals as cognitively impaired. Indeed, Norman, Evans, Miller, and Heaton (2000) found that in the absence of demographically corrected norms on a test of memory (i.e., California Verbal Learning Test [CVLT]), 46% of neurologically intact African Americans were classified as cognitively impaired, whereas with race and ethnicity corrections, only 17.8% of African Americans were impaired. These findings demonstrate that using race-based CVLT norms clearly improved the rates of misdiagnosis. Despite these improvements, however, we still continue to lack appropriate norms for Native American, Middle Eastern, and Asian Pacific Islander groups because a majority of the work on the use of ethnicity and race norms thus far has been conducted on U.S. African American and Hispanic groups.

Although there are clear clinical advantages in using adjusted norms for diagnostic purposes, several limitations inherent in adjusted norms warrant attention (Manly, 2005; Reitan & Wolfson, 2005). Discrepancies in performance scores are not fully accounted for by equating demographic variables such as years of education or SES across groups (Manly, Jacobs, Touradji, Small, & Stern, 2002). Matching groups on such metrics is an oversimplified attempt to control for group differences that neglects important psychosocial aspects. For example, although many studies match for years of education, recent studies have reported that quality of education is a more important influence on IQ test performance (Manly et al., 2002, 2004).

EDUCATIONAL QUALITY

Individuals from minority cultural and linguistic backgrounds demonstrate greater variability in the quality of their educational experiences. The Coleman report (Coleman et al., 1966) was among the first of papers to demonstrate that quality of education can account for differences in out-comes between African Americans and Caucasians, and findings have since been extensively replicated (Manly et al., 2002; Manly, Byrd, Touradji, & Stern, 2004).

Even within the educational system in the United States, those attend-ing schools populated by large numbers of low-income minority children may have distinctly different educational opportunities as a result of the lower per-pupil expenditures that are common in these schools (Darling-Hammond, 2007). This is significant when one considers the finding that education can account for up to 15% of the variance in scores on particu-lar neuropsychological assessments among adults (Dick, Teng, Kempler, Davis, & Taussig, 2002). Furthermore, Manly and colleagues (2002, 2004) conducted a series of investigations that demonstrated that older African Americans performed significantly lower than their White counterparts across measures of memory, word list learning, abstract reasoning, figure memory, fluency, and visuospatial skills, even when controlling for years of education. However, when the analysis adjusted scores based on the Wide Range Achievement Test–Revision 3 (Wilkinson, 1993) reading recog-nition subtest score (a proxy for educational quality), the effect of race overall was reduced and all group differences were found to be nonsignifi-cant (except for performance on a drawing measure and category fluency). Findings from this study indicate that simply using years of education as a covariate may not be an appropriate way of adequately controlling for education among diverse older populations and that reading recognition performance (a proxy of the quality of education received) may increase specificity for neuropsychological measures (Manly et al., 2002). Although these findings were based on a sample of older African Americans, there is reason to believe that these factors apply to ethnic and racial minority children as well.

CULTURALLY FAIR CONTENT

If someone told you that they were going to give you a *lagniappe*, would you be angry or delighted? If you reacted to this question by scratching your head or entering this word into Google's search engine, you are not alone. Most people do not know what *lagniappe* means, because this is an uncommon word used in our society. Nevertheless, if you were tested on your knowledge of words such as *lagniappe* and failed, what does that say about intelligence and/or verbal aptitude? Familiarity with the content of the assessment measures being used can have a significant impact on test performance. Characteristics such as the use of colloquial language, inclusion of geographically relevant information, and even the method of assessing a purported construct are often factors that are taken for granted when assessing individuals from the mainstream culture on which most existing tests are normed.

The idea of "culturally fair" tests has been under scrutiny after observations of ethnic, racial, and cultural differences on tests that were once thought to contain culturally fair content (e.g., Raven's Progressive Matrices). It has become increasingly recognized that cultural familiarity with test content is an important component to maintaining construct validity. For instance, Sternberg et al. (2002) found that among a group of African children who scored highly on a test of knowledge about medicinal herbs—a measure of practical intelligence—many tended to score poorly on tests of academic intelligence, suggesting that practical and academic intelligence can develop independently and that the values of a culture influence the direction in which a child develops. Osuji (1982) compared the performance of Nigerian children with that of Canadian children on construction of geometric patterns and found that both groups demonstrated similar aptitude but that the Nigerian children achieved the construction skills at a slightly younger age. Mulenga, Ahonen, and Aro (2001) compared the performance of Zambian children on the developmental neuropsychological assessment (NEPSY) with the norms available from the United States and found that the Zambian children performed significantly better on visuospatial tasks (design copying) but worse on tasks in the domains of attention, language, and executive function. Notably, the authors reported that although the children were instructed to complete the task as fast as possible, the majority of children worked slowly, suggesting that some cultures may trade accuracy and precision over speed.

Indeed, there is evidence to suggest that even widely used tests such as the Digit Span test are influenced by formal education as well as age and country of origin (Ostrosky-Solís & Lozano, 2006). Subtle nuances in cultural variables, such as the quality of education received and language, potentially contribute to the differences found between the different countries of origin and performance on the Digit Span test. For instance, although some studies have documented a trend for English speakers to outperform Spanish speakers on the Digit Span task, other research has suggested that phonological length (or the number of phonemes per item) accounts for some of these differences (Puente & Ardila, 2000; Wheeler, 2011). In sum, although the field remains hopeful about the continued development of more culturally fair measures, the development process requires a deep familiarity with each culture's values, practices, and language.

USE OF TRANSLATED TESTS AND TRANSLATORS OR INTERPRETERS

Appropriate use of translation practices is critical when assessing ethnic minority children from diverse linguistic backgrounds, and two important issues should be considered in each circumstance. One pertains to the appropriateness of the measures being used such that they are congruent with the child's linguistic and cultural background, whereas the other refers to the neuropsychologist's cultural competency and ability to fluently converse with the child in his or her native language. In the event that neither of these issues can be ideally addressed (i.e., clinician and child are not culturally or linguistically compatible), translation practices may be used. This can be accomplished through the use of translated measures, translators, or interpreters.

Not all translation practices are equally advisable. Ideal translation practices are the ones that adhere to the guidelines provided in the APA's *Ethical Principles of Psychologists and Code of Conduct* (APA, 2010) and *Standards for Educational and Psychological Testing* (American Educational Research Association, APA, & National Council on Measurement in Education, 2014). Translators and interpreters require proper training and should demonstrate linguistic and cultural competency. Translated tests should be administered under the supervision of a panel of linguistically and culturally competent trained professionals, appropriately validated, and properly normed using a sample that is representative of the target group. Using bilingual translators, even when they are properly trained, to translate English text into Spanish is not recommended, because the process of translating a test in such a manner can severely limit the validity and reliability of the assessment being performed. An even less desirable practice, and one that should be avoided whenever possible, is allowing a person known to the child, such as a family member or caregiver, to act as an interpreter (Judd et al., 2009); doing so is likely to interfere with accurate assessment of the child's responses.

The issue of translation practices has increasingly become an area of focus in the assessment literature, particularly with regard to the assessment of Hispanic children. Unfortunately, given the limited number of neuropsychological instruments that have been appropriately translated, normed, and validated for Spanish speakers, less desirable practices are more often used (Artiola I Fortuny et al., 2005; Rivera Mindt, Byrd, Saez, & Manly, 2010). These include using inappropriately adapted or translated tests. As a general rule, it is recommended that any form of adaptation or translation of testing materials be implemented by trained professionals during the test development phase (Artiola I Fortuny et al., 2005).

There are a minimal number of ethnic and racial minority neuro-psychologists in the United States, and the number of bilingual neuro-psychologists is even smaller (Echemendia & Harris, 2004). Although testing clients in their common language is most optimal, there are a number of financial and logistical hardships that may interfere with access to a bilingual neuropsychologist (for more detail, see Casas et al., 2012) and therefore require the use of an interpreter (Judd et al., 2009). However, the use of interpreters has been shown to influence performance outcome. A study by Casas and colleagues (2012) using four common verbal and nonverbal tests from the Wechsler Adult Intelligence Scale–Third Edition revealed that interpreter use adversely affected scores on verbal-mediated neuropsychological tests (i.e., vocabulary and similarities). As such, verbal tests may be more sensitive than nonverbal tests to measurement error associated with interpreter use, perhaps due to the increased verbal exchanges between the interpreter, patient, and examiner, which increases the chances for miscommunication. Although not nearly as widely available and numerous as English language measures, there are a number of empirically validated neuropsychological measures available in languages other than English that can be used in pediatric evaluations (see Table 8.1).

BILINGUAL CONSIDERATIONS

The degree to which language proficiency affects performance on neuro-psychological assessments is a critical area of inquiry. Most neuropsychologists would agree that it is important to account for an individual's language facility in both English and his or her native language; however, debate persists about the most appropriate methods for evaluating language proficiency. Language proficiency should not be assumed on the basis of clients' informal conversational skills or self-report, because this may not reflect their objective performance on verbal-mediated neuropsychological tasks (Acevedo & Loewenstein 2007). To address this issue, objective measurements of language proficiency have been proposed. One such proposed measure includes verbal phonemic/letter fluency (i.e., F-A-S in English and P-M-R in Spanish), because the ability to access words from one's lexicon is a key component of human language processing and production (Artiola I Fortuny, Romo, Heaton, & Pardee, 1999). There is also evidence that semantically driven language tasks (e.g., confrontational naming) may also provide an objective measure of bilingual status (Roberts, Garcia, Desrochers, & Hernandez, 2002). A recent study by Suarez and colleagues (2014) used a language dominance index, a metric that calculates the number of total words produced in English compared with total words produced in English and Spanish, to

TABLE 8.1

Examples of Pediatric Neuropsychology Measures Commonly Used in the United States

Test	Constructs measured	Age range	Normative sample	Available languages
Cognitive batteries (verbal)				
Batería III Woodcock-Muñoz: Pruebas de Habilidades Cognitivas (Muñoz-Sandoval, Woodcock, McGrew, & Mather, 2005)	Cognitive and verbal abilities	2–90+ years	N = 1,413 Native Spanish speakers (30% Mexico, 20% United States, 18% Costa Rica, 11% Panama, 8% Argentina, 7% Columbia, 6% Puerto Rico, <1% Spain)	Spanish
NEPSY–II (Korkman, Kirk, & Kemp, 2007)	Attention and executive functions, language, sensorimotor functions, visuospatial processing, memory and learning, social perception	3–16 years	N = 1,200 Based on the October 2003 U.S. Census data	English, French (Canada), Swedish, German (Austria)
Stanford–Binet Intelligence Scales (SB5), Fifth Edition (Roid, 2003)	Fluid reasoning, knowledge, quantitative reasoning, visual–spatial processing, working memory, nonverbal IQ, verbal IQ, full scale IQ	2–23 years	N = 4,800 (69% White/Anglo American, 12% Black/African American, 12% Hispanic, 4% Asian, 3% Other)	English
Wechsler Adult Intelligence Scales—Fourth Edition (WAIS–IV; Wechsler, 2008)	Processing speed, perceptual reasoning, working memory, verbal abilities	16–89 years	N = 2,200 Proportions of White, African Americans, Hispanics, Asians, and Other on the basis of 2005 U.S. Census data	English, Spanish (Spain). A Spanish-adapted version of the previous WAIS–III (Wechsler, 1997) is considered acceptable for use with U.S. Spanish speakers
Wechsler Abbreviated Scale of Intelligence—Second Edition (WASI–II; Wechsler, 2011)	Global cognitive ability, verbal reasoning, nonverbal reasoning	6–90 years	N = 2,300 Based on 2010 U.S. Census data	English

Test	Domain/abilities	Age	Sample	Language
Wechsler Intelligence Scales for Children—Fourth Edition (WISC–IV; Wechsler, 2003)	Verbal comprehension, perceptual reasoning, working memory, processing speed, general intelligence	6–16 years	N = 2,200 children Ages 6–16 (63.5% Caucasian, 15.5% African American, 15% Hispanic, 4.5% Asian, 1.5% Other) Based on 2000 U.S. Census	English, Spanish, French German, Dutch, Welsh, Japanese, Chinese, etc.
Wechsler Preschool and Primary Scale of Intelligence—Fourth Edition (WPPSI–IV; Wechsler, 2012)	Verbal comprehension, visual spatial abilities	2.6–7.7 years	N = 1,700 Nationally stratified sample based on age, sex/ gender, race/ethnicity, parent education levels, geographic region	English
Woodcock–Johnson III Normative Update: Tests of Cognitive Abilities (WJ III NU; Woodcock, McGrew, Schrank, & Mather, 2001, 2007)	General intellectual ability	2–90+ years	N = 8,782 Ethnically/racially stratified on the basis of 2005 U.S. Census data	English

Cognitive batteries (nonverbal)

Test	Domain/abilities	Age	Sample	Language
Children's Category Test (CCT; Boll, 1993)	Nonverbal learning and memory, concept formation, problem-solving abilities	5–16 years	N = 920 (69.7% White, 14.7% African American, 11.9% Hispanic, 3.7% Other) Stratified on the basis of data from 1988 U.S. Census	English
Leiter International Performance Scale, Third Edition (Leiter-3; Roid & Miller, 2013)	Memory attention, fluid intelligence	3–75+ years	N = 1,600 Representative of general population as of 2006, in terms of ethnicity/ race, gender, age	English
Universal Nonverbal Intelligence Test (UNIT; Bracken & McCallum, 1998)	Nonverbal general intelligence	5–17 years	N = 2,100 Collected across 38 states; stratified on the basis of U.S. Census data	English

(continues)

TABLE 8.1
Examples of Pediatric Neuropsychology Measures Commonly Used in the United States (Continued)

Test	Constructs measured	Age range	Normative sample	Available languages
Wechsler Nonverbal Scale of Ability (WNV; Wechsler & Naglieri, 2006)	Nonverbal abilities	4–21 years	N = 1323 (U.S.) N = 875 (Canada) Both samples match respective populations	English
Learning and memory				
Children's Memory Scale (CMS; Cohen, 1997)	Learning and memory	5–16 years	N = 1,000 (68.4% Caucasian, 16.1% African American, 11.6% Hispanic, 3.9% Other) Based on 1995 U.S. Census data	English
California Verbal Learning Test—Second Edition (CVLT–II; Delis, Kramer, Kaplan, & Ober, 2000)	Verbal learning and memory	16–89 years	N = 920 (69.7% White, 14.7% African American, 11.9% Hispanic, 3.7% Other) Stratified on the basis of 1988 U.S. Census data.	English
California Verbal Learning Test—Children's Version (CVLT–C; Delis, Kramer, Kaplan, & Ober, 1994)	Verbal learning and memory	5–16 years	N = 678 (46% Caucasian, 30% Hispanic American, 2% African American, 15% Other) Data collected from healthy children from the Downey Unified School District in Los Angeles, CA	English
Attention/executive function				
Children's Color Trails Test (CCTT; Llorente, Williams, Satz, & D'Elia, 2003)	Attention, executive functioning	8–16 years	N = 1,000 (68.4% Caucasian, 16.1% African American, 11.6% Hispanic, 3.9% Other) Stratified on the basis of 1995 U.S. Census data	English

Test	Domain	Age range	Normative data	Language
Conners' Continuous Performance Test II (CPT–II; Conners, 1992)	Attention	6–70 years	$N = 1{,}920$ (47% White, 27% Black, 21.4% Other,[a] 4.6% Asian)	English
Delis-Kaplan Executive Function System (D-KEFS; Delis, Kaplan, & Kramer, 2001)	Executive functioning	8–89 years	$N = 1{,}750$ Stratified on the basis of 2000 U.S. Census data	English
Stroop Color and Word Test (Golden, 1978)	Executive functioning	5–14 (children's version) 15+ years (adult)	Due to variability in administration, multiple normative data exist (see Homack & Riccio, 2004)	English, Spanish, Chinese, Czechoslovakian, German, Hebrew, Swedish, Japanese
Wisconsin Card Sorting Test (WCST; Grant & Berg, 1981)	Executive functioning	6 years, 6 months–89 years	$N = 899$ Stratified on the basis of 2010 U.S. Census data	English, Spanish (United States, Spain)

Language (Spanish & bilingual)

Test	Domain	Age range	Normative data	Language
Clinical Evaluation of Language Fundamentals—Fifth Edition (CELF–5; Wiig, Semel, & Secord, 2013)	Language comprehension	5–21 years	Based on 2010 U.S. Census data	English, Spanish
Expressive One-Word Picture Vocabulary Test—Spanish-Bilingual Edition (EOWPVT–SBE; Brownell, 2001a)	Expressive language	2–18 years	$N = 1{,}050$ (84.5% Mexican, 5% Puerto Rican, 6.6% Central/South American, 3% Cuban, 0.9% Other Hispanic)	English, Spanish bilingual

(continues)

TABLE 8.1
Examples of Pediatric Neuropsychology Measures Commonly Used in the United States *(Continued)*

Test	Constructs measured	Age range	Normative sample	Available languages
Preschool Language Scales, Fifth Edition (PLS–5; Zimmerman, Steiner, & Pond, 2011)	Receptive language, expressive language	0–7 years	Based on 2008 U.S. Census data	English, Spanish
Receptive One-Word Picture Vocabulary Test–Spanish-Bilingual Edition (ROWPVT–SBE; Brownell, 2001b)	Receptive language	4–12 years	$N = 1,050$ (84.5% Mexican, 5% Puerto Rican, 6.6% Central/South American, 3% Cuban, 0.9% Other Hispanic)	English, Spanish
Spanish Language Assessment Procedures–SLAP (3rd ed.; Mattes, 1995)	Receptive language, expressive language, verbal reasoning	3–8 years	Norms for Spanish speaking and English–Spanish bilingual students	English, Spanish
Spanish Test for Assessing Morphologic Production (STAMP; Nugent, Shipley, & Provencio, 1991)	Spanish language proficiency	5–11 years	Norms for Spanish-speaking students	Spanish
Woodcock-Muñoz Language Survey–Revised (Alvarado, Ruef, & Schrank, 2005)	Reading, writing, language comprehension	2–90 years	$N = 8,800$ (77.8% White, 16.2% Black, 4.7% Asian/Pacific Islander, 1.0% American Indian, 16.4% Hispanic heritage)	English, Spanish

Visuospatial functioning				
Beery-Buktenica Developmental Test of Visual Motor Integration, Sixth Edition (Beery VMI; Beery, Buktenica, & Beery, 2010)	Visuospatial ability, motor coordination, visual perception	2–18 years	$N = 1,737$ Ages 1–18 (59% White, 18% Hispanic, 16% Black, 4% Asian, 3% Other) Stratified according to projected 2010 U.S. Census	English
Rey Complex Figure Test (RCFT; Meyers & Meyers, 1995)	Visuospatial ability	6–93 years	Due to variability in administration, multiple normative data exist. See Demsky, Carone, & Burns (2000) for child normative data or Palomo et al. (2013) for normative data for young adult Spanish speakers.	Nonverbal measure; test instructions can be administered in multiple languages

Note. This list is not meant to be exhaustive, but rather it is meant to provide some common assessment options for those interested in assessment of ethnic minority children. For those specifically interested in assessment with Latino/a Spanish-speaking children, a more comprehensive list of appropriate tests and measures can be found through the Hispanic Neuropsychological Society website.
[a]The epidemiological sample classified individuals as "African American" or "Other," producing a large percentage of "Other" classifications.

assess language proficiency. In this study, it was found that participants with greater relative second-language ability were better at suppressing the automatic reading response (as measured by the Stroop test) in their native language, providing support for the notion that second language fluency confers a true advantage in the ability to suppress the unwanted prepotent response in the native language.

The question of whether bilingualism confers an overall advantage or disadvantage to cognitive performance has mixed answers. Significant differences in performance have been reported to be absent in some studies but present in others, which may be due to methodological confounds (e.g., small sample sizes, failure to account for educational and acculturative differences). Some have found that performance differences between bilingual and monolingual children on tests of vocabulary diminish quickly after they enter school (Collier, 1995; Hamayan & Damico, 1991), whereas others have found no change (Bialystok, Craik, & Luk, 2008; Bialystok, Luk, Peets, &Yang, 2010). Bilingual children have been demonstrated to acquire conversational proficiency in the nondominant language similar to that of monolingual children (Kan & Kohnert, 2005; Kohnert, 2010), though it may take longer to acquire higher order language knowledge (e.g., syntax, grammatical structure). Hence, when formally tested in their nondominant language, such as in an educational or neuropsychological evaluation, they may perform worse than native English-speaking monolinguals. This has been demonstrated in a few studies using the NEPSY with children in the United Kingdom and Zambia. In these studies, bilingual children scored significantly lower than monolingual children on the Language domain, which was thought to be a result of the timed nature of the tests (Mulenga, Ahonen, & Aro, 2001). In addition, the number of years that one has been exposed to the nondominant language has been demonstrated to be a critical factor in performance (Portocarrero, Burright, & Donovick, 2007).

Studies across groups of bilingual children from Hispanic/Latino, French, and Italian backgrounds have demonstrated that bilingual children outperform monolingual children on tasks of executive functioning, such as inhibitory control of attention and task switching (Kloo & Perner, 2005; Zelazo et al., 2003). Gasquoine, Croyle, Cavazos-Gonzalez, and Sandoval (2007) found that for *balanced bilinguals* (those who are equally fluent in both languages), language of administration had no significant effect on performance for any of the neuropsychological tests. When allowed to use both languages during testing, bilinguals who were equally fluent in both native language and nonnative language demonstrated optimal performance, though this benefit was restricted to performance on untimed tasks (Gollan, Fennema-Notestine, Montoya, & Jernigan, 2007).

OTHER PSYCHOSOCIAL CONSIDERATIONS AND RECOMMENDATIONS FOR RESEARCH, PRACTICE, AND EDUCATION

Claude Steele and Joshua Aronson were the first to experimentally demonstrate the profound effects of stereotype threat among African American students from Stanford University (Steele & Aronson, 1995). *Stereotype threat* refers to the anxiety that one experiences when belonging to a group for which there is a negative stereotype and which may result in suboptimal performance in the domain to which the stereotype threat pertains. In this classic study, when African Americans were exposed to the threat condition, they underperformed on a verbal aptitude test compared with African Americans who were in the non-threat condition. This study was replicated in the context of neuropsychological assessment, and similar results were found, in that African Americans in the stereotype threat condition performed significantly worse than African Americans in the non-threat condition (Thames et al., 2013).

Test-taking anxiety, which has been demonstrated among ethnic and racial minority schoolchildren, may account for lower neuropsychological performance as well. In a study examining the effects of test-taking anxiety and neuropsychological performance among African American adults, it was found that African Americans compared with White participants reported higher levels of test-taking anxiety because of concerns of negative performance evaluation. Furthermore, anxiety about negative performance evaluation was associated with lower performance on neuropsychological testing (Thames et al., 2014).

In sum, there is a dire need for more research in the neuropsychological assessment of ethnic and racial minority children in order to fully appreciate the complex developmental and psychosocial issues that are characteristic of this population. To advance the field, there must be continued efforts to develop culturally appropriate tests in a manner that reduces bias and increases validity. In addition, we must increase the availability of normative data consisting of ethnically and linguistically heterogeneous subgroups. As the numbers of individuals from ethnic and racial, cultural, and linguistic backgrounds increase, we have a professional and ethical responsibility to adapt and refine our assessment approaches accordingly. This includes, but is not limited to, keeping up with the literature on cultural assessment, developing and implementing guidelines for the education and training in the neuropsychological assessment of ethnic and racial minority children, and critical evaluation of current assessment tools that may or may not measure the intended constructs of interest.

REFERENCES

Acevedo, A., & Loewenstein, D. A. (2007). Performance on the Boston Naming Test in English–Spanish bilingual older adults: Some considerations. *Journal of the International Neuropsychological Society, 13*, 212–214. http://dx.doi.org/10.1017/S1355617707070415

Alvarado, R. Ruef, M. L., & Schrank, F. A. (2005). *Woodcock-Muñoz Language Survey–Revised*. Itasca, IL: Riverside.

American Educational Research Association, American Psychological Association, & National Council on Measurement in Education. (2014). *Standards for educational and psychological testing*. Washington, DC: Author.

American Psychological Association. (2010). *Ethical principles of psychologists and code of conduct (2002, Amended June 1, 2010)*. Retrieved from http://www.apa.org/ethics/code/index.aspx

Artiola I Fortuny, L., Garolera, M., Hermosillo Romo, D., Feldman, E., Fernández Barillas, H., Keefe, R., . . . Verger Maestre, K. (2005). Research with Spanish-speaking populations in the United States: Lost in the translation. A commentary and a plea. *Journal of Clinical and Experimental Neuropsychology, 27*, 555–564. http://dx.doi.org/10.1080/13803390490918282

Artiola I Fortuny, L., Romo, D., Heaton, R., & Pardee, R. (1999). *Manual de normas y procedimientos para la bateria neuropsicologica en espanol* [Manual of norms and procedures for the Spanish neuropsychological battery]. New York, NY: Psychology Press.

Beery, K., Buktenica, N., & Beery, N. (2010). *The Beery-Buktenica Developmental Test of Visual Motor Integration*. (6th ed). Minneapolis, MN: Pearson.

Berkman, D. S., Lescano, A. G., Gilman, R. H., Lopez, S. L., & Black, M. M. (2002, February 16). Effects of stunting, diarrhoeal disease, and parasitic infection during infancy on cognition in late childhood: A follow-up study. *The Lancet, 359*, 564–571. http://dx.doi.org/10.1016/S0140-6736(02)07744-9

Bialystok, E., Craik, F. I. M., & Luk, G. (2008). Cognitive control and lexical access in younger and older bilinguals. *Journal of Experimental Psychology: Learning, Memory, and Cognition, 34*, 859–873. http://dx.doi.org/10.1037/0278-7393.34.4.859

Bialystok, E., Luk, G., Peets, K. F., & Yang, S. (2010). Receptive vocabulary differences in monolingual and bilingual children. *Bilingualism: Language and Cognition, 13*, 525–531. http://dx.doi.org/10.1017/S1366728909990423

Bolger, D. J., Perfetti, C. A., & Schneider, W. (2005). Cross-cultural effect on the brain revisited: Universal structures plus writing system variation. *Human Brain Mapping, 25*, 92–104. http://dx.doi.org/10.1002/hbm.20124

Boll, T. (1993). *Children's Category Test (CCT)*. San Antonio, TX: Pearson.

Bracken, B. A., & McCallum, R. S. (1998). *Universal Nonverbal Intelligence Test (UNIT)*. Lutz, FL: PAR.

Brownell, R. (2001a). *Expressive One-Word Picture Vocabulary Test–Spanish-Bilingual Edition (EOWPVT–SBE)*. Novato, CA: Academic Therapy Publications.

Brownell, R. (2001b). *Receptive One-Word Picture Vocabulary Test–Spanish-Bilingual Edition (ROWPVT–SBE)*. Novato, CA: Academic Therapy Publications.

Byrd, D., Arentoft, A., Scheiner, D., Westerveld, M., & Baron, I. (2008). State of multicultural neuropsychological assessment in children: Current research issues. *Neuropsychology Review, 18*, 214–222. http://dx.doi.org/10.1007/s11065-008-9065-y

Casas, R., Guzmán-Vélez, E., Cardona-Rodriguez, J., Rodriguez, N., Quiñones, G., Izaguirre, B., & Tranel, D. (2012). Interpreter-mediated neuropsychological testing of monolingual Spanish speakers. *The Clinical Neuropsychologist, 26*, 88–101.

Casey, B. J., Jones, R. M., & Hare, T. A. (2008). The adolescent brain. *Annals of the New York Academy of Sciences, 1124*, 111–126. http://dx.doi.org/10.1196/annals.1440.010

Cohen, M. (1997). *Children's Memory Scale (CMS)*. San Antonio, TX: Pearson.

Coleman, J. S., Campbell, E. Q., Hobson, C. J., McPartland, J., Mood, A. M., Weinfeld, F. D., & York, R. (1966). *Equality of educational opportunity*. Washington, DC: U.S. Department of Health, Education & Welfare,

Collier, V. P. (1995). Acquiring a second language for school. *Directions in language and education, 4*, 1–12.

Conners, C. K. (1992). *Conners' Continuous Performance Test Computer Program, Version 2.0*. North Tonawanda, NY: Multi-Health Systems.

Darling-Hammond, L. (2007). Race, inequality and educational accountability: The irony of "No Child Left Behind." *Race, Ethnicity and Education, 10*, 245–260. http://dx.doi.org/10.1080/13613320701503207

Delis, D. C., Kaplan, E., & Kramer, J. H. (2001). *Delis-Kaplan Executive Function System (D-KEFS)*. San Antonio, TX: Pearson.

Delis, D. C., Kramer, J. H., Kaplan, E., & Ober, B. A. (1994). *California Verbal Learning Test–Children's Version (CVLT–C)*. San Antonio, TX: Pearson.

Delis, D. C., Kramer, J. H., Kaplan, E., & Ober, B. A. (2000). *California Verbal Learning Test–Second Edition (CVLT–II)*. San Antonio, TX: Pearson.

Dellinger, A. M., & Kresnow, M.-J. (2010). Bicycle helmet use among children in the United States: The effects of legislation, personal and household factors. *Journal of Safety Research, 41*, 375–380. http://dx.doi.org/10.1016/j.jsr.2010.05.003

Demsky, Y., Carone, D., & Burns, W. J. (2000). Assessment of visual–motor coordination in 6- to 11-year-olds. *Perceptual and Motor Skills, 91*, 311–332.

Dick, M. B., Teng, E. L., Kempler, D., Davis, D. S., & Taussig, I. M. (2002). The cross-cultural neuropsychological test battery (CCNB): Effects of age, education, ethnicity, and cognitive status on performance. In F. R. Ferraro (Ed.), *Minority and cross-cultural aspects of neuropsychological assessment* (pp. 17–41). Lisse, Netherlands: Swets & Zeitlinger.

Echemendia, R. J., & Harris, J. G. (2004). Neuropsychological test use with Hispanic/Latino populations in the United States: Part II of a national survey. *Applied Neuropsychology, 11*, 4–12. http://dx.doi.org/10.1207/s15324826an1101_2

Education for All Handicapped Children Act of 1975, Pub. L. No. 94-142, 89 Stat. 773 (1975).

Environmental Protection Agency. (2013). *America's children and the environment*. Retrieved from http://www2.epa.gov/ace

Evans, G. W., & English, K. (2002). The environment of poverty: Multiple stressor exposure, psychophysiological stress, and socioemotional adjustment. *Child Development, 73*, 1238–1248. http://dx.doi.org/10.1111/1467-8624.00469

Gasquoine, P. G., Croyle, K. L., Cavazos-Gonzalez, C., & Sandoval, O. (2007). Language of administration and neuropsychological test performance in neurologically intact Hispanic American bilingual adults. *Archives of Clinical Neuropsychology, 22*, 991–1001. http://dx.doi.org/10.1016/j.acn.2007.08.003

Golden, C. J. (1978). *Stroop Color and Word Test: A manual for clinical and experimental uses*. Chicago, IL: Stoelting.

Gollan, T. H., Fennema-Notestine, C., Montoya, R. I., & Jernigan, T. L. (2007). The bilingual effect on Boston Naming Test performance. *Journal of the International Neuropsychological Society, 13*, 197–208.

Goswami, U., Wang, H. L. S., Cruz, A., Fosker, T., Mead, N., & Huss, M. (2011). Language-universal sensory deficits in developmental dyslexia: English, Spanish, and Chinese. *Journal of Cognitive Neuroscience, 23*, 325–337. http://dx.doi.org/10.1162/jocn.2010.21453

Grant, D. A., & Berg, E. A. (1981). *Wisconsin Card Sorting Test (WCST)*. Torrance, CA: WPS.

Hamayan, E. V., & Damico, J. S. (1991). *Limiting bias in the assessment of bilingual students*. Austin, TX: Pro Ed.

Han, S., & Northoff, G. (2008). Culture-sensitive neural substrates of human cognition: A transcultural neuroimaging approach. *Nature Reviews Neuroscience, 9*, 646–654. http://dx.doi.org/10.1038/nrn2456

Hart, B., & Risley, T. R. (1999). *The social world of children: Learning to talk*. Baltimore, MD: Paul H. Brookes.

Heaton, R. K., Grant, I., Butters, N., White, D. A., Kirson, D., Atkinson, J. H., . . ., & the HIV Neurobehavioral Research Center. (1995). The HNRC 500—neuropsychology of HIV infection at different disease stages. *Journal of the International Neuropsychological Society, 1*(3), 231–251.

Heaton, R. K., Grant, I., & Matthews, C. G. (1991). *Comprehensive norms for an expanded Halstead-Reitan Battery: Demographic corrections, research findings, and clinical applications*. Odessa, FL: Psychological Assessment Resources.

Heaton, R. K., Taylor, M. J., & Manly, J. J. (2003). Demographic effects and use of demographically corrected norms with the WAIS–III and WMS–III. In D. S. Tulsky, D. H. Saklofske, G. J. Chelune, R. K. Heaton, R. J. Ivnik, R. Bornstein, . . . Ledbetter, M. (Eds.), *Clinical interpretation of the WAIS–III and WMS–III* (pp. 181–210). San Diego, CA: Academic Press. http://dx.doi.org/10.1016/B978-012703570-3/50010-9

Hoeft, F., Meyler, A., Hernandez, A., Juel, C., Taylor-Hill, H., Martindale, J. L., . . . Gabrieli, J. D. (2007). Functional and morphometric brain dissociation between dyslexia and reading ability. *Proceedings of the National Academy of Sciences of the United States of America, 104,* 4234–4239. http://dx.doi.org/10.1073/pnas.0609399104

Hoff, E. (2003). The specificity of environmental influence: Socioeconomic status affects early vocabulary development via maternal speech. *Child Development, 74,* 1368–1378. http://dx.doi.org/10.1111/1467-8624.00612

Homack, S., & Riccio, C. A. (2004). A meta-analysis of the sensitivity and specificity of the Stroop Color and Word Test with children. *Archives of Clinical Neuropsychology, 19,* 725–743. http://dx.doi.org/10.1016/j.acn.2003.09.003

Hynd, G. W., Snow, J., & Becker, M. G. (1986). *Neuropsychological assessment in clinical child psychology* (pp. 35–86). New York, NY: Springer. http://dx.doi.org/10.1007/978-1-4613-9823-3_2

Individuals With Disabilities Education Act, 20 U.S.C. § 1400 (2004).

Jones, K. L. (2011). The effects of alcohol on fetal development. *Birth Defects Research, Part C: Embryo Today, 93,* 3–11.

Judd, T., Capetillo, D., Carrión-Baralt, J., Mármol, L. M., Miguel-Montes, L. S., Navarrete, M. G., . . . the NAN Policy and Planning Committee. (2009). Professional considerations for improving the neuropsychological evaluation of Hispanics: A National Academy of Neuropsychology education paper. *Archives of Clinical Neuropsychology, 24,* 127–135. http://dx.doi.org/10.1093/arclin/acp016

Kan, P. F., & Kohnert, K. (2005). Preschoolers learning Hmong and English: Lexical–semantic skills in L1 and L2. *Journal of Speech, Language, and Hearing Research, 48,* 372–383. http://dx.doi.org/10.1044/1092-4388(2005/026)

Kloo, D., & Perner, J. (2005). Disentangling dimensions in the dimensional change card-sorting task. *Developmental Science, 8,* 44–56. http://dx.doi.org/10.1111/j.1467-7687.2005.00392.x

Kohnert, K. (2010). Bilingual children with primary language impairment: Issues, evidence and implications for clinical actions. *Journal of Communication Disorders, 43,* 456–473. http://dx.doi.org/10.1016/j.jcomdis.2010.02.002

Korkman, M., Kirk, U., & Kemp, S. (2007). *NEPSY–II: A developmental neuropsychological assessment.* San Antonio, TX: The Psychological Corporation.

Kuhl, P. K., Stevens, E., Hayashi, A., Deguchi, T., Kiritani, S., & Iverson, P. (2006). Infants show a facilitation effect for native language phonetic perception between 6 and 12 months. *Developmental Science, 9,* F13–F21. http://dx.doi.org/10.1111/j.1467-7687.2006.00468.x

Llorente, A. M., Williams, J., Satz, P., & D'Elia, L. F. (2003). *Children's Color Trail Test (CCTT).* Odessa, FL: PAR.

Manly, J. J. (2005). Advantages and disadvantages of separate norms for African Americans. *The Clinical Neuropsychologist, 19,* 270–275. http://dx.doi.org/10.1080/13854040590945346

Manly, J. J., Byrd, D. A., Touradji, P., & Stern, Y. (2004). Acculturation, reading level, and neuropsychological test performance among African American elders. *Applied Neuropsychology, 11*, 37–46. http://dx.doi.org/10.1207/s15324826an1101_5

Manly, J. J., Jacobs, D. M., Touradji, P., Small, S. A., & Stern, Y. (2002). Reading level attenuates differences in neuropsychological test performance between African American and White elders. *Journal of the International Neuropsychological Society, 8*, 341–348. http://dx.doi.org/10.1017/S1355617702813157

Manly, J. J., Schupf, N., Tang, M. X., & Stern, Y. (2005). Cognitive decline and literacy among ethnically diverse elders. *Journal of Geriatric Psychiatry and Neurology, 18*, 213–217. http://dx.doi.org/10.1177/0891988705281868

Mattes, L. J. (1995). *Spanish Language Assessment Procedures–SLAP* (3rd ed.). Oceanside, CA: Academic Communication Associates.

Meyers, J. E., & Meyers, K. R. (1995). *Rey Complex Figure Test and the Recognition Trial*. Odessa, FL: Psychological Assessment Resources.

Minnes, S., Lang, A., & Singer, L. (2011). Prenatal tobacco, marijuana, stimulant, and opiate exposure: Outcomes and practice implications. *Addiction science & clinical practice, 6*, 57–70.

Mulenga, K., Ahonen, T., & Aro, M. (2001). Performance of Zambian children on the NEPSY: A pilot study. *Developmental Neuropsychology, 20*, 375–383. http://dx.doi.org/10.1207/S15326942DN2001_4

Muñoz-Sandoval, A. F., Woodcock, R. W., McGrew, K. S., & Mather, N. (2005). *Batería III Woodcock-Muñoz: Pruebas de habilidades cognitivas* [Battery III Woodcock-Muñoz: Test of cognitive abilities]. Itasca, IL: Riverside.

Norman, M. A., Evans, J. D., Miller, W. S., & Heaton, R. K. (2000). Demographically corrected norms for the California Verbal Learning Test. *Journal of Clinical and Experimental Neuropsychology, 22*, 80–94. http://dx.doi.org/10.1076/1380-3395(200002)22:1;1-8;FT080

Nugent T., Shipley K., & Provencio, D. (1991). *Spanish Test for Assessing Morphologic Production (STAMP)*. Oceanside, CA: Academic Communication Associates.

Ostrosky-Solís, F., & Lozano, A. (2006). Digit span: Effect of education and culture. *International Journal of Psychology, 41*, 333–341. http://dx.doi.org/10.1080/00207590500345724

Osuji, O. N. (1982). Constructing complex geometric patterns: A study of age and ability among Igbo children of Eastern Nigeria. *Journal of Cross-Cultural Psychology, 13*, 481–489. http://dx.doi.org/10.1177/0022002182013004007

Palomo, R., Casals-Coli, M., Sanchez-Benavides, G., Quintana, M., Manero, R. M., Rognoni, T., . . . Pena-Casanova, J. (2013). Spanish normative studies in young adults (NEURONORMA young adults project): Norms for Rey-Osterrieth Complex Figure (copy and memory) and Free Cued Selective Reminding Test. *Neurologia, 28*, 226–35. http://dx.doi.org/10.1016/j.nrleng.2012.03.017

Pan, B. A., Rowe, M. L., Singer, J. D., & Snow, C. E. (2005). Maternal correlates of growth in toddler vocabulary production in low-income families. *Child Development, 76,* 763–782.

Paolicelli, R. C., Bolasco, G., Pagani, F., Maggi, L., Scianni, M., Panzanelli, P., . . . Gross, C. T. (2011). Synaptic pruning by microglia is necessary for normal brain development. *Science, 333,* 1456–1458. http://dx.doi.org/10.1126/science. 1202529

Paulesu, E., McCrory, E., Fazio, F., Menoncello, L., Brunswick, N., Cappa, S. F., . . . Frith, U. (2000). A cultural effect on brain function. *Nature Neuroscience, 3,* 91–96. http://dx.doi.org/10.1038/71163

Pedraza, O., & Mungas, D. (2008). Measurement in cross-cultural neuropsychology. *Neuropsychology Review, 18,* 184–193. http://dx.doi.org/10.1007/s11065-008-9067-9

Portocarrero, J. S., Burright, R. G., & Donovick, P. J. (2007). Vocabulary and verbal fluency of bilingual and monolingual college students. *Archives of Clinical Neuropsychology, 22,* 415–422. http://dx.doi.org/10.1016/j.acn.2007.01.015

Puente, A. E., & Ardila, A. (2000). Neuropsychological assessment of Hispanics. In E. Fletcher-Janzen, T. L. Strickland, & C. R. Reynolds (Eds.), *Handbook of cross-cultural neuropsychology* (pp. 87–104). New York, NY: Kluwer Academic/Plenum. http://dx.doi.org/10.1007/978-1-4615-4219-3_7

Rakic, P., Bourgeois, J. P., Eckenhoff, M. F., Zecevic, N., & Goldman-Rakic, P. S. (1986). Concurrent overproduction of synapses in diverse regions of the primate cerebral cortex. *Science, 232,* 232–235. http://dx.doi.org/10.1126/science. 3952506

Reitan, R. M., & Wolfson, D. (2005). The effect of age and education transformations on neuropsychological test scores of persons with diffuse or bilateral brain damage. *Applied Neuropsychology, 12,* 181–189. http://dx.doi.org/10.1207/s15324826an1204_1

Rivera Mindt, M., Byrd, D., Saez, P., & Manly, J. (2010). Increasing culturally competent neuropsychological services for ethnic minority populations: A call to action. *The Clinical Neuropsychologist, 24,* 429–453. http://dx.doi.org/10.1080/13854040903058960

Roberts, P. M., Garcia, L. J., Desrochers, A., & Hernandez, D. (2002). English performance of proficient bilingual adults on the Boston Naming Test. *Aphasiology, 16,* 635–645. http://dx.doi.org/10.1080/02687030244000220

Roid, G. H. (2003). *Stanford-Binet Intelligence Scales (SB5), Fifth Edition.* Itasca, IL: Riverside.

Roid, G. H., & Miller, L. J. (2013). *Leiter International Performance Scale, Third Edition (Leiter-3).* Torrance, CA: WPS.

Root, K. A., D'Amato, R. C., & Reynolds, C. R. (2005). Providing neurodevelopmental, collaborative, consultative, and crisis intervention school neuropsychology services. In R. C. D'Amato, E. Fletcher-Janzen, & C. R. Reynolds (Eds.), *Handbook of school neuropsychology* (pp. 15–40). Hoboken, NJ: Wiley.

Seymour, P. H., Aro, M., & Erskine, J. M. (2003). Foundation literacy acquisition in European orthographies. *British Journal of Psychology, 94*, 143–174. http://dx.doi.org/10.1348/000712603321661859

Shaywitz, S. E., Shaywitz, B. A., Pugh, K. R., Fulbright, R. K., Constable, R. T., Mencl, W. E., . . . Gore, J. C. (1998). Functional disruption in the organization of the brain for reading in dyslexia. *Proceedings of the National Academy of Sciences of the United States of America, 95*, 2636–2641. http://dx.doi.org/10.1073/pnas.95.5.2636

Siok, W. T., Niu, Z., Jin, Z., Perfetti, C. A., & Tan, L. H. (2008). A structural-functional basis for dyslexia in the cortex of Chinese readers. *Proceedings of the National Academy of Sciences of the United States of America, 105*, 5561–5566. http://dx.doi.org/10.1073/pnas.0801750105

Siok, W. T., Perfetti, C. A., Jin, Z., & Tan, L. H. (2004). Biological abnormality of impaired reading is constrained by culture. *Nature, 431*, 71–76. http://dx.doi.org/10.1038/nature02865

Steele, C. M., & Aronson, J. (1995). Stereotype threat and the intellectual test performance of African Americans. *Journal of Personality and Social Psychology, 69*, 797–811. http://dx.doi.org/10.1037/0022-3514.69.5.797

Sternberg, R. J., Grigorenko, E. L., Ngorosho, D., Tantufuye, E., Mbise, A., Nokes, C., . . . Bundy, D. A. (2002). Assessing intellectual potential in rural Tanzanian school children. *Intelligence, 30*, 141–162. http://dx.doi.org/10.1016/S0160-2896(01)00091-5

Suarez, P. A., Gollan, T. H., Heaton, R., Grant, I., & Cherner, M., & the HNRC Group. (2014). Second-language fluency predicts native language Stroop effects: Evidence from Spanish–English bilinguals. *Journal of the International Neuropsychological Society, 20*, 342–348. http://dx.doi.org/10.1017/S1355617714000058

Tan, L. H., Laird, A. R., Li, K., & Fox, P. T. (2005). Neuroanatomical correlates of phonological processing of Chinese characters and alphabetic words: A meta-analysis. *Human Brain Mapping, 25*, 83–91. http://dx.doi.org/10.1002/hbm.20134

Tang, Y., Zhang, W., Chen, K., Feng, S., Ji, Y., Shen, J., . . . Liu, Y. (2006). Arithmetic processing in the brain shaped by cultures. *Proceedings of the National Academy of Sciences of the United States of America, 103*, 10775–10780.

Thames, A. D., Hinkin, C. H., Byrd, D. A., Bilder, R. M., Duff, K. J., Mindt, M. R., . . . Streiff, V. (2013). Effects of stereotype threat, perceived discrimination, and examiner race on neuropsychological performance: Simple as black and white? *Journal of the International Neuropsychological Society, 19*, 583–593. http://dx.doi.org/10.1017/S1355617713000076

Thames, A. D., Panos, S. E., Arentoft, A., Byrd, D. A., Hinkin, C. H., & Arbid, N. (2014). Mild test anxiety influences neurocognitive performance among African Americans and European Americans: Identifying interfering and facilitating sources. *Cultural Diversity and Ethnic Minority Psychology, 21*, 105–113. http://dx.doi.org/10.1037/a0037530

Tsao, F. M., Liu, H. M., & Kuhl, P. K. (2006). Perception of native and non-native affricate-fricative contrasts: Cross-language tests on adults and infants. *The Journal of the Acoustical Society of America, 120,* 2285–2294. http://dx.doi.org/10.1121/1.2338290

Wechsler, D. (1997). *Wechsler Adult Intelligence Scale—Third Edition (WAIS–III).* San Antonio, TX: Pearson.

Wechsler, D. (2003). *Wechsler Intelligence Scale for Children—Fourth Edition (WISC–IV).* San Antonio, TX: Pearson.

Wechsler, D. (2008). *Wechsler Adult Intelligence Scale—Fourth Edition (WAIS–IV).* San Antonio, TX: Pearson.

Wechsler, D. (2011). *Wechsler Abbreviated Scale of Intelligence—Second Edition (WASI–II).* San Antonio, TX: Pearson.

Wechsler, D. (2012). *Wechsler Preschool and Primary Scale of Intelligence—Fourth Edition (WPPSI–IV).* San Antonio, TX: Pearson.

Wechsler, D., & Naglieri, J. A. (2006). *Wechsler Nonverbal Scale of Ability (WNV).* San Antonio, TX: Pearson.

Wheeler, D. K. (2011). *Digit span with a linguistically diverse Latina/Latino population: A cross-language study.* Retrieved from http://search.proquest.com/docview/855633123

Wiig, E. H., Semel, E., & Secord, W. A. (2013). *Clinical Evaluation of Language Fundamentals—5th Edition (CELF–5).* San Antonio, TX: Pearson.

Wilkinson, G. S. (1993). *Wide Range Achievement Test–Revision 3.* Wilmington, DE: Jastak.

Woodcock, R. W., McGrew, K. S., Schrank. F. A., & Mather, N. (2001, 2007). *Woodcock–Johnson III Normative Update.* Rolling Meadows, IL: Riverside.

Yeates, K. O. (2000). Closed-head injury. In K. O. Yeates, M. D. Ris, & H. G. Taylor (Eds.), *Pediatric neuropsychology: Research, theory, and practice* (pp. 92–116). New York, NY: Guilford Press.

Zelazo, P. D., Müller, U., Frye, D., Marcovitch, S., Argitis, G., Boseovski, J., . . . Sutherland, A. (2003). The development of executive function in early childhood. *Monographs of the Society for Research in Child Development, 68,* vii–137. http://dx.doi.org/10.1111/j.0037-976X.2003.00269.x

Zhang, L. J., & Annul, S. (2008). The role of vocabulary in reading comprehension: The case of secondary school students learning English in Singapore. *RELC Journal: A Journal of Language Teaching and Research, 39,* 51–76.

Zimmerman, I. L., Steiner, V. G., & Pond, R. V. (2011). *Preschool Language Scales, Fifth Edition (PLS–5).* San Antonio, TX: Pearson.

III

PROMISING PRACTICES IN INTERVENTION FOR ETHNIC MINORITY STUDENTS

9

ASSESSMENT-BASED INTERVENTION FRAMEWORKS: AN EXAMPLE OF A TIER 1 READING INTERVENTION IN AN URBAN SCHOOL

MATTHEW K. BURNS, SANDRA M. PULLES, LORI HELMAN, AND JENNIFER McCOMAS

An alarming number of students in urban settings cannot read proficiently, and 83% of African American fourth graders in this country cannot read at grade level (Children's Defense Fund, 2014), which is particularly a concern for urban schools, given that they tend to serve populations that are mostly ethnically diverse and economically disadvantaged (National Center for Educational Statistics, 2011). There are many potential reasons for the low reading scores of students attending an urban school, including institutional bias and stereotypic impressions of minority families (Harry & Klingner, 2014). Moreover, schools in urban intensive (i.e., concentrated in large metropolitan areas) and urban emergent (large population but less than 1 million people) environments often lack resources because the existing infrastructure cannot adequately address the large number of students (Milner, 2012).

Unfortunately, efforts to reverse academic trends for students in urban settings have not been generally successful because they often did not adequately

http://dx.doi.org/10.1037/14855-010
Psychoeducational Assessment and Intervention for Ethnic Minority Children: Evidence-Based Approaches,
S. L. Graves, Jr., and J. J. Blake (Editors)

consider the context in which the education occurs (Tatum & Muhammad, 2012). Multitiered systems of support (MTSS), such as response to intervention and positive behavior interventions and supports, have been advocated as methods to better address the needs of urban schools and the children from minority backgrounds who attend them (Hosp & Madyun, 2007) and have demonstrated some success (Slavin, Lake, Davis, & Madden, 2011). Most readers will be familiar with the three-tiered triangle associated with MTSS, including the entire school (Tier 1), supplemental interventions delivered to small groups (Tier 2), and individualized interventions for students with the most severe needs (Tier 3). Most MTSS implementation efforts and research have focused on small groups (Tier 2) and individual students (Tier 3) rather than the context and system in which students are educated. For example, multiple states have identified a specific problem-solving process that varies across states, but all have discussed identifying and analyzing problems for individual students without an explicit reference to the overall instructional environment (Berkeley, Bender, Gregg Peaster, & Saunders, 2009).

The focus on individual students within many MTSS models is especially problematic for urban schools because it could exacerbate the lack of resources to address the needs of a greater number of students (Milner, 2012). On average, 20% of students in an elementary school require additional support despite research-based curriculum and effective teaching practices (Burns, Appleton, & Stehouwer, 2005), but the standard deviation was quite large and suggested considerable variability across schools. It is reasonable to assume that urban schools may have as much as 50%, 66%, or even 75% of students needing extra support. Thus, if a school had 600 students and 66% were below the seasonal benchmark, school personnel would have to conduct individual problem analysis and problem solving for approximately 400 students. MTSS models rely on approximately 80% of the students demonstrating proficiency because it would be practically difficult or even impossible to deliver interventions to more than 20% to 25% of the student population (Batsche et al., 2005), especially in a school already experiencing staffing challenges.

Efforts to improve achievement in urban schools should consider the context in which the education occurs (Tatum & Muhammad, 2012). It is important to evaluate and remediate core instructional issues as part of the overall plan for implementing small-group and individual reading interventions. There is certainly more to examining the context of an urban education, but core instruction is one aspect on which school personnel could focus to increase the effectiveness of reading interventions. Therefore, the purpose of this chapter is to demonstrate how screening data from the curriculum-based measurement of oral reading fluency (CBM-R) with first-grade students could be used to evaluate student response to the core curriculum and to identify the need for a Tier 1 intervention.

Effective Tier 2 interventions decrease the number of students who need individualized interventions, and effective core instruction (Tier 1) can reduce the number of students who need supplemental support. The first step in delivering interventions is to identify who needs them through *universal screening*, which is defined as using data to identify which students need intervention and determining whether current school practices are meeting students' needs (Kettler, Glover, Albers, & Feeney-Kettler, 2014). Many schools collect screening data at three seasonal benchmarks during the fall, winter, and spring (Ikeda, Neesen, & Witt, 2008) using a 2-week window each time to collect the data with an equal interval (e.g., 16 weeks) between each benchmark assessment (Parisi, Ihlo, & Glover, 2014).

Most elementary schools use CBM-R to screen the reading skills of their students (Nese, Park, Alonzo, & Tindal, 2011). There is considerable research supporting the use of CBM-R as a screening tool; Minneapolis Public Schools were among the first to adopt it (Marston, 2012). Thus, much of the early research on the validity of CBM-R occurred in an urban setting. Research has consistently demonstrated that CBM-R results in reliable data and valid conclusions among African American students (Keller-Margulis, Shapiro, & Hintze, 2008), and English language learners (Baker, Plasencia-Peinado, & Lezcano-Lytle, 1998) and with samples taken from urban schools (Francis et al., 2008).

Screening has long been conceptualized as the first step in identifying whether a problem exists (Marston, Lau, & Muyskens, 2007) and can occur school wide, grade wide, or within an individual classroom (Newell & Kratochwill, 2007). Thus, most schools only use screening data to identify who needs additional support in reading, but this does not fully tap into the potential of the data (Kettler et al., 2014). Screening data for reading can help to differentiate whether students need a Tier 2 intervention that focuses on phonemic awareness, phonics, fluency, or comprehension (Burns, Haegele, & Petersen-Brown, 2014), which suggests how to address student needs in Tier 2. Parisi and colleagues (2014) discussed how screening data can be used to determine whether changes in core instruction are needed at Tier 1, but they only discussed identifying a need and not using the data to determine how to address the need.

VanDerHeyden and colleagues (VanDerHeyden & Burns, 2005; VanDerHeyden, Witt, & Naquin, 2003) provided a potential model for analyzing screening data at Tier 1 by identifying and remediating class-wide problems. A class-wide problem occurs when systems issues are the cause of individual student difficulties (VanDerHeyden et al., 2003) and is often identified by computing a class median for the benchmark data and comparing the median with a standard (VanDerHeyden & Burns, 2010). For example, each student in a third-grade classroom is screened for oral reading fluency by the Aimsweb curriculum-based measurement (CBM; Pearson, 2010) system. Of the 25 students screened in the fall assessment, 17 score below the fall benchmark criterion of 70 words read correctly (WRC) per minute and are identified as needing an intervention. The median for this hypothetical group of students is 61 WRC per minute. Thus, the class median falls below the fall benchmark criterion, suggesting that a class-wide problem exists. It would be more efficient to apply an intervention to the class than it would be to plan and execute Tier 2 interventions for 17 of 25 students. Moreover, previous research has shown that the number of students who need supplemental support can be decreased from as many as 23 of 41 (56%) across two classrooms to 10 (24%; Burns et al., 2015).

CLASS-WIDE READING INTERVENTIONS BASED ON SCREENING DATA

Although quality core reading instruction is critical to success in kindergarten to 12th grade schools and within any MTSS model, many urban schools do not provide effective core instruction because they tend to emphasize vocabulary development at the expense of teaching decoding skills (Ripp, Jean-Pierre, & Fergus, n.d.). Although vocabulary knowledge is essential to reading comprehension, instruction in phonological awareness and decoding, word recognition, and reading fluency, along with explicit instruction in comprehension strategies, are also critical during the early grades in urban schools (Teale, Paciga, & Hoffman, 2007). Thus, class-wide interventions for reading in kindergarten and first and second grades should supplement the code-based aspects of reading and should be implemented before students receive small-group interventions (Tier 2). Peer-Assisted Learning Strategies (PALS; Mathes, Howard, Allen, & Fuchs, 1998) is a reading intervention in which students work as partners to complete a 26-week curriculum that involves practicing letter sounds, segmenting and blending words, reading sight words, and reading a brief story that has key words that the student practiced reading in the previous section.

Research has consistently demonstrated the effectiveness of the PALS model with first-grade students who are at risk of reading failure (Mathes et al., 1998), but it has not examined the effect within an MTSS framework. Burns et al. (2015) found that implementing a class-wide intervention for students in second and third grade increased the reading skills of the participating students but also reduced the percentage of students who needed supplemental support (Tier 2). Similar research has consistently demonstrated the effectiveness of identifying and remediating class-wide problems before beginning

Tier 2 interventions (VanDerHeyden et al., 2003; VanDerHeyden, Witt, & Gilbertson, 2007). Moreover, identifying class-wide problems could help evaluate the instructional environment (Tier 1), which is also the purpose of collecting screening data (Parisi et al., 2014) and is the first step in any assessment intervention model, including MTSS (Burns & Gibbons, 2012). However, most of the previous research was conducted with math rather than reading (VanDerHeyden & Burns, 2005; VanDerHeyden et al., 2003, 2007) or with students in second and third grades (Burns et al., 2015).

SCREENING AND CLASS-WIDE INTERVENTION AT JOHNSON ELEMENTARY SCHOOL

The current research was conducted during the third year of a 3-year partnership (Path to Reading Excellence in School Sites; PRESS) among six urban schools, a research university, a statewide service organization, and a national corporation. The PRESS partnership involved implementation of MTSS, with the goal of having every student on grade level for reading by the end of third grade. The model focused on tiered interventions, universal screening, and monitoring student progress, but also placed emphasis on quality core instruction and embedded professional development.

Participating School

Johnson Elementary is a kindergarten to eighth-grade school that serves 250 students in kindergarten through Grade 5. It is a magnet school for Native American students; at the time of the study 86% of the students were Native American, 5% were Hispanic, 4% were African American, 3% were White, and 2% were listed as other or multiracial. Almost every student (99.4%) who attended Johnson Elementary received a free or reduced-price lunch. The data from the current demonstration were obtained from 34 students from the school's two first-grade classrooms. A total of 40 students attended first grade in the building, but 10 were absent during one or two of the data collection sessions or had moved during the intervention period, leaving a total of 30 students. Johnson Elementary is part of a large urban school district that serves over 35,000 students in 92 schools.

Core literacy instruction was delivered with a balanced literacy approach based on the Fountas and Pinnell (1996) reading program. Instruction occurred for 90 minutes each day and consisted of reader's workshop, writer's workshop, and word study to teach grade-level reading standards, all of which were delivered in daily guided reading groups. The reading instruction in all classrooms was observed multiple times throughout the school year with a

54-item observation protocol to assess the quality of the core instruction. The scale included 28 items that addressed the classroom environment (e.g., accessibility of writing tools and varied reading materials) and 26 items that addressed the instructional practice (e.g., explains the purpose of the lesson, fosters discussion). Each item was rated on a 0–3 scale, with 3 indicating that the item was implemented at an expert level. The mean rating for the classrooms on the final observation, which occurred in May of the school year, was 1.25 for environment items and .73 for instructional practice. Thus, overall, the schools seemed to use some effective instructional practices within the reading curriculum used for core instruction, but the quality of the core instruction was likely somewhat poor.

Universal Screening

Johnson Elementary School screened the reading skills of its students with CBM-R from the Formative Assessment System for Teachers (FAST; Christ, Ardoin, & Eckert, 2011) three times each year. Data for the current demonstration were collected in January. The FAST CBM-R assessment was developed at the University of Minnesota and consisted of having students read grade-level passages for 1 minute and recording the number of WRC (Christ, Ardoin, & Eckert, 2011). Reliability estimates for data from FAST CBM-R are generally above .90, and validity coefficients meet or exceed .70 (see http://www.rti4success.org/formative-assessment-system-teachers-fast-cbmreading-english).

Screening Process

School psychology graduate students working for the PRESS project collected all data. Each data collector was trained in the administration of the project measures for 1 hour and had completed a semester-long course on CBM and general assessment procedures. The assessment administration procedures were evaluated before the graduate students began collecting data. Each graduate student was observed by a literacy coach while conducting an assessment to determine interobserver agreement (IOA). The literacy coach also recorded WRC, and all words that were consistently rated as correct or incorrect across both observers were counted as agreements. Inconsistent ratings were counted as disagreements. The total number of agreements was divided by the total number of words and multiplied by 100 to obtain IOA. All data collectors demonstrated at least 95% IOA before they began collecting data.

Each student was individually assessed with three grade-level probes, and the median WRC and the median errors were recorded. In addition to the number of WRC, accuracy was also computed by dividing the total WRC by the number of WRC plus the number of errors (e.g., 45 WRC and 5 errors is 45/50 = 90%). There is considerable research regarding the importance of students being able to read the words with high accuracy, and 93% to 97% has consistently been demonstrated to be an effective criterion with which to interpret accuracy data (Burns, 2007; Treptow, Burns, & McComas, 2007). Previous research used 93% accuracy as a criterion to determine whether the student was reading slowly and inaccurately and would likely need a reading decoding intervention, or slowly and accurately and would likely require an intervention that focused on reading more fluently (Burns et al., 2014).

Identifying Class-Wide Problems

The first step in determining a class-wide problem is to calculate the class median score on the screening measure for each classroom and to compare that score with the benchmark standard. Class medians are used because small data sets (i.e., less than 30) can be too heavily influenced by outlying data and medians are not as susceptible to outliers. Median classroom scores that fall below the seasonal benchmark criterion suggest that a class-wide problem exists. Readers are referred to VanDerHeyden and Burns (2010) for more information about computing class medians and determining class-wide problems.

The seasonal criterion for the project was developed a priori by using the previous year's data and computing a receiver operating characteristics (ROC) analysis that specified points on the coordinate curve. The criterion selected at fall, winter, and spring was the score at which there was an 80% probability that students who obtained that score or higher would pass the state accountability test in reading. However, most criteria used by schools, such as national norms (e.g., 25th or 40th percentile on norms provided by Aimsweb [Pearson, 2010] or risk categories associated with the Dynamic Indicators of Basic Early Literacy produced by the University of Oregon Center on Teaching and Learning; Good et al., 2012), would be sufficient for identifying class-wide problems.

After the universal screening process was completed, the data were ranked on a spreadsheet with the WRC score listed from lowest to highest (see Tables 9.1 and 9.2). Next, the class-wide median was calculated by identifying the middle score in the class list and was compared with the criterion for the winter benchmark of 35 WRC. The class medians were 23 WRC and 18 WRC, both of which were below the criterion of 35 WRC, suggesting class-wide problems.

Implementing the Class-Wide Intervention

Both classrooms demonstrated a class-wide problem because the medians were below the seasonal benchmark criterion. The next step was to use

TABLE 9.1
Winter Screening and Postintervention Scores for Classroom 1

Student	Pre-intervention WRC	Pre-intervention accuracy	Post-intervention WRC	Post-intervention accuracy	Growth
A	2	20%	2	14%	0.00
B	2	20%	2	15%	0.00
C	11	58%	10	53%	−0.50
D	16	70%	24	83%	4.00
E	17	71%	24	83%	3.50
F	17	63%	46	94%	14.50
G	18	62%	19	68%	0.50
H	20	69%	31	89%	5.50
I	26	70%	42	88%	8.00
J	35	90%	64	96%	14.50
K	39	85%	64	94%	12.50
L	43	86%	54	93%	5.50
M	55	98%	59	98%	2.00
N	69	96%	80	100%	5.50
O	87	99%	102	95%	7.50
P	107	98%	113	99%	3.00
Median	23	70.5%	44	91%	

Note. WRC = words correct per minute; expected growth rate for first grade is 1.37 WRC per week.

TABLE 9.2
Winter Screening and Postintervention Scores for Classroom 2

Student	Pre-intervention WRC	Pre-intervention accuracy	Post-intervention WRC	Post-intervention accuracy	Growth
A	6	40%	18	67%	6.00
B	7	54%	10	50%	1.50
C	7	47%	16	67%	4.50
D	9	53%	13	59%	2.00
E	9	47%	24	77%	7.50
F	13	100%	10	56%	−1.50
G	14	70%	10	71%	−2.00
H	22	76%	37	93%	7.50
I	27	82%	63	95%	18.00
J	28	78%	63	94%	17.50
K	29	74%	63	98%	17.00
L	30	86%	49	98%	9.50
M	116	100%	113	100%	−1.50
N	122	100%	144	99%	11.00
Median	18	75%	31	85%	

Note. WRC = words correct per minute; expected growth rate for first grade is 1.37 WRC per week.

the screening data to determine what type of intervention was needed. The median accuracy score was 70.5% and 75%, which fell below the criterion of 93%. Therefore, it was determined that these two classrooms needed additional support with decoding skills. Had the median accuracy been 93% or higher, the intervention would have focused on building fluency through partner reading activities (Burns et al., 2015).

The intervention was delivered in heterogeneous dyads. To create the appropriate student partnerships, the class list with student screening scores was divided into the top half and bottom half; the highest student of the top half was partnered with the highest student in the bottom half, the second highest student in the top half with the second highest student in the bottom half, and so on (see Table 9.3). In the case where there was an uneven split, the student without a partner could join an existing partnership or work with an adult.

The intervention occurred each day for 10 school days and required 20 minutes per day to complete. Each student in the dyad was assigned to be Reader A or Reader B. Reader A was the higher reader (from the top half) and Reader B was the lower reader (from the bottom half). The intervention was based on PALS and each dyad received a student sheet that contained four main sections. First, the dyads would practice letter sounds for 1 minute.

TABLE 9.3
Creating the Appropriate Partner Match for Classroom 1

Student	Screening words read correctly per minute	Resulting dyads
	Top half	
A	2	A & I
B	2	B & J
C	11	C & K
D	16	D & L
E	17	E & M
F	17	F & N
G	18	G & O
H	20	H & P
	Bottom half	
I	26	
J	35	
K	39	
L	43	
M	55	
N	69	
O	87	
P	107	

Second, each dyad practiced segmenting and blending words that contained target sounds. Students were instructed to sound out each word and then "read it fast" by blending all the sounds. Third, the students practiced reading first-grade sight words for 1 minute. Finally, the students practiced reading a brief story that contained the sight words that they practiced. Reader A always went first and served as the model. Reader B then completed the four steps again with Reader A serving as the coach. Both students provided error correction when needed and called on the teacher when neither knew the correct response. All materials for each dyad were placed into a folder with their names on it. The procedures for getting the materials and moving to a quiet place in the classroom to work were practiced during the first two sessions.

All students were again assessed with a FAST CBM-R probe after implementing the intervention for 10 school days. However, the second time we did not use three grade-level probes and record the median score, we used just one probe for each student and recorded the WRC and accuracy from that measure.

RESULTS

On completion of the 2-week intervention, we examined four sets of data: changes in median WRC scores, growth in WRC across 2 weeks, accuracy, and the number of students needing intervention. The data for the students are included in Tables 9.1 and 9.2.

Median Words Read Correctly

As shown in Tables 9.1 and 9.2, the median WRC for each classroom before the intervention was 23 and 18, which were well below the criterion of 35. After implementing the 2-week intervention, the medians increased to 44 and 31, which almost doubled the previous score for each classroom. It is important to note that the class median for Classroom 1 now exceeded the criterion, but the score for Classroom 2 did not. In practice, Classroom 2 should have continued the intervention and reassessed each student every 5 school days until the median exceeded the seasonal benchmark criterion. Because the median increased from 18 to 31 in just 10 school days, it is reasonable to predict that the median would have met or surpassed 35 with 5 more days of intervention.

Growth

Growth was evaluated by subtracting the screening WRC score (pretest) from the posttest WRC score and dividing by two, to equal an average growth per week. The expected increase in WRC per week was 1.37, which was computed with ordinary least squares regression with the three seasonal benchmark criterion scores for fall, winter, and spring and the number that represented the week of the school year when those data were collected (e.g., 3, 19, and 35). Thus, the expected growth rate was based on the amount of growth required to maintain a score that would at least meet the seasonal benchmarks. A total of 23 students (77%) demonstrated growth that met or exceeded 1.37, and all but one of those students increased by at least 2.00 words per minute per week. One student who did not increase the WRC score had a screening score of 116, which was considerably above the target score. The average rate of growth was 6.1 ($SD = 5.95$) words per minute per week, which was much higher than the expected growth rate of 1.37. In Classroom 1, Students A and B made zero growth, and Student C decreased in WRC. An examination of these three students' attendance during the intervention indicated that attendance was at or below 80% during the intervention period for these three students. Thus, with a few notable exceptions, the students increased their WRC score at an acceptable rate.

Accuracy

The accuracy with which students read connected text is an important variable. Students who read 93% to 97% of the words correctly tended to have higher comprehension, task completion, time on task (Treptow et al., 2007), and reading growth (Burns, 2007). Moreover, students who read less than 93% of the words correctly likely required a different intervention than those who read at least 93% of the words correctly, despite similar WRC scores on an oral reading fluency measure (Burns et al., 2014). The median accuracy increased for each classroom from 70.5% and 75% to 91% and 85%, respectively. Neither median exceeded the criterion of 93%, but the number of students who exceeded the criterion went from 7 (23%) to 15 (50%). Thus, the students seemed to increase the accuracy with which they read the words. However, the intervention could perhaps have continued for another 5 school days for each classroom in order to attempt to have more students reading at a higher rate of accuracy.

Number of Students Who Need Intervention

Any student who scored less than 35 WRC was identified as needing an intervention. Prior to the start of the intervention, 21 out of 30 (70%) students were below the seasonal benchmark criterion of 35. That number decreased to 14 of 30 (47%) at the end of the intervention, which was an average of seven students per classroom. The goal was to reduce the number of students needing intervention to three per classroom (six total), which would have represented 20%. It is reasonable to implement an intervention with five to seven students from each classroom, but with classrooms of less than 20 students, the number should have been lower.

IMPLICATIONS

The students in these two classrooms increased their reading skills with a brief intervention for 10 school days. They grew at an acceptable rate in WRC and increased the accuracy with which they read words. Given that the intervention did not require much time or many resources, it seems to be a possible option for resource-stretched urban schools. Nonetheless, growth may not be the critical goal. Most of the students made considerable growth, but 14 of them still were not at the seasonal benchmark. High expectations have long been identified as an important component of effective urban schools (Edmonds, 1979), and reading interventions and instruction should be evaluated by how frequently they achieve proficiency rather than by how much they increase student learning. A student who substantially increases his or her reading skills but is not proficient will not perform well in future academic and career endeavors despite the positive growth.

In some cases, a 2-week intervention may not be sufficient. In our example, the class median was above the criterion for one classroom but not the other. Moreover, too many students remained below the benchmark score and their accuracy did not meet or exceed 93%. Screening data can be interpreted many ways, including by the median score and the score for each student. Practitioners are also encouraged to examine screening data to determine the accuracy and number of students still identified as needing support. Overall, the intervention was successful. Within an MTSS, there are usually one of three decisions made based on intervention data: (a) the intervention was successful because the student is now proficient and the intervention is no longer needed; (b) the intervention was effective because the student is demonstrating sufficient growth, but the student is not proficient yet and the intervention should continue; or (c) the intervention was ineffective and a different intervention should be attempted (Riley-Tillman & Burns, 2009). In this example, the intervention was effective but should have continued in both classrooms, even though the class median was 44 for Classroom 1. An additional 5 school days of intervention may have positively affected the number of students needing intervention and their individual accuracy levels.

Research

Screening is becoming common practice in kindergarten to Grade 12 schools, and there is increasing research regarding how to best to implement this, but most of the research correlates screeners with other measures and does not adequately address screening in urban schools. For example, previous research has found that English language learners demonstrate a lower growth rate on CBM-R than English-speaking students (de Ramirez & Shapiro, 2006), which could challenge the notion of using the same seasonal benchmark criteria for reading screenings among both groups. Although none of the students in the current sample were English learners, approximately 25% of the nation's students who are English learners attend an urban school, and 17% of the population within urban schools is English learners (Uro & Barrio, 2013). There seems to be considerable evidence that there is little bias within CBM data regarding gender and ethnicity within early grades (Baker & Good, 1995), but differences in scores for African American students and students from poverty in fifth grade were noted (Kranzler, Miller, & Jordan, 1999). Thus, more research is needed to verify that CBM-R data result in valid conclusions for students from urban schools and to develop criteria with which the data can be compared.

Kane (2013) suggested that validity be a line of inquiry and that correlations between two measures represents weak evidence for the validity of the decisions being made. Researchers could examine issues such as the diagnostic accuracy of CBM-R with urban populations, the frequency of types of screening decisions made with urban populations compared with the general population, and the effect of various potential cultural biases on the data.

Practice

The class-wide intervention described here led to increased reading proficiency and seems to have promise, especially combined with previous research that has shown positive effects (Burns et al., 2015; VanDerHeyden et al., 2007). Thus, practitioners could consider working within professional learning communities to interpret screening data in the manner described here and to use the data to implement a class-wide intervention when needed.

Assessment practices in schools are informed by ethical standards (e.g., American Psychological Association, 2010; National Association of School Psychologists, 2010) and standards for assessment and testing (American Educational Research Association, American Psychological Association, & National Council on Measurement in Education, 1999). Although there are points of inconsistency across standards, all call for nondiscriminatory assessment practices. Schools can easily determine whether language is a potential source of bias and select screeners in different languages as needed, however, language alone does not account for differences in culture and race.

Ortiz (2008) suggested that assessments must be conducted for intervention, not just placement; should consider the ecology of the student;

should converge with multiple data sources; and assessors should "begin with the hypothesis that the examinee's difficulties are not intrinsic in nature, but rather that they are more likely attributable to external or environmental problems" (p. 664). Examiners must use their knowledge of a student's unique experiences and background to evaluate and interpret all information gathered. The hypothesis of normality is not rejected unless the data strongly suggest the contrary. Universal screening to identify class-wide problems addresses several of these recommendations because (a) the data are used to drive intervention, (b) the process begins to assess the instructional environment, and (c) it assumes that student learning issues are related to the system in which students are being instructed. However, school personnel should be cautious about making screening decisions with students in urban settings on the basis of only one source of data. Screening data such as CBM-R should be combined with other types of data, such as additional measures of the same construct, teacher assessments, and historical data. Moreover, screening decisions could also be informed by growth data, which would base decisions on comparisons with the student's previous data rather than comparing him or her with a norm group; this would likely reduce the likelihood of bias for an individual student (Ortiz, 2008).

The criteria developed for the demonstration we describe here were derived from the relationship between the state test and the screener for this specific population. Using norms derived from the population being assessed, or local norms, seems especially advantageous for urban schools because the norm group will then have similar educational and background experiences as the students being assessed, reducing the influence of bias (Little & Akin-Little, 2014). Thus, practitioners could develop proficiency criteria for their own school using ROC with CBM-R and their state test (or some other meaningful criterion) and determine the point at which binary decisions (e.g., pass/fail or at-risk/not at-risk) are best made. It would go beyond the scope of this chapter to explain ROC curves, but less statistically sophisticated practitioners could simply take a normative approach in which local norms are used to determine risk (e.g., at or below the 25th percentile on the local norm), although the data would have to meet assumptions necessary to compute local norms, such as sufficient size of the sample, sufficient representation of the population being assessed, and a normal distribution.

CONCLUSION

The current data demonstrated how to identify student needs with screening data and that implementing class-wide interventions for 10 days improved the overall reading skills in two classrooms, thus reducing the overall number of students needing Tier 2 interventions. Urban classrooms with more than half of students reading below grade level should consider implementing a research-based intervention to reduce the number of students needing Tier 2 interventions and to limit using unnecessary resources that would be spent implementing more Tier 2 interventions than necessary. Given that resources are often lacking in urban schools, the efforts described here seemed warranted.

REFERENCES

American Educational Research Association, American Psychological Association, & National Council on Measurement in Education. (1999). *Standards for educational and psychological testing* (2nd ed.). Washington, DC: American Educational Research Association.

American Psychological Association. (2010). *Ethical principles of psychologists and code of conduct (2002, Amended June 1, 2010)*. Retrieved from http://www.apa.org/ethics/code/index.aspx

Baker, S. K., & Good, R. (1995). Curriculum-based measurement of English reading with bilingual Hispanic students: A validation study with second-grade students. *School Psychology Review, 24,* 561–578.

Baker, S. K., Plasencia-Peinado, J., & Lezcano-Lytle, V. (1998). The use of curriculum-based measurement with language-minority students. In M. R. Shinn (Ed.), *Advanced applications of curriculum-based measurement* (pp. 175–213). New York, NY: Guilford Press.

Batsche, G., Elliott, J., Graden, J. L., Grimes, J., Kovaleski, J. F., Prasse, D., & Tilly, W. D. (2005). *Response to intervention: Policy considerations and implementation*. Reston, VA: National Association of State Directors of Special Education.

Berkeley, S., Bender, W. N., Gregg Peaster, L., & Saunders, L. (2009). Implementation of response to intervention: A snapshot of progress. *Journal of Learning Disabilities, 42,* 85–95. http://dx.doi.org/10.1177/0022219408326214

Burns, M. K. (2007). Reading at the instructional level with children identified as learning disabled: Potential implications for response-to-intervention. *School Psychology Quarterly, 22,* 297–313. http://dx.doi.org/10.1037/1045-3830.22.3.297

Burns, M. K., Appleton, J. J., & Stehouwer, J. D. (2005). Meta-analytic review of responsiveness-to-intervention research: Examining field-based and research-implemented models. *Journal of Psychoeducational Assessment, 23,* 381–394. http://dx.doi.org/10.1177/073428290502300406

Burns, M. K., & Gibbons, K. (2012). *Response to intervention implementation in elementary and secondary schools: Procedures to assure scientific-based practices* (2nd ed.). New York, NY: Routledge.

Burns, M. K., Haegele, K., & Petersen-Brown, S. (2014). Screening for early reading skills: Using data to guide resources and instruction. In R. J. Kettler, T. A. Glover, C. A. Albers, & K. A. Feeney-Kettler (Eds.), *Universal screening in educational settings: Evidence-based decision making for schools* (pp. 171–197). Washington, DC: American Psychological Association. http://dx.doi.org/10.1037/14316-007

Burns, M. K., Karich, A. C., Maki, K. E., Anderson, A., Pulles, S. M., Ittner, A., . . . Helman, L. (2015). Identifying classwide problems in reading with screening data. *Journal of Evidence Based Practices for Schools, 14,* 186–204.

Children's Defense Fund. (2014). *The state of America's children.* Retrieved from http://www.childrensdefense.org/library/state-of-americas-children/2014-soac.pdf?utm_source=2014-SOAC-PDF&utm_medium=link&utm_campaign=2014-SOAC

Christ, T. J., Ardoin, S. A., & Eckert, T. (2011). *Formative Assessment and Instrumentation for Reading (FAIP-R): Curriculum based measurement for reading.* Minneapolis: University of Minnesota.

de Ramirez, R. D., & Shapiro, E. S. (2006). Curriculum-based measurement and the evaluation of reading skills of Spanish-speaking English language learners. *School Psychology Review, 35,* 356–369.

Edmonds, R. (1979). Effective schools for the urban poor. *Educational Leadership, 37,* 15–27.

Fountas, I. C., & Pinnell, G. S. (1996). *Guided reading: Good first teaching for all children.* Portsmouth, NH: Heinemann.

Francis, D. J., Santi, K. L., Barr, C., Fletcher, J. M., Varisco, A., & Foorman, B. R. (2008). Form effects on the estimation of students' oral reading fluency using DIBELS. *Journal of School Psychology, 46,* 315–342. http://dx.doi.org/10.1016/j.jsp.2007.06.003

Good, R. H., III, Kaminski, R. A., Cummings, K. D., Dufour-Martel, C., Peterson, K., Powell-Smith, K. A., . . . Wallin, J. (2012). *DIBELS Next assessment manual.* Eugene, OR: Dynamic Measurement Group.

Harry, B., & Klingner, J. (2014). *Why are so many minority students in special education? Understanding race & disability in schools* (2nd ed.). New York, NY: Teachers College.

Hosp, J. L., & Madyun, N. (2007). Addressing disproportionality with response to intervention. In S. Jimerson, M. Burns, & A. VanDerHeyden (Eds.), *Handbook of response to intervention: The science and practice of assessment and intervention* (pp. 172–181). New York, NY: Springer. http://dx.doi.org/10.1007/978-0-387-49053-3_13

Ikeda, M. J., Neesen, E., & Witt, J. C. (2008). Best practices in universal screening. In A. Thomas & J. Grimes (Eds.), *Best practices in school psychology V* (pp. 721–734). Bethesda, MD: National Association of School Psychologists.

Kane, M. (2013). The argument-based approach to validation. *School Psychology Review, 42,* 448–457.

Keller-Margulis, M., Shapiro, E. S., & Hintze, J. M. (2008). Long term diagnostic accuracy of curriculum-based measures in reading and mathematics. *School Psychology Review, 37,* 374–390.

Kettler, R. J., Glover, T. A., Albers, C. A., & Feeney-Kettler, K. A. (2014). An introduction to universal screening in educational settings. In R. J. Kettler, T. A. Glover, C. A. Albers, & K. A. Feeney-Kettler (Eds.), *Universal screening in educational settings: Evidence-based decision making for schools* (pp. 3–16). Washington, DC: American Psychological Association. http://dx.doi.org/10.1037/14316-001

Kranzler, J. H., Miller, M. D., & Jordan, L. (1999). An examination of racial/ethnic and gender bias on curriculum-based measurement of reading. *School Psychology Quarterly, 14,* 327–342. http://dx.doi.org/10.1037/h0089012

Little, S. G., & Akin-Little, A. (2014). Methods of academic assessment. In S. G. Little & A. Akin-Little (Eds.), *Academic assessment and intervention* (pp. 3–6). New York, NY: Routledge.

Marston, D. (2012). School- and district-wide implementation of curriculum-based measurement in the Minneapolis Public Schools. In C. Espin, K. McMaster, S. Rose, & M. M. Wayman (Eds.), *A measure of success: The influence of curriculum-based measurement on education* (pp. 59–78). Minneapolis: University of Minnesota Press.

Marston, D., Lau, M., & Muyskens, P. (2007). Implementation of the problem-solving model in the Minneapolis public schools. In S. R. Jimerson, M. K. Burns, & A. M. VanDerHeyden (Eds.), *Handbook of response to intervention* (pp. 270–287). New York, NY: Springer. http://dx.doi.org/10.1007/978-0-387-49053-3_21

Mathes, P. G., Howard, J. K., Allen, S. H., & Fuchs, D. (1998). Peer-Assisted Learning Strategies for First-Grade Readers: Responding to the needs of diverse learners. *Reading Research Quarterly, 33,* 62–94. http://dx.doi.org/10.1598/RRQ.33.1.4

Milner, H. R. (2012). But what is urban education? *Urban Education, 47,* 556–561. http://dx.doi.org/10.1177/0042085912447516

National Association of School Psychologists. (2010). *Principles for professional ethics.* Bethesda, MD: Author.

National Center for Educational Statistics. (2011). *School attendance boundary survey: 2010–2011.* Washington, DC: Institute for Education Science.

Nese, J. F. T., Park, B. J., Alonzo, J., & Tindal, G. (2011). Applied curriculum-based measures as a predictor of high-stakes assessment: Implications for researchers and teachers. *The Elementary School Journal, 111,* 608–624. http://dx.doi.org/10.1086/659034

Newell, M., & Kratochwill, T. R. (2007). The integration of response to intervention and critical race theory-disability studies: A robust approach to reducing racial discrimination in evaluation decisions. In S. R. Jimerson, M. K. Burns, & A. M. VanDerHeyden (Eds.), *Handbook of response to intervention* (pp. 65–79). New York, NY: Springer. http://dx.doi.org/10.1007/978-0-387-49053-3_5

Ortiz, S. O. (2008). Best practices in nondiscriminatory assessment. In A. Thomas & J. Grimes (Eds.), *Best practices in school psychology V* (pp. 661–678). Bethesda, MD: National Association of School Psychologists.

Parisi, D. M., Ihlo, T., & Glover, T. (2014). Screening within a multitiered early prevention model: Using assessment to inform instruction and promote students' response to intervention. In R. J. Kettler, T. A. Glover, C. A. Albers, & K. A. Feeney-Kettler (Eds.), *Universal screening in educational settings: Evidence-based decision making for schools* (pp. 19–46). Washington, DC: American Psychological Association. http://dx.doi.org/10.1037/14316-002

Pearson. (2010). *Aimsweb*. Bloomington, MN: Author.

Riley-Tillman, T. C., & Burns, M. K. (2009). *Single case design for measuring response to educational intervention*. New York, NY: Guilford Press.

Ripp, A., Jean-Pierre, P., & Fergus, E. (n.d.). *Promising examples of RtI practices for urban schools*. Retrieved from http://www.rtinetwork.org/learn/diversity/promising-examples-of-rti-practices-for-urban-schools

Slavin, R. E., Lake, C., Davis, S., & Madden, N. A. (2011). Effective programs for struggling readers: A best-evidence synthesis. *Educational Research Review, 6*, 1–26. http://dx.doi.org/10.1016/j.edurev.2010.07.002

Tatum, A. W., & Muhammad, G. E. (2012). African-American males and literacy development in contexts that are characteristically urban. *Urban Education, 47*, 434–463. http://dx.doi.org/10.1177/0042085911429471

Teale, W. H., Paciga, K. A., & Hoffman, J. L. (2007). Beginning reading instruction in urban schools: The curriculum gape ensures a continuing achievement gap. *The Reading Teacher, 61*, 344–348. http://dx.doi.org/10.1598/RT.61.4.8

Treptow, M. A., Burns, M. K., & McComas, J. J. (2007). Reading at the frustration, instructional, and independent levels: Effects on student time on task and comprehension. *School Psychology Review, 36*, 159–166.

Uro, G., & Barrio, A. (2013). *English language learners in America's great city schools: Demographics, achievement, and staffing*. Washington, DC: Council of the Great City Schools.

VanDerHeyden, A. M., & Burns, M. K. (2005). Using curriculum-based assessment and curriculum-based measurement to guide elementary mathematics instruction: Effect on individual and group accountability scores. *Assessment for Effective Intervention, 30*, 15–31. http://dx.doi.org/10.1177/073724770503000302

VanDerHeyden, A. M., & Burns, M. K. (2010). *Essentials of response to intervention*. New York, NY: Wiley.

VanDerHeyden, A. M., Witt, J. C., & Gilbertson, D. (2007). A multi-year evaluation of the effects of a response to intervention (RTI) model on identification of children for special education. *Journal of School Psychology, 45*, 225–256. http://dx.doi.org/10.1016/j.jsp.2006.11.004

VanDerHeyden, A. M., Witt, J. C., & Naquin, G. (2003). Development and validation of a process for screening referrals to special education. *School Psychology Review, 32*, 204–227.

10

MANUALIZED SCHOOL-BASED SOCIAL–EMOTIONAL CURRICULA FOR ETHNIC MINORITY POPULATIONS

SARA M. CASTRO-OLIVO, KRISTINE CRAMER,
AND NICOLE M. GARCIA

For more than 50 years the consistent reporting of negative outcomes in the areas of academics, social, emotional, behavioral, and overall quality of life has held steady for culturally and linguistically diverse (CLD) students when compared with their non-Hispanic White peers (Castro-Olivo, Preciado, Sanford, & Perry, 2011). Since the early 1970s, educational research has highlighted the disparities in academic success between CLD students (specifically African Americans, Latinos, and Native Americans) and their non-Hispanic White peers, consistently demonstrating an achievement gap in the areas of math and reading (Kena et al., 2014). Along with lower test scores in core academic areas, CLD youth are also found to drop out of high school at higher rates than their non-Hispanic White peers. For more than 30 years Latino youth in particular have had the highest percentages of dropouts compared with all other races, and

http://dx.doi.org/10.1037/14855-011
Psychoeducational Assessment and Intervention for Ethnic Minority Children: Evidence-Based Approaches,
S. L. Graves, Jr., and J. J. Blake (Editors)

those percentages continue to increase for Latino students who are born outside the United States (Chapman, Laird, Ifill, & KewalRamani, 2011). Suárez-Orozco and Suárez-Orozco (2001) estimated that nearly 80% of Latino immigrant youth (those who qualified as English language learners [ELLs]) never obtain a high school diploma. In addition, the National Center for Education Statistics (NCES; 2014) reported that 13% of non-ELL Hispanics never obtain a high school diploma or GED.

It has also been suggested that CLD youth are at higher risk of developing social, emotional, and behavioral problems (U.S. Department of Health and Human Services, 2001). This is evident in the overrepresentation of African American and Latino youth subject to school disciplinary practices (e.g., office referrals, suspensions, expulsions) and within the juvenile justice system (Armour & Hammond, 2009; Gregory, Skiba, & Noguera, 2010; Skiba et al., 2011). In addition, reports have continued to link ethnic minority youth to risky behavior and signs of emotional distress (Centers for Disease Control and Prevention, 2014).

African American and Latino youth are more likely to be poor, live in neighborhoods marked by disorganization and violence, attend poor quality and potentially violent schools, and have families in which parents report higher levels of stress (Cauce, Cruz, Corona, & Conger, 2011). These environmental factors put CLD youth who come from disadvantaged backgrounds at a higher risk of academic, behavioral, and social–emotional problems. Given that African American and Latino youth are more likely to come from disadvantaged environments, more needs to be done in schools to increase protective factors and build resiliency within their home, neighborhood, and school environments (Cauce et al., 2011).

Schools are an ideal setting in which to address these issues. Research has found that schools can be successful settings for promoting social–emotional resiliency (Durlak, Weissberg, Dymnicki, Taylor, & Schellinger, 2011; Jones, Brown, & Aber, 2011; Zins, Weissberg, Wang, & Walberg, 2004), which can be defined as having a combination of a multitude of positive social–emotional traits such as social and emotional knowledge and competence, peer acceptance and relationships, ability to bounce back in the face of difficulties, coping skills, problem-solving abilities, empathy, and global self-concept (Merrell, 2010). Higher levels of social–emotional competency have been linked to lower levels of high-risk behaviors such as delinquency, alcohol and drug use, high school dropout, poor attendance, conduct problems, suspensions, and school disciplinary actions, and to improved academic performance (Ali, Dwyer, Vanner, & Lopez, 2010; Durlak et al., 2011; Najaka, Gottfredson, & Wilson, 2001).

SCHOOL-BASED MANUALIZED
SOCIAL–EMOTIONAL INTERVENTIONS

The promotion and teaching of social–emotional resiliency has been best achieved in schools through the implementation of manualized programs. For over a decade, the development and validation of manualized social–emotional learning programs that can be implemented in schools at the school-wide (universal) level has become a major focus of prevention researchers who aim to increase social–emotional competence and resilience among all youth (Durlak et al., 2011). Developing manuals for such interventions has been found to be best practice. Manualized programs have been found to be more effective than nonmanualized interventions at increasing treatment fidelity, skill development, and generalizations of skills to different settings (Durlak et al., 2011; Merrell, 2010). In their meta-analysis of social–emotional learning (SEL) school-based programs, Durlak and colleagues (2011) found 213 articles summarizing the results of school-based controlled trials. Of those studies, programs that followed the sequenced active focused and explicit framework were found to be more effective at improving students' social–emotional and academic outcomes than those that did not. Although Durlak and colleagues conducted a comprehensive review of those universal school-based SEL programs, data presented in the original studies limited their ability to examine intervention effects across members of different ethnic groups. Examining the effects of SEL interventions of CLD populations must be a main focus of SEL prevention research given that these populations have historically been found to be at higher risk of social–emotional and academic problems and without explicit interventions are likely to continue to lag behind. In a country where CLD populations are projected to become the majority, not focusing on their needs constitutes a great risk for the future of the entire nation. The current chapter describes a research agenda that aims to address the gap in SEL research for CLD populations by (a) addressing the need to adapt SEL programming for one of the most vulnerable populations in the United States (Latino ELLs), (b) describing a validated SEL program for Latino ELLs, (c) summarizing the results of the validated *jóvenes fuertes* (strong teens) SEL program (Castro-Olivo, Blanco-Vega, & Merrell, 2006; discussed later), and (d) discussing future directions to best serve the social–emotional and academic needs of CLD populations.

NEED TO ADAPT SOCIAL–EMOTIONAL LEARNING
FOR LATINO ENGLISH LANGUAGE LEARNERS

As previously mentioned, efforts to promote social–emotional resiliency in the United States have been significantly notable in the last few years. For example, two bills have been introduced to the U.S. House of

Representatives that would allow federal funds to be available for the research and implementation of SEL (CASEL, 2014). An increasing number of states are starting to include SEL standards in their core kindergarten to Grade 12 curriculum (Dusenbury, Weissberg, Goren, & Domitrovich, 2014). The National Association of School Psychologists (NASP) also endorsed promoting and teaching social–emotional skills at the universal level (Tier 1 from a multitiered level of support system; NASP, 2009). Although support from the federal government and reputable national associations demonstrates how established SEL has become, little research has evaluated the effects of these interventions on some of our nation's most vulnerable populations, CLD students. To date, most of the research conducted in school settings addressing the social–emotional and behavioral needs of CLD students has combined them in the overall sample without examining ethnic group differences (Jones et al., 2011; Jones, Brown, Hoglund, & Aber, 2010). Few have examined the effects of SEL on CLD groups; to our knowledge the only SEL program that has been adapted and studied with a CLD population is *jóvenes fuertes* (Castro-Olivo, 2014; Castro-Olivo & Merrell, 2012). Although this line of research is important, methodological and population constraints limit the generalizations that can be made about it and the unique effects of these interventions on CLD students' diverse and intense needs.

A subpopulation of particular interest are Latino ELLs. Although most research on ethnic disparities combines all Latinos (U.S. born and foreign born) in the same category, research has suggested that Latino ELLs (those who are immigrants or first-generation U.S. born) are at higher risk of social–emotional and academic problems than their second and later generation counterparts (Blanco-Vega, Castro-Olivo, & Merrell, 2008; Kulis, Marsiglia, & Nieri, 2009; Suárez-Orozco & Suárez-Orozco, 2001). Latino ELLs have been identified as a fast growing (over 11% of the U.S. school-aged population; NCES, 2014) and high-risk population in terms of both academic and social–emotional issues (Balagna, Young, & Smith, 2013; Castro-Olivo et al., 2011). Language barriers, parents who are unfamiliar with the U.S. school system, familial acculturation gaps, acculturative stress, and perceived discrimination are believed to negatively influence the development and outcomes of Latino ELLs (Albeg & Castro-Olivo, 2014; Blanco-Vega et al., 2008; Suárez-Orozco & Suárez-Orozco, 2001). To effectively address the unique needs of these students, Castro-Olivo and Merrell (2012) suggested that school-based interventions should be adapted to incorporate the cultural reality of the students served in school settings.

Identifying culturally competent best practices for serving the needs of at-risk CLD students has become a priority for school-based mental health care providers (American Psychological Association, 2002; NASP, 2000). However, few research studies have been conducted to evaluate the effects of

SEL programs on Latino ELLs. Blanco-Vega et al. (2008) argued that Latino ELLs are a unique population who can benefit from culturally adapted SEL interventions because of the many sociocultural challenges that they face in U.S. schools and society. Blanco-Vega and colleagues noted that culturally adapted interventions for adolescent Latino ELLs must explicitly teach skills to cope with these challenges, especially during challenging stages of life such as adolescence.

The need to make programs culturally relevant or responsive has been clearly articulated; however, there is little existing research on applied culturally responsive practices in school psychology (Forman et al., 2013). The efficacy of making cultural adaptations to existing evidence-based programs is supported by Vygotsky's (1962) social–cultural theory, which posits that humans' overall development is highly influenced by their cultural environments. A solid body of research already exists in what is often called *cultural adaptations of existing evidence-based treatments/interventions* (EBT/I; Griner & Smith; 2006; Smith, Domenech Rodríguez, & Bernal, 2011). However, most of this research has been conducted primarily with adults in community-based or clinical settings. Research on culturally adapted EBTs for adults has shown that such adaptations improve client outcomes, treatment acceptability, and participation rates when compared with nonadapted interventions (Bernal, Jiménez-Chafey, & Domenech Rodríguez, 2009; Griner & Smith, 2006; Smith et al., 2011).

CULTURALLY ADAPTED EVIDENCE-BASED TREATMENTS FOR CHILDREN

Despite the evidence of research on adults and the theoretical rationale for making cultural adaptations of SEL programming, few empirical studies have been conducted in the area of culturally adapted EBTs with children and adolescents (Huey & Polo, 2008). In addition, Latino ELLs are rarely represented in this research (Castro-Olivo & Merrell, 2012). Most worrisome is that most of the extant literature on cultural adaptations of mental health interventions for youth has significant methodological limitations. Although a significant number of publications have described the process of tailoring cultural adaptations for use with ethnic minorities (e.g., Ford-Paz, Reinhard, Kuebbeler, Contreras, & Sánchez, 2013; Nicolas, Arntz, Hirsch, & Schmiedigen, 2009), few design-intensive investigations have been published showing the outcomes of these adapted interventions. To date, published research in this domain is mostly limited to pilot investigations and case studies.

Two studies have used controlled group-based designs to evaluate culturally adapted youth intervention programs. Botvin, Schinke, Epstein, Diaz,

and Botvin (1995) reported the follow-up results of a school-based substance abuse prevention program targeting a minority sample composed
of primarily Black and Latino youths. The culturally adapted intervention
included materials and activities related to ethnic pride and the development of cultural identity. In comparison with the general skills program
approach and control groups, the culturally focused prevention approach
showed stronger effects in the reduction of drinking behaviors. O'Donnell,
Jurecska, and Dyer (2012) delivered a culturally adapted coping skills program to an at-risk sample of Mexican American youth. When compared with
controls (a European American sample receiving the nonadapted intervention), no differences were detected in intervention outcomes and retention
rates. Despite the lack of a true comparable control group, these authors concluded that cultural adaptations are needed to augment EBTs when working
with minority samples.

Few published studies of culturally adapted interventions using less
intensive research designs have shown promising results. For example,
Wood, Chiu, Hwang, Jacobs, and Ifekwunigwe (2008) reported the results of
a clinical case study in which a Mexican American student participated in
a culturally modified cognitive–behavior therapy program aimed at reducing
anxiety. After 12 weeks of treatment, significant reductions were noted
in the child's symptoms of anxiety, and positive behavioral changes were
reported both at home and at school. BigFoot and Schmidt (2010) adapted
a trauma-focused cognitive–behavioral intervention for use with American
Indian and Alaska Native children by incorporating traditional teachings
involving the cultural groups' beliefs, practices, and spirituality. These
authors presented a case illustration and described how tribal-specific cultural practice adaptations enhanced the effectiveness of the intervention in
the areas of affect management, relaxation, and coping. Both of these investigations demonstrated the importance of developing culturally appropriate
interventions to improve the effectiveness of EBTs for ethnically diverse
populations.

Additional empirical investigations are needed to support the efficacy
of culturally adapted EBTs for youth in school settings. Although a number
of studies have ascertained the need for cultural adaptations, few publications
have explored the outcomes of these developed interventions. Limitations
of current research include small sample sizes and the lack of high-quality
research designs (e.g., randomized controlled trials). Furthermore, much of
the published literature on culturally adapted interventions has been conducted in clinical settings. Future research should explore outcomes of culturally adapted interventions using larger samples and more sophisticated
research designs and include interventions delivered in other settings, such
as schools.

JÓVENES FUERTES: A VALIDATED SOCIAL–EMOTIONAL LEARNING PROGRAM FOR ENGLISH LANGUAGE LEARNERS

An intervention shown to be effective at teaching SEL skills in a culturally responsive manner to Latino ELL students is the *jóvenes fuertes* intervention by Castro-Olivo and colleagues (2006). The *jóvenes fuertes* program is a validated culturally adapted version of the strong teens program, originally developed by Merrell, Carrizales, Feuerborn, Gueldener, and Tran (2007). The strong teens/kids curriculum is a semi-scripted, 12-lesson (one lesson per week), SEL program that teaches students key social–emotional skills, such as self-awareness, social awareness, empathy, problem solving, anger management, responsible decision making, goal setting, and reframing of destructive thoughts (see Table 10.1 for a summary of lessons and cultural adaptations performed).

The *jóvenes fuertes* program was initially validated by Castro-Olivo and Merrell (2012) for use with Latino immigrant adolescents in a high school setting. Castro-Olivo and Merrell culturally adapted the core EBT program using the ecological validity model by Bernal, Bonilla, and Bellido (1995) to validate its effectiveness with this population. The ecological validity model requires interventionists interested in adapting EBT/Is to be used with CLD populations to consider the following dimensions: language, persons, metaphors, content, concepts, goals, methods, and context of the intervention (see Table 10.2 for a description of each dimension in this model). To validate this school-based program for use with Latino ELL adolescents, Castro-Olivo and Merrell first identified the theory-based culturally relevant content and concepts to add to the original program (i.e., a lesson on ethnic pride, explicit examples of how to use problem solving and reframing skills to cope with acculturative stress and familial acculturative gaps). Next, they held a series of focus groups and consulted a panel of experts to ensure that the adaptations were aligned with the goals and values of the target population and to verify that the planned methods of delivery and context were appropriate. Once this process had been completed, Castro-Olivo and Merrell conducted a pre–post pilot study with 40 recent immigrant high school students to assess the preliminary efficacy of the program. The results suggested that participants perceived that the program was socially valid, had improved their knowledge of SEL, and showed preventive effects for acculturative stress and low sense of school belonging. Although the results of the pilot study were promising, the small sample size and the lack of a control group limited the ability of the researchers to generalize their findings.

As a follow-up to the initial pilot study, Castro-Olivo (2014) conducted an additional randomized controlled study in which 121 Latino ELLs in Southern California participated in either an intervention or

TABLE 10.1
Lessons and Cultural Adaptations

Lesson name and number	Skills focus of *Strong Teens*	Focus of cultural adaptation
Strong Latino Roots (Lesson 1)	Overview of program, build rapport, behavior expectations	Strengthening ethnic pride
Understanding Your Feelings (Lessons 2 and 3)	Increasing awareness of one's own emotions and emotional variability	Learning to certain culturally related emotions (i.e., acculturative stress) as comfortable or uncomfortable
Dealing with Anger (Lesson 4)	Anger management, learning steps to avoid overreacting to triggers	Learning to deal with culturally related situations that might trigger anger
Understanding Other People's Feelings (Lesson 5)	Empathy training (understanding others' perspectives)	Learning to cope with familial acculturative gaps
Clear Thinking (Lesson 6)	Learning to recognize thinking errors	Examples related to English proficiency and other culturally specific situations
The Power of Positive Thinking (Lesson 8)	Replacing irrational thoughts with positive thinking	Examples related to English proficiency and other culturally specific situations
Solving People Problems (Lesson 9)	Conflict resolution model	Culturally specific examples and role playing in school and home settings
Letting Go of Stress (Lesson 10)	Relaxation training	Culturally specific examples and discussions related to letting go of acculturative stress
Behavior Change (Lesson 11)	Learning to set and attain goals	Culturally specific examples
Finishing Up (Lesson 12)	Review of all main concepts	Emphasizing the use of skills to reduce accultura-tive stress and other cultural conflicts in school and at home

Note. From "Validating Cultural Adaptations of a School-Based Social-Emotional Learning Programme for Use With Latino Immigrant Adolescents," by S. M. Castro-Olivo and K. W. Merrell, 2012, *Advances in School Mental Health Promotion, 5,* p. 82. Copyright 2012 by Taylor & Francis. Adapted with permission.

TABLE 10.2

Dimensions of Adaptation: Making *Jóvenes Fuertes* Culturally Relevant
for Latino English Language Learners

Dimension	Performed adaptations
Language	Fully translated into Spanish
Persons	Conducted by bicultural or bilingual Spanish speaking interventionists
Metaphors	Included concepts specific to the Latino culture and ELL experience
Content	Included a lesson on ethnic pride; changed examples to relate the taught skills to common social experiences of ELLs
Concepts	Included concepts related to the risk and protective factors of Latino populations (e.g., acculturation, acculturative stress, acculturative gap, ethic pride, *familism*)
Goals	Provided examples on how to use the skills taught to maintain adaptive and positive values of Latino culture (i.e., *familism* and *respeto*)
Methods	Included examples that illustrated Latino folk tales and customs
Context	Considered the context of target population in relation to their immigrant experiences, country of origin, acculturative stress, and language challenges

Note. ELL = English language learner.

waitlist control group. The results showed not only that the program was perceived as socially valid by participating students and teachers but also that it improved students' knowledge of SEL skills and reports of social–emotional resiliency.

Additional studies have been conducted in school settings using *jóvenes fuertes* with other Latino ELLs and CLD populations using a response-to-intervention framework (Castro-Olivo, Cramer, Lopez, & Benitez, 2014). The most recent studies have shown that *jóvenes fuertes* can effectively be implemented as a Tier 1 intervention for Latino ELLs and other CLD students. In these studies, Castro-Olivo and colleagues (2014) provided *jóvenes fuertes* to a group of 86 CLD students (including 56 Latino ELLs and 24 mixed CLD students). Students who participated in Tier 1 (receiving all 12 lessons of the culturally adapted program) reported improved outcomes in the areas of resiliency and social–emotional knowledge post intervention. In addition, students who participated in the Tier 2 intervention of the program, which consisted of an additional three one-on-one booster sessions, reported improved levels of internalizing symptoms and acculturative stress.

CONCLUSION AND FUTURE DIRECTIONS

School-based SEL programs have been found to be effective at promoting social–emotional and academic resiliency among all youth, including some of those most at risk (Jones et al., 2011). However, more research is needed to ensure that school-based practices are truly addressing the needs of the most vulnerable CLD populations. CLD students are the future of the United States; promoting their success must become a priority in our educational and research agenda. A way to ensure that CLD populations do not continue to lag behind their White counterparts is through the implementation of culturally responsive resiliency building programs (Blanco-Vega et al., 2008). For school-based SEL programs to be considered truly effective, they must not only yield positive effects on important outcomes but must also allow the students the opportunity to be fully engaged and feel that the instruction is truly applicable to their daily lives and to challenging environments. Although the research on the culturally adapted strong kids/*jóvenes fuertes* program has shown promising results in multiple studies, more research is needed to identify whether following the ecological validity model is applicable for members of other CLD groups (e.g., Asian Americans, Native Americans, African Americans). Jones and colleagues (2011) have shown that SEL programs are effective when delivered to disadvantaged students (including CLD populations); however, little research has been conducted to examine the effects of cultural adaptations (enhanced cultural responsiveness in delivery) on students' outcomes and the potential added values of such adaptations. More research is needed to examine whether adapted SEL programs are as effective and as socially valid as nonadapted SEL programs.

Theoretically, making adaptations to SEL programs makes sense. Students respond well to adapted programs, but more research is needed to establish their added effects. Research in community settings has already established this with adults (Griner & Smith, 2006; Smith et al., 2011). Current research has supported the adoption of models for making cultural adaptations to evidence-based and manualized treatments for youth. Evidence has suggested that these cultural adaptations are not only effective but also feasible to implement in school settings. Although some argue that more randomized trials are needed to evaluate the added value of making cultural adaptations to manualized treatments, the practice is supported by theory, and the few studies available have shown it to be effective (Castro-Olivo, 2014; Castro-Olivo & Merrell, 2012; McClure, Connell, Griffith, & Kaslow, 2005). In addition, as psychologists, we are required by our ethical guidelines to engage in practices that are not only evidence based but also culturally sensitive, responsive, and competent. Simply stating that we are culturally aware and are taking a few classes on cultural sensitivity or responsiveness does not make us culturally competent. We must engage in practices that are replicable and observable. Following models that have been shown to be effective at adapting evidence-based interventions for CLD populations is the first step in meeting the needs of populations that have been neglected for decades; these needs must be addressed to ensure the success of our nation and future generations.

REFERENCES

Albeg, L. J., & Castro-Olivo, S. M. (2014). The relationship between mental health, acculturative stress, and academic performance in a Latino middle school sample. *Contemporary School Psychology*, *18*, 178–186. http://dx.doi.org/10.1007/s40688-014-0010-1

Ali, M. M., Dwyer, D. S., Vanner, E. A., & Lopez, A. (2010). Adolescent propensity to engage in health risky behaviors: The role of individual resilience. *International Journal of Environmental Research and Public Health*, *7*, 2161–2176. http://dx.doi.org/10.3390/ijerph7052161

American Psychological Association. (2002). *APA guidelines on multicultural education, training, research, practice, and organizational change for psychologists*. Retrieved from http://www.apa.org/pi/oema/resources/policy/multicultural-guidelines.aspx

Armour, J., & Hammond, S. (2009). *Minority youth in the juvenile justice system: Disproportionate minority contact*. Retrieved from http://www.ncsl.org/print/cj/minoritiesinjj.pdf

Balagna, R. M., Young, E. L., & Smith, T. B. (2013). School experiences of early adolescent Latinos/as at risk for emotional and behavioral disorders. *School Psychology Quarterly*, *28*, 101–121. http://dx.doi.org/10.1037/spq0000018

Bernal, G., Bonilla, J., & Bellido, C. (1995). Ecological validity and cultural sensitivity for outcome research: Issues for the cultural adaptation and development of psychosocial treatments with Hispanics. *Journal of Abnormal Child Psychology*, *23*, 67–82. http://dx.doi.org/10.1007/BF01447045

Bernal, G., Jiménez-Chafey, M. I., & Domenech Rodríguez, M. M. D. (2009). Cultural adaptation of treatments: A resource for considering culture in evidence-based practice. *Professional Psychology: Research and Practice*, *40*, 361–368. http://dx.doi.org/10.1037/a0016401

BigFoot, D. S., & Schmidt, S. R. (2010). Honoring children, mending the circle: Cultural adaptation of trauma-focused cognitive–behavioral therapy for American Indian and Alaska Native Children. *Journal of Clinical Psychology: In Session*, *66*, 847–856.

Blanco-Vega, C. O., Castro-Olivo, S. M., & Merrell, K. W. (2008). Social and emotional needs of Latino immigrant adolescents: An ecological model for developing planning and implementing culturally sensitive interventions. *Journal of Latinos and Education*, *1*, 43–61.

Botvin, G. J., Schinke, S. P., Epstein, J. A., Diaz, T., & Botvin, E. M. (1995). Effectiveness of culturally focused and generic skills training approaches to alcohol and drug abuse prevention among minority adolescents: Two-year follow-up results. *Psychology of Addictive Behaviors*, *9*, 183–194. http://dx.doi.org/10.1037/0893-164X.9.3.183

CASEL. (2014). *Federal legislation to promote social and emotional learning*. Retrieved from https://casel.squarespace.com/federal-policy-and-legislation/

Castro-Olivo, S. (2014). Promoting social–emotional learning in Latino ELLs: A study of the culturally adapted *Strong Teens* program. *School Psychology Quarterly, 29*, 567–577. http://dx.doi.org/10.1037/spq0000055

Castro-Olivo, S. M., Blanco-Vega, C. O., & Merrell, K. W. (2006). *Cultural adaptation of the Strong Kids/Teens program: A culturally responsive SEL intervention for use with Latino ELL populations (Manuscript written in Spanish)*. Unpublished manuscript, University of Oregon, Eugene.

Castro-Olivo, S. M., Cramer, K., Lopez, V., & Benitez, S. (2014, February). *Culturally responsive SEL interventions: From screening to targeting interventions*. Paper presented at the meeting of the National Association of School Psychology, Washington, DC.

Castro-Olivo, S. M., & Merrell, K. W. (2012). Validating cultural adaptations of a school-based social–emotional learning program for use with Latino immigrant adolescents. *Advances in School Mental Health Promotion, 5*, 78–92. http://dx.doi.org/10.1080/1754730X.2012.689193

Castro-Olivo, S. M., Preciado, J., Sanford, A. K., & Perry, V. (2011). The academic and social–emotional needs of secondary Latino English learners: Implications for screening, identification, and instructional planning. *Exceptionality, 19*, 160–174. http://dx.doi.org/10.1080/09362835.2011.579846

Cauce, A. M., Cruz, R., Corona, M., & Conger, R. (2011). The face of the future: Risk and resilience in minority youth. In G. Carlo, L. J. Crocket, & M. Carranza (Eds.), *Health disparities in youth and families: Research and applications* (pp. 13–32). New York, NY: Springer. http://dx.doi.org/10.1007/978-1-4419-7092-3_2

Centers for Disease Control and Prevention. (2014). *Youth risk behavior surveillance: United States, 2013*. Retrieved from http://www.cdc.gov/mmwr/preview/mmwrhtml/ss6304a1.htm

Chapman, C., Laird, J., Ifill, N., & KewalRamani, A. (2011). *Trends in high school dropout and completion rates in the United States: 1972–2009* (NCES 2012-006). Retrieved from http://nces.ed.gov/pubs2012/2012006.pdf

Durlak, J. A., Weissberg, R. P., Dymnicki, A. B., Taylor, R. D., & Schellinger, K. B. (2011). The impact of enhancing students' social and emotional learning: A meta-analysis of school-based universal interventions. *Child Development, 82*, 405–432. http://dx.doi.org/10.1111/j.1467-8624.2010.01564.x

Dusenbury, L., Weissberg, R. P., Goren, P., & Domitrovich, C. (2014). *State standards to advance social and emotional learning: Findings from CASEL's state scan of social and emotional learning standards, preschool through high school, 2014*. Retrieved from http://www.casel.org/library/2014/2/10/state-standards-to-advance-social-and-emotional-learning

Ford-Paz, R. E., Reinhard, C., Kuebbeler, A., Contreras, R., & Sánchez, B. (2013, October). Culturally tailored depression/suicide prevention in Latino youth: Community perspectives. *The Journal of Behavioral Health Services & Research*, 1–15. http://dx.doi.org/10.1007/s11414-013-9368-5

Forman, S. G., Shapiro, E. S., Codding, R. S., Gonzales, J. E., Reddy, L. A., Rosenfield, S. A., . . . Stoiber, K. C. (2013). Implementation science and school psychology. *School Psychology Quarterly, 28*, 77–100. http://dx.doi.org/10.1037/spq0000019

Gregory, A., Skiba, R. J., & Noguera, P. A. (2010). The achievement gap and the discipline gap: Two sides of the same coin? *Educational Researcher, 39*, 59–68. http://dx.doi.org/10.3102/0013189X09357621

Griner, D., & Smith, T. B. (2006). Culturally adapted mental health intervention: A meta-analytic review. *Psychotherapy: Theory, Research, Practice, Training, 43*, 531–548. http://dx.doi.org/10.1037/0033-3204.43.4.531

Huey, S. J., Jr., & Polo, A. J. (2008). Evidence-based psychosocial treatments for ethnic minority youth. *Journal of Clinical Child and Adolescent Psychology, 37*, 262–301. http://dx.doi.org/10.1080/15374410701820174

Jones, S. M., Brown, J. L., & Aber, J. L. (2011). Two-year impacts of a universal school-based social–emotional and literacy intervention: An experiment in translational developmental research. *Child Development, 82*, 533–554. http://dx.doi.org/10.1111/j.1467-8624.2010.01560.x

Jones, S. M., Brown, J. L., Hoglund, W. L. G., & Aber, J. L. (2010). A school-randomized clinical trial of an integrated social–emotional learning and literacy intervention: Impacts after 1 school year. *Journal of Consulting and Clinical Psychology, 78*, 829–842. http://dx.doi.org/10.1037/a0021383

Kena, G., Aud, S., Johnson, F., Wang, X., Zhang, J., Rathbun, A., & Kristapovich, P. (2014). *The condition of education 2014* (NCES 2014-083). Retrieved from http://nces.ed.gov/pubs2014/2014083.pdf

Kulis, S., Marsiglia, F. F., & Nieri, T. (2009). Perceived ethnic discrimination versus acculturation stress: Influences on substance use among Latino youth in the Southwest. *Journal of Health and Social Behavior, 50*, 443–459. http://dx.doi.org/10.1177/002214650905000405

McClure, E. B., Connell, A. M., Griffith, J. R., & Kaslow, N. J. (2005). The adolescent depression empowerment project (ADEPT): A culturally sensitive family treatment for depressed African American girls. In E. D. Hibbs & P. S. Jensen (Eds.), *Psychosocial treatments for child and adolescent disorders: Empirically based strategies for clinical practice* (2nd ed., pp. 149–164). Washington, DC: American Psychological Association.

Merrell, K. W. (2010). Linking prevention science and social and emotional learning: The Oregon Resiliency Project. *Psychology in the Schools, 47*, 55–70.

Merrell, K. W., Carrizales, D., Feuerborn, L., Gueldener, B. A., & Tran, O. K. (2007). *Strong Teens: A social & emotional learning curriculum*. Baltimore, MD: Brookes.

Najaka, S. S., Gottfredson, D. C., & Wilson, D. B. (2001). A meta-analytic inquiry into the relationship between selected risk factors and problem behavior. *Prevention Science, 2*, 257–271. http://dx.doi.org/10.1023/A:1013610115351

National Association of School Psychologists. (2000). *Professional code manual: Principles for professional ethics guidelines for the provision of school psychological services*. Retrieved from http://nasponline.org/standards/ProfessionalCond.pdf

National Association of School Psychologists. (2009). *Position statement: Appropriate behavioral, social, and emotional supports to meet the needs of all students.* Retrieved from http://www.nasponline.org/about_nasp/positionpapers/appropriatebehavioralsupports.pdf

National Center for Education Statistics. (2014). *Number and percentage of public school students participating in programs for English language learners, by state: Selected years, 2002–03 through 2011–12.* Retrieved from http://nces.ed.gov/programs/digest/d13/tables/dt13_204.20.asp

Nicolas, G., Arntz, D. L., Hirsch, B., & Schmiedigen, A. (2009). Cultural adaptation of a group treatment for Haitian American adolescents. *Professional Psychology: Research and Practice, 40,* 378–384. http://dx.doi.org/10.1037/a0016307

O'Donnell, S. L., Jurecska, D. E., & Dyer, R. (2012). Effectiveness of the coping power program in a Mexican-American sample: Distinctive cultural considerations. *International Journal of Culture and Mental Health, 5,* 30–39. http://dx.doi.org/10.1080/17542863.2010.547272

Skiba, R. J., Homer, R. H., Chung, C. G., Rausch, M. K., May, S. L., & Tobin, T. (2011). Race is not neutral: A national investigation of African American and Latino disproportionality in school discipline. *School Psychology Review, 40,* 85–107.

Smith, T. B., Domenech Rodríguez, M., & Bernal, G. (2011). Culture. *Journal of Clinical Psychology, 67,* 166–175. http://dx.doi.org/10.1002/jclp.20757

Suárez-Orozco, C., & Suárez-Orozco, M. M. (2001). *Children of immigration.* Cambridge, MA: Harvard University Press.

U.S. Department of Health and Human Services. (2001). *Mental health: Culture, race, and ethnicity.* Retrieved from http://www.ncbi.nlm.nih.gov/books/NBK44243/pdf/TOC.pdf

Vygotsky, L. S. (1962). *Thought and language.* Cambridge, MA: MIT Press. http://dx.doi.org/10.1037/11193-000

Wood, J. J., Chiu, A. W., Hwang, W.-C., Jacobs, J., & Ifekwunigwe, M. (2008). Adapting cognitive–behavioral therapy for Mexican American students with anxiety disorders: Recommendations for school psychologists. *School Psychology Quarterly, 23,* 515–532. http://dx.doi.org/10.1037/1045-3830.23.4.515

Zins, J. E., Weissberg, R. P., Wang, M. C., & Walberg, H. J. (2004). *Building academic success on social and emotional learning: What does the research say?* New York, NY: Teachers College Press.

11

CONSULTATION-BASED INTERVENTION SERVICES FOR RACIAL MINORITY STUDENTS

MARKEDA NEWELL

For decades, researchers and practitioners in the field of school psychology and other education-related fields have used various approaches to serving racial minority students to improve their academic, behavioral, social–emotional, and mental health outcomes. Nevertheless, these gaps in performance outcomes persist, which beg the question, why have researchers and practitioners in school psychology been unable to reduce or eliminate racial gaps in education? The reason, in large part, might lie in how school psychology researchers and practitioners have approached service delivery with minority students.

There has been a longstanding, seemingly intractable gap in academic performance between racial minority students (i.e., Black, Hispanic, and Native American) and White students (Kena et al., 2014). In addition to the achievement gap, Black, Hispanic, and Native American students also have been and continue to be overrepresented in specific special education

http://dx.doi.org/10.1037/14855-012
Psychoeducational Assessment and Intervention for Ethnic Minority Children: Evidence-Based Approaches,
S. L. Graves, Jr., and J. J. Blake (Editors)

categories (U.S. Department of Education, 2014). Overrepresentation is a concern because these students may be inappropriately placed in special education, thereby limiting their academic and postsecondary education outcomes. In addition, a significant number of Black, Hispanic, and Native American students may not be receiving the school-based services they need (Waitoller, Artiles, & Cheney, 2010).

School consultation is a process of providing psychological and educational services in which a specialist (consultant) works cooperatively with a staff member (consultee) to improve the learning and adjustment of a student (client) or group of students (Erchul & Sheridan, 2014). For the purpose of this review, the consultant is a school psychology student or practitioner who consults with a classroom teacher. In some cases (i.e., conjoint consultation), the consultant is also consulting with a caregiver in addition to the teacher.

Research has shown that consultation can effectively improve academic, behavioral, and social–emotional outcomes while also reducing referrals for special education evaluations (see Erchul & Sheridan, 2014, for a review). However, school psychologists spend more of their time engaged in assessment and less of their time consulting (Castillo, Curtis, Chappel, & Cunningham, 2011). Therefore, one of the primary reasons school psychologists may not be effectively reducing racial or ethnic gaps in achievement is that the one service that has been empirically shown to improve performance and reduce referrals is not being used very often by practitioners. The problem is not only that consultation is a promising, yet underutilized service, but also that the quality of the evidence base on the effectiveness of consultation with racial minority students is unknown. Understanding the evidence base of consultation research with racial minority students is important because the types of approaches or strategies that are optimal for improving outcomes among ethnically diverse students are unknown. For this reason, researchers have embarked on developing and testing multicultural models of consultation and related strategies (Ingraham, 2014; Newell, 2012; Newell, Newell, & Looser, 2013). The purpose of this line of multicultural research is to ensure that school psychologists have the knowledge, attitude, and skills to understand cultural differences, view differences not as deficiencies, and use these differences to maximize the effectiveness of the consultation process as well as the interventions that are implemented. With that being said, the overall goal of multicultural models of consultation is to understand how to best provide consultation to racial minority students. Therefore, the purpose of this chapter is twofold: (a) to review the evidence-base on consultation with racial minority students and (b) to explain methods and approaches for conducting high-quality consultation research with racial minority students.

EVIDENCE BASE ON CONSULTATION WITH RACIAL MINORITY STUDENTS

The results of several meta-analyses spanning 3 decades have shown that consultation is an effective approach to improving student performance (Batts, 1988; Jackson, 1986; Medway & Updyke, 1985; Reddy, Barboza-Whitehead, Files, & Rubel, 2000; Sibley, 1986). Across all of these meta-analyses, the average effect sizes for client outcomes ranged from .39 to 1.30. Although this is a rather large range, all of the effects are in the positive direction indicating that consultation is effective in improving client outcomes and does no harm. However, none of the meta-analyses to date have included data on the effectiveness of consultation with racial minority students. The one exception is a meta-analysis conducted by Reddy and colleagues (2000). Reddy et al. were the only authors to mention the lack of reporting on sample demographics in their review of consultation outcome research. In fact, of the 35 studies included in their review only 10 reported the race or ethnic background of the students targeted for consultations. Schulte, Murr, Tunstall, and Mudholkar (2014) explained that demographic data is woefully underreported in consultation research, which poses significant challenges to establishing the efficacy of consultation with diverse populations. Therein lies a major concern for use of consultation with racial minority students. Specifically, it is unknown whether current consultation models are effective with racial minority students or whether one consultation model is more effective than another with racial minority students. More important, it is unclear how the race of the client (as well as consultees and consultants) could influence the consultation process. Given these concerns coupled with the strong potential of consultation to significantly impact outcomes for racial minority students, it is important to review the existing evidence-base to identify school-based consultation research with racial minority students.

To identify school-based consultation research studies with racial minority students, a search framework had to be created. For this chapter, we searched the PsycINFO database using various combinations of the following terms: *school, consultation, race, minority, multicultural, diverse, culture,* and *ethnic* to identify studies that met the following criteria: (a) implementation of a school-based consultation model (consultation had to be the primary method of developing and delivering the intervention), (b) reporting of intervention outcomes for students, and (c) inclusion of racial minorities in the client sample. In addition to searching PsycINFO, studies from the previously mentioned meta-analysis were also searched. If the study was not school-based, did not report client intervention outcomes, or did not report race of students in the sample, it is not included in this review. It is important to note that there are several high-quality qualitative studies examining consultation with racial minority students; however, given space limitations, only the quantitative outcome studies are included in this review. After an exhaustive search, a total of 11 studies met all criteria for this review.

Across the 11 studies, one of four consultation models was used. To explain, three studies used a conjoint behavioral consultation model, three used an instructional consultation (IC) team-based model, three studies used a behavioral or problem-solving consultation model, and two studies used a multicultural or social justice model.

Behavioral Consultation

Behavioral consultation is the most researched form of school-based consultation, and the evidence indicates that it is the most effective form of school-based research (see Martens, Reed, & Magnuson, 2014). Although the consultation literature is replete with behavioral consultation research, only two outcome studies reported including racial minority students in the sample. In the first study, Schulte, Osborne, and McKinney (1990) examined the effectiveness of consultation on academic outcomes among students with learning disabilities. Students were randomly assigned to one of four treatment conditions: one period of resource room per day, two periods of resource room per day, consultation with classroom teacher and direct instruction with client, and consultation with classroom teacher only. A total of 67 students were assigned to one of these conditions, and 11 of these 67 students were identified as Black. The results indicated that the students who received consultation with direct instruction had significantly higher overall academic gains compared with the students who received one resource room period per day. No other comparisons were significant. However, given the small number of Black students in the sample, it was not possible to conduct any analysis with the racial minority students in the sample. Therefore, it is unclear whether this effect was the same for the racial minority students in the sample.

Dunson, Hughes, and Jackson (1994) also examined the effectiveness of behavioral consultation; however, they looked at behavioral outcomes instead of academic outcomes. Specifically, Dunson and colleagues examined whether behavioral consultation could be used to reduce attention-deficit/hyperactivity disorder (ADHD)-type symptoms among kindergarten–fifth-grade students. In this study, 20 classroom teachers were randomly assigned to the behavioral consultation condition or no-treatment condition. To participate in the study, the teachers had to have a student with significant ADHD-type behaviors in his or her classroom. Approximately 60% of the students were White, 15% were African American, and 25% were Hispanic. The results indicated that the students in the behavioral consultation condition had significantly lower ADHD-type behaviors compared with the control group by the end of treatment. However, it is difficult to say whether these findings are reflective of the racial minority students in the sample because there was no specific analysis of the intervention effects with these students. On the basis of the results of these three studies, behavioral consultation is a promising practice with racial minority students; however, the lack of analysis with racial minority students makes it difficult to draw conclusions about the exact effective upon racial minority students.

Conjoint Behavioral Consultation

According to Sheridan and Kratochwill (1992), *conjoint behavioral consultation* (CBC) is "a structured, indirect form of service delivery, in which parents and teachers are joined to work together to address the academic, social, or behavioral needs of an individual for who both parties bear some responsibility" (p. 122). Therefore, CBC involves the home and school environments working together to address the needs of students. Just like behavioral consultation, there is a rather extensive evidence of research demonstrating the effectiveness of CBC for a range of outcomes. According to Sheridan, Clarke, and Ransom (2014), a total of 21 outcome studies of CBC were conducted between 1990 and 2013. However, only three studies of CBC were identified that reported the race of the students in the sample, and two of those studies are dissertations.

Both dissertations examined the effectiveness of CBC with racial minority students for externalizing behavior problems. To explain, Cagle (2003) examined CBC with four Hispanic students who were all in HeadStart. A single-participant AB design was used to analyze whether the consultative interventions effectively improved client's social skills and reduced problem behaviors. Although the data indicated that parents and teachers were satisfied with the CBC process, the client outcomes were mixed across the home and school environments. For example, only one client evidenced significant improvements in social skills at home and school, but the remaining three students only showed improvement at school. Regarding reductions in the problem behavior, only two students showed significant improvement in home and school. The remaining two students showed improvement at home but not at school because the target behaviors were primarily occurring at home.

Beckman (2009) also examined the effect of CBC with racial minority students, but the Beckman study differed from that of Cagle (2003) in that all students were African American and all consultees were caregivers. Caregivers and teachers reported being satisfied with the CBC process, and all students showed significantly lower parent and teacher Behavior Assessment for Children (2nd ed.; BASC-2; Reynolds & Kamphaus, 2004) scores from pre- to postintervention and significantly lower incidents of behavioral disruptions at home and school.

Sheridan, Eagle, and Doll (2006) examined the effectiveness of CBC with diverse students; however, instead of studying the effect with racial minorities alone, they examined the cumulative effect of diversity. To explain, they organized student outcomes by categories of cumulative diversity (i.e., no diversity factors, one diversity factor, and two or more diversity factors). Factors included, but were not limited to racial minority status, income, maternal education, and English language proficiency. The results indicated that regardless of the number of diversity factors students possessed the consultation interventions were effective, with effect sizes ranging from 1.21 to 1.51. On the basis of the results of these three studies, CBC is a promising form of consultation with racial minority students. However, it is difficult to be conclusive about the effectiveness of CBC with racial minorities because of the small number of studies and small sample sizes.

Instructional Consultation

Instructional consultation (IC) is based on the four-stage consultation process; however, the focus of IC is on using the instructional triangle to develop the most effective interventions to meet the academic and behavioral needs of students in the classroom (Gravois & Rosenfield, 2006). The instructional triangle is the relationship between the instruction, curriculum, and the learner. IC can be delivered via individual consultee-centered consultation or a team-based format. Individual consultee-centered consultation occurs when the school psychologist uses the IC approach with the classroom teacher to address the concerns of a student. Team-based IC includes a school-based team that works with a classroom teacher to address a student concern. Both formats are represented in this review. Fuchs, Fuchs, Hamlett, and Ferguson (1992) used individual IC to examine reading performance. Specifically, Fuchs and colleagues assigned 33 special education teachers (i.e., consultees) to one of three conditions: (a) curriculum-based measurement (CBM) with expert IC, (b) CBM without consultation, and (c) no CBM or consultation. Each consultee had two students. There were a total of 63 students (3 dropped out) across Grades 2 through 8. Approximately 19 of the students were of a racial minority. The results indicated that students in the CBM groups outperformed the control groups; students in the CBM with expert IC outperformed the other two groups in tasks requiring written recalls.

Gravois and Rosenfield (2006) and McDonough (2010) used IC teams in their outcome studies. The primary difference is that when using IC teams, the delivery format is via an interdisciplinary team instead of a single professional.

In these two studies, the researchers examined the impact of the use of IC teams on special education referrals and placement. Gravois and Rosenfield (2006) found that 2 years after implementing IC teams in 13 schools, racial minority students were significantly less likely to be referred to or placed in special education compared with students in the nine schools that were not using IC. They also found that the composition index was significantly lower for racial minority students in IC schools compared with those in the non-IC schools. McDonough did not compare the use of IC teams between schools, instead, she compared IC teams with traditional student assistance teams that were being used within the same school. The results showed that racial minority students had a lower risk of being placed in special education in the IC teams as compared with those in the traditional student assistance teams.

The IC consultation teams provide the most direct assessment of the impact of consultation on racial minority students' outcomes because they examine the direct effect on racial minority students. Therefore, IC consultation teams as well as CBC show the most promising evidence as being an effective consultation approach with minority students. However, to be conclusive, much more research is needed.

Multicultural/Social Justice Consultation

Multicultural consultation research and related approaches, such as social justice consultation, are in their infancy. According to Tarver Behring and Ingraham (1998), *multicultural consultation* is "a culturally-sensitive, indirect service in which the consultant adjusts the consultation service to address the needs and cultural values of the consultee, the client, or both" (p. 58). Clearly, multicultural consultation is not a specific set of strategies, rather it is a process of learning about the self, the consultee, and the student to maximize the effectiveness of the consultation process. *Social justice consultation* extends the responsibility of the consultant from within the consultation triad to the larger school and social context. Shriberg and Fenning (2009) explained that school consultants who practice within a social justice framework should

> . . . strive to find areas of common ground among people and to iden-
> tify and support that which makes us different. School consultants do
> this toward the end of finding just solutions to challenging problems and
> opportunities facing individuals and schools, with particular attention to
> students and families who have been disenfranchised through larger sys-
> temic and institutional biases and barriers. School consultants will strive
> to bring their training, experiences, and talents to bear toward actively

resisting the status quo in schools and institutions when these actions result in the perpetuation of injustice. School consultants strive to support justice and to resist injustice and they seek to do this in collaborative partnership with students, families, school personnel, community members, and the larger social institutions that perpetuate bias. (pp. 4–5)

Multicultural and social justice approaches to consultation explicitly compel the consultant to analyze the cultural and social contextual factors that can include the consultation process and outcomes, and these factors are not as expressed mentioned in traditional consultation models (e.g., behavioral, problem-solving, instructional). Unlike the other models reviewed, there is not extensive evidence on these consultation approaches in school-based settings; however, there is a strong theoretical basis for advancing this line of research (Ingraham, 2014). The literature on these models is reflective of the infancy of this line of research in that many of the articles on multicultural consultation and social justice approaches to consultation are conceptual or qualitative; therefore, they do not provide direct evidence of the effectiveness of these approaches in improving client outcomes. However, two studies provide some emerging evidence on the potential of these approaches. Ingraham (2003) conducted a qualitative analysis of multicultural consultation with three novice consultants who were working with culturally different consultees and students. Although the purpose of Ingraham's study was to examine how novice consultants used multicultural consultation to address cultural hypotheses, she did anecdotally report client outcomes. Specifically, she reported that all students improved as a result of the multicultural consultation process, especially when consultants could effectively address cultural hypotheses for the target concerns with the consultee. However, more objective client outcome data are needed before strong conclusions about effectiveness can be drawn.

Hazel, Pfaff, Albanes, and Gallagher (2014) studied the effect of consultation using a social justice framework on reducing risk for dropout among ninth-grade students in an urban high school. Hazel and colleagues used the social justice consultation process to work with school staff to identify the level of risk of the incoming ninth-grade cohort on the basis of their performance in eighth grade. On categorizing students on the basis of risk for school dropout, Hazel and colleagues worked with school professionals to implement interventions to reduce students' risk for dropping out. The results of this analysis indicated that 76% of the students entered ninth grade with an intermediate level of risk (two to three risk factors present); by the end of the fall semester, only 29% of students fell into this category. However, not all of the students demonstrated lower risk; in fact, the risk for some students increased by the end of the fall semester. That is, only 5% of students entered ninth grade with four risk factors (i.e., the highest level of risk); by the end of the fall semester, 35% of students fell into this category. Therefore, many of the students who were at intermediate risk moved to the highest risk category, whereas the number of students in the lowest risk group increased from 16% to 36% by the end of the fall semester. The ninth-grade cohort sample was racially diverse, so the exact impact on racial minority students is unclear. More research is needed to draw conclusions.

SUMMARY OF THE EVIDENCE BASE

A total of 11 consultation studies met the criteria to be included in this review. In all 11 studies, consultation significantly improved client outcomes. These demonstrate the potential of consultation to improve academic, behavioral, and social–emotional difficulties as well as special education referral and placement rates among racial minorities across several grade levels. The most commonly used consultation approaches were behavioral consultation, CBC, and IC. Most of the authors from these studies did not make modifications to the behavioral, conjoint, or IC processes to serve racial minority students. Cagle (2003) and Beckman (2009) noted that they made modifications such as making phone calls home to maintain contact and engagement with the parent or caregiver during conjoint consultation process. However, the structure of the consultation process remained intact. There were only two articles on multicultural or social justice approaches to consultation; however, this is to be expected given that these consultation approaches are still relatively new to the field.

Given that all of these studies included racial minorities in the sample, there is promising evidence that consultation can be effective with racial minority students. However, because of the limitations of the current evidence the effectiveness of consultation for improving academic and behavioral outcomes for racial minority students is not conclusive.

First, the limited number of studies is a fundamental problem with the current evidence-base. Noltemeyer, Proctor, and Dempsey (2013) conducted a content analysis of the three major journals in school psychology (i.e., *Journal of School Psychology*, *School Psychology Review*, and *School Psychology Quarterly*) and found that only 9.2% of the articles published in these journals between 2008–2010 focused on racial or ethnic diversity. Moreover, Albers, Hoffman, and Lundahl (2009) found that only 6.5% of articles published in school psychology journals focused on English Language Learners, whereas Brown, Shriberg, and Wang (2007) found that only 16.9% of articles published in school psychology focused on any form of diversity. Furthermore, consultation has garnered the least amount of attention in school psychology literature, representing only 8.7% of literature published between the years 2000 and 2003 (Brown et al., 2007). Given the limited research on consultation in school psychology, there is a significant dearth of research on consultation with racial minorities. The limited research has significant implications because consultation is a prevention-based strategy that has the potential to address major concerns regarding racial minority students, who are low in academic performance and referral to or placement in special education. The potential benefits of consultation provide a strong impetus for school psychology researchers and practitioners to prioritize this line of research. That notwithstanding, in addition to the limited evidence base itself, there are also concerns about how extant research has been conducted with racial minorities.

To explain, the lack of focused analysis on the impact of consultation on outcomes among racial minority students is a serious flaw in the current evidence base. In the evidence-based intervention movement, there have been numerous calls for more racially diverse samples (Bernal & Domenech Rodríguez, 2012; Ingraham & Oka, 2006). As Ingraham and Oka (2006) explained, we are not saying that evidence-based interventions will not work with minority populations; the point is that we do not know if they will work, thus they must be tested. However, simply including racial minority students in the sample is not sufficient; researchers must ensure that they are appropriately conducting research with racial minorities to produce valid and reliable results.

According to the American Psychological Association (2003) *Guidelines on Multicultural Education, Training, Research, Practice, and Organizational Change for Psychologists*, researchers in psychology ignored race as a variable of interest, which is in large part because of the belief, historically, that research with White males generalized to all populations. However, as that view was increasingly challenged, researchers included racial minorities in research samples, though significant concerns remain.

Often, when researchers have a racially diverse sample, they will statistically control for race, which essentially conceptualizes race as a nuisance variable or problem (APA, 2003). When race is a control variable, researchers are not able to see the effects of this variable on the outcomes; therefore, it is unclear what impact, if any, race has on the outcomes (e.g., whether outcomes differed by race). In addition to treating race as a nuisance variable, researchers also do not acknowledge within-group diversity in their research designs, analyses, and interpretations (APA, 2003). As a result, results are generalized to all Black students or all Asian students, which is problematic because Black students from different socioeconomic statuses, geographical locations, or religious backgrounds can differ significantly. The lack of addressing within-group diversity is compounded by the fact that researchers also frequently use samples of convenience, which means the results likely will not be reflective of the target population of interest (APA, 2003).

Beyond these limitations, researchers also lack a clearly articulated theoretical basis for how they are approaching their research with racial minorities. Helms, Jernigan, and Mascher (2005) explained that the use of racial categories (e.g., Black, White, Native American, Asian) in psychology is inappropriate because there is no consensus about the meaning of the concept of race; that is, different theorists have different definitions of race (e.g., biological theories, social theories). Therefore, "equating race with racial categories gives scientific legitimacy to the conceptually meaningless construct of race, thereby perpetuating racial stereotypes and associated problems in society" (Helms, Jernigan, & Mascher, 2005, p. 27). Hence, "racial categories should not be used to explain psychological phenomenon because the categories have no conceptual meaning" (p. 30). As a result, decades of research in psychology communicate race-based differences in performance and mental health without a clear conceptual or theoretical rationale for why these differences exist and what they mean. Helms and colleagues did not argue that race does not matter; instead, they asserted that psychologists must be much more theoretically and conceptually-driven in their endeavor to understand the relationship between race and various outcomes.

For these reasons, researchers and practitioners must first ask, "What is the relationship between the student's race and their performance?" And second, "Why is race a central variable in understanding the effect of consultation outcomes?"

CONCLUSION

There is a paucity of consultation research with racial minorities. Although existing studies show promising results, we argue that the evidence is not conclusive because of the limited number of studies and the lack of adherence to guidelines on how to conduct research with racial minorities. Therefore, more research is needed; however, the quality of the research must also be considered, such as studies with racially diverse populations, studies that analyze the impact of consultation on specific racial groups, and studies with a clearly articulated theoretical model for understanding racial and ethnic differences in achievement and behavioral outcomes. Most important, "psychologists are encouraged to consider the multidimensionality of ethnic, linguistic, and racial minority individuals and groups when planning research" (APA, 2003, p. 389), such as racial identity, ethnic identity, socioeconomic status, and geographic location. For more information on how to conduct appropriate research with minority populations, the readers are referred to APA's (2003) *Guidelines* and the Council of National Psychological Associations for the Advancement of Ethnic Minority Interests' *Guidelines* (2000).

In sum, consultation is a promising practice that has the potential to significantly improve outcomes for racial minority students. For this reason, it is imperative that more research is conducted to better understand how effective current models are, what modifications or adaptations might be necessary, and to create new models to actualize the promise of consultation with racial minority students.

REFERENCES

Albers, C. A., Hoffman, A. J., & Lundahl, A. A. (2009). Journal coverage of issues related to English language learners across student-service professions. *School Psychology Review, 38*, 121–134.

American Psychological Association. (2003). Guidelines on multicultural education, training, research, practice, and organizational change for Psychologists. *American Psychologist, 58*, 377–402.

Batts, J. W. (1988). The effects of teacher consultation: A meta-analysis of controlled studies. *Dissertation Abstracts International, 49*, 1404.

Beckman, T. (2009). Treatment integrity and child outcomes: Conjoint behavioral consultation in an urban setting with clients of ethnic minority status. *Dissertation Abstracts International: Section B: The Sciences and Engineering, 69*, 7796.

Bernal, G., & Domenech Rodríguez, M. M. (Eds.). (2012). *Cultural adaptations: Tools for evidence-based practice with diverse populations.* Washington, DC: American Psychological Association. http://dx.doi.org/10.1037/13752-000

Brown, S. L., Shriberg, D., & Wang, A. (2007). Diversity research literature on the rise? A review of school psychology journals from 2000 to 2003. *Psychology in the Schools, 44*, 639–650. http://dx.doi.org/10.1002/pits.20253

Cagle, M. (2003). Conjoint behavioral consultation with parents and teachers of Hispanic children: A study of acceptability, integrity, and effectiveness. *Dissertation Abstracts International: Section A: Humanities and Social Sciences, 64*, 394.

Castillo, J. M., Curtis, M. J., Chappel, A., & Cunningham, J. (2011, February). *School psychology 2010: Results of the national membership study.* Special session conducted at the National Association of School Psychologists Annual Convention, San Francisco, CA.

Council of National Psychological Associations for the Advancement of Ethnic Minority Interests. (2000). *Guidelines for research in ethnic minority communities.* Washington, DC: American Psychological Association.

Dunson, R. M., III, Hughes, J. N., & Jackson, T. W. (1994). Effect of behavioral consultation on student and teacher behavior. *Journal of School Psychology, 32*, 247–266. http://dx.doi.org/10.1016/0022-4405(94)90017-5

Erchul, W., & Sheridan, S. (Eds.). (2014). *Handbook of research in school consultation* (2nd ed.). New York, NY: Routledge.

Fuchs, L. S., Fuchs, D., Hamlett, C. L., & Ferguson, C. (1992). Effects of expert system consultation within curriculum-based measurement, using a reading maze task. *Exceptional Children, 58*, 436–450.

Gravois, T. A., & Rosenfield, S. A. (2006). Impact of instructional consultation teams on the disproportionate referral and placement of minority students in special education. *Remedial and Special Education, 27*, 42–52. http://dx.doi.org/10.1177/07419325060270010501

Hazel, C. E., Pfaff, K., Albanes, J., & Gallagher, J. (2014). Multi-level consultation with an urban school district to promote 9th grade supports for on-time graduation. *Psychology in the Schools, 51*, 395–420. http://dx.doi.org/10.1002/pits.21752

Helms, J. E., Jernigan, M., & Mascher, J. (2005). The meaning of race in psychology and how to change it: A methodological perspective. *American Psychologist, 60*, 27–36. http://dx.doi.org/10.1037/0003-066X.60.1.27

Ingraham, C. L. (2003). Multicultural consultee-centered consultation: When novice consultants explore cultural hypotheses with experienced teacher consultees. *Journal of Educational & Psychological Consultation, 14*(3–4), 329–362. http://dx.doi.org/10.1080/10474412.2003.9669492

Ingraham, C. L. (2014). Studying multicultural aspects of consultation. In W. P. Erchul & S. M. Sheridan (Eds.), *Handbook of research in school consultation* (2nd ed., pp. 33–348). New York, NY: Routledge. http://dx.doi.org/10.4324/9780203133170.ch13

Ingraham, C. L., & Oka, E. R. (2006). Multicultural issues in evidence-based interventions. *Journal of Applied School Psychology, 22*, 127–149. http://dx.doi.org/10.1300/J370v22n02_07

Jackson, E. P. (1986, December). A meta-analysis of school-based consultation outcome research. *Dissertation Abstracts International: Section A: Humanities and Social Sciences, 17*, 1087.

Kena, G., Aud, S., Johnson, F., Wang, X., Zhang, J., Rathbun, A., . . . Kristapovich, P. (2014). *The condition of education 2014* (NCES 2014-083). Washington, DC: U.S. Department of Education, National Center for Education Statistics. Retrieved from http://nces.ed.gov/pubsearch

Martens, B., Reed, F., & Magnuson, J. (2014). Behavioral consultation: Contemporary research and emerging challenges. In W. Erchul & S. Sheridan (Eds.), *Handbook of research in school consultation* (pp. 180–209). New York, NY: Routledge.

McDonough, E. (2010). An examination of differences between instructional consultation teams and traditional student assistance teams in evaluation and identification of minority students for special education. *Dissertation Abstracts International: Section A: Humanities and Social Sciences, 70*, 2460.

Medway, F. J., & Updyke, J. F. (1985). Meta-analysis of consultation outcome studies. *American Journal of Community Psychology, 13,* 489–505. http://dx.doi.org/10.1007/BF00923263

Newell, M. L. (2012). Transforming knowledge to skills: Evaluating the consultation competence of novice school-based consultants. *The Consulting Psychology Journal: Research and Practice, 64,* 8–28. http://dx.doi.org/10.1037/a0027741

Newell, M. L., Newell, T. S., & Looser, J. A. (2013). Examining how novice consultants address cultural factors during consultation: Illustration of a computer-simulated case-study method. *Consulting Psychology Journal: Practice and Research, 65,* 74–86. http://dx.doi.org/10.1037/a0032598

Noltemeyer, A. L., Proctor, S. L., & Dempsey, A. (2013). Race and ethnicity in school psychology publications: A content analysis and comparison to publications in related disciplines. *Contemporary School Psychology, 17,* 129–142.

Reddy, L. A., Barboza-Whitehead, S., Files, T., & Rubel, E. (2000). Clinical focus of consultation outcome research with children and adolescents. *Special Services in the Schools, 16*(1–2), 1–22. http://dx.doi.org/10.1300/J008v16n01_01

Reynolds, C. R., & Kamphaus, R. W. (2004). *Behavior assessment system for children* (2nd ed.). Old Tappan, NJ: Pearson.

Schulte, A. C., Murr, N., Tunstall, K., & Mudholkar, P. (2014). Measurement in school consultation research. In W. Erchul & S. Sheridan (Eds.), *Handbook of research in school consultation* (2nd ed., pp. 43–78). New York, NY: Routledge.

Schulte, A. C., Osborne, S. S., & McKinney, J. D. (1990). Academic outcomes for students with learning disabilities in consultation and resource programs. *Exceptional Children, 57,* 162–172.

Sheridan, S. M., Clarke, B. L., & Ransom, K. A. (2014). Bringing instructional consultation to scale: Research and development of IC and IC teams. In W. Erchul & S. Sheridan (Eds.), *Handbook of research in school consultation* (pp. 210–247). New York, NY: Routledge.

Sheridan, S. M., Eagle, J. W., & Doll, B. (2006). An examination of the efficacy of conjoint behavioral consultation with diverse clients. *School Psychology Quarterly, 21,* 396–417. http://dx.doi.org/10.1037/h0084130

Sheridan, S. M., & Kratochwill, T. R. (1992). Behavioral parent–teacher consultation: Conceptual and research considerations. *Journal of School Psychology, 30,* 117–139. http://dx.doi.org/10.1016/0022-4405(92)90025-Z

Shriberg, D., & Fenning, P. A. (2009). School consultants as agents of social justice: Implications for practice: Introduction to the special issue. *Journal of Educational & Psychological Consultation, 19,* 1–7. http://dx.doi.org/10.1080/10474410802462751

Sibley, S. L. (1986, November). A meta-analysis of school consultation research. *Dissertation Abstracts International, 47,* 2145.

Tarver Behring, S., & Ingraham, C. L. (1998). Culture as a central component of consultation: A call to the field. *Journal of Educational & Psychological Consultation*, 9, 57–72. http://dx.doi.org/10.1207/s1532768xjepc0901_3

U.S. Department of Education. (2014). *35th annual report to Congress on the implementation of the Individuals with Disabilities Education Act, 2013.* Washington, DC: Author.

Waitoller, F., Artiles, A. J., & Cheney, D. (2010). The miner's canary: A review of overrepresentation research and explanations. *The Journal of Special Education*, 44, 29–49. http://dx.doi.org/10.1177/0022466908329226

12

IMPLEMENTING COMMUNITY-BASED RESEARCH AND PREVENTION PROGRAMS TO DECREASE HEALTH DISPARITIES

TIFFANY G. TOWNSEND AND STEPHANIE HARGROVE

There has long been a concern regarding health inequities among people of color in the United States, particularly African Americans (Heckler, 1985). Epidemiological studies continue to demonstrate that African Americans across the lifespan suffer much higher disease and death rates than do other ethnic groups in this country (Kawachi, Daniels, & Robinson, 2005). In fact, scholars and researchers dating as far back as W. E. B. Du Bois (2003) have commented on the poorer health status of African Americans compared with their White counterparts, providing a literal translation for the old adage, "When America catches a cold, African Americans catch pneumonia." A comprehensive analysis of health disparities in America requires a full examination of the social structure in which these disparities emerge, although the adverse influence of racism is frequently cited as a primary contributor to health inequities in the United States (Williams & Williams-Morris, 2000). Intersectionality theorists posit that the life experiences of people of color are shaped by the

http://dx.doi.org/10.1037/14855-013
Psychoeducational Assessment and Intervention for Ethnic Minority Children: Evidence-Based Approaches,
S. L. Graves, Jr., and J. J. Blake (Editors)

213

intersection of multiple systems of oppression. These systems are organized along axes of race, class, gender, sexuality, ethnicity, nation, and age (Collins, 1998, 2000), and it is the interplay of these systems that creates the unique life experiences that contribute to health inequities and ultimately poorer health among African Americans (Jackson, Knight, & Rafferty, 2010).

This chapter explores health vulnerabilities that are faced by African American girls. Using a framework of intersectionality, we examine the social structure and context in which health disparities emerge among this population. In addition, we offer a conceptual model that considers contextual factors that researchers may find helpful in guiding intervention development efforts with this population. Community collaborative approaches to research and intervention development are also discussed, as community knowledge and input work to enhance the cultural specificity and ultimately the efficacy of theory-based models and interventions. Later in the chapter, we present a detailed analysis of our community-based work to illustrate the way in which community collaboration can inform the development of culturally specific intervention strategies. It is hoped that this analysis can serve as a model for understanding and addressing health inequities among other populations of color.

HEALTH DISPARITIES AMONG AFRICAN AMERICAN GIRLS

Because of their race, gender, and age, African American girls are members of three subjugated groups and are particularly vulnerable to several health disparities. Epidemiological studies of mental health outcomes among adolescents consistently point to a higher prevalence of depression, eating disorders, and other depressive symptomatology (i.e., suicidal ideation and suicide attempts) among adolescent girls when compared with their male counterparts (Afifi, 2007). This gender-based disparity seems to emerge and widen with age. According to Prinstein, Borelli, Cheah, Simon, and Aikins (2005), the prevalence of depression is fairly consistent across gender in childhood. However, depressive symptoms among girls begin to increase during preadolescence, and by late adolescence girls are twice as likely to experience depression than are boys of the same age. In addition, adolescent girls are two to three times more likely to develop posttraumatic stress disorder (PTSD) than are their male counterparts, and their symptoms are more likely to persist following a traumatic event (Afifi, 2007). This is particularly significant for African American adolescent girls who have been found to experience high rates of interpersonal violence, trauma, and sexual abuse. According to the Centers for Disease Control and Prevention (CDC, 2006b), African American adolescent girls report higher rates of involuntary first intercourse than do European American and Latina girls. Similarly, Teitelman, Tennille, Bohinski, Jemmott, and Jemmott (2011) found that 59% of African American girls ages 14 through 17 reported having experienced some form of sexual abuse in their lives. This abuse included threats, verbal coercion, condom coercion, and physical violence.

In the physical health domain, increased risks in sexual and nutritional health have given rise to two major epidemics among this population. For instance, in 2004 African American adolescent girls ages 10 to 14 and 15 to 19 were more likely to be infected with chlamydia and gonorrhea than were their White counterparts (CDC, 2005). In 2009, African American adolescents accounted for 65% of newly diagnosed cases of HIV infection among the 13-to-24 age group (CDC, 2011), whereas African American adolescent girls and young women ages 15 to 24 accounted for 70% of the HIV diagnoses among girls and women in this age group (CDC, 2006a). The new face of HIV is young, Black, and female.

Similarly, obesity is alarmingly high among African American girls. The prevalence rates of obesity have more than doubled among girls in the United States in the last 40 years, with the greatest increase seen among girls of African descent (Kimm et al., 2002). In a study on the decline of physical activity in adolescent girls, Kimm and colleagues (2002) found that Black girls had a significantly higher body-mass index than did their White counterparts. The increase in obesity and overweight status among African American girls is a significant concern (Eisenmann, Wickel, Welk, & Blair, 2005; O'Connor, Yang, & Nicklas, 2006), particularly because of its association with an increased incidence of Type II diabetes in children (CDC, 2009). Childhood obesity is a predictor of adult disease and chronic illnesses, such as high blood pressure, diabetes, and cardiovascular disease. Clearly obesity, like HIV, poses a significant health risk for African American girls.

INSTITUTIONAL OPPRESSION AND HEALTH DISPARITIES AMONG AFRICAN AMERICAN GIRLS

Modifiable behaviors, such as risky sexual practices, poor eating habits and limited physical activity contribute to many of these health concerns (Kimm et al., 2002; Naylor & McKay, 2008; Townsend et al., 2006). However, it would be inaccurate to assert that African American girls are solely responsible for their health vulnerabilities. Instead, it is the complex interaction of contextual forces and modifiable lifestyle factors that contribute to their poorer health status. According to Jackson et al. (2010), unhealthy behaviors that contribute to health disparities often develop among African Americans as a strategy to cope with the by-products of institutional oppression (i.e., chronic stress and psychological distress). Other scholars suggest that oppressive systems create situations that limit opportunities and resources, which may encourage certain unhealthy choices. In the case of obesity, the inaccessibility of quality grocery stores or supermarkets in some African American communities; the high cost of fresh fruit, vegetables, and lean cuts of meat; and the greater availably of packaged or processed foods make the choice of unhealthy comfort foods more likely (Basiotis, Lino, & Anand, 1999; Goyan Kittler, & Sucher, 1989; Popkin, Siega-Riz, & Haines, 1996), particularly among African American girls and women who tend to consume large quantities of comfort foods in response to chronic stress (Jackson et al., 2010).

In some instances, oppressive contextual forces may totally remove free will and unrestricted choice. As previously mentioned, sexual activity among African American girls is frequently forced or coerced. Even when sexual activity may seem consensual, a traumatic history may have influenced that choice. Studies have shown that sexual abuse or trauma in childhood has been associated with interpersonal difficulties (e.g., social isolation or a lack of self-protection) later in life (Miner, Flitter, & Robinson, 2006), limiting a girl's perceived control over sexual decisions and behaviors. It is this environment of coercion and abuse that contributes to the epidemic rates of sexually transmitted infections among this population (Teitelman et al., 2011) and increases the risk of mental health vulnerabilities described above (e.g., chronic stress, PTSD, depression).

MODELS TO GUIDE HEALTH DISPARITIES INTERVENTIONS WITH AFRICAN AMERICAN GIRLS

Several social cognitive models (e.g., health belief model, theory of planned behavior, self-efficacy theory) have been used to examine factors that may be significant in predicting health behaviors (Albarracín, Johnson, Fishbein, & Muellerleile, 2001). Interventions based on these social cognitive models have shown some effectiveness in preventing or reducing health risks among African American adolescents (Barker, Battle, Cummings, & Bankroft, 1998; Jemmott & Jemmott, 1996; Jemmott, Jemmott, & Hacker, 1992; Rotherham-Borus, Gwadz, Fernandez, & Srinivasan, 1998). But many of these models focus exclusively on cognitive components (e.g., social norms, attitudes, perceived behavioral control, behavioral intentions) and fail to address contextual factors specific to African Americans or gender-based vulnerabilities (gender inequities and history of abuse or trauma) that may represent barriers to risk reduction for girls. To effectively address health disparities, developers of interventions that target African American girls need to consider the influence of contextual factors (e.g., ethnicity, socioeconomic factors, social discrimination), and gender-based vulnerabilities (e.g., power imbalance due to gender disparities, relationship maintenance concerns, and history of physical or sexual abuse) on cognitive constructs. For instance, Townsend et al. (2006) found the ability of the theory of planned behavior to predict sexual outcomes among African American adolescents improved when the theory was examined in conjunction with culturally and developmentally relevant components (i.e., cultural values and ethnic identity). It therefore becomes exceedingly important to find an appropriate model that will guide intervention efforts with this population.

On the basis of the literature and the first author's extensive community-based work with African American girls, we offer a model to guide health risk reduction efforts with African American girls. This health risk prevention model, which has been used as the foundation for many of the first author's community-based prevention efforts with African American girls, is grounded in theory from several fields. Feminist perspectives on female development point to the importance of relationships to the healthy development of female identity, and African American mothers have been reported to be crucial to helping black girls negotiate intersecting systems of oppression (e.g., Collins, 2000; Gilligan, 1990; Miller, 1986). Bronfenbrenner's (1986) ecological perspective highlights the different levels of contextual influences on adolescents; those that have indirect or more distal influence, such as the community context and culture; and those that have more direct and proximal influence, such as the family, peers, and school environment. Connell's theory of gender and power (Wingood & DiClemente, 2000) acknowledges the impact of trauma and other gender-based vulnerabilities on girls' ability to perceive control over their health decisions, particularly in the sexual domain. Finally, social cognitive models, such as the theory of planned behavior (Ajzen & Fishbein, 1980), emphasize the significance of social norms, perceptions, and peer influences in predicting health behaviors and health risks.

This health risk prevention model integrates aspects of the theory of planned behavior with Donenberg and Pao's (2004) social–personal framework. Their social–personal framework, which focuses specifically on sexual risks, considers both individual and social factors. Specifically, the model proposes that adolescent risk behaviors are a function of the interplay of adolescent emotional and psychological concerns, family context (the parent–adolescent relationship and parenting styles), personal attributes (e.g., trauma and abuse history, personality characteristics), relationship concerns (teens' feelings about relationships, e.g., need for intimacy, fear of rejection, peer influence), and broader environmental factors (e.g., access to economic resources, social discrimination).

In the health risk prevention model that guides this intervention, a strong identity and an appreciation of culture are the first steps to achieving less risky behaviors. Identity, along with belief-based values and expectations (e.g., cultural values, gender roles, social norms), are aspects of the adolescent's worldview, and her worldview serves as a mediator between intervention efforts and behavioral outcomes. Together, the cognitive constructs that comprise the worldview influence interpersonal interactions, behavioral decisions and ultimately health behavior. Equally as important, the constructs directly affect each other. In other words, the way in which an African American girl views herself is often affected by her value system and her beliefs concerning her expected roles and behaviors. In turn, these values and expectations are influenced by the girl's identity, along with other external factors, such as broader environmental conditions (e.g., culture, community, economic status, social discrimination), personal attributes (e.g., trauma histories and interpersonal difficulties), and family context (e.g., parental relationships, parental communication).

Even though this framework has a sound theoretical basis, it has been the first author's successful collaborations with community partners that helped to translate this theoretical framework into culturally relevant, efficacious interventions. Partnering with communities for research and intervention development ensures that the norms, values, and beliefs of that community are considered, resulting in a deeper appreciation for the unique experience of the population and a better understanding of the ways in which that experience shapes health concerns (Grills, 2003). Thus, integrating community partners into the research process is a promising strategy to develop appropriate models and interventions that address health disparities among adolescents of color.

APPROACHES TO COMMUNITY-BASED RESEARCH TO REDUCE HEALTH RISKS AMONG AFRICAN AMERICAN GIRLS

Research based on collaborative inquiry that purposively and systematically integrates community members into the research process has been identified as an important approach by which to address documented health disparities, particularly among communities of color. These approaches are effective because they use the knowledge of the community to identify relevant sociopolitical or contextual factors that influence the target population, resulting in a culturally tailored intervention (Viswanathan et al., 2004).

Community collaborative approaches such as Community Action Research (CAR) and Community-Based Participatory Research (CBPR) are designed to ensure community involvement and engagement in the research process. Although both CAR and CBPR place importance on a process of research, action, and education, CBPR provides a more radical framework that regards community members as true partners in a mutual process of learning between academic researchers and community members (Minkler, 2000). In this approach, research is done collaboratively with communities, affirming the value of the community's knowledge and cocreation of knowledge by the community and academic researchers (Leung, Yen, & Minkler, 2004). By focusing on social action and mutual ownership of the research process, CBPR empowers communities to take part in ensuring their own health and well-being.

Thus, CBPR provides a process model that, if used appropriately, ensures the involvement of community members and other community stakeholders in all aspects of research and intervention development (Sloane et al., 2003). Established CBPR principles include mutuality and equality among all partners, an open and transparent process, and the development of community informed research and intervention strategies that build on the strengths of all partners (Israel, Schulz, Parker, & Becker, 1998; Seifer & Maurana, 2000). Mutuality and equity serve to foster ownership and empowerment among all partners; and can be established using several strategies which include (a) developing a shared mission among community and academic partners, (b) ensuring shared power through mutual decision making, and (c) fostering capacity building through learning exchanges that capitalize on the strengths of each partner (Coker-Appiah, Davis, & Townsend, 2013). Although these principles appear to have wide acceptance among researchers and have been applied in health research (Wells, Miranda, Bruce, Alegría, & Wallerstein, 2004), putting them into practice can be challenging.

In the following section, the ISIS (Intelligent Sisters Improving them-Selves) Project, an integrated HIV/substance abuse prevention program for African American girls developed and implemented by the first author is discussed and the community engagement process is described in detail. As the community became more involved in the planning and implementation of the ISIS Project, the program become much more tailored to the specific culture of the southwest Philadelphia community in which the project was housed. This likely increased the program's effectiveness. In recounting the community engagement process for the ISIS Project, the goal is to highlight practical strategies that can be used to empower communities of color to take control over their health and the health of their children by becoming active participants in the intervention development and implementation process.

THE ISIS PROJECT: COMMUNITY EMPOWERMENT THROUGH COMMUNITY ENGAGEMENT

The ISIS Project was born out of a partnership between Tiffany G. Townsend and the Philadelphia satellite office of the Progressive Life Center (PLC)—a community-based mental health agency headquartered in Washington DC—that uses a unique Africentric approach in the delivery of therapeutic services and psychoeducational programs. The ISIS Project was administered in all of the middle schools in the southwest Philadelphia community from 2004 to 2008. Initially, it was designed as a 26-week program in which ISIS staff would meet with participating girls for an hour after school on a weekly basis, providing psychoeducational material related to HIV and substance use prevention.

Using the aforementioned theoretical perspectives as a foundation, the ISIS Project was designed by Tiffany G. Townsend to incorporate (a) the social developmental context of pre- and early-adolescence in which there is declining (but not absent) centrality of parents and increasing influence of peers; (b) female gender orientations where there is a value on meaningful and supportive relationships with a significant adult woman and on connections and mutually positive relationships with peers; (c) ecological factors including ethnic beliefs and cultural orientations (i.e., African American identity and Africentric values), as well as other contextual factors that may be present in low resource communities (e.g., limited access to quality health care, high rates of crime and drug use); and (d) social structural factors, such as gender based power inequities in heterosexual relationships that may make it difficult for young girls to exert control over their health decisions, particularly in the sexual domain.

In addition to the content, the structure of the curriculum was designed to be attractive and engaging to this population. Consistent with a relational, Africentric perspective, the feelings of self and others were acknowledged and sensitivity to affect and emotional state were emphasized. All direct line intervention staff were African American women that modeled relational and Africentric orientations in their behavior and interactions with each other and the participants. The program was designed to instill ISIS participants with the skills necessary to enhance identity, promote healthy behavior, and reduce risk. But more than that, it was hoped that the project would empower this population to make fundamental, lifelong changes regarding healthy attitudes and behaviors.

According to Zimmerman (2000), empowerment is the process through which people with limited access to resources gain greater access to and control over those resources. Thus, community outreach and capacity building was a necessary component of the program. For true empowerment, ISIS participants, in particular, and the southwest Philadelphia community, in general, needed to experience a level of ownership of the ISIS Project and the knowledge or information conveyed. Accordingly, a plan of community engagement was developed that was intended to increase community input, involvement, and ultimately buy-in. This constituted the planning phase of the ISIS Project, which spanned the 2003–2004 academic year.

During the initial phases of project planning, it was important to connect with key community members and stakeholders to foster community trust. As a result, the Southwest Action Coalition (SWAC) was contacted. SWAC is 30-member community advisory board and planning group composed of community members, service providers and community activists dedicated to improving the quality of life for residents in the southwest Philadelphia area. After providing the mission and goals of the ISIS Project, the ISIS project director was asked to join SWAC. Forging a relationship with SWAC was an extremely important step to ensure that ISIS's efforts were coordinated with the larger community. It also was a crucial step in obtaining community feedback. Using the connections developed through SWAC, we coordinated a community needs assessment.

The needs assessment included focus groups, workshops, and forums designed to increase the understanding of the problems faced by African American girls in the southwest Philadelphia region. Members of several community organizations based in southwest Philadelphia were in attendance. In addition to providing basic information on girls, the focus groups and forums served as an opportunity for community members and stakeholders to voice their concerns and provide suggestions on working with adolescent girls in the southwest Philadelphia community. To obtain feedback from the target population, a pilot administration was conducted during the spring of 2004. The pilot, which lasted 5 weeks, was used to assess implementation and evaluation adequacy. In addition, the pilot gave the project staff an opportunity to fine-tune implementation techniques and activities. It also provided an opportunity for the target girls to indicate the topics they wanted to see addressed in the full ISIS Project implementation.

Every effort was devoted to ensuring that the feedback received from the community during this planning phase was used to make changes and fine-tune the program. However, it is important to note that at this point, true community ownership of the ISIS Project had not been achieved, primarily because the level of community engagement was limited. To facilitate engagement and community ownership, the community needed to be integrated more substantively into the planning and implementation process. To this end, an ISIS Community Advisory Board (CAB) was created in the beginning of 2005.

In developing the CAB, there was an effort to make sure there were members representing different sectors from the community (i.e., faith-based organizations, law enforcement, the school system, etc.). The plan was to develop a diverse community entity that could provide ongoing feedback concerning the progress of the ISIS Project. However, the lack of a truly collaborative relationship with the community became quite apparent very early on in the process as many of the CAB members questioned the very structure of the CAB. Not only had the community not been fully integrated into the planning process, but the community was not even consulted as to the membership of the CAB. According to CAB members, the Board was "top heavy" (i.e., too many organizational representatives and not enough community members who have a direct stake in the program, such as parents, teachers), and the absence of target girls at the planning table was a major oversight in the composition of the Board. At the urging of our CAB, the ISIS Project began to become much more grounded in the community. The changes that were made to the partnership, the infrastructure and the communication loop pushed the project toward a model in which there was shared decision making and open communication between the community and the project. It was hoped this would facilitate community ownership and ultimately improve project outcomes.

While not the original plan, it became clear that a CBPR approach was warranted to garner the desired project effects. As previously mentioned, when done properly, CBPR lends itself to the development of culturally appropriate intervention methods (Viswanathan et al., 2004). Accordingly, ISIS Project staff re-conceptualized the project based on these principals which helped to guide subsequent program changes.

The first changes instituted were changes to the CAB infrastructure. Based on the strong recommendations of the board, a Girls' Advisory Board (GAB) was added, and the concentration of parents, teachers and community youth service providers on the main CAB was increased. In addition, meetings were held more frequently (from quarterly to monthly) and an email list serve was developed for more efficient communication between meetings. These minor alterations made a noticeable change in the level of CAB participation. By including community members more substantively in the planning and implementation process, an implicit message was communicated that the ISIS Project valued them as integral members of the ISIS team. Members that feel personally validated and respected are more likely to participate in the group, and feel a sense of ownership. These changes moved the ISIS Project closer to true community engagement and collaboration, which prompted more dramatic changes to the project infrastructure. For instance, advisory board members began to be incorporated into program implementation. In fact, a community member from the board was hired to serve as a paid project coordinator. Although it didn't happen immediately, signs of community ownership began to emerge.

For instance, ISIS and the work of the project began to receive media coverage. In March and April of 2005, the first author was asked to speak about African American adolescent girls' development on *Dialogues*, a radio program featured on a local radio station in Philadelphia. In addition, the ISIS Project was featured in the Tribune, a local newspaper in Philadelphia that focuses on African American issues. The emerging community presence of the program prompted other community-based organizations to seek out co-sponsored outreach activities. In 2006, ISIS in partnership with MEE Productions and the Blueprint Project for a Safer Philadelphia hosted a Community Action Team (CAT) workshop. The goal of the workshop was to help young adults learn ways to combat youth risks, particularly youth violence. During that implementation year, many of the ISIS participants were also participants in the CAT workshop. Slowly, ISIS began moving from a narrowly focused after-school program, to a more holistic risk prevention program with broader reach in the community. ISIS was truly becoming tailored to meet the needs of southwest Philadelphia.

Program delivery was also altered as a result of our GAB and CAB. CAB representatives from the school system were instrumental in helping to move ISIS from an after-school program, to an in-school activity. The youth requested more contact with the program, so intervention sessions increased from once a week to twice a week. The 26-session program, changed to a 46-session program. This increase in participant contact could have been cost prohibitive, if the CAB hadn't stepped in. The CAB took the lead in developing the content and administering the program for the second intervention day, which was called the "Culture Day." For several weeks, African American women from the community (many were from the advisory board) served as guest speakers or workshop facilitators. Each workshop covered various topics designed to enhance African American girls' self-image and self-worth (some of the workshop covered topics such as hair care, jewelry making, and quilting). In addition, based on a suggestion from our GAB members, a video project was administered on the "Culture Days" during the spring semesters of the program.

This project consisted of 12 weekly sessions. A video producer from the community met with participants to provide an overview of "what happens behind the making of a video." Participants received a basic understanding of how a video is made from conception to the finish product. Participants also received instructional lessons on how to operate cameras, lights, sound, video dubbing, and editing. The girls then developed a music video that conveyed a positive image or message concerning African American girls and women. The finished product was "premiered" to their family, friends, and broader community at the ISIS Graduation Ceremony, which was held at the end of each ISIS program administration.

As time progressed, the ISIS CAB served less in an advisory capacity, and instead began to function more as a true collaborator. In addition to the changes outlined above, the ISIS CAB began sponsoring its own outreach activities. In 2007, CAB members organized a community forum to raise HIV awareness and they hosted a walk-a-thon entitled "Walk for a Teenage Girl," again, to raise awareness concerning the impact of HIV on African American girls, while also raising money for ISIS program activities. However, it was noticed that the most consistent and enthusiastic board members were parents of ISIS participants. Given the strength and enthusiasm of the parent board members, a Parent Community Council was developed to increase the power and input of the parents. In the final year, much of the advising from the community was provided by the Parent's Council. In fact, at the urging of the Council, parent-led workshops were instituted during the final year to encourage parent participation in the program delivery, and to address topics of concern for interested parents. One workshop even focused on parental stress management techniques. As the parents became more involved in program planning and program implementation, it appeared that community ownership had taken place, a necessary component to ensuring that the program would be maintained even after the project funding had expired.

By the final year, 2007–2008, it was clear that ISIS had completely transformed from a narrowly focused, academically run after-school risk prevention program to a broad reaching program, deeply grounded in the community. Ownership of the program had shifted from the project staff to enthusiastic community members. In fact, other than curriculum administration many of the ISIS sponsored programs during the final year of the project, were initiated by the Parent Community Council. In the summer of 2008, the ISIS project director held a 6 hour training session to teach interested parents, teachers and community members how to administer the ISIS curriculum, on their own and the "passing of the baton" was complete. At last report, some ISIS activities were still administered to girls on a limited basis in a southwest Philadelphia recreation center and one of the CAB members used the principals from ISIS to develop a complementary program for boys, called T.H.E. NUBIANS (Teaching, Healing, Empowering—Never Underestimating Brothers' Intelligence, Ambitions, & Natural Strengths). Although in altered form, ISIS lives on in southwest Philadelphia and this longevity can be credited to the strong involvement of the community.

LESSONS LEARNED FROM THE ISIS PROJECT

The community collaborative process of the ISIS Project was presented as an illustration of the ways in which the knowledge and experience of the community can be successfully incorporated into a theory based intervention model to create a culturally specific intervention program. It is hoped that the information garnered from this process will encourage other scholars to consider engaging community partners into research and intervention development as a means of enhancing intervention specificity and relevance. The collaborative process itself can also be used as an effective community empowerment strategy that encourages communities of color to take an active role in addressing their health vulnerabilities.

As demonstrated in the ISIS Project example, a sound theoretical framework or conceptual model is a necessary starting point for any community-based work. In fact, St. Lawrence et al. (1997) suggested that theory based interventions are more effective and enable sounder evaluation than interventions that are not grounded in theory. However, there needs to be flexibility in the guiding framework to allow community input (e.g., additional constructs to consider, alternative implementation strategies that work better with the target population) to help realize the model. Frequently, it is the input from the community that brings the theoretical constructs to life for the target population. Community involvement seemed to be the key ingredient to the success and eventual effectiveness of the ISIS Project. Analysis of program outcomes over the 4 years of program implementation evidenced modest improvements. However, the most significant results were found in the final year of program implementation once the community became well integrated into the process and the intervention was tailored to the specific southwest Philadelphia community.

Repeated measure analyses of variance were performed to determine between and within group changes from pre- to posttest. Analysis of the final cohort revealed a significant interaction between pre/posttest differences in self-esteem and the group variable, $F(1, 96) = 5.60$, $p < .05$, such that increases in self-esteem from pre- to posttest were more significant among those girls in the ISIS Project than among girls in the comparison group. In fact, self-esteem decreased among girls in the comparison group, whereas there was an increase in self-esteem among the ISIS Project girls. On the basis of the first author's health risk prevention model, identity enhancement represents the first most proximal step in fostering the necessary skills in girls to resist health risks. Accordingly, ISIS Project participants endorsed significantly higher levels of risk perception from pre- to posttest, $F(1, 91) = 7.31$, $p < .01$, and this difference was higher than the increase found among comparison group participants. In other words, girls who participated in the ISIS program were more likely to perceive certain sexual and substance use behaviors as risky (i.e., intercourse without a condom, smoking marijuana, etc.) than were the comparison girls who did not participate in the program. In addition to these outcome findings, parents, guardians and family members of ISIS Project participants provided anecdotal accounts stating the project had a positive influence on their daughters (Townsend & Curtis, 2008). These results lend support to the benefit of community engagement, and underscore the power of community collaborative approaches to increase the relevance and effectiveness of interventions that result from these collaborations.

Additional lessons learned from the ISIS Project are subsequently highlighted. First, community-based researchers may find it helpful to adopt a community participatory model and involve the community early in the process. True coalition building requires time and effort before partners feel completely open and trusting of each other and the partnership process. Once an environment of trust and open communication has been established, community partners should be able to effectively discuss their needs and what they are willing to contribute to the research and program implementation process (Gitlin & Lyons, 2003). In this way, an interdependent relationship and team approach can be established. This should foster community investment and ownership of the resulting product. Including community members in program development and fundraising is also a good way to foster ownership.

Second, collaboration and partnership building can be challenging. It involves consistent negotiation and renegotiation of specific goals, roles, and responsibilities of all partners. Therefore, when establishing a community advisory board, it is important that roles and responsibilities of each group member are clearly defined. Unclear roles and poorly defined areas of responsibility lead to group conflict and dissatisfaction of individual members. In addition, it is important for the community to feel that decisions of the board are balanced and that there is shared power between the community and the research scholars. To achieve this with the ISIS CAB, it was helpful to encourage each board member to raise issues or concerns in the group (formally through addition of agenda items or informally during group meetings). Developing a formal process for addressing and resolving conflicts was also helpful.

By highlighting the influence of intersecting systems of oppression on the lives of African American girls, it is hoped that psychologists and other mental health service providers are made aware of the many factors that affect the health behavior of this population and can use this knowledge when developing and designing culturally appropriate community-based interventions. Hence, description of the community collaborative strategies used with the ISIS Project was intended to illustrate the ways in which shared knowledge between an academic researcher and the community can create an effective, culturally tailored intervention program. In addition to enhancing intervention effectiveness, community collaborative approaches have been shown to empower communities of color to take control over their health by becoming active partners in health-based research and the resulting interventions that are brought to their communities. Given the contextual forces that have been shown to negatively influence the health of African American girls, strategies that help to empower these girls and their families are likely to be most effective and most beneficial to this population.

REFERENCES

Afifi, M. (2007). Gender differences in mental health. *Singapore Medical Journal, 48,* 385–391.

Ajzen, I., & Fishbein, M. (1980). *Understanding attitudes and predicting social behavior.* Englewood Cliffs, NJ: Prentice-Hall.

Albarracín, D., Johnson, B. T., Fishbein, M., & Muellerleile, P. A. (2001). Theories of reasoned action and planned behavior as models of condom use: A meta-analysis. *Psychological Bulletin, 127,* 142–161. http://dx.doi.org/10.1037/0033-2909.127.1.142

Barker, J. C., Battle, R. S., Cummings, G. L., & Bankroft, K. N. (1998). Condoms and consequences: HIV/AIDS education and African American women. *Human Organization, 57,* 273–283. http://dx.doi.org/10.17730/humo.57.3.4064h66n46811451

Basiotis, P. P., Lino, M., & Anand, R. S. (1999). Eating breakfast greatly improves schoolchildren's diet quality. *Family Economics Review, 12*(3), 81–84.

Bronfenbrenner, U. (1986). Ecology of the family as a context for human development: Research perspectives. *Developmental Psychology, 22,* 723–742. http://dx.doi.org/10.1037/0012-1649.22.6.723

Centers for Disease Control and Prevention. (2005). *Sexually transmitted disease surveillance, 2004.* Atlanta, GA: U.S. Department of Health and Human Services.

Centers for Disease Control and Prevention. (2006a). Racial/ethnic disparities in diagnoses of HIV/AIDS—33 states, 2001–2004. *MMWR, 55*(5), 121–125.

Centers for Disease Control and Prevention. (2006b). *Youth risk behavior surveillance—United States, 2005.* Retrieved from http://www.cdc.gov/mmwr/preview/mmwrhtml/ss5505a1.htm

Centers for Disease Control and Prevention. (2009). *Diabetes projects: Children and diabetes, SEARCH for diabetes in youth.* Retrieved from http://www.searchfordiabetes.org/public/dsphome.cfm

Centers for Disease Control and Prevention. (2011). *National Center for HIV/AIDS, Viral Hepatitis, STD and TB Prevention: HIV among youth.* Retrieved from http://www.cdc.gov/nchhstp

Coker-Appiah, D. S., Davis, D. S., & Townsend, T. G. (2013). Using community-based partnerships to enhance prevention research among African American youth: A focus on child/adolescent health. In P. J. Kinsey & D. Louden (Eds.), *Health, ethnicity, and well-being: An African American perspective* (pp. 268–302). Bloomington, IN: Xlibris.

Collins, P. H. (1998). Intersections of race, class, gender, and nation: Some implications for Black family studies. *Journal of Comparative Family Studies, 29,* 27–36.

Collins, P. H. (2000). *Black feminist theory: Knowledge, consciousness, and the politics of empowerment.* New York, NY: Routledge.

Donenberg, G., & Pao, M. (2004). HIV/AIDS prevention and intervention: Youths and psychiatric illness. *Contemporary Psychiatry, 2,* 1–8.

DuBois, W. E. B. (2003). The health and physique of the Negro American. 1906. *American Journal of Public Health, 93,* 272–276. http://dx.doi.org/10.2105/AJPH.93.2.272

Eisenmann, J. C., Wickel, E. E., Welk, G. J., & Blair, S. N. (2005). Relationship between adolescent fitness and fatness and cardiovascular disease risk factors in adulthood: The Aerobics Center Longitudinal Study (ACLS). *American Heart Journal, 149*, 46–53. http://dx.doi.org/10.1016/j.ahj.2004.07.016

Gilligan, C. (1990). Joining the resistance: Psychology, politics, girls and women. *Michigan Quarterly Review, 24*, 501–536.

Gitlin, L. N., & Lyons, K. J. (2003). *Successful grant writing: Strategies for health and human service professionals* (2nd ed.). New York, NY: Springer.

Goyan Kittler, P., & Sucher, K. (1989). *Food and culture in America: A nutrition handbook*. New York, NY: Van Nostrand Reinhold.

Grills, C. T. (2003). Substance abuse and African Americans: The need for Africentric-based substance abuse treatment models. In D. J. Gilbert & E. M. Wright (Eds.), *African American women and HIV/AIDS: Critical responses* (pp. 51–72). Westport, CT: Praeger.

Heckler, M. M. (1985). *Report of the secretary's task force on Black & minority health*. Washington, DC: United States Department of Health and Human Services.

Israel, B. A., Schulz, A. J., Parker, E. A., & Becker, A. B. (1998). Review of community-based research: Assessing partnership approaches to improve public health. *Annual Review of Public Health, 19*, 173–202. http://dx.doi.org/10.1146/annurev.publhealth.19.1.173

Jackson, J. S., Knight, K. M., & Rafferty, J. A. (2010). Race and unhealthy behaviors: Chronic stress, the HPA axis, and physical and mental health disparities over the life course. *American Journal of Public Health, 100*, 933–939. http://dx.doi.org/10.2105/AJPH.2008.143446

Jemmott, J. B., III, & Jemmott, L. S. (1996). Strategies to reduce the risk of HIV infection, sexually transmitted diseases, and pregnancy among African American adolescents. In R. J. Resnick & R. H. Rosensky (Eds.), *Health through the life span: Practice and research opportunities* (pp. 395–422). Washington, DC: American Psychological Association. http://dx.doi.org/10.1037/10220-024

Jemmott, J. B., III, Jemmott, L. S., & Hacker, C. I. (1992). Predicting intentions to use condoms among African-American adolescents: The theory of planned behavior as a model of HIV risk-associated behavior. *Ethnicity & Disease, 2*, 371–380.

Kawachi, I., Daniels, N., & Robinson, D. E. (2005). Health disparities by race and class: Why both matter. *Health Affairs, 24*, 343–352. http://dx.doi.org/10.1377/hlthaff.24.2.343

Kimm, S. Y., Glynn, N. W., Kriska, A. M., Barton, B. A., Kronsberg, S. S., Daniels, S. R., . . . Liu, K. (2002). Decline in physical activity in black girls and white girls during adolescence. *The New England Journal of Medicine, 347*, 709–715. http://dx.doi.org/10.1056/NEJMoa003277

Leung, M. W., Yen, I. H., & Minkler, M. (2004). Community based participatory research: A promising approach for increasing epidemiology's relevance in the 21st century. *International Journal of Epidemiology, 33*, 499–506. http://dx.doi.org/10.1093/ije/dyh010

Miller, J. (1986). *What do we mean by relationships?* Wellesley, MA: Stone Center, Wellesley College.

Miner, M. H., Flitter, J. M. K., & Robinson, B. B. E. (2006). Association of sexual revictimization with sexuality and psychological function. *Journal of Interpersonal Violence, 21*, 503–524. http://dx.doi.org/10.1177/0886260505285913

Minkler, M. (2000). Using participatory action research to build healthy communities. *Public Health Reports, 115*(2–3), 191–198. Retrieved from http://www.jstor.org/stable/4598511

Naylor, P. J., & McKay, H. A. (2008). Prevention in the first place: Schools a setting for action on physical inactivity. *British Journal of Sports Medicine, 43*, 10–13. http://dx.doi.org/10.1136/bjsm.2008.053447

O'Connor, T. M., Yang, S. J., & Nicklas, T. A. (2006). Beverage intake among preschool children and its effect on weight status. *Pediatrics, 118*, e1010–e1018. http://dx.doi.org/10.1542/peds.2005-2348

Popkin, B. M., Siega-Riz, A. M., & Haines, P. S. (1996). A comparison of dietary trends among racial and socioeconomic groups in the United States. *The New England Journal of Medicine, 335*, 716–720. http://dx.doi.org/10.1056/NEJM199609053351006

Prinstein, M. J., Borelli, J. L., Cheah, C. S., Simon, V. A., & Aikins, J. W. (2005). Adolescent girls' interpersonal vulnerability to depressive symptoms: A longitudinal examination of reassurance-seeking and peer relationships. *Journal of Abnormal Psychology, 114*, 676–688. http://dx.doi.org/10.1037/0021-843X.114.4.676

Rotherham-Borus, M. J., Gwadz, M., Fernandez, M. I., & Srinivasan, S. (1998). Timing of HIV interventions on reductions in sexual risk among adolescents. *American Journal of Community Psychology, 26*, 73–96. http://dx.doi.org/10.1023/A:1021834224454

Seifer, S., & Maurana, C. (2000). Developing and sustaining community campus partnerships: Putting principles into practice. *Partnership Perspectives, 1*(2), 7–11.

Sloane, D. C., Diamant, A. L., Lewis, L. B., Yancey, A. K., Flynn, G., Nascimento, L. M., . . . Cousineau, M. R., & the REACH Coalition of the African American Building a Legacy of Health Project. (2003). Improving the nutritional resource environment for healthy living through community-based participatory research. *Journal of General Internal Medicine, 18*, 568–575. http://dx.doi.org/10.1046/j.1525-1497.2003.21022.x

St. Lawrence, J., Eldridge, G. D., Shelby, M. C., Little, C. E., Brasfield, T. L., & O'Bannon, R. E., III. (1997). HIV risk reduction for incarcerated women: A comparison of brief interventions based on two theoretical models. *Journal of Consulting and Clinical Psychology, 65*, 504–509. http://dx.doi.org/10.1037/0022-006X.65.3.504

Teitelman, A. M., Tennille, J., Bohinski, J. M., Jemmott, L. S., & Jemmott, J. B., III. (2011). Unwanted unprotected sex: Condom coercion by male partners and self-silencing of condom negotiation among adolescent girls. *Advances in Nursing Science, 34*, 243–259. http://dx.doi.org/10.1097/ANS.0b013e31822723a3

Townsend, T. G., & Curtis, S. B. (2008). *I.S.I.S. program: A cultural-based HIV/ substance abuse prevention program for African American adolescent girls, 5 H79 SP10687* (p. 20857). Rockville, MD: Center of Substance Abuse Prevention.

Townsend, T. G., Grange, C., Belgrave, F. Z., Wilson, K. D., Fitzgerald, A., & Owens, K. (2006). Understanding HIV risk among African American adolescents: The role of Africentric values and ethnic identity in the theory of planned behavior. *Humboldt Journal of Social Relations, 30*, 89–120.

Viswanathan, M., Ammerman, A., Eng, E., Gartlehner, G., Lohr, K., Griffith, D., . . . Whitener, L. (2004). *Community-based participatory research: Assessing the evidence. Summary, Evidence Report/Technology Assessment No. 99* (AHRQ Publication 04-E022-1). Rockville, MD: Agency for Healthcare Research and Quality.

Wells, K., Miranda, J., Bruce, M. L., Alegría, M., & Wallerstein, N. (2004). Bridging community intervention and mental health services research. *The American Journal of Psychiatry, 161*, 955–963. http://dx.doi.org/10.1176/appi.ajp.161.6.955

Williams, D. R., & Williams-Morris, R. (2000). Racism and mental health: The African American experience. *Ethnicity & Health, 5*(3–4), 243–268. http://dx.doi.org/10.1080/713667453

Wingood, G. M., & DiClemente, R. J. (2000). Application of the theory of gender and power to examine HIV-related exposures, risk factors, and effective interventions for women. *Health Education & Behavior, 27*, 539–565. http://dx.doi.org/10.1177/109019810002700502

Zimmerman, M. (2000). Empowerment theory. In J. Rappaport & E. Seidman (Eds.), *Handbook of community psychology* (pp. 43–63). New York, NY: Kluwer Academic/ Plenum. http://dx.doi.org/10.1007/978-1-4615-4193-6_2

13

INCREASING ACADEMIC PERFORMANCE OF ETHNICALLY DIVERSE LEARNERS THROUGH SINGLE-SUBJECT RESEARCH

LAURICE M. JOSEPH

Across the nation, there is an ever-increasing emphasis on school districts being accountable for assisting all enrolled students in meeting common core academic standards. In fact, a national report card—the National Assessment of Educational Progress (NAEP)—is periodically generated and specifies how well students in all states are meeting common core standards across grade levels, subject areas, disability types, and ethnic and racial groups. This report indicates that some ethnic and/or linguistically diverse groups of students, such as English language learners, are functioning below expected academic standards (NAEP, 2013). This is the case even for those districts meeting academic standards in most other areas (NAEP, 2013). These school districts need to develop plans and document efforts to increase the academic performance of ethnically and/or linguistically diverse groups of students. A way to document efforts toward this end is by systematically assessing and monitoring their academic progress (Joseph et al., 2014).

http://dx.doi.org/10.1037/14855-014
Psychoeducational Assessment and Intervention for Ethnic Minority Children: Evidence-Based Approaches,
S. L. Graves, Jr., and J. J. Blake (Editors)

Systematically assessing and monitoring students' academic progress over time assists educators in making instructional decisions that could have an influence on the rate of progress students are making on performing academic tasks. For all students with diverse learning needs, including those who are ethnically and/or linguistically diverse, it is imperative that academic performance be assessed and monitored frequently to provide an indicator as to whether or not appropriate high-quality types and amounts of instruction (i.e., levels of intensity) are being delivered. One way to assess and monitor if these have been implemented is through the use of single-subject research designs (SSRDs), which provides a way to identify evidence-supported interventions (Horner et al., 2005). Over the past decade, there has been an emphasis on implementing evidence-based instruction within a multitiered response to intervention instructional delivery systems in schools partly due to the reauthorization of both the Individuals With Disabilities Education Improvement Act and the No Child Left Behind Act of 2011. Due to this emphasis, single-subject designs are increasingly gaining the attention of members of the educational community (Casey et al., 2012). In 2010, the What Works Clearinghouse (see http:// ies.ed.gov/ncee/wwc/) deemed these designs to be valuable tools for educators and published the resource *Single-Case Design Technical Documentation* (Kratochwill et al., 2010). This resource describes criteria and standards for evaluating evidence-based practices through SSRDs. The American Psychological Association (http://www.apa.org/education/k12/index.aspx), Rizvi and Ferraioli (2012), and the Council for Exceptional Children (2014) also provide resources for evaluating evidence-based practices through studies involving single-subject designs. Knowledge of SSRDs and their contributions to evidence-based practices provides practitioners and researchers alike with a strong foundation for evaluating the effectiveness of interventions for students who have language, cultural, academic, cognitive, social, or emotional needs (e.g., Perry, Albeg, & Tung, 2012). This chapter discusses the advantages and usefulness of SSRDs with ethnically and/or linguistically diverse populations.

ADVANTAGES OF USING SINGLE-SUBJECT DESIGNS

There are advantages to using SSRDs to examine the effectiveness of the types and amount of instruction in improving ethnically diverse students' academic performance. First, SSRDs are useful for studying assorted samples of students for which it is challenging and costly to obtain a large, homogeneous sample in one study. For instance, there may only be five primary grade students in a Midwestern rural school district who are English language learners (ELLs), or there may be only one Spanish-speaking student diagnosed with autism in an urban school district. Moreover, these designs are useful for monitoring the progress of diverse learners who do not learn in the same manner and at the same rate as their peers in the classroom (Casey et al., 2012). Second, SSRDs are helpful when one wishes to examine specific targeted academic or social behaviors that are emitted by a small group or by individual students. For example, these research designs may be used when examining the effectiveness of a phonemic awareness instructional technique on phoneme awareness performance for a small sample of ELLs having limited command of both their first and their second language.

Third, these research designs are helpful when one wishes to examine how students are performing over time while interventions are being implemented rather than only prior (e.g., pretest) to or after (e.g., posttest) implementation. Examining students' performance over time in this manner permits one to formatively note changes in students' academic performance on an ongoing basis and make systematic changes to an intervention if performance is not progressing in the desired direction. In other words, with the use of single-subject designs, the process of assessing and intervening is dynamic.

Fourth, SSRDs permit one to compare differences in each student's performance between two or more experimental conditions rather than between two or more groups of students, as with large-groups comparison designs. Stated another way, with SSRDs, one can examine how each student participant performed during conditions when a targeted intervention was implemented against conditions when the targeted intervention was not implemented (i.e., baseline). With these designs, every participant receives the targeted intervention, whereas, in large-group comparison research, one group receives the targeted intervention while the other group serves as a control. When diverse learners are the participants of interest in a study in which a similar control group is not attainable, it may be more feasible to use single-subject designs. Moreover, their use may minimize ethical concerns when including human subjects as participants in research studies, as all SSRD participants receive an intervention that potentially has positive effects. This is particularly critical for diverse learners because it is essential, given the limited time for instruction within a school day, that time is spent implementing methods that have great potential to increase academic performance.

COMMON COMPONENTS OF SINGLE-SUBJECT DESIGNS

There are various types of single-subject designs that can be used to increase the academic performance of ethnically diverse learners. The single-subject designs most commonly employed to examine academic performance variables are *simple baseline–intervention* (A-B), *withdrawal* (A-B-A-B), *multiple baseline*, and *alternating treatments designs*, which are described in detail subsequently.

Tankersley, Harjusola-Webb, and Landrum (2008) discussed three critical components that are commonly used across these designs. The first component is assessing academic performance repeatedly using direct measures of behavior (e.g., basic addition math fact probes, high-frequency word recognition probes). By directly and repeatedly assessing academic performance of ethnically diverse students in the same way over time, one can observe a true representation of each student's performance pattern and trend before and during intervention. The second component is systematically implementing and removing the intervention. Interventions are carefully designed and implemented with integrity, and changes are made purposefully, meaning that changes are made based on data obtained through repeated assessments. The third component is that each student's performance assessment data are analyzed across baseline and intervention conditions; changes in academic performance are based on the intervention and not on other environmental variables.

STAGES OF BASELINE LOGIC

In addition to the common components of SSRDs, general guidelines are used when examining the students' performance data across baseline and intervention conditions within those designs. These guidelines are often referred to as the *stages of baseline logic* and include (a) *making a prediction*, (b) *affirming the consequent*, (c) *verifying the prediction*, and (d) *replicating by affirming the consequent* (Riley-Tillman & Burns, 2009).

Making a Prediction

Prediction in single-subject research refers to making a data-based estimate of how the targeted behavior will change when the intervention is implemented. A prediction is made once a sufficient amount of preintervention data are gathered to form a baseline of academic performance against which academic performance data gathered during the intervention will be measured. Several data points need to be gathered prior to implementing an intervention to clearly obtain level, trend, and variability of a student's academic performance data. A student's academic performance level, trend, and variability over time are analyzed in a way to form a basis for making a prediction about how academic performance data will remain the same if an intervention is not implemented and how academic performance may change if an intervention is implemented. Without sufficient amounts of baseline data to measure against performance during intervention, one cannot claim that it was the intervention that produced a desired change in the student's academic performance.

Affirming the Consequent

Affirming the consequent refers to observing a desired change in a series of data depicting a student's academic performance during intervention sessions. In this stage, we may begin to link the change in the student's performance to the intervention. However, we cannot say with certainty that this change occurred due to the intervention so we need to verify the prediction.

Verifying the Prediction

Verifying the prediction refers to examining the data when the intervention has been removed (i.e., a return to baseline phase). If the data resemble the data depicted during the initial baseline, then one can verify the prediction that the student's performance would remain the same without the implementation of the intervention and that it was likely the intervention that produced the change in performance and not other external factors.

Replicating by Affirming the Consequent

Replicating the affirmation of the consequent refers to reimplementing the intervention and examining whether the student's performance returns to the level that was observed when the intervention was initially implemented, before its withdrawal. If the student's performance returned to the level that was observed the first time the intervention was implemented, then one affirms that it was the intervention and not other factors that produced the desired change in the student's performance. Kratochwill et al. (2010) recommended that, within a design, a minimum of one replication of a functional relationship between the outcome variable and the intervention be evident.

TYPES OF SSRDs

There are various types of SSRDs, along with a common coding system used to describe their elements. The A refers to the baseline phase; B refers to the intervention phase; C and D and so on refer to subsequent and varying intervention phases. A hyphen between the letters signifies a change in phases (e.g., A-B). Two letters presented together (e.g., BC) signifies that two intervention phases are being implemented concurrently. When a superscript is placed next to a letter (e.g., B^1, B^2), it signifies minor changes to the intervention.

Baseline-Intervention (A-B) Design

A-B design is the most basic of the SSRDs. The baseline phase involves the measurement of academic performance without the implementation of the intervention. Baseline data are collected for a number of sessions. It is recommended that a minimum of three to five academic performance data points (the more the better) are collected frequently (i.e., on a daily, biweekly, or weekly basis) during this phase to accurately assess levels, trends, and variability in the data path. Next, the intervention is implemented systematically and with integrity for several sessions while academic performance data (e.g., a minimum of five data points) are gathered on a frequent basis (i.e., daily, biweekly, or weekly). Figure 13.1 illustrates an A-B design in which baseline data are gathered for a number of sessions before the intervention (e.g., story mapping) is implemented. In this example, there was a desired change in the student's performance when the intervention was implemented. However, because it is difficult to know with certainty that it was the intervention and not some other extraneous factor that contributed to the desired change. Experimental control cannot be achieved with this design.

Essentially, A-B designs permit one to apply two stages of baseline logic: making a prediction and affirming the consequent. During the baseline phase, prediction about the student's performance can be made—particularly if there was a consistent pattern observed in the data path. Affirming the consequent occurs during the intervention phase if the student's academic performance increased above baseline levels. One cannot verify the prediction or replicate the affirmation of the consequent with A-B designs. Practitioners mostly

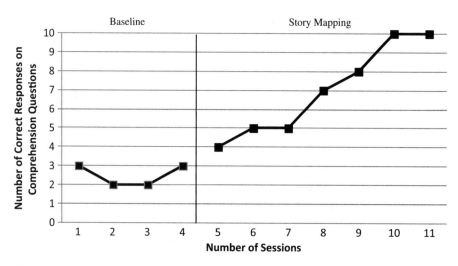

Figure 13.1. Example of an A-B design.

apply A-B designs when working with students or clients who are referred to them in school or clinical settings where experimental control is challenging to achieve. Even though they cannot claim with absolute certainty that the increase in academic performance was due to the intervention, they can report whether there was a change in academic performance from baseline to intervention phases and the nature of that change with regards to the level, trend and variability of the student's performance over time.

Withdrawal Designs (A-B-A and A-B-A-B)

Other designs that could be feasibly applied in school and clinical settings are A-B-A and A-B-A-B, if the target behavior is one that could be reversed when the intervention is removed. For most academic skills, this is not possible because certain skills cannot be unlearned once they are learned (e.g., basic math facts, letter–sound correspondences). This is the reason that withdrawal designs are typically used when dealing with social behaviors rather than with academic behaviors. However, there are some academic behaviors for which these designs may be used, such as behaviors that are context dependent. Figure 13.2 depicts an example of how A-B-A-B designs can be used to examine the effectiveness of an intervention on academic performance. In this example, a graphic organizer such as story mapping is used to increase the number of correctly answered comprehension questions. One can observe a student's reading comprehension performance when the story map is implemented and when it is removed. The passages and comprehension questions are similar in type and difficulty level; however, they are distinct from one session to another across and within experimental phases, making it potentially possible for the student's performance to reverse when the

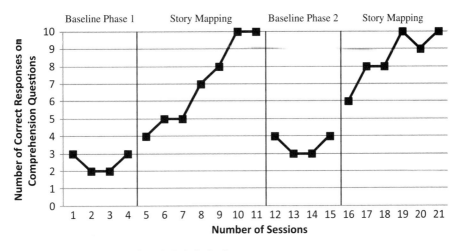

Figure 13.2. Example of an A-B-A-B design.

intervention is removed. This will not be the case for academic skills such as word recognition and math calculations in which it is difficult to unlearn skills once they have been taught even though the intervention has been removed.

An A-B-A design refers to observing a student's academic performance during baseline phase, during intervention phase, and then during a return to baseline phase. An A-B-A-B design refers to the same phases but with one added phase, which is a return to the intervention phase. It is recommended in most instances that the intervention be reimplemented once it has been removed to restore desired academic performance levels. All stages of baseline logic can be applied when using A-B-A-B designs, making this design strong as it has the potential to depict a functional relationship between the implementation of the intervention and changes in performance (Tankersley, Harjusola-Webb, & Landrum, 2008). Prediction is made during the initial baseline phase; affirming the consequent is done during the first intervention phase; verification is made during the second baseline phase; and affirming the consequent with replication is done during the final intervention phase.

Patterson's (2005) study is an example of one that implemented an A-B-A-B *withdrawal* SSRD to increase students' academic performance. The participants were eight African American students; seven had been identified with behavior disorders and one had been identified with learning disabilities. The purpose of the study was to examine the effects of using guided notes versus students' own notes on weekly quizzes in an inclusive science classroom. Guided notes consisted of preprinted lecture notes with blanks inserted throughout for the students to record key concepts as they were presented during a class lecture. This form of note taking reduces the chances of students omitting important content from the lecture while remaining actively engaged during the lecture by following it along with their guided notes and recording key concepts in the inserted blanks. In Patterson's study, the first and second baseline phases consisted of students listening to a class lecture and taking their own notes. The first and second intervention phases consisted of the students listening to a class lecture and using the preprinted guided notes to record key concepts in the blank spaces inserted throughout the notes. Findings revealed that, generally, the students performed above baseline levels on quizzes when they used guided notes versus when they took their own notes. Moreover, classroom observation data revealed that the students preferred the guided-notes method over taking their own notes, as they were observed to be listening to the lecture while taking guided notes and would often emit loud sighs while taking their own notes.

Multiple Baseline Designs

One of the most common SSRDs is the *multiple baseline* design. The fact that many academic skills such as those in the areas of math, reading, and written expression cannot be reversed once learned makes the multiple baseline design a popular one. Multiple baseline designs are essentially a series of at least three A-B designs, except that the intervention is staggered sequentially across a set of variables, such as three participants, three types of settings (e.g., classroom, lunch room, playground), or each type of behavior/skill (e.g., addition, subtraction, multiplication facts). The intervention is sequentially implemented at different points in time, for instance, across each of the three participants. The possible variables—such as whether they are participants, settings, and behaviors (e.g., academic, social)—need to be as similar as possible in relation to the intervention for a logical effect on each variable to occur. For instance, a series of A-B designs may be implemented across three students of Hispanic origin in an urban elementary school (e.g., José, Maria, Pedro) who have basic division-fact calculation difficulties. Specifically, the targeted academic outcome may be the number of division facts that are correctly solved. The intervention may be cover, copy, and compare. With multiple baseline designs across participants, José, Maria, and Pedro will be given the same number and type of division facts to solve during several sessions in the baseline phase. Next, the cover, copy, and compare intervention is implemented with José while Maria and Pedro remain in the baseline phase. The division facts continue to be administered to all participants throughout all phases. Once José demonstrates a level and trend in performance in the desired direction, the cover, copy, and compare intervention is also implemented with Maria while Pedro remains in baseline. Once Maria demonstrates a trend in performance in the desired direction, Pedro receives the intervention. Changes in performance are expected only when the intervention is implemented across the participants and not during baseline phases. Figure 13.3 presents an example of a multiple baseline design across three participants in which a change in performance (number of correct division facts) occurred only when the intervention (cover, copy, and compare) was implemented. Experimental control is possible with multiple baseline designs when there are no observed changes in performance during the baseline phases across each of the participants. In other words, changes in academic performance are observed only when the intervention is introduced to each student.

With multiple baseline designs, prediction is made about performance through examination of the data points on the first participant's baseline phase. Affirming the consequent is done through observation of the data points depicted on the first participant's intervention phase. Verifying the prediction is done through observing data points during the second and third participants' baseline phases if their performance remained stable. Replicating the affirmation of the consequent occurs when examining the data points in the second and third participants' intervention phases if a desired change in performance is observed only when the intervention is implemented.

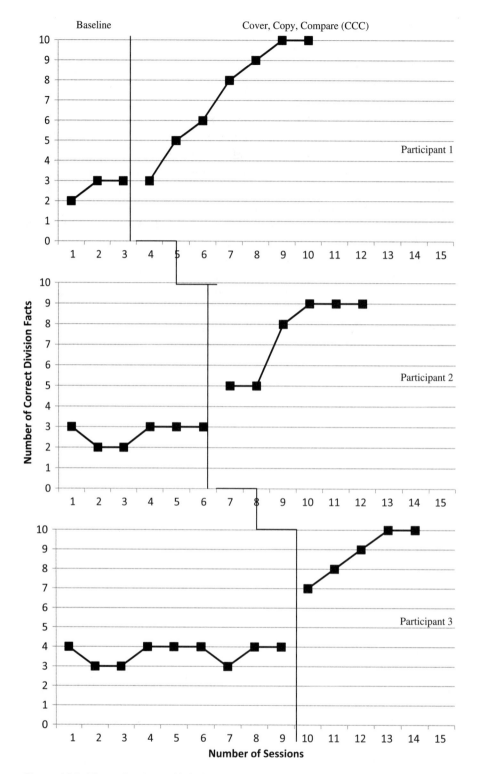

Figure 13.3. Example of a multiple baseline design across participants.

An example of a study using a multiple baseline design across culturally diverse students is one conducted by Huennekens and Xu (2010). These researchers explored the effects of a cross-linguistic parent–child dialogic reading intervention on the frequency and length of English language utterances made in the classroom. The students were two 4-year-old ELLs enrolled in a Head Start preschool program. Parents were trained to read and engage in discussion of stories written in their child's native language (i.e., Spanish). Pages of the storybooks were marked with stop points to prompt parents to ask their child questions pertaining to the story. Findings revealed that students increased the frequency and length of their utterances. However, there was considerable overlap in data between the baseline and intervention conditions, so it was difficult to claim that any increases were due to the intervention.

Joseph (2002) employed multiple baseline designs across participants to examine the combined effects of word boxes and word sorts, two techniques targeted to help children develop phonological skills. The participants included two African American children who improved on their word recognition and spelling performance when these phonological techniques were implemented.

Peterson et al. (2014) contains an example of a multiple baseline design across behaviors/skills. These researchers investigated the effects of an incremental rehearsal strategy on helping three kindergartners who were ELLs acquire three distinct sets of letter–sound correspondences. Thus, the incremental rehearsal intervention was examined across performance on three sets of letter-sound correspondences. The participants in the study each possessed a different first language (i.e., Polish, Spanish, Hmong), and each performed below benchmark levels on making letter-sound correspondences. The incremental rehearsal intervention involved presenting a ratio of 10% unknown to 90% known letter–sound correspondences in an incremental rehearsal fashion. Findings revealed that the intervention was consistently effective across all three sets of letter-sound correspondences for each of the students.

One of the challenges of implementing multiple baseline designs across participants is the prolonged period that the third participant remains in baseline and experiences a substantial lag in time before receiving the intervention. The third participant may also experience monotony in being administered assessments multiple times and not experiencing changes in performance before receiving the intervention. For this reason and others, variations of multiple baseline designs may be used. Common variations of the multiple baseline design include multiple probe designs, multielement designs, and changing criterion designs.

Multiple Probe Designs

A *multiple probe* design involves administering assessments intermittently during the baseline phases within the design (Byiers, Reichle, & Symons, 2012). A few assessments may be administered at the beginning of the baseline phase, then again after a number of sessions have elapsed, and again right before the intervention is implemented. A multiple probe design may be more feasible with regard to preventing the administration of prolonged repeated assessments during baseline phases for the second and third participants. However, if there is considerable variability in the data in the baseline phases, the multiple baseline design rather than the multiple probe design is recommended, as highly variable data make it challenging to establish a functional relationship between the intervention and the outcome variable (Byiers, Reichle, & Symons, 2012).

Gibson, Cartledge, Keyes, and Yawn's (2014) study is an example of implementing a multiple probe design to demonstrate an increase in academic performance. These researchers implemented this design with eight African American first graders who struggled with reading skills. In their study, this design was used to examine the effectiveness of the *Read Naturally Software Edition* program on the students' oral-reading fluency and word-retell fluency on both training and generalization passages. Findings revealed that all students improved their performance on those reading measures.

Spooner, Rivera, Browder, Baker, and Salas (2009) used a multiple probe design across skill sets to examine the effectiveness of story-based lessons on emergent literacy skills for a 6-year-old ELL with moderate intellectual disability. The lessons consisted of several emergent literacy-instructional components that were divided into skill sets. Some components involved instruction on concepts about print (e.g., modeling proper book orientation, identifying the title of a story), identifying vocabulary words (e.g., having students point to particular words), and asking comprehension questions (e.g., questioning what happens next in the text and verifying predictions). The stories that were chosen for the lessons pertained to the student's heritage. The lessons were initially instructed in the child's native language (i.e., Spanish). The instructor gradually taught the lessons in English. While instructing the first skill set, the book that was selected was written and read aloud in Spanish. For the second skill set, the book selected was written and read aloud in Spanish and then in English. For the third skill set, the book chosen was written and read aloud in English. Findings revealed that the story-based lessons generally helped the student improve and maintain emergent literacy skills across the three skill sets. However, it was noted that the student's trend in data descended a bit on the English-only story-based skill set.

In another study using multiple probe designs, researchers explored the effectiveness of main-idea summarization coupled with self-monitoring instruction on reading comprehension performance of two Hispanic and two African American sixth graders with learning disabilities (Jitendra, Cole, Hoppes, & Wilson, 1998). The researchers demonstrated the students' increase in academic performance by directly teaching them through scripted lessons how to identify the main idea in passages and how to self-monitor their performance.

Multielement Designs

Multielement designs are similar to multiple baseline designs, except that an additional intervention phase or two may be added. Typically, the additional phase is systematically added to boost academic performance if performance has not improved at the most desirable levels in the first intervention phase. For example, more opportunities for practice on academic skills may be added in an additional intervention phase to boost students' performance.

Changing Criterion Designs

Another design that is similar to the multiple baseline design is the *changing criterion* design. The changing criterion design is used when it is appropriate to change the performance criterion of the outcome variable. This occurs when the student meets the preestablished criterion and it is beneficial to her or him to incrementally increase or decrease the criterion depending on the nature of the outcome variable. For instance, when ELLs are first learning to compose a written story in English, it may be reasonable to set the criterion at writing five English words on a page, and once students meet that criterion level, increase the level to writing 10 English words, and then to writing 15 English words, and so on. In this instance, each changing criterion phase (i.e., Phase 1: five words, Phase 2: 10 words, Phase 3: 15 words) serves as the baseline phase for the next phase. Experimental control is achieved when the student's performance repeatedly moves in the desired direction of meeting the criterion established in each phase (Byiers, Reichle, & Symons, 2012).

Alternating Treatments Design

An *alternating treatments* design is used to compare the effectiveness of two or more interventions. This design may be particularly useful in research and practical settings where it is important to identify which intervention is producing the most desirable outcomes for students. Determining this is important when working with ethnically diverse students as "getting the most bang for your buck" is critical under the instructional time constraints of a school day. Typically, with an alternating treatments design, a comparison among two interventions and a baseline phase is conducted (e.g., A-B-A-C-A-B-A-C-A or A-B-A-C-A-C-A-B-A or some other combination of these phases). To minimize intervention interference, it is recommended that the interventions be implemented in a counterbalanced order. Figure 13.4 presents an example of an alternating treatments design where the cover, copy, and compare (CCC)

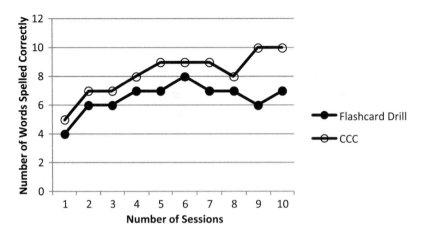

Figure 13.4. Example of an alternating treatments design.

technique was compared with a traditional flashcard drill and practice technique on helping a student learn to spell words. While both procedures seemed to help the student improve over time on the number of correct words they were able to spell, the CCC technique appeared to have greater influence over time on the student's level of performance. In fact, in this example, there were no overlapping data points on performance between the two interventions, indicating that CCC was a more effective method of teaching spelling for this particular student. In these designs, prediction is made during the first baseline phase and verification of the prediction is made in the return-to-baseline phase. Additionally, in the return-to-baseline phase, a new prediction is made about the second intervention. Affirming the consequent occurs after several data points are gathered for each intervention. Replicating the affirmation of the consequent can occur when another student demonstrates similar performance outcomes when the interventions are altered in the same manner.

Taylor, Alber, and Walker (2002) provided an example of a study using an alternating treatments design that included African American fifth-grade students who were receiving special education services. Their study examined the alternating effects of story mapping, a self-questioning strategy, and a no-intervention condition on answering literal and inferential comprehension questions. The story-mapping condition consisted of having the students record details about critical elements (e.g., characters, settings, plot, problem, resolution) of a story on a graphic organizer. The self-questioning condition involved having students read a passage, stop at the marked stopping points, and then ask themselves 10 generic questions that were printed on a laminated card. Students were also required to record their responses to the questions on an audio recorder. Students performed better under both the story-mapping and self-questioning strategy intervention conditions than in the no-intervention condition. Interestingly, when the students' performance on literal versus inferential comprehension questions was compared, the students performed slightly better on answering inferential comprehension questions under the self-questioning condition than in the story-mapping and no-intervention conditions.

Alternating treatments designs have also been used to compare the effects of response topographies on individual students' academic performance. For instance, a recent study used an alternating treatments design to make comparisons between having each student practice spelling words by orally rehearsing them and by repeatedly writing them (Garcia et al., 2014). Findings revealed that, for most of the children, orally spelling words during practice trials was a more efficient way to learn the words than writing them during practice trials. Response-topography comparisons such as this may have important implications on how to best teach culturally and linguistically diverse students skills and content that are new to them.

In addition to examining instructional-effectiveness variables, alternating treatment designs have also been used to measure instructional-efficiency variables. For example, over the past decade, several studies have compared two or more interventions to determine which one took the least amount of time to implement and which one yielded the highest rate in student performance (e.g., Cates et al., 2003; Joseph & Nist, 2006; Joseph et al., 2012; Nist & Joseph, 2008). Examining instructional efficiency similar to the way it was examined in those studies would likely have practical implications for selecting and implementing efficacious instruction to students who are culturally and linguistically diverse.

Repeated Acquisition Design

A variation of the alternating treatment design is the *repeated acquisition design*. Repeated acquisition designs are used to determine how quickly skills can be acquired under at least two different conditions (Boren, 1963). For instance, the first intervention is implemented for a total of five successive sessions. Outcome data are gathered on those five successive sessions. Next, the second intervention is implemented for a total of five successive trials or sessions, and outcome data are once again gathered during those trials or sessions. These distinct conditions, however—equivalent in the number of trials or sessions under each—are delivered in a counterbalanced order until it is clear as to which intervention produces the highest rate of learning. So, a student may reach the criterion level by the third trial and remain at that level during the fourth and fifth trials under the first intervention, but that same student may not even reach the criterion level by the fifth trial under the second intervention.

ANALYSIS OF INTERVENTION EFFECTS

The most common method for analyzing academic performance effects in single-subject designs is visual inspection of data obtained during the baseline and intervention conditions. The data are typically depicted on graphs. Graphs are a powerful way of depicting and communicating about student progress as they provide a visual (i.e., a picture) that transcends cultural and linguistic barriers (Casey et al., 2012). There is usually a separate graph containing performance data across baseline and intervention conditions for each student. Changes across baseline and intervention conditions are commonly assessed through the examination of the level, variability, trend, and latency of each student's performance across those conditions. These graphic forms of analyses, taken together, provide a good visual depiction of the student's performance (Casey et al., 2012).

The *change in level* refers to the change in performance that is observed once the intervention is implemented or removed. A strong response to the intervention is observed when the student makes an immediate and a high level of change in performance from the final sessions of the baseline phase to the beginning sessions of the intervention phase. Often, the set of data points within a condition is averaged to obtain the mean performance level for that condition. In some instances, the level is calculated using the median (the middle) data point. Although the level is critical when analyzing the data, the level does not represent how varied the data points may be from another. *Variability in the data* means that there was fluctuation in the vertical spread across consecutive data points within or across conditions. In most studies that employ single-subject designs, there is some variability among data points; however, high variability within any condition likely signifies that variables other than the intervention may be influencing student performance (Kratochwill et al., 2010).

The *trend* (sometimes referred to as *slope*) is the direction of a series of data points. A trend in data may be ascending or descending over time during the implementation or removal of the intervention.

Latency of change refers to the rapidness of the change in a student's performance data when the baseline phase ended and the intervention phase began. Intervention is said to have strong effects if it takes only a few trials before changes in performance are observed.

Magnitude of intervention effects or *effect sizes* can also be measured with SSRDs. The most common effect-size metrics include percentage of nonoverlapping data (PND), percentage of all nonoverlapping data (PAND), and the improvement rate difference (IRD). PND is calculated by first identifying the highest (if the desired goal is an increase in performance) or the lowest (if the desired goal is a decrease in performance) baseline data point. Next, a straight line is drawn from that point through the intervention data. The number of intervention data points that are above or below the line, depending on the direction of the desired performance goal, is divided by the total number of intervention data points (Riley-Tillman & Burns, 2009). PAND is a nonparametric approach that accounts for some idiosyncratic data that are not captured when calculating PNDs (see Parker, Hagan-Burke, & Vannest, 2007, for a description of how to compute this metric). IRDs are calculated by subtracting the improvement rate obtained from performance in the baseline phase from the improvement rate of performance in the intervention phase (see Parker, Vannest, & Brown, 2009, for a thorough discussion on this metric).

CONCLUSION

SSRDs provide viable alternative methods to large-group comparison designs for examining intervention effectiveness and increasing the academic performance of ethnically diverse learners. The type of single-subject design selected depends on the purpose of the evaluation. For example, when comparing the effectiveness of two or more interventions in increasing students' academic performance, the most likely design chosen would be an alternating treatments design. Multiple baseline designs may be the design of choice if the goal is to examine the effectiveness of an intervention across learners, skills, or settings for which academic skills or content is not likely to be unlearned.

Examples of published research that consisted of implementing some of these designs with samples of ethnically diverse learners were provided in this chapter. Clearly, however, there is a need for more SSRD studies that aim to increase the academic performance of ethnically diverse samples of students.

REFERENCES

Boren, J. J. (1963). The repeated acquisition of new behavioral chains. *American Psychologist, 18,* 421.

Byiers, B. J., Reichle, J., & Symons, F. J. (2012). Single-subject experimental design for evidence-based practice. *American Journal of Speech-Language Pathology, 21,* 397–414. http://dx.doi.org/10.1044/1058-0360(2012/11-0036)

Casey, L. B., Meindl, J. N., Frame, K., Elswick, S., Hayes, J., & Wyatt, J. (2012). Current trends in education: How single-subject research can help middle and high school educators keep up with the zeitgeist. *The Clearing House: A Journal of Educational Strategies, Issues and Ideas, 85,* 109–116.

Cates, G. L., Skinner, C. H., Watson, S. T., Meadows, T. J., Weaver, A., & Jackson, B. (2003). Instructional effectiveness and instructional efficiency as considerations for data-based decision making: An evaluation of interspersing procedures. *School Psychology Review, 32,* 601–616.

Council for Exceptional Children. (2014). *Council for Exceptional Children standards for evidence-based practices in special education.* Arlington, VA: Council for Exceptional Children.

Garcia, D., Joseph, L. M., Alber-Morgan, S., & Konrad, M. (2014). Efficiency of oral incremental rehearsal versus written incremental rehearsal on students' rate, retention, and generalization of spelling words. *School Psychology Forum, 8,* 113–129.

Gibson, L., Cartledge, G., Keyes, S. E., & Yawn, C. D. (2014). The effects of a supplementary computerized fluency intervention on the generalization of the oral reading fluency and comprehension of first grade students. *Education & Treatment of Children, 37,* 25–51. http://dx.doi.org/10.1353/etc.2014.0003

Horner, R. H., Carr, E. G., Halle, J., McGee, G., Odom, S., & Wolery, M. (2005). The use of single-subject research to identify evidence based practice in special education. *Exceptional Children, 71,* 165–179. http://dx.doi.org/10.1177/001440290507100203

Huennekens, M. E., & Xu, Y. (2010). Effects of a cross-linguistic storybook intervention on the second language development of two preschool English language learners. *Early Childhood Educ J, 38,* 19–26. http://dx.doi.org/10.1007/s10643-010-0385-1

Individuals With Disabilities Education Act. (2011). SpringerReference. http://dx.doi.org/10.1007/springerreference_223925

Jitendra, A. K., Cole, C. L., Hoppes, M. K., & Wilson, B. (1998). Effects of a direct instruction main idea summarization program and self-monitoring on reading comprehension of middle school students with learning disabilities. *Reading & Writing Quarterly, 14,* 379–396. http://dx.doi.org/10.1080/1057356980140403

Joseph, L. M. (2002). Facilitating word recognition and spelling using word boxes and word sort phonic procedures. *School Psychology Review, 31,* 122–129.

Joseph, L. M., Eveleigh, E., Konrad, M., Neef, N., & Volpe, R. (2012). Comparison of the efficiency of two flashcard drill methods on children's reading performance. *Journal of Applied School Psychology, 28,* 317–337. http://dx.doi.org/10.1080/15377903.2012.669742

Joseph, L. M., Kastein, L. A., Konrad, M., Chan, P. E., Peters, M. T., & Ressa, V. A. (2014). Collecting and documenting evidence: Methods for helping teachers improve instruction and promote academic success. *Intervention in School and Clinic, 50,* 86–95. http://dx.doi.org/10.1177/1053451214536043

Joseph, L. M., & Nist, L. (2006). Comparing the effects of unknown-known ratios on word reading learning versus learning rates. *Journal of Behavioral Education, 15,* 69–79. http://dx.doi.org/10.1007/s10864-006-9008-8

Kratochwill, T., Hitchcock, J., Horner, R., Levin, J., Odom, S., Rindskopf, D., & Shadish, W. (2010). *Single-case design technical documentation.* Retrieved from http://ies.ed.gov/ncee/wwc/pdf/reference_resources/wwc_scd.pdf

National Assessment of Educational Progress. (2013). *The nation's report card: Reading and Math 2013*. Washington, DC: National Center for Education Statistics.

Nist, L., & Joseph, L. M. (2008). Effectiveness and efficiency of flashcard drill instructional methods on urban first-grades' word recognition, acquisition, maintenance and generalization. *School Psychology Review, 37*, 294–308.

No Child Left Behind Act. (2011). SpringerReference. http://dx.doi.org/10.1007/springerreference_223926

Parker, R. I., Hagan-Burke, S., & Vannest, K. (2007). Percent of all non-overlapping data (PAND): An alternative to PND. *The Journal of Special Education, 40*, 194–204. http://dx.doi.org/10.1177/00224669070400040101

Parker, R. I., Vannest, K. J., & Brown, L. (2009). The improvement rate difference for the single-case research. *Exceptional Children, 75*, 135–150.

Patterson, K. B. (2005). Increasing positive outcomes for African American males in special education with the use of guided notes. *Journal of Negro Education, 74*, 311–320.

Perry, V., Albeg, L., & Tung, C. (2012). Meta-analysis of single-case design research on self-regulatory intervention for academic performance. *Journal of Behavioral Education, 21*, 217–229. http://dx.doi.org/10.1007/s10864-012-9156-y

Peterson, M., Brandes, D., Kunkel, A., Wilson, J., Rahn, N. L., Egan, A., & McComas, J. (2014). Teaching letter sounds to kindergarten English language learners using incremental rehearsal. *Journal of School Psychology, 52*, 97–107. http://dx.doi.org/10.1016/j.jsp.2013.11.001

Riley-Tillman, T. C., & Burns, M. K. (2009). *Evaluating educational interventions: Single-case design for measuring response to intervention*. New York, NY: Guilford Press.

Rizvi, S. L., & Ferraioli, S. J. (2012). Single-case experimental designs. In H. Cooper (Ed.), *APA handbook of research methods in psychology: Vol. 2. Research designs* (pp. 589–611). http://dx.doi.org/10.1037/13620-031

Spooner, R., Rivera, C. J., Browder, D. M., Baker, J. N., & Salas, S. (2009). Teaching emergent literacy skills using cultural contextual story-based lessons. *Research and Practice for Persons With Severe Disabilities, 34*, 102–112. http://dx.doi.org/10.2511/rpsd.34.3-4.102

Tankersley, M., Harjusola-Webb, S., & Landrum, T. J. (2008). Using single-subject research to establish the evidence base of special education. *Intervention in School and Clinic, 44*, 83–90. http://dx.doi.org/10.1177/1053451208321600

Taylor, L. K., Alber, S. R., & Walker, D. W. (2002). The comparative effects of a modified self-questioning strategy and story mapping on the reading comprehension of elementary students with learning disabilities. *Journal of Behavioral Education, 11*, 69–87. http://dx.doi.org/10.1023/A:1015409508939

14

IMPROVING SERVICE DELIVERY TO ETHNIC AND RACIAL MINORITY STUDENTS THROUGH MULTICULTURAL PROGRAM TRAINING

SHERRIE L. PROCTOR AND CHAMANE SIMPSON

Schools in the United States are becoming increasingly diverse in terms of students' disability status, ethnicity, language, race, religion, sexual orientation, socioeconomic status, and other characteristics (Lopez & Bursztyn, 2013; National Center for Education Statistics [NCES], 2014). This diversity provides educators opportunities to teach students how to live in a pluralistic U.S. society and global world (Proctor & Meyers, 2014). Yet, student diversity also creates challenges for educators, including psychologists, who seek to provide culturally competent services in the schools (Ford, 2014). These challenges include a lack of understanding of the unique obstacles that diverse student populations must negotiate as they interface with U.S. educational systems (see Proctor & Meyers, 2014). Given the increase in the numbers of ethnically and racially diverse students, it is critical for psychologists to be prepared to competently serve these diverse children and their families. Such preparation should begin in psychology graduate programs (Proctor & Truscott, 2012).

http://dx.doi.org/10.1037/14855-015
Psychoeducational Assessment and Intervention for Ethnic Minority Children: Evidence-Based Approaches,
S. L. Graves, Jr., and J. J. Blake (Editors)

The purpose of this chapter is to elucidate how multicultural training within psychology graduate programs can improve service delivery to ethnically and racially diverse prekindergarten to 12th-grade students. We begin with a brief overview of the demographics of ethnically and racially diverse students in U.S. public schools, then we define multiculturalism within school settings. Next, we advocate for improving service delivery to ethnically and racially diverse students by incorporating multiculturalism into graduate psychology programs. Finally, we offer concrete recommendations for multicultural practices that can be initiated to prepare psychologists to work with ethnically and racially diverse school-age students.

DEMOGRAPHICS OF ETHNICALLY AND RACIALLY DIVERSE STUDENTS IN U.S. SCHOOLS

The shifting ethnic and racial demographics of the United States are reflected in the school-age population. During the 2011–2012 school year, White students represented 52% of the prekindergarten to 12th-grade public school population; Hispanic/Latino students accounted for 24%; African Americans, 16%; and Asian/Pacific Islander, Native American/Alaska Native, Native Hawaiian, and students of two or more races accounted for almost 9% (NCES, 2014). Linguistic diversity is also evident with over 400 languages spoken in public schools, Spanish being the most prevalent non-English language (NCES, 2014). Approximately 4.4 million students, or 9.1%, are English language learners (NCES, 2014). Regarding socioeconomic status (SES), compared with Asian and White children, higher percentages of African American/Black, Hispanic/Latino, American Indian/Alaska Native, Native Hawaiian/Pacific Islander children, and children of two or more races live in families below the poverty line (NCES, 2014). In terms of religious affiliation, Lopez and Bursztyn (2013) noted that 78% of Americans identify as Christian, but the influence of immigrant populations who are Buddhist, Catholic, Hindu, and Islamic is expanding the religions and belief systems observed in the public-school student population. Proctor and Meyers (2014) explained that psychologists' understanding of a student's intersecting identities (e.g., ethnicity, race, gender, sexual orientation, SES, religion) is a key aspect of providing multiculturally competent school-based psychological services.

MULTICULTURALISM IN U.S. PUBLIC SCHOOLS

Multicultural refers to individuals from varying sociodemographic backgrounds occupying the same environment or setting (Newell et al., 2010). *Multiculturalism*, as practiced in schools, is a worldview that recognizes and values diverse learners, including their intersecting dimensions of individual identity and cultural background (Carroll, 2009). When effectively implemented, multiculturalism permeates a school and results in educational policies, procedures, and practices that take into account the needs of diverse learners who present with multiple needs (Carroll, 2009). Proctor and Meyers (2014) noted the importance of psychologists understanding, valuing, and engaging in multicultural practices, as well as developing multicultural competencies in regard to all domains of school-based service delivery. Newell et al. (2010) discussed multicultural competency development in terms of psychologists moving beyond sensitivity to multicultural issues to knowledge acquisition and attitude shifts about diverse populations, and engagement in behaviors that facilitate successful interaction with diverse populations in multicultural settings.

Indeed, most professional standards and other documents that guide psychologists' work emphasize the importance of multiculturalism in serving diverse populations (Miranda, 2014). For instance, the American Psychological Association's (APA's) *Guidelines on Multicultural Education, Training, Research, Practice, and Organizational Change for Psychologists* (APA, 2003) direct psychologists to (a) recognize how their worldview influences perceptions of and service delivery to multicultural populations, (b) consider sociocultural factors when selecting assessment tools, and (c) implement culturally sensitive interventions. Further, the National Association of School Psychologists (NASP; 2010a) and APA's (2010) standards for ethical behavior require that psychologists provide fair and just services that respect differences based on ethnicity, race, SES, religion, and other dimensions of human diversity. Carroll (2009) noted that educators who practice using multiculturalism as a framework "see learners, their families, and communities within the context of culture, race, ethnicity, gender, sexual orientation, and all those other cultural lenses that give meaning to students' daily learning experiences" (p. 5). U.S. public school demographics require that all educators and mental health service providers have the dispositions, knowledge, and skills to work with an increasingly diverse student population.

To train future psychologists to deliver effective services to ethnically and racially diverse students, multicultural practices must be modeled and enacted at the program level. This presents a challenge for some graduate psychology programs because many faculty are not equipped with the knowledge and skills to do this (Lopez & Bursztyn, 2013; Newell et al., 2010; Proctor & Truscott, 2012). A relevant question, then, is: How should programs implement multiculturalism? The discussion that follows explores the answer to this question. In our discussion, we rely on previous work we have done in relation to ethnically and racially diverse school age, postsecondary, and professional populations and recent research related to multicultural training practices in psychology graduate programs.

Incorporating Multiculturalism Into Psychology Graduate Programs

Theoretical and research articles have explored promising practices in multicultural psychology graduate training (Jones, Sander, & Booker, 2013; Lopez & Bursztyn, 2013; Moy et al., 2014; Newell et al., 2010). Most recently, Moy et al. (2014) studied how one school psychology graduate program instituted social justice training that incorporated service-learning opportunities in multicultural schools and communities. The 37 students who served as participants offered feedback on training components salient to their development as social justice agents, according to which the researchers outlined a social-justice training model for psychology graduate programs. This model includes institutional variables (e.g., faculty commitment to social justice and university partnerships within local communities and schools with multicultural populations), curricular variables (e.g., classroom activities, discussions, readings), as well as service learning and practical experiences with social justice foci. The model also illustrates the importance of clear goals related to training outcomes, applied outcomes, and educational and social outcomes for clients. Moy et al. described a training outcome goal as preparing graduates to advocate for and deliver fair and equitable services to children and families in culturally and economically diverse schools and communities—the foundation of multicultural service delivery.

Additionally, Lopez and Bursztyn (2013) discussed challenges and opportunities related to multicultural psychology training. They described four specific challenges and then reframed them as opportunities for psychology faculty to meet the needs of an increasingly diverse school-age population: (a) embedding multicultural education theory into a training philosophy, (b) reframing education and psychological theory using a multicultural approach, (c) defining the scope of multicultural training, and (d) articulating multicultural competencies that must be mastered within the context of preexisting professional psychology training standards. It is noteworthy that Lopez and Bursztyn explored aligning multicultural competencies within the context of the NASP (2010b) training standards. School psychology faculty and faculty from other psychology disciplines that prepare clinicians to work with children and youth can also reference the APA (2003) *Guidelines on Multicultural Education, Training, Research, Practice, and Organizational Change for Psychologists.* While professional guidelines differ from professional standards (i.e., guidelines are not mandatory and enforceable, whereas standards are), APA's (2003) multicultural guidelines can be used alongside discipline-specific training standards to help faculty structure discussions around defining the scope of multicultural training and identifying desired training outcomes.

Finally, Newell et al. (2010) provided a comprehensive and critical review of the research related to multicultural training within psychology graduate programs. Their review yielded evidence-based recommendations for multicultural training focused on two levels: *program/faculty* (i.e., integration-separate course model of training, multicultural research, recruitment and retention, and faculty professional development) and *student* (i.e., knowledge about different groups, translation of knowledge to school psychological services, practical experiences with diverse populations, and evaluation of students' multicultural knowledge and skills). To frame the remainder of this chapter's content, we use the key components of multicultural psychology graduate training identified by Newell et al. Findings from across the multicultural psychology graduate training literature are integrated into the discussion.

Recruiting and Retaining Diverse School Psychology Students

Recruitment and retention of racially and ethnically diverse students have been cited as methods to promote multicultural competence among psychologists (Proctor & Truscott, 2012). The importance of recruiting and retaining an ethnically diverse workforce is well established given the changing cultural landscape of U.S. schools. Moreover, it is recognized that ethnically and racially diverse individuals often enter the field of psychology with a commitment to serving those within their communities (Proctor, Simpson, Levin, & Hackimer, 2014). As Hill-Briggs, Evans, and Norman (2004) noted, "to achieve cultural competence, trainees and professionals need not only textbook knowledge and curricula, but also experiences within a diverse academic environment analogous to the diversity of the society and environment in which they will be expected to practice" (p. 14). Thus, we provide strategies below for faculty to use for recruiting and retaining ethnically and racially diverse psychology graduate students.

Recruitment

For decades, scholars across psychology disciplines have studied ways to increase the number of ethnically, racially, and linguistically diverse psychologists (Proctor et al., 2014). Much of this work has been focused at the psychology graduate program level. Psychology graduate program administrators across psychology disciplines have reported using personal contacts with minority candidates; referrals from current students, alumni, and practitioners; minority faculty and students during recruitment season; and preadmission workshops and open houses as recruitment methods to attract minority graduate students

(Hammond & Yung, 1993). Recently, Smith, Blake, and Graves (2013) surveyed directors of school psychology programs to determine what strategies they used to recruit culturally diverse students. Findings indicated that of the 69 respondents, 45 indicated utilizing specific efforts to recruit culturally diverse students, such as relying primarily on program websites and student organizations for recruitment.

Rogers and Molina (2006) studied the recruitment strategies used by counseling, clinical, clinical/community, and school psychology programs known for their exemplary multicultural training. These programs reported using a variety of strategies to recruit ethnically and racially diverse graduate students, including inviting minority faculty members and students to participate in recruitment activities, publicizing the availability of funding via the Internet, and establishing personal contacts at historically black colleges and universities (HBCUs) to create a pipeline into their graduate programs. Notably, each of the programs mentioned by Rogers and Molina had a high percentage of racially and ethnically diverse psychology graduate students.

Most recently, several studies have focused on recruiting ethnically and racially diverse students, particularly Black/African Americans, into school psychology programs. Findings related to this body of research are particularly relevant here since school psychologists are key providers of psychological services to ethnically and racially diverse children (Proctor & Truscott, 2012). Results suggest that Black/African Americans do not know about the field of school psychology. Graves and Wright (2009) found that HBCU students' knowledge of school psychology was significantly lower than their knowledge of other psychology subfields, while African American School Psychologists (AASPs) in Proctor and Truscott (2013) noted that one barrier to African Americans' entry into the field is their general lack of knowledge about the profession. Both HBCU students and faculty in Graves and Wright reported that school psychology programs do not actively recruit students from their universities. HBCU students in Chandler (2011) recommended that programs use Black-specific recruitment strategies that emphasize the need for African Americans/Blacks in the field. Both Chandler and Proctor and Truscott's (2013) participants suggested that recruitment activities should highlight how African American/Black school psychologists might positively impact the significant issues facing students of color in U.S. public schools, including issues like disproportionate placement of Black students in special education.

From a broader perspective, Bidell, Ragen, Broach, and Carrillo (2007) studied the diversity-related content on clinical, counseling, school, and combined psychology graduate programs' web pages. Their findings suggested that clinical and counseling psychology programs included more diversity-related content (e.g., financial aid for minority students, statement indicating commitment to diversity) than school and combined programs. These researchers noted that including diversity-related content on psychology graduate programs' webpages is a cost-efficient method for attracting racially and ethnically diverse students.

Retention

An emerging body of work explores factors related to retaining ethnically and racially diverse individuals in school psychology graduate programs. For example, Clark, Mercer, Zeigler-Hill, and Dufrene (2012) studied factors that present as barriers to the retention of ethnic minority (i.e., Asian American, Hispanic American, Native American) and majority (i.e., European American) students in school psychology programs. They found that ethnic minority students reported more negative race-related program experiences, leading to feeling higher levels of emotional stress and lower levels of belongingness than majority students. To facilitate student retention, Clark and colleagues recommended that programs cultivate and maintain environments wherein there is acceptance and support of ethnic minority students. One way in which programs can demonstrate this is via inclusive and diverse social and professional activities. Participants in Proctor and Truscott's (2012) study of African American student attrition from school psychology programs suggested that an inclusive program environment might have encouraged their retention.

Rogers and Molina (2006) noted that the counseling, clinical, clinical/community, and school psychology programs they sampled used retention strategies that included assigning student mentors, exposing students to minority populations during assistantships and externships, having a critical mass of ethnic and racial minority students, encouraging student involvement with faculty in diversity-related research, and offering at least one diversity course. Further, all programs in Rogers and Molina offered some form of financial support, which ranged from full tuition for students' entire matriculation to financial support for a limited period. AASPs in Proctor and Truscott (2013) also emphasized the importance of providing financial support and mentoring to ethnically and racially diverse students.

Finally, Maton et al. (2011) investigated the graduate program experiences and program satisfaction of African American, Asian American, Latina/o, and European American students enrolled in doctoral (PhD and PsyD) programs across psychology disciplines. Compared with European American students, minority students perceived more academic barriers as a result of their race. However, they felt more satisfied with a program when they perceived that it was responsive to diversity as indicated by the presence of minority students, faculty, and staff; diversity-related courses; and opportunities to work with clients of color in practice settings. Overall, findings across studies indicated the salience of financial support and faculty and student mentors for ethnically and racially diverse graduate students, and program environments that are accepting of diversity.

Engaging in Faculty Professional Development

To facilitate multicultural competency in psychology students, faculty must be knowledgeable about the unique challenges facing students from ethnically and racially diverse backgrounds and emphasize to trainees the importance of up-to-date knowledge about educational and social issues that impact students from diverse groups (Lopez & Bursztyn, 2013; Proctor & Meyers, 2014). Proctor and Truscott (2012) noted that psychology faculty must evaluate their knowledge regarding ethnically and racially diverse populations; reflect on their personal biases and prejudices pertaining to ethnically and racially diverse populations; and seek resources that will help develop their knowledge, skills, and dispositions regarding issues relevant to the history, education, and mental health of ethnically and racially diverse students. Newell et al. (2010) recommended that faculty identify diversity-related professional development opportunities at conferences, consume research about diverse populations, and seek out community resources that can be accessed to enhance multicultural knowledge. To develop knowledge about diverse populations, Proctor and Meyers (2014) suggested that psychologists connect with colleagues who are engaged in work on key issues relevant to ethnically and racially diverse student populations, join professional communities and interest groups focused on issues relevant to diverse populations (e.g., APA's Division 45, Society for the Study of Culture, Ethnicity, and Race), and access resources (e.g., books, conferences, websites, videos) that address diversity issues. As indicated by Moy et al.'s (2014) findings, to successfully implement a training model that results in practitioners who are prepared to competently serve and advocate for multicultural populations, program faculty must be committed to understanding issues of equity, fairness, and justice in relation to ethnically and racially diverse populations and other marginalized groups.

Integrating Multicultural Content and Developing Students' Knowledge about Diverse Groups

Multicultural Content Integration

One significant consideration for faculty is how to integrate multicultural content into existing program structures. Lopez and Bursztyn (2013) argued that multicultural training in psychology should extend beyond teaching only culture-specific knowledge to facilitating students' critical thinking skills about how cultural values, beliefs, and behaviors interact with other factors such as SES, language, and religion. Since interactions between such variables influence student outcomes at the primary and secondary levels (Noltemeyer, Proctor, & Dempsey, 2013), Lopez and Bursztyn's approach to multicultural psychology training is recommended for programs that aim to improve outcomes for the populations their graduates will serve—ethnically and racially diverse school-age students.

Some researchers (e.g., Proctor & Truscott, 2012; Proctor et al., 2014) have suggested that psychology programs should develop specialty tracks focused on specific student populations. However, Newell et al. (2010) cautioned that when program officials elect to use specialty tracks, they should also prepare students to serve a range of populations. Based on their review of the research, Newell et al. suggested an integration-separate course model for multicultural training. This model requires faculty to integrate multicultural content into all courses and to also have separate courses that have a targeted focus on multicultural issues.

The integration-separate course model for multicultural education is an approach that may be ideal for programs that have faculty expertise related to specific ethnic and/or racial groups. Using this model, separate courses focus on developing graduate students' awareness, knowledge, and skills about specific ethnic and/or racial groups, while dedicated content about these groups is also integrated throughout core coursework. For instance, a program that has faculty with expertise regarding African American youth might offer a separate topical course that focuses on educational and sociocultural issues relevant to African American students (e.g., disproportionality in school discipline). Simultaneously, content in core courses (e.g., Behavioral Assessment and Intervention; Consultation) would integrate films, readings, lectures, and class discussions to enhance students' knowledge about how to prevent and intervene when faced with discipline disproportionality for African American students. As Lopez and Bursztyn (2013) recommended, all courses would aim to build not only knowledge about African Americans as a cultural group, but also students' critical thinking skills about how issues such as racial identity, SES, religion, and sexual orientation interact with African American students' school-based experiences and outcomes.

Multicultural Knowledge Development

Another key consideration for faculty is how to build psychology students' multicultural knowledge. A number of teaching tools, techniques, and strategies can be utilized in this area. Faculty must first encourage students' cultural self-awareness since those with more established cultural self-awareness are better able to build cultural knowledge about others (Jones, Sander, & Booker, 2013).

Jones, Sander, and Booker (2013) described valuable resources, including self-assessment tools, films, and readings that can facilitate critical classroom discussions aimed at building cultural self-awareness.

It is important that faculty who teach multicultural content should use strategies to create classroom environments that are safe for all students (Jones et al., 2013; Proctor & Truscott, 2012). For instance, when utilizing films about sensitive racial topics to encourage cultural self-awareness, faculty can offer students an opportunity to submit anonymous questions to decrease potential fear and/or anxiety about discussing ethnic and/or racial issues (Jones et al., 2013). Anonymous questions, which should be phased out to increase student accountability once safety is established, can serve as a springboard for class discussion (Jones et al., 2013). Further, faculty should acknowledge that conversations around multicultural issues are often difficult and that anxiety, fear, and other emotional responses occur and are expected (Jones et al., 2013).

Readings, films, discussions, experiential activities, and journaling can be used to build multicultural knowledge about specific ethnic and racial groups (Jones et al., 2013; Proctor & Truscott, 2012). Newell et al. (2010) noted that multicultural knowledge development should focus on the beliefs, values, customs, and histories of culturally and linguistically diverse groups. Miranda (2014) cautioned that there is the potential to engage in positive or negative stereotyping of ethnic and racial groups while acquiring knowledge about these groups. To prevent this, faculty should ensure that students understand that differences exist within ethnic and racial groups, as well as between groups (Miranda, 2014; Proctor & Meyers, 2014). This requires what Miranda described as deep cultural knowledge of a group. That is, the development of cultural knowledge that extends beyond surface level (e.g., foods and celebrations associated with a group) to a broader understanding of a group's beliefs, customs, values, and how individuals within the group can differ along a continuum (Miranda, 2014).

Miranda (2014) recommended cultural immersion experiences as one way to develop deep cultural knowledge. Similarly, Proctor et al. (2014) encouraged psychology faculty to support psychology graduate students' attendance at summer immersion programs designed to strengthen multicultural competencies with racially, ethnically, and linguistically diverse populations. Of course, such programs should be carefully vetted to ensure quality training. Finally, as discussed next, practical experiences with multiculturally competent field-based psychology supervisors can also serve to develop and enhance psychology students' knowledge about and skills with specific ethnic and racial groups.

Translating Multicultural Knowledge Into Service Delivery

As part of training in applied psychology programs, students are expected to translate knowledge into service delivery. To improve outcomes for ethnically and racially diverse school-age populations, psychology faculty should, as previously discussed, develop multicultural training activities in content areas that align with their accrediting bodies' training standards. However, in light of educational injustices that have occurred for ethnically and racially diverse students in U.S. public schools, particular attention should be given to developing students' skills in nondiscriminatory assessment, culturally relevant counseling and educational intervention, and multicultural consultation and systems intervention (Newell et al., 2010; Proctor, Graves, & Esch, 2012). Newell et al. (2010) noted that during the beginning of students' training, most activities are didactic in nature. Jones et al. (2013) recommended didactic activities that include having students engage in multicultural assessment case conceptualizations, teaching students to conduct culturally relevant clinical interviews prior to engaging in counseling with clients, and exposing students to case studies that include cultural variables that can potentially impact school-based consultation at the organizational, classroom, and teacher level.

Field-based practical experiences, including internships, should provide students with opportunities to serve ethnically and racially diverse school-age populations. Depending on the psychology discipline, practical experiences might occur in a university or community-based clinic, hospital, and/or school setting. Despite the setting, faculty must develop and communicate clearly defined training goals for field-based practical experiences with ethnically and racially diverse populations. For example, in settings in which students work with school-age children who are recent immigrants, goals could be set to help students translate knowledge related to immigrant populations into multiculturally competent service delivery. Such goals might include accurate assessment of a child's acculturation level using standardized acculturation measures, structured interviews, and records review; appropriate interpretation of acculturation assessments; and a written report of the findings, including implications for teacher consultation and educational intervention. Finally, it is psychology faculty's responsibility to ensure that multiculturally competent field-based psychology supervisors direct students' practical experiences with ethnically and racially diverse children (Newell et al., 2010).

Evaluating Students' Multicultural Knowledge and Skills

Newell et al. (2010) suggested that faculty should assess psychology students' multicultural awareness, knowledge, and skills just as diligently as other desired professional competencies are assessed. In terms of multicultural training, Jones et al. (2013) described knowledge as the most basic level of understanding and noted that psychology students' multicultural knowledge can be assessed and monitored using classroom tests, research papers, presentations, and reports. They recommended assessing students' knowledge of concepts such as racism, prejudice, stereotyping, marginalization, acculturation, and so on; racial and ethnic groups, including knowledge about variability that exists within ethnic and racial groups; and historical and contemporary issues related to testing and measurement with minority populations.

To evaluate multicultural skills Jones et al. (2013) and Newell et al. (2010) recommended the use of multicultural competency scales (for more detail on multicultural competency scales, readers are referred to these authors), multicultural guidelines provided by psychology programs' accrediting bodies, and faculty-made assessments based on programs' curricula. For faculty who choose to create their own assessments, the use of a four-level model rubric that describes multicultural skills as Emerging, Basic, Proficient, or Advanced is recommended (Newell et al., 2010). Jones et al. recommended against using self-assessments to evaluate students' multicultural skill development, but encouraged the development and use of treatment integrity checklists that integrate cultural factors, particularly when assessing multicultural skills during counseling and consultation sessions. Since students do not likely enter psychology programs with deep cultural knowledge of ethnically and racially diverse groups, ongoing, formative assessments of their multicultural knowledge and skills can help uncover gaps in their knowledge, direct instructional practices, demonstrate student progress towards multicultural skills development, and provide programs with outcome data related to preparing students to serve ethnically and racially diverse school-age populations.

ENHANCING MULTICULTURAL RESEARCH

Another way for faculty to improve multicultural training that will impact service delivery to ethnically and racially diverse school-age students is to value and implement multicultural research. This involves attending to issues of culture throughout study design, implementation, and evaluation of results (Newell et al., 2010). Newell et al. (2010) recommended that faculty identify how cultural considerations are related to their areas of research and interests (Newell et al., 2010). *Guidelines for Research in Ethnic Minority Communities* may be helpful to faculty seeking basic knowledge about research issues relevant to ethnically and racially diverse populations (Council of National Psychological Associations for the Advancement of Ethnic Minority Interests, 2000). Similarly, the APA (2003) *Guidelines on Multicultural Education, Training, Research, Practice, and Organizational Change for Psychologists* offer guidance regarding conducting multicultural research. One important recommendation in this document is that researchers develop relationships with leaders or cultural brokers within communities. Faculty interested in research with ethnically and racially diverse student populations should be cognizant of the potential mistrust some ethnic and racial minority group members feel towards those within the scientific community. Ethnically and racially diverse parents may be particularly wary of faculty interested in doing research with their children. In these situations, we recommend connecting with a cultural broker (i.e., respected individual within the community of interest who can provide knowledge about and entry into the community).

Additionally, Newell et al. (2010) noted that psychology programs often do not train students in how to use culturally appropriate research methods and designs (e.g., qualitative research). Faculty who do not have the skills to conduct multicultural research should consider cross-institutional collaborations with researchers who possess multicultural and qualitative skills (e.g., case study, ethnography, and participatory action research) (Lopez & Bursztyn, 2013). Such collaborations are critical since multicultural research often uses alternative methodology to understand the nuances (including intersecting identities) of ethnically and racially diverse populations.

CONCLUSION

The increased population diversity in the United States necessitates the training of psychologists whose practices reflect a deep understanding of and commitment to multiculturalism. One way to enhance the delivery of psychological services to ethnically and racially diverse children is to improve multicultural training in psychology graduate programs. This chapter has presented research-based recommendations that faculty can use to reflect on their current multicultural training practices and improve future efforts. By engaging in such reflection and implementing strategic, structural changes in multicultural training practices, faculty can prepare future psychologists to respond to an ethical responsibility: the provision of fair and just services that respect differences based on client characteristics to the racially and ethnically diverse children they will inevitably serve.

REFERENCES

American Psychological Association. (2003). Guidelines on multicultural education, training, research, practice, and organizational change for psychologists. *American Psychologist*, 58, 377–402.

American Psychological Association (2010). *Ethical principles of psychologists and code of conduct (2002, Amended June 1, 2010)*. Retrieved from http://www.apa.org/ethics/code/index.aspx

Bidell, M. P., Ragen, J. K., Broach, C. D., & Carrillo, E. A. (2007). First impressions: A multicultural content analysis of professional psychology program web sites. *Training and Education in Professional Psychology, 1*, 204–214. http://dx.doi. org/10.1037/1931-3918.1.3.204

Carroll, D. W. (2009). Toward multicultural competence: A practical model for implementation in the schools. In J. M. Jones (Ed.), *The psychology of multiculturalism in schools* (pp. 1–16). Bethesda, MD: National Association of School Psychologists.

Chandler, D. R. (2011). Proactively addressing the shortage of blacks in psychology: Highlighting the school psychology subfield. *Journal of Black Psychology, 37*, 99–127. http://dx.doi.org/10.1177/0095798409359774

Clark, C. R., Mercer, S. H., Zeigler-Hill, V., & Dufrene, B. A. (2012). Barriers to the success of ethnic minority students in school psychology graduate programs. *School Psychology Review, 41*, 176–192.

Council of National Psychological Associations for the Advancement of Ethnic Minority Interests. (2000). *Guidelines for research in ethnic minority communities*. Washington, DC: American Psychological Association.

Ford, D. Y. (2014). Segregation and the underrepresentation of Blacks and Hispanics in gifted education: Social inequality and deficit paradigms. *Roeper Review, 36*, 143–154. http://dx.doi.org/10.1080/02783193.2014.919563

Graves, S. L., Jr., & Wright, L. B. (2009). Historically black colleges and university students' and faculties' views of school psychology: Implications for increasing diversity in higher education. *Psychology in the Schools, 46*, 616–626. http://dx.doi.org/10.1002/pits.20402

Hammond, R. W., & Yung, B. (1993). Minority student recruitment and retention practices among schools of professional psychology: A national survey and analysis. *Professional Psychology: Research and Practice, 24*, 3–12. http://dx.doi. org/10.1037/0735-7028.24.1.3

Hill-Briggs, F., Evans, J. D., & Norman, M. A. (2004). Racial and ethnic diversity among trainees and professionals in psychology and neuropsychology: Needs, trends, and challenges. *Applied Neuropsychology, 11*, 13–22. http://dx.doi.org/10.1207/s15324826an1101_3

Jones, J. M., Sander, J. B., & Booker, K. W. (2013). Multicultural competency building: Practical solutions for training and evaluating student progress. *Training and Education in Professional Psychology, 7*, 12–22. http://dx.doi.org/10.1037/a0030880

Lopez, E. C., & Bursztyn, A. M. (2013). Future challenges and opportunities: Toward culturally responsive training in school psychology. *Psychology in the Schools, 50*, 212–228. http://dx.doi.org/10.1002/pits.21674

Maton, K. I., Wimms, H. E., Grant, S. K., Wittig, M. A., Rogers, M. R., & Vasquez, M. J. T. (2011). Experiences and perspectives of African American, Latina/o, Asian American, and European American psychology graduate students: A national study. *Cultural Diversity and Ethnic Minority Psychology, 17*, 68–78. http://dx.doi.org/10.1037/a0021668

Miranda, A. H. (2014). Best practices in increasing cross-cultural competency. In P. L. Harrison & A. Thomas (Eds.), *Best practices in school psychology: Foundations* (pp. 9–19). Bethesda, MD: National Association of School Psychologists.

Moy, G. E., Briggs, A., Shriberg, D., Furrey, K. J., Smith, P., & Tompkins, N. (2014). Developing school psychologists as agents of social justice: A qualitative analysis of student understanding across three years. *Journal of School Psychology*. Advance on-line publication. http://dx.doi.org/10.1016/j.jsp.2014/03.001

National Association of School Psychologists. (2010a). *Principles for professional ethics*. Retrieved from http://www.nasponline.org/publications/periodicals/spr/volume-26/volume-26-issue-4/principles-for-professional-ethics

National Association of School Psychologists. (2010b). *Standards for the graduate preparation of school psychologists*. Retrieved from http://www.nasponline.org/standards/2010standards/1_Graduate_Preparation.pdf

National Center for Educational Statistics. (2014). *Condition of education 2014*. Washington, DC: Author.

Newell, M. L., Nastasi, B. K., Hatzichristou, C., Jones, J. M., Schanding, G. T., Jr., & Yetter, G. (2010). Evidence on multicultural training in school psychology: Recommendations for future directions. *School Psychology Quarterly*, *25*, 249–278. http://dx.doi.org/10.1037/a0021542

Noltemeyer, A. L., Proctor, S. L., & Dempsey, A. (2013). Race and ethnicity in school psychology publications: A content analysis and comparison to publications in related disciplines. *Contemporary School Psychology*, *17*, 129–142.

Proctor, S. L., Graves, S. L., Jr., & Esch, R. C. (2012). Assessing African American students for specific learning disabilities: The promises and perils of response to intervention. *The Journal of Negro Education*, *81*, 268–282.

Proctor, S. L., & Meyers, J. (2014). Best practices in primary prevention in diverse schools and communities. In P. L. Harrison & A. Thomas (Eds.), *Best practices in school psychology: Foundations*, 33–47. Bethesda, MD: National Association of School Psychologists.

Proctor, S. L., Simpson, C. M., Levin, J., & Hackimer, L. (2014). Recruitment of diverse students in school psychology programs: Direction for future research and practice. *Contemporary School Psychology*, 117–126. http://dx.doi.org/10.1007/s40688-014-0012-z

Proctor, S. L., & Truscott, S. D. (2012). Reasons for African American student attrition from school psychology programs. *Journal of School Psychology*, *50*, 655–679. http://dx.doi.org/10.1016/j.jsp.2012.06.002

Proctor, S. L., & Truscott, S. D. (2013). Missing voices: African American school psychologists' perspectives on increasing professional diversity. *The Urban Review*, *45*, 355–375. http://dx.doi.org/10.1007/s11256-012-0232-3

Rogers, M. R., & Molina, L. E. (2006). Exemplary efforts in psychology to recruit and retain graduate students of color. *American Psychologist*, *61*, 143–156. http://dx.doi.org/10.1037/0003-066X.61.2.143

Smith, L., Blake, J., & Graves, S. L. (2013). School psychology programs' efforts to recruit culturally diverse students. *Trainers' Forum*, *31*, 4–23.

INDEX

Alter, P. J., 17

Alternating treatments design, 233, 243–245

American Indians. *See also* Native Americans
achievement gap for, 23
in doctoral study in psychology, 14
low-income, barriers to psychological support for, 95
in treatment efficacy studies, 17

American Indians/Alaska Natives
culturally adapted intervention for, 188
Society of Indian Psychologists, 15

American Psychiatric Association, 67

American Psychological Association (APA), 3–4, 206–207, 232, 253–255, 262

Anxiety
assessment of, 102–104
and stereotype threat, 32

Aptitude–achievement discrepancy, diagnosing, 68–69

Army Alpha test, 11, 62

Army Beta test, 11, 62

Aro, M., 143

Aronson, Joshua, 153

Asian American Journal of Psychology, 14

Asian American Psychological Association (AAPA), 15

Asian Americans
anxiety in, 104
depression in, 27, 101–102
in doctoral psychology programs, 14, 257
emotional disturbance among, 97
and intellectual test score gap, 64
intelligence scores of, 65
stereotype threat for, 32, 34
in treatment efficacy studies, 17

Asian/Pacific Islanders
demographics of, 252
neuropsychological assessment of, 141

Asian psychologists, 15

ASQ3 (Ages and Stages Questionnaire, 3rd ed.), 121–122

Assessment. *See also specific types of assessment, e.g.*: Intellectual assessment

criticisms of test scores in minority populations, 42–43
early history of, 9–10
standards for, 177. *See also Standards for Educational and Psychological Testing*

Association of Black Psychologists (ABPsi), 13, 14

Association of Psychologists Por La Raza, 14

Athanasiou, M. S., 86

Attention-deficit/hyperactivity disorder (ADHD)
and behavioral consultation, 200–201
efficacy of treatment studies of, 17

Attneave, Carolyn, 15

Austin, A. A., 101, 104

Baker, J. N., 242

Balanced bilinguals, 152

BASC-2 (Behavior Assessment for Children, 2nd ed.), 201–202

Baseline-intervention (A-B) design, 233, 236–237

Battelle Developmental Inventory (BDI), 122, 123

Battelle Developmental Inventory, Second Edition (BDI–2), 123–124

Battelle Developmental Inventory Screening Test (BDIST), 122–123

Bay Area Association of Black Psychologists, 13

Bayley Scales of Infant Development, Second Edition, 124

BDI (Battelle Developmental Inventory), 122, 123

BDI–2 (Battelle Developmental Inventory, Second Edition), 123–124

BDIST (Battelle Developmental Inventory Screening Test), 122–123

Beckham, Albert, 12

Beckman, T., 201–202, 205

Beem, S., 86

Behavioral assessment. *See* Social–emotional and behavioral assessment

Behavioral consultation, 200–202

Blacks/African Americans, *continued*
  in special education, 12–14, 43, 69, 70, 197–198
  STEM achievement of males, 27
  stereotype threat for, 32, 33, 153
  strengths and assets of, 30
  suicidality among, 101
  teacher feedback for, 31
  test-taking anxiety among adults, 153
  in treatment efficacy studies, 17
  unmet mental health needs of, 98–99
  violence in males, 27
Blake, J., 256
Blanco-Vega, C. O., 187
Boehm, A. E., 116–117
Bohinski, J. M., 214–215
Bond, Horace Mann, 12
Bongar, B., 101
Bonilla, J., 189
Booker, K. W., 259–260
Borelli, J. L., 214
Borman, G. D., 33–34
Bos, A. F., 122
Botvin, E. M., 187–188
Botvin, G. J., 187–188
Boykin, A. W., 28
Bradley, M. H., 63
Brassard, M. R., 116–117
Brigance Early Childhood Screens III, 124–125
Broach, C. D., 256–257
Browder, D. N., 242
Brown, S. L., 79, 205
Brown v. Board of Education, 69
Bruch, S. K., 33–34
Burns, M. K., 168, 171
Bursztyn, A. M., 252, 254, 258–259
Byrne, K. E., 123

Cagle, M., 201, 205
California Verbal leaning Test (CVLT), 141
Callahan, J. E., 87
Camara, W. J., 49
Canadian children, 143
CAR (Community Action Research), 218
Caretaking responsibilities, 29

Carlson, J. S., 64
Carrillo, E. A., 256–257
Carrizales, D., 189
Carroll, D. W., 253
Cartledge, G., 242
Casas, R., 145
Casavantes, Edward, 14
Castro-Olivo, S. M., 186, 189–191
Cattell, James McKeen, 10
Caucasians. *See also* Whites
  CBM in assessment of, 87
  depression among, 99
  feelings of sadness among, 100
  high-stakes assessments of, 86
  and intellectual test score gap, 63, 64
  quality of education for, 142
Cavazos-Gonzalez, C., 152
CBA (curriculum-based assessment), 85
CBA-ID (curriculum-based assessment for instructional design), 85–86
CBC (conjoint behavioral consultation), 201–202
CBM. *See* Curriculum-based measurement
CBPR (Community-Based Participatory Research), 218–219, 222
CCC (cover, copy, and compare) technique, 243–244
CDC (Centers for Disease Control and Prevention), 214
CD students. *See* Culturally diverse students
Cell proliferation and migration, in neurodevelopment, 134–135
Cellular zones, 134
Centers for Disease Control and Prevention (CDC), 214
Chandler, D. R., 256
Changing criterion design, 243
Cheah, C. S., 214
Cheng, Y., 102
Child neuropsychology, 134. *See also* Neuropsychological assessment
Children of color, 10. *See also specific groups*, *e.g.*: Blacks/African Americans
Chinese Americans, 101, 102, 104
Chinese speakers, neurodevelopment in, 136–138
Chisholm, Shirley, 3

Digit Span test, 143
Disability(-ies). *See also* Learning disabilities diagnosis
    determining presence of, 84–85
    in early childhood, 115
    standards for individuals with, 49
    vague or lacking definitions of, 87–88
Discipline practices, for Black and Latino students, 24
Diversity
    among ethnic minority students, 4
    challenges created by, 251
    conceptualizing of, 78–79
    and conjoint behavioral consultation research results, 202
    dimensions of, 78
    within-group, 206
Documentation, of need for specialized instruction/services, 85
Dolan, C. V., 64, 66
Doll, B., 202
Donovan, S., 16
Dowdy, E., 107–108
DP-3 (Developmental Profile 3), 126
Dropout rates. *See* High school dropout rates
DSM–5 (*Diagnostic and Statistical Manual of Mental Disorders, 5th ed.*), 67–68, 96
DuBois, W. E. B., 12, 213
Dufrene, B. A., 257
Dunlap, G., 17
Dunn, Lloyd, 69
Dunson, R. M., III, 200–201
Duran, M., 30
Durlak, J. A., 185
Dyer, R., 188
Dynamic Indicators of Basic Early Literacy, 171
Dyslexia, 137

Eagle, J. W., 202
EAHCA (Education for All Handicapped Children Act of 1975), 69, 138
Early childhood assessment, 115–129
    Ages and Stages Questionnaire, 121–122
    approaches to, 116–117
    assumptions guiding, 116–117

Battelle Developmental Inventory, Second Edition, 123–124
Battelle Developmental Inventory Screening Test, 122–123
Brigance Early Childhood Screens III, 124–125
considerations in, 118–120
Developmental Assessment of Young Children-2, 126–127
Developmental Profile 3, 126
Differential Ability Scales, Second Edition, 127–128
observations, 121
primary step in, 120
Wechsler Preschool and Primary Scale of Intelligence, Fourth Edition, 128–129
Eating disorders, 214
EB students. *See* Emerging bilingual students
EBT/I. *See* Evidence-based treatments/interventions
Ecological framework, 85
Ecological validity model, 189
ED. *See* Emotional disturbance
Educational quality
    for CLD students, 184
    and neuropsychological assessment, 141–142
Education for All Handicapped Children Act of 1975 (EAHCA), 69, 138
Education of the Handicapped Act Amendments of 1986, 115
Educators. *See also* Specialized staff; Teachers
    academic assessment and training/professional competency of, 84
    multicultural training to improve service delivery by, 258
Edwards, O. W., 63, 65
Efficacy of interventions, research on, 16–18
EL. *See* English learners
Elbaum, B., 123
ELL. *See* English language learners
Emerging bilingual (EB) students
    culturally diverse students vs., 79
    language of assessment for, 81–82

Evidence-based treatments/
interventions (EBT/I)
consultation, 198–207
cultural adaptations of, 187, 188
Expectations
achievement and, 29
in effective urban schools, 176

Faculty professional development, 258
Fairness in testing
1999 *Standards* on, 50–51
2014 *Standards* on, 51–53
academic assessments, 82
culturally fair instruments, 107–108,
142–143
as lack of bias, 62
Familism, 101
Family involvement, 88–89
Farrell, A. D., 102–103
FAS (fetal alcohol syndrome), 135–136
FBAs (functional behavioral assess-
ments), 107
Feedback, academic valuing and, 31
Females
health disparities among African
American girls, 213–226
IT and STEM program for, 30
stereotype threat for, 32
Fenning, P. A., 203–204
Ferguson, C., 202
Fetal alcohol syndrome (FAS),
135–136
Feuerborn, L., 189
Field-based practical experiences, 261
Figueroa, R. A., 83
Filipino Americans, depression among,
101, 102
Flanagan, D. P., 82, 83
Floyd, R., 101
Floyd, R. G., 66
Flynn, J. R., 64
Fountas, I. C., 169
Four-level multicultural skills model,
262
Francis, D. J., 81
French-background children, 152
Fuchs, D., 202
Fuchs, L. S., 202
Functional behavioral assessments
(FBAs), 107

Gallagher, J., 204–205
Gamoran, A., 33–34
Gasquoine, P. G., 152
GATE programs. *See* Gifted education
Gender-based health disparities, 214,
216. *See also* Health disparities
among African American girls
Generalization of treatments, 17–18
Genetic explanations
for cognitive abilities differences,
65–66
for racial differences, 12
Gibson, L., 242
Gifted education (GATE programs)
African American students in, 43
outcomes of, 16
underrepresentation of certain racial/
ethnic groups in, 78
Glascoe, F. P., 123
Glioblasts, 134
Goldblum, P., 101
Graduate psychology programs, multi-
cultural training in. *See* Multicul-
tural training
Grant, Igor, 141
Graphic analyses, 246–247
Graves, S. L., 256
Graves, S. L., Jr., 256
Gravois, T. A., 202–203
Grunewald, S., 17
Gueldener, B. A., 189
*Guidelines for Research in Ethnic
Minority Communities* (Council
of National Psychology Associa-
tions for the Advancement of
Ethnic Minority Interests), 4,
208, 262
*Guidelines on Multicultural Education,
Training, Research, Practice, and
Organizational Change for Psy-
chologists* (American Psychologi-
cal Association), 3–4, 206–207,
253–255, 262

Hall, B., 29
Halstead-Reitan Battery, 141
Hamlett, C. L., 202
Hanselman, P., 33–34
Harjusola-Webb, S., 234
Harry, B., 83

Indigenous American students, unmet mental health needs of, 98–99
Individualized Education Plans (IEPs)
information collection for, 85
and neuropsychological assessment, 139
for students with social, emotional, or behavioral symptoms, 96
Individuals With Disabilities Education Act (IDEA), 70, 81, 84, 138–139
Individuals With Disabilities Educational Improvement Act of 2004 (IDEIA), 70, 96–98, 232
Infants. See Early childhood assessment
Information technology (IT) after-school program, 30
Ingraham, C. L., 203–204, 206
Institutional oppression, health disparities among African American girls and, 215–216
Instructional consultation (IC), 202–203
Instructional efficiency, 245
Instructional triangle, 202
Integration-separate course model (for multicultural education), 259
Intellectual assessment(s), 61–72. See also Intelligence testing
bias in, 62–64
differences among, 65–67
ethnic minority performance on, 64–65
historical context of, 62
of learning disabilities, 67–71
Intellectual test score gap, 64, 65
Intelligence quotient (IQ), 10, 66
and aptitude–achievement discrepancy model, 68–69
and malnutrition, 135
and quality of education, 141
Intelligence testing, 18. See also Intellectual assessment(s); individual instruments
of African American children, 12–14
Binet–Simon and Stanford–Binet scales, 10
controversy over, 42
in identifying learning disability, 70, 71
standardization of tests, 10, 61, 62
during World War I, 11–12, 62

International Classification of Diseases (10th rev.; ICD–10), 67, 68
Interpreters
in neuropsychological assessment, 145
training for, 108, 144
Intersectionality framework, 96
factors in life experiences for people of color, 213–214
for health disparities among African American girls, 213–226
Intervention-based intellectual assessment, 70–71
Intervention efficacy research, 16–18
Intervention research
consultation-based, 197–208
historical issues with minority populations, 16–18
single-subject designs, 236–237, 246–247
Interventions
for health disparities among African American girls, 216–218
history of, with minority populations, 9–18
manualized vs. nonmanualized, 185. See also Manualized school-based social–emotional interventions
to monitor/improve academic performance. See Single-subject research designs [SSRDs]
reading, 165–179
self-affirmation, and stereotype threat, 33–34
theory- vs. nontheory-based, 225
universal screening for need for, 167
Interviews
in early childhood assessment, 120
in social–emotional and behavioral assessment, 106–107
IQ. See Intelligence quotient
IRD (improvement rate difference), 246, 247
ISIS (Intelligent Sisters Improving themSelves) Project, 219–226
lessons learned from, 224–226
theoretical perspectives for, 219–220

IT (information technology) after-school
program, 30
Italian-background children, 152

Jackson, J. S., 215
Jackson, T. W., 200–201
Jacobs, J., 188
Japanese Americans, depression among,
101, 102
Jemmott, J. B., III, 214–215
Jemmott, L. S., 214–215
Jernigan, M., 207
Johnson Elementary School reading
intervention, 169–178
and core literacy instruction,
169–170
implementing class-wide interven-
tion, 171, 173–174
implications of, 176–178
results of, 174–176
and student population characteris-
tics, 169
universal screening, 170–172
Jones, J. M., 259–262
Jones, S. M., 192
Jordan, L., 86
Joseph, L. M., 241
Journal content, 17, 79
Journal of Black Psychology, 14
Journal of Indigenous Research, 14
Journal of Latina/o Psychology, 14
Journal of School Psychology, 205
Jóvenes fuertes intervention, 186, 189–191
Jurecska, D. E., 188

KABC–II (Kaufman Assessment Battery
for Children, 2nd ed.), 63
Kamin, L. J., 64–65
Kamphaus, R. W., 107–108
Kan, K. J., 66
Kane, M., 177
Kaufman Assessment Battery for Chil-
dren (2nd ed.; KABC–II), 63
Kerstjens, J. M., 122
Keyes, S. E., 242
Kimm, S. Y., 215
Kingery, J. N., 103
Klingner, J. K., 83
Korean Americans, depression among,
101–102

Kranzler, J. H., 86
Kratochwill, T. R., 201, 235
Kuhl, P. K., 136
Kuo, W. H., 101–102

Landrum, T. J., 234
Lane, S., 49
Language minority, 78
Language proficiency
in bilingual children, 152
objective measures of, 145, 152
Languages, used in assessment, 81–82
Larry P. v. Riles, 12–13
Latinas/os
achievement gap for, 23–25.
See also Achievement
frameworks
anxiety in, 103–104
bilingual, test performance of, 152
and deficit-based achievement
frameworks, 26
demographics of, 252
depression in, 27, 100–101
development and achievement in,
28
disciplinary actions against, 184
in doctoral psychology programs,
14, 257
emotional disturbance among,
97, 98
functional behavioral assessments
with, 107
high school dropout rates for,
183–184
and intellectual test score gap, 64
intelligence scores of, 65
low-income, barriers to psychological
support for, 95
National Latina/o Psychological
Association, 14–15
negative outcomes for, 183
poverty among, 98
school-based substance abuse prevention for, 188
stereotype threat for, 32, 33
suicidality among, 101
teacher feedback for, 31
in treatment efficacy studies, 17
unmet mental health needs of,
98–99

Latino English language learners, 185–187
 culturally adapted evidence-based treatments for, 187–188
 jóvenes fuertes intervention for, 189–191
 manualized school-based social–emotional interventions for, 185–187
Lawson, D. B., 30
Leadership, ethnic identity and, 28
Learning, connected to life and future job security, 31
Learning disabilities diagnosis, 67–71
 of African Americans, 70
 aptitude–achievement discrepancy, 68–69
 in clinical settings, 67–68
 distinguishing between low-language proficiency and, 83, 84
 response to intervention, 69–71
 in schools, 68–71
Learning disorders, neurodevelopment and, 137
LEP (limited English proficient), 78
Lesaux, N. K., 81
Lichtenstein, R., 88
Limited English proficient (LEP), 78
Linguistically diverse students
 assessing/monitoring academic performance of. *See* Single-subject research designs [SSRDs]
 assessment challenges and concerns with, 79–84
 in culturally and linguistically diverse group, 78
 demographics of, 252
 identifying disability in, 84–85
Linguistic minorities, standards for, 49
Linguistic skills, cultural differences in, 136–137
Liu, H. M., 136
Lopez, E. C., 252, 254, 258–259
Lundahl, A. A., 205
Lynn, R., 64

Malnutrition, 135
Manly, J. J., 142

Manualized school-based social–emotional interventions, 183–192
 culturally adapted evidence-based treatments, 187–188
 jóvenes fuertes intervention for Latino ELL students, 189–191
 for Latino English language learners, 185–187
Mascher, J., 207
Maton, K. I., 257
Matthews, W. J., 87
McClelland, M. M., 122
McCloskey, D., 86
McDonough, E., 202–203
McGee, E. O., 27
McIntosh, D. E., 63
McKinney, M. D., 200
Measurement bias, fairness as lack of, 53
Medjahed, B., 30
Mental age, of Army recruits in World War I, 11
Mental disorders, efficacy of treatment studies, 17
Mental Health (Surgeon General), 17
Mental health assessment. *See* Social–emotional and behavioral assessment
Mental test (term), 9–10
Mercer, S. H., 257
Merrell, K. W., 186, 189
Mexican Americans
 bilingual programs for, 29
 culturally adapted interventions for, 188
 and intelligence testing standardization, 10
Meyers, J., 252, 253, 258
Mickelson, R. A., 31
Middle Eastern Americans, neuropsychological assessment of, 141
Miller, M. D., 86
Miller, W. S., 141
Minneapolis Public Schools, 167
Minority group (term), 47
Miranda, A. H., 260
Molina, L. E., 256, 257
Moughamian, A. C., 81
Moy, G. E., 254, 258
MTSS. *See* Multitiered systems of support

Mudholkar, P., 199
Mulenga, K., 143
Multicultural (term), 252
Multicultural competency scales, 262
Multicultural consultation, 203–204
Multicultural content integration,
     258–259
Multiculturalism, 252–253
     as practiced in U.S. public schools,
          252–261
     standards on importance of, 253
Multicultural knowledge
     development of, 259–260
     of students, evaluating, 261–262
     translated into service delivery,
          260–261
Multicultural research, 198, 262–263
Multicultural training, 251–263
     demographics of ethnically and
          racially diverse students in
          U.S. public schools, 252
     enhancing multicultural research,
          262–263
     evaluating students' multicultural
          knowledge and skills, 261–262
     faculty professional development,
          258
     multicultural content integration,
          258–259
     multiculturalism as practiced in U.S.
          public schools, 252–261
     multicultural knowledge develop-
          ment, 259–260
     in psychology graduate programs,
          254–255
     recruitment of diverse school psy-
          chology students, 255–257
     retention of diverse school
          psychology students, 255,
          257–258
     translating multicultural knowledge
          into service delivery,
          260–261
Multielement designs, 243
Multifactor eco-cultural model of
     assessment, 117
Multiple baseline designs, 233, 238–243
     changing criterion design, 243
     multielement designs, 243
     multiple probe designs, 241–243

Multiple probe designs, 241–243
Multitiered systems of support (MTSS),
     166, 168–169, 176
Murr, N., 199

Nadler, J. T., 32
NAEP (National Assessment for
     Educational Progress), 231
NAEYC (National Association for the
     Education of Young Children),
     116
Nakano, S., 63
NASP. See National Association of
     School Psychologists
Nation, M., 16
National Assessment for Educational
     Progress (NAEP), 231
National Association for the Advance-
     ment of Colored People, 12
National Association for the Education
     of Young Children (NAEYC),
     116
National Association of School Psy-
     chologists (NASP), 116, 186,
     253, 254
National Center for Learning Disabili-
     ties/RTI Action Network, 71
National Dissemination Center for
     Children with Disabilities, 84
National Latina/o Psychological Asso-
     ciation, 14–15
National Research Council, 16, 70
Native Americans. See also American
     Indians
     academic performance of, 197
     display of internalizing and psychotic
          symptoms among, 99
     fetal alcohol syndrome among, 136
     intelligence scores of, 65
     at Johnson Elementary School, 169
     negative outcomes for, 183
     neuropsychological assessment of,
          141
     in special education categories,
          197–198
     and validity of WISC–IV, 63
Native Americans/Alaska Natives, 252
Native Hawaiians, 252. See also
     Hawaiians
Native Hawaiians/Pacific Islanders, 252

People of color. *See also individual racial/ ethnic groups*
  health inequities among, 213–214
  intelligence testing standardization for children, 10
Percentage of all nonoverlapping data (PAND), 246, 247
Percentage of nonoverlapping data (PND), 246–247
Perez, M., 29
Personal assets, 29
Peruvian children, 135
Peterson, M., 241
Pfaff, K., 204–205
Phenomenological variant of ecological systems theory (PVEST), 26–28
Pinnell, G. S., 169
Pitoniak, M. J., 81–82
PLC (Progressive Life Center), 219
PND (percentage of nonoverlapping data), 246–247
Positive youth development (PYD) research, 27–28
Posttraumatic stress disorder (PTSD), 214
Poverty
  among Latino youth, 98
  and CBM-R results, 177
  of CLD students, 184
  depression and, 99–100
  and neurodevelopment, 135
  of U.S. school students, 252
Pratt, C., 122
Predictive bias, 43, 63
Prereferral team, in social–emotional and behavioral assessment, 105–106
Preschool children. *See* Early childhood assessment
PRESS (Path to Reading Excellence in School Sites), 169
Prinstein, M. J., 214
Problem suppression–facilitation model, 101
Proctor, S. L., 79, 205, 252, 253, 256–258, 260
Professional competency, in academic assessment, 83, 84
Professional judgment, 87–88
Professional organizations, 14–15

Progressive Life Center (PLC), 219
Protective factors, 26–27
Pruning (segregation), in neuro-development, 135
Psych Discourse, 14
Psychological assessment. *See* Assessment
Psychology graduate programs, multi-cultural training in, 254–255. *See also* Multicultural training
Psychometric movement, 10
PTSD (posttraumatic stress disorder), 214
PVEST (phenomenological variant of ecological systems theory), 26–28
PYD (positive youth development) research, 27–28

Quality of academic assessment, 87–89
Questionnaires, in early childhood assessment, 120
Quirk, M., 86

Race, as a control variable in research, 206
Racial categories, 207
Racial differences
  in emotional disturbance, 97–98
  genetic explanations for, 12
  in intellectual assessment scores, 62–63
Racial inferiority, 12
Racially diverse students, demographics of, 252. *See also specific topics*
Racial minority students. *See also* Ethni-cally diverse students
  consultation-based interventions for, 197–208
  in U.S. public school population, 3
Racism, 213–214
Ragen, J. K., 256–257
Ramirez, M., 29
Ransom, K. A., 201
Rating scales, in early childhood assess-ment, 120
Reading intervention, 165–179
  class-wide, based on screening data, 168–169
  at Johnson Elementary School, 169–178
  screening reading skills, 167–168

Reading proficiency
    of Black and Latino students, 24
    of English learners, 84
    of urban students, 165
Reading-related learning disabilities,
        among ELs, 84
Receiver operating characteristics
        (ROC) analysis, 171, 178
Recruitment, of diverse school psychol-
        ogy students, 255–257
Reddy, L. A., 199
Reijneveld, S. A., 122
Reliability
    1985 *Standards* on, 48, 49
    of instruments developed for pre-
        school children, 119, 123–
        125, 127–129
    of reading assessments, 167, 170
Religious affiliation of U.S. school stu-
        dents, 252
Repeated acquisition design, 245
Resiliency, social–emotional, 184, 185
Response-related sources of bias, 51
Response to intervention (RTI), 69–71
    in academic assessment, 84
    jóvenes fuertes intervention with, 191
    use of CBM for, 86
Response-topography comparisons, 245
Retention of diverse school psychology
        students, 255, 257–258
Rhodes, R. L., 84
Rivera, C. J., 242
Rivera, M. O., 81
ROC (receiver operating characteris-
        tics) analysis, 171, 178
Rogers, M. R., 256, 257
Rosenfield, S. A., 202–203
Rothlisberg, B. A., 63
RTI. *See* Response to intervention

Salas, S., 242
Salend, S. J., 88–89
Salinas, A., 88–89
Sander, J. B., 259–260
Sando, L., 124
Sandoval, O., 152
Schinke, S. P., 187–188
Schizophrenia
    assessment of, 104–105
    efficacy of treatment studies of, 17

Schmidt, S. R., 188
School consultation, 198. *See also*
        Consultation-based intervention
        services
School procedures/practices, for aca-
        demic assessment, 82–83
School professionals, academic assess-
        ment competency of, 83. *See also*
        Specialized staff
School Psychology Quarterly, 205
School Psychology Review, 205
School psychology students
    diverse, recruitment of, 255–257
    diverse, retention of, 255, 257–258
    multicultural training for. *See* Multi-
        cultural training
Schulte, A. C., 199, 200
Science, technology, engineering, and
        math (STEM), 27, 30
Screening, 167
    in early childhood assessment,
        120–129
    to evaluate student response to core
        curriculum, 166
    in kindergarten to Grade 12 schools,
        176–177
    for reading skills, 167–169. *See also*
        Johnson Elementary School
        reading intervention
    universal, 167
Segregation (pruning), in neurodevel-
        opment, 135
Self-affirmation intervention, stereotype
        threat and, 33–34
Self-efficacy theory, 216
SEL programs. *See* Social–emotional
        learning programs
SES. *See* Socioeconomic status
Sexual abuse, of African American girls,
        214–216
Sexual health, in African American
        girls, 215, 217
Shadish, W. R., 66
Sheridan, S. M., 201, 202
Shriberg, D., 79, 203–205
Significant disproportionality
        (term), 70
Silverman, W., 66
Simon, Theodore, 10
Simon, V. A., 214

Simple baseline-intervention (A-B) design, 233
Single-Case Design Technical Documentation (What Works Clearinghouse), 232
Single-subject research designs (SSRDs), 231–247
   advantages of using, 232–233
   alternating treatments design, 243–245
   analysis of intervention effects, 246–247
   baseline-intervention design, 236–237
   common components of, 233–234
   multiple baseline designs, 238–243
   repeated acquisition design, 245
   stages of baseline logic in, 234–235
   types of, 235
   withdrawal designs, 237–238
Skin color, performance on intelligence tests and, 12
Smith, L., 256
Social cognitive models, 216
Social–cultural theory, 187
Social–emotional and behavioral assessment, 95–108
   administration and interpretation of, 108
   anxiety, 102–104
   best practices in, 105–108
   clinical interviews, 106–107
   cultural manifestations of ED symptomatology, 98–105
   depression, 99–102
   functional behavioral assessments, 107
   IDEIA emotional disturbance framework for, 96–98
   prereferral team in, 105–106
   schizophrenia, 104–105
   selecting culturally fair instruments, 107–108
Social–emotional learning (SEL) programs, 185. *See also* Manualized school-based social–emotional interventions

adapted for Latino ELLs, 185–187
   for CLD students, research on, 186
Social–emotional outcomes, consultation and, 198
Social–emotional resiliency, 184
   for Latino ELLs, 186
   promotion and teaching of, 185–186. *See also* Manualized school-based social–emotional interventions
Socialization, ethnic and racial, 27
Social justice consultation, 203–205
Social justice training model, 254
"Socially maladjusted" children (in IDEIA), 97
Social support, 30
Society of Indian Psychologists, 15
Socioeconomic status (SES). *See also* Poverty
   of Black youth, 99
   and emotional disturbance, 95, 97–98
   and neuropsychological assessment, 135–136
   and stereotype threat, 32
   of U.S. school students, 252
   and vocabulary development, 137
Soles, T., 124
Southwest Action Coalition (SWAC), 221
Spanish speakers
   Digit Span performance of, 143
   effectiveness of story-based lessons for, 242
   translation practices in assessment of, 144
   in U.S. schools, 252
Special education outcomes, 16
Special education referral/placement
   academic assessments, 82–89
   of African Americans, 69, 70
   based on intelligence test scores, 42–43
   under the category of ED, 105
   CBM in, 86
   clarity of practices in, 87–88
   under EAHCA, 69
   ecological framework in evaluating, 85

Task performance, stereotype threat
    and, 32
Taylor, L. K., 244–245
TBI (traumatic brain injury), 136,
    139
TDM (talent development model of
    schooling), 28–31
Teachers
    building morale of, 30
    feedback from, 31
    lack of bilingual education
        training for, 84
Team-based instructional
    consultation, 202–203
Teaming, 88–89
*Technical Recommendations for
    Achievement Tests* (1955),
    44, 45
*Technical Recommendations for Psy-
    chological Tests and Diagnostics*
    (1954), 43
Teitelman, A. M., 214–215
Tennille, J., 214–215
Terman, Lewis, 10
Test administration
    for BDI–2, 124
    at Johnson Elementary School,
        170
    for preschoolers, 119
    for social–emotional and
        behavioral assessment,
        108
    for WPPSI–IV, 129
Test content
    2014 *Standards* on, 53
    culturally fair, 142–143
    in early childhood assessment,
        119
Test context
    2014 *Standards* on, 53
    in early childhood assessment,
        119–120
Testing environment, in early childhood
    assessment, 119–120
Testing process, fair treatment during,
    52–53
Test interpretations
    in neuropsychological assessment,
        133, 140–141

and observations of preschoolers,
    121
with preschoolers, 119
with social–emotional and behav-
    ioral assessment, 108
validity of, 53
Test response, 2014 *Standards* on, 53
Test scores
    appropriate use of, 42, 47
    in minority populations, criticisms
        of, 42–43
Test-taking anxiety, neuropsychological
    assessment and, 153
T.H.E. NUBIANS (Teaching, Healing,
    Empowering—Never Under-
    estimating Brothers' Intelligence,
    Ambitions & Natural Strengths),
    224
Theory of planned behavior, 216, 217
Tier 1 interventions, 166, 169–178
Tier 2 interventions, 166–168
Tier 3 interventions, 166
Tobin, K. G., 87
Toddlers. *See* Early childhood assessment
Townsend, T. G., 217, 219, 220
Tran, O. K., 189
Translation practices
    in academic assessment, 81–82
    in neuropsychological assessment,
        144–151
    in social–emotional and behavioral
        assessment, 108
Traumatic brain injury (TBI), 136, 139
True peers (term), 86
Truscott, S. D., 256–258
Tsai, H. A., 122
Tsao, F. M., 136
Tunstall, K., 199
Twyford, J. M., 107–108

Unemployment rates, 24
United Kingdom, tests of bilingual
    children in, 152
United States Surgeon General, 17
Universal screening, 167
    to identify class-wide problems, 178
    at Johnson Elementary School,
        170–172
University of Minnesota, 170

University of Oregon Center on
    Teaching and Learning, 171
Urban schools
    CBM-R screening in, 167
    combining types of data for decision
        making in, 178
    reading proficiency of students in,
        165
    students needing extra support in,
        166
    Tier 1 reading intervention at
        Johnson Elementary School,
        169–178
U.S. Army intelligence testing
    program, 11
U.S. Bureau of the Census, 15
U.S. Department of Education, 69

Valdez, G., 29
Validity
    1974 *Standards* on, 47
    1985 *Standards* on, 48–49
    1999 *Standards* on, 50
    of academic assessment measures,
        79–81
    of academic assessments, 82
    defined, 80
    in early childhood assessment, 124
    of instruments developed for
        preschool-age children, 119,
        122–124, 127–129
    and measurement invariance, 63
    of reading assessments, 167,
        170, 177
    of test score interpretations, 53
VanDerHeyden, A. M., 167, 171
Van der Maas, H. L. J., 64, 66
Variance, construct-irrelevant, 80
Vineland Social–Emotional Early
    Childhood Scales, 124
Violence, racial/ethnic socialization
    and, 27
Vygotsky, L. S., 187

WAIS (Wechsler Adult Intelligence
    Scale), 66
"Wait-to-fail model," 69
Walker, D. W., 244–245
Wang, A., 79, 205

Ward, K. E., 63
Watkins, M. W., 63
Wechsler Adult Intelligence Scale
    (WAIS), 66
Wechsler Adult Intelligence Scale–
    Third Edition, 145
Wechsler Intelligence Scale for
    Children (4th ed.; WISC–V),
    63
Wechsler Intelligence Scale for
    Children (revised), 12
Wechsler Intelligence Scale for
    Children (WISC), 12, 65
Wechsler Preschool and Primary Scale
    of Intelligence, Fourth Edition
    (WPPSI–IV), 128–129
Weinstein, R. S., 30–31
Whaley, A. L., 104–105
What Works Clearinghouse, 232
White, K. S., 102–103
Whites. *See also* Caucasians
    academic performance of, 197
    academic performance of CLD
        students vs., 183
    behavioral consultation for
        ADHD-type behaviors in,
        200–201
    demographics of, 252
    emotional disturbance among, 97
    and intelligence testing
        standardization, 10
    IQ difference between Blacks and,
        64, 65
    at Johnson Elementary School, 169
    quality of education for, 142
    in racial/ethnic group comparisons,
        25
    stereotype threat for, 32, 34
    suicidality among, 101
WHO (World Health Organization),
    67
Wicherts, J. M., 64, 66
Wide Range Achievement Test–
    Revision 3, 142
Williams, M. E., 124, 129
Williams, S. A., 87, 101
WISC (Wechsler Intelligence Scale for
    Children), 12, 65
WISC–V (Wechsler Intelligence Scale
    for Children, 4th ed.), 63

ABOUT THE EDITORS

Scott L. Graves, Jr., PhD, is an associate professor in the Department of Counseling, Psychology and Special Education at Duquesne University. He earned his doctorate in educational psychology from the University of Kentucky in 2006. His interests can be broadly categorized as understanding protective factors that lead to appropriate development in early childhood. His research agenda is focused on identifying strengths in African American children that lead to positive social–emotional and academic outcomes. Dr. Graves has published widely in these areas. Currently, he is an elected member of the APA Committee on Ethnic Minority Affairs.

Jamilia J. Blake, PhD, LSSP, is a licensed psychologist and associate professor at Texas A&M University in the school psychology program. She earned her doctoral degree from the University of Georgia in educational psychology. Dr. Blake's research examines the developmental trajectory of peer-directed aggression, bullying, and victimization in socially marginalized youth; and racial disparities in school discipline. She has published studies examining the social and psychological consequences of aggression for African American girls and the degree to which parental beliefs about aggression differentially influence African American and European American girls' use of aggression. She teaches courses in emotional and behavioral assessment, child therapy, consultation, educational disparities, and multicultural counseling.